liber

ROBERT HENRYSON

MEDIEVAL AND RENAISSANCE AUTHORS

Robert Henryson

DOUGLAS GRAY

Fellow of Pembroke College,
Oxford

LEIDEN / E. J. BRILL / 1979

ISBN 90 04 05917 2

PRINTED IN GREAT BRITAIN AT THE UNIVERSITY PRESS, CAMBRIDGE

CONTENTS

GENERAL PREFACE

The Medieval and Renaissance Authors Series is intended to fulfil two aims: first, to produce a detailed critical evaluation of the literary achievements of the most important English and Scots authors of the later Middle Ages and the Renaissance; second, to contribute towards a generous and systematic account of the literature of the period *c.* 1100–1600.

The original concentration on Medieval authors (when the series was published by Routledge & Kegan Paul) was a deliberate attempt to remind a rapidly growing criticism of the worth of an humane medievalism—of the continuity and originality of an individual, personal contribution to our literature, of the extent to which the individuality of Renaissance authors is anticipated and largely made possible by that of Middle English and Middle Scots writers. The extending of the series to include the Renaissance completes the editors' original design. The order of appearance of volumes does not represent an historical chronology or grouping.

University of Dundee — JOHN NORTON-SMITH
Pembroke College, Oxford — DOUGLAS GRAY

AUTHOR'S NOTE

My indebtedness to the many scholars who have written on Henryson will be evident from the text and the notes of this book. To two, however, I owe special thanks—to Professor Denton Fox for generously allowing me to use the draft of his forthcoming edition, and to Dr. Ian Jamieson for permitting me to consult his unpublished Ph.D. thesis, and for a number of stimulating discussions. I am deeply grateful also to Mrs. Margaret Twycross for allowing me to read her unpublished B.Litt. thesis. I regret that some recent studies—notably the essays in *Bards and Makars*, Professor MacQueen's article on *Orpheus and Eurydice*, and the books of Peter Richards on lepers and R. A. Dwyer on Boethian narratives—came to hand too late for me to take account of them in the text. My thanks are also due to the Bodleian Library, the British Library, the National Library of Scotland, the Bibliothèque Nationale, Paris, the Warburg Institute and the English Faculty Library, Oxford. Plates 4, 5(*b*) and 6 are reproduced by permission of the British Library Board, plates 1, 2, 3, 5(*a*), 7, and 8–13 by permission of the Curators of the Bodleian Library. The general editor of the series, Professor John Norton-Smith, has provided constant encouragement and a flow of learned and helpful suggestions. I am grateful also to my wife for much careful reading and criticism. Finally, I must thank Miss Sue Robb for coping with a particularly untidy manuscript.

ABBREVIATIONS

EETS	Early English Text Society (ES: Extra Series)
ELH	*Journal of English Literary History*
ELN	*English Language Notes*
JEGP	*Journal of English and Germanic Philology*
JWCI	*Journal of the Warburg and Courtauld Institutes*
MÆ	*Medium Ævum*
MLN	*Modern Language Notes*
MLR	*Modern Language Review*
MP	*Modern Philology*
NQ	*Notes and Queries*
OED	*Oxford English Dictionary*
PL	*Patrologia Latina*
PMLA	*Publications of the Modern Language Association*
PQ	*Philological Quarterly*
RES	*Review of English Studies*
SHR	*Scottish Historical Review*
SP	*Studies in Philology*
SSL	*Studies in Scottish Literature*
STS	Scottish Text Society
TLS	*Times Literary Supplement*
Whiting	B. J. Whiting, *Proverbs, Sentences, and Proverbial Phrases from English Writings Mainly before 1500* (Cambridge, Mass., London, 1968)

CHAPTER ONE

Dunfermline and Beyond

'Henryson', says Edwin Muir (speaking of the 'high concise style' of *The Testament of Cresseid*), 'embodies more strikingly than any poet who has lived since the fundamental seriousness, humanity and strength of the Scottish imagination.'[1] True seriousness, he says, later passed from the poet to the theologian; '...the Scottish poets followed the tradition of Dunbar, who expressed the exuberance, wildness and eccentricity of the Middle Ages, not that of Henryson, who inherited the medieval completeness and harmony, and the power to see life whole, without taking refuge in the facetious and the grotesque'. Henryson, it should be said at once, does not always speak with the same voice, and is not always grave and strong—Muir elsewhere in his excellent essay writes appreciatively of the humour of the *Fables*, where seriousness and comedy are inextricably intertwined. And while it is true that in Henryson we do not find so often or so stridently the startling contrasts of style and emotion characteristic of Dunbar, contrasts undoubtedly exist. Henryson is capable of sardonic humour, and of sharp satire, and sometimes (as in *Robene and Makene*) of a wit which would have delighted another younger contemporary, Thomas More. Occasionally, he can be exuberant, wild and eccentric. Some lines of *Ane Prayer for the Pest* combine aureate and homely diction with the virtuosity found later in Dunbar's 'Hale sterne superne', and the burlesque *Sum Practysis of Medecyne* takes off in a rumbustious, Rabelaisian swirl of words and comic impersonation. Yet there is a unity and a coherence about his *œuvre* which allows us to talk of him in the way Muir does, as of a distinct poetic individuality. We need not follow the tendency of some modern criticism—in revulsion from the pseudo-biographical 'personalities' (whether the 'gentlest and most

1 Edwin Muir, 'Robert Henryson' in *Essays on Literature and Society* (1949, revised ed. London, 1965), p. 21.

lovable of all the old Scots makars', or the severe Calvinist before his time) invented by earlier writers frustrated by the dearth of real biographical information—to reduce his poetry to a level plain of universal rhetorical devices and literary commonplaces. We should look in vain for that long and intense preoccupation with the artist's individual self which marks his contemporary Dürer, who portrayed himself from the mirror 'when he was still a child', but Henryson has a poetic individuality none the less real for being modest and self-effacing. He emerges as a superb craftsman, but as something much more, a boldly imaginative and original poet, who accepts, moulds and transforms the literary traditions and the 'mental sets' of his own age, a poet who is European as well as Scottish.

Of Henryson the man we know very little.[2] Our biography consists, essentially, of two lines by Dunbar in his *Lament for the Makars*, in which he says of Death:

> In Dunfermelyne he hes done roune
> With Maister Robert Henrisoun

These lines tell us for certain that he was dead by the time Dunbar wrote this poem, *c.* 1505,[3] and since Dunbar calls him 'Maister', we may assume that he was a university graduate (but of which university we do not know). He is here associated with Dunfermline; the later tradition that he was a schoolmaster there is quite likely to be correct. Two further scraps of information support the association with this locality: in the table of contents of the early sixteenth-century Asloan MS. there is a reference to a lost poem, 'Master Robert Hendersonnis Dreme On fut by forth', and in *Sum Practysis of Medecyne* there is what sounds like a local adaptation of the common formula 'from x to y' (i.e. everywhere), 'fra lawdian to lundin', which is often taken as 'from Lothian to Lundin (Fife)'. Apart from the fact that he lived in the second half of the fifteenth century, more precise biographical details

[2] Cf. Laing's 'Memoir' in *The Poems and Fables of Robert Henryson* (Edinburgh, 1864), H. Harvey Wood, *The Poems and Fables of Robert Henryson* (Edinburgh, 1933, revised ed. 1958), pp. xi–xiv, Denton Fox, *The Testament of Cresseid* (London, 1968), pp. 16–17.

[3] Fox, *Testament*, p. 17 n., suggests that the fact that Henryson's name appears late in Dunbar's list may indicate that his death is not referred to as a recent event, and that 'a death-date of about 1500 would not be far wrong'. Perhaps we may be permitted to wonder if the solemn and unmacabre image of Death speaking to the 'maister' is an allusion to the *Ressoning betuix Deth and Man*.

are unproven. The name is not uncommon. The several contenders include a Magister Robertus Henrisone who in 1462 was incorporated in the University of Glasgow as a licentiate in arts and a bachelor in decrees (i.e. Canon Law), who has found favour with some scholars, and a Magister Robertus Henrison who was a notary public, and witnessed charters of the Abbot of Dunfermline in 1477–8. These may very well be the same person, and may well be our poet, but it is not finally certain. The callings of schoolmaster and notary public would certainly have brought the poet into contact with many walks of life and no doubt encouraged his interest in the vagaries of human nature. Sir Francis Kynaston, who translated *The Testament of Cresseid* into Latin in the early seventeenth century, tells a nice story about Henryson's death of a 'diarrhea or fluxe',

> that all phisitians having given him over & he lying drawing his last breath there came an old woman unto him, who was held a witch, & asked him whether he would be cured, to whome he sayed very willingly. then quod shee there is a whikey tree in the lower end of your orchard, & if you will goe and walke but thrice about it, & thrice repeate theis wordes whikey tree whikey tree take away this fluxe from me you shall be presently cured, he told her that beside he was extreme faint and weake it was extreme frost & snowe & that it was impossible for him to go: She told him that unles he did so it was impossible he should recover. Mr Henderson then lifting upp himselfe, & pointing to an Oken table that was in the roome, asked her & seied gude dame I pray ye tell me, if it would not do as well if I repeated thrice theis words oken burd oken burd garre me shit a hard turde. the woman seing herselfe derided & scorned ran out of the house in a great passion & Mr Henderson within halfe a quarter of an houre departed this life.[4]

In the light of *Sum Practysis of Medecyne*, 'this merry, though somewhat unsavoury tale', as Kynaston calls it, is not so fundamentally un-Henrysonian as has been alleged. But there is, alas, no evidence that it is anything other than apocryphal.

The authenticity of the canon of his major poetry is reasonably well

[4] Wood, p. xii. The MS. (Add. C 287, Bodleian), is printed in G. Gregory Smith, *The Poems of Robert Henryson*, STS lxiv (1904–1910), I, pp. ciiiff.

attested,[5] but it is impossible to know—apart from 'Master Robert Hendersonnis Dreme'—how much has been lost. Furthermore, the text of his poems is hard to establish. Apart from a few poems and fragments in early MSS., and those published by Scotland's first printers, Chepman and Myllar, full copies of his major works are found only in MSS. or editions made long after his death, as the Bannatyne MS. (1568), the sixteenth-century prints of Bassandyne and Charteris, or the sixteenth-century English editions of Chaucer.[6]

The difficulties of piecing together some picture of Henryson's *milieu* in late medieval Scotland are not quite as daunting as those facing a would-be biographer, but they are none the less considerable. On the one hand, the remains and the records are fragmentary; on the other, it is difficult in any brief attempt at a cultural history of his time to do justice to its complexities and its changing patterns. What follows, therefore, is not a neatly organized or inclusive account, but rather a series of notes and suggestions for the reader of his poetry.

Although medieval Scotland was, culturally as well as geographically, part of Europe, from a European or even from an English viewpoint it often seemed a remote and mysterious region, especially in its further reaches.[7] A careful map, that of Matthew Paris in the thirteenth century, says of the North-West coast that it 'looks only towards a sea where there is nought but the abode of monsters'; it is a 'country marshy and impassable, fit for cattle and shepherds'. On another thirteenth-century map the West coast bears the forbidding, but no doubt accurate, note *Hic habundant lupi*, and among the marvels of Loch Tay is recorded a 'swimming island'. The Loch Ness monster does not yet appear to have been noticed, but the humanist Aeneas Silvius who visited the country in the earlier fifteenth century enquired (without success) about the mythical barnacle geese. French romancers thought of it as a desolate wilderness.[8] It was poor and backward; Jean

[5] That of some of the shorter poems is rather less secure (on *The Want of Wyse Men* cf. p. 241 below). D. McDonald (*Neophilologus* li, 168–177) argues on internal grounds for Henryson's authorship of *The Thre Preistis of Peblis*.

[6] For fuller information on the MSS. and printed books, see the editions of Gregory Smith, Wood (pp. xix–xxx), C. Elliott, *Robert Henryson, Poems* (Oxford, Clarendon Medieval and Tudor Series, 1963, 2nd ed. 1974), pp. xxiiiff., Fox, *Testament* (pp. 2–13). Professor Fox's forthcoming Oxford edition will contain an account of the textual problems.

[7] See P. Hume Brown, *Early Travellers in Scotland* (Edinburgh, 1891), M. Lindsay, *The Discovery of Scotland* (London, 1961).

[8] P. Rickard, *Britain in Medieval French Literature* (Cambridge, 1956), chapter ix.

de Meun made it the home of Hunger. The Scots were wild and dangerous: one of a series of Latin sentences devised for translation at Eton in the early sixteenth century reads baldly: 'he was robbed as he entered Scotland'.[9]

Scots were known abroad as students, scholars, merchants, pilgrims and—especially—as soldiers. Scottish archers formed the bodyguard of the kings of France; one of their famous leaders, Lord Bernard Stewart, Seigneur d'Aubigny, 'un grand chevalier sans reproche', is celebrated by Dunbar as 'the flour of chevelrie'.[10] Ordinary soldiers enjoyed a less happy reputation, being thought of as truculent tavern-haunters and plunderers. 'Fier comme un escossois' was a French proverb of the time; in one of the stories in the *Cent Nouvelles Nouvelles* a Scottish archer has his way with a wife, while her husband is too terrified to emerge from hiding because of his fearsome threats.[11] The Scottish soldier's treatment of the French language is the subject of many jokes, but it is once used to make a rather touching poem, *Le Testament du gentil Cossois* (1499).[12] In this work, an example of the very popular 'Testament' form, written in a kind of Scottish-French, a dying archer makes his last will. He leaves his equipment to his page, commends his soul to St. Ninian, and asks his comrades to bear his body to its rest. He bids farewell to his friends, his leader, and the poor land of Scotland—'le povre pais de Cos'.

Poverty and backwardness were what most impressed the majority of early foreign visitors to Scotland. Aeneas Silvius (who was clearly relieved when he returned south of the border) says that

> 'it is a cold country where few things will grow and for the most part has no trees...the houses are usually constructed without

[9] Horman, *Vulgaria* ed. M. R. James (Roxburghe Club, Oxford, 1926), p. 357.

[10] Cf. Gray, 'A Scottish "Flower of Chivalry" and his Book', *Words. Wai-te-ata Studies in English* iv (1974), 22–34; A. I. Dunlop, *Scots Abroad in the Fifteenth Century* (Hist. Ass. Pamphlet 124, London, 1942), F. Michel, *Les Écossais en France, les Français en Écosse* (London, Bordeaux, 1862), R. J. Mitchell, 'Scottish Law Students in Italy in the later Middle Ages', *Juridical Review* xlix (1937), 19–24.

[11] Ed. P. Champion (Paris, 1928), Nouvelle 4 (tr. R. H. Robbins, *The Hundred Tales* (New York, 1960)).

[12] See Rickard, pp. 214, 252–6, D. Baird Smith, *SHR* xvii (1919–20), 190–8. Cf. Chastellain's nice story (Rickard, p. 213) of Queen Margaret, a fugitive in France, being so poor that she had to borrow money for the offering at mass from a Scottish archer, 'qui a demy à dur et à regret luy tira ung gros d'Escosse de sa bourse et le luy presta'.

> mortar; their roofs are covered with turf; and in the country doorways are closed with oxhides. The common people, who are poor and rude, stuff themselves with meat and fish, but eat bread as a luxury.'[13]

Peasants' houses, indeed, remained very primitive for centuries. The Reverend Patrick Graham describes them in the late eighteenth century as

> wretched huts, thatched with fern or straw; having two apartments only, the one a kitchen...the other a sort of room... where strangers were occasionally received, and where the heads of family generally slept. The byre and the stable were generally under the same roof, and separated from the kitchen by a partition of osiers...plastered with clay. A glass window and a chimney were esteemed a luxury.[14]

Scotland appears rather less as its stereotype of a rugged wilderness in the account (from a period which was perhaps promising a greater prosperity) of Pedro de Ayala, the Spanish ambassador to the court of James IV. He seems to have known—and liked—the country as well as its ruler (who could speak, he says with some admiration, not only Latin, French, German, Flemish, Italian and Spanish, but also 'the language of the savages who live in some parts of Scotland and on the islands'), and his task was to provide a full report for Ferdinand and Isabella. He is struck by the plenitude of fish, the immense flocks of sheep, the friendliness of the people ('vain and ostentatious by nature', 'courageous, strong, quick and agile'), by the prosperity of the towns—which were populous, with good houses made of 'hewn stone, and provided with excellent doors, glass windows, and a great number of chimneys'—the magnificence of the abbeys and the religious houses, and by the power of the Scottish prelates.[15]

As in the rest of Europe, life in medieval Scotland was marked not only by poverty, but by violence and turbulence. In the fifteenth

[13] *Commentarii* (Rome, 1584), p. 5, tr. F. A. Cragg, *Memoirs of a Renaissance Pope* (abridged ed. New York, 1962), p. 33.

[14] *General View of the Agriculture of Stirlingshire* (1812), quoted Royal Commission on the Ancient and Historical Monuments of Scotland, *Stirlingshire* (Edinburgh, 1963), p. 47; cf. J. G. Dunbar, *The Historic Architecture of Scotland* (London, 1966), pp. 224ff.

[15] Hume Brown, p. 39.

century four Stewart kings met violent deaths. James I (1406–1437) and James III (1460–1488) were murdered; James II (1437–1460) was accidentally killed by a bombard at the siege of Roxburgh, and James IV (1488–1513) died in battle. Strife was both external—in the campaigns against the English which culminated in the disaster of Flodden—and internal—in the struggles of young kings against over-mighty nobles and powerful families: the Grahams, the Livingstones, the Douglases.[16] In Henryson's lifetime, James III was challenged by nobles who seized him at Lauder Bridge, and he died in a renewed outbreak of civil war.

It would be misleading, however, to suggest that Henryson's age was one of unmitigated disaster and of constant turmoil. The extra-ordinary capacity of ordinary people to survive was refreshed by periods of peace and comparative prosperity. Beside the tensions of rural life, the old agricultural rhythms (so memorably caught by Henryson in the *Fables*) continued to bring livelihood and reward. Towns and the characteristic Scottish Burghs—trading centres with privileges and monopolies—became more numerous and more important. Henryson's contrast of town and country in 'The Two Mice', where the town mouse is a 'gildbrother' and a 'fre burges'—

> Toll-fre als, but custum mair or les,
> And fredome had to ga quhair ever scho list,
> Amang the cheis in ark, and meill in kist (173–5)[17]

—wittily draws on these mercantile privileges, and is more pointed than in versions from the earlier Middle Ages.[18] The ledger of Andrew

[16] Cf. *Liber Pluscardensis* ed. F. J. H. Skene (Edinburgh, 1877), I, p. 391: justicia regno Scociae est debilis et tepida, in defectu regum juvenum et baronum insipiencium. See R. Nicholson, *Scotland. The Later Middle Ages* (Edinburgh, 1974), W. C. Dickinson, *Scotland from the Earliest Times to 1603* (Edinburgh, 1961, revised A. A. M. Duncan, Oxford, 1977), R. L. Mackie, *King James IV of Scotland* (Edinburgh, 1958), J. M. Brown (ed.), *Scottish Society in the XVth Century* (London, 1977).

[17] All quotations from Henryson (except for *The Testament of Cresseid*) are from the edition of H. Harvey Wood. I have modernized the usage of such letters as u/v, i/j, 3, and I have occasionally altered the punctuation. Thanks to the generosity of Professor Fox, I have been able to see a typescript of his new edition. I have adopted a number of the most important of the many superior readings he offers, and have indicated these in the footnotes.

[18] On burghs, see Nicholson, esp. pp. 263–5, Cosmo Innes, *Scotland in the Middle Ages* (Edinburgh, 1860), chapter 5, W. Ross, *Burgh Life in Dunfermline in the Olden Time* (Edinburgh, 1864). On the following section, cf. *Ledger of Andrew*

Halyburton, a merchant of Middleburgh at the end of the fifteenth century shows a traditional pattern of exports—wool, skins, and fish (including barrels of salmon and trout from the Bishop of Aberdeen)—and imports of luxury goods, including silver chalices, gowns, 'a kynkyn of olyffis', 'a pip of claret vyne', almonds, saffron, and pepper. For Bishop Elphinstone, Halyburton provided 'the mendyn of an oralag and the cais new'.

One of Henryson's great strengths as a writer is his precise use of the details and the texture of everyday domestic life. In 'The Two Mice', for instance, the cat lets the mouse run under the straw (which would have covered the floor) and it finally escapes between 'ane burde and the wall', climbing quickly 'behind ane parraling' (a partition wall). At the beginning of *The Testament of Cresseid* Henryson presents himself as an aged poet in his 'oratur' (which has 'glas') before moving to his 'chalmer' and a warm fire and a drink. From legal records, historians have reconstructed the details of the dwelling of the wealthy 'persone of Stobo', Maister Adam Colquhoun (d. 1542), in Drygate, Glasgow. In his bedchamber (with fireplace) he had a decorated bed, with feather mattress, 'pladis' and blankets, with curtains of damask of divers hues, fastened with silk and tasselled with gold, and a carved chest. Rather charmingly, he also had 'ane bird, videlicet: parrok', and, besides 'ane round preists bonet' he had some stylish clothes (e.g. 'ane hat of silk with ane tippet'). He was evidently a man of sporting taste, interested in archery and hare-coursing. He had another room, 'the oratour within his duelling place', with altar, vessels and vestments, a desk with his 'orasoun buke coverit with grene velvot', and his collection of 'librell bukis' including 'tua courss of the law with utheris doctoris thairupone', with 'bukis of theologie and uthir science'. It seems to have been usual to keep books in the oratory, and to 'make use of it as a quiet study for secular as well as religious reading'. Later in the *Testament* Cresseid retires to 'ane secreit orature', which sounds as if it is in the house of her father, the priest Calchas. Like Calchas (cf. ll. 358–9), Colquhoun had a hall, with the 'burde' or dining-table. He also had a well-stocked kitchen: his stores included 'ane pipe of beif', a pipe of salmon (eight dozen), a pipe of Loch Fyne herring, 'ane ark full of mele', six stone of butter, and 'ane kebboc of

Halyburton 1492–1503 (Edinburgh, 1867), H. Warrack, *Domestic Life in Scotland 1488–1688* (London, 1920), esp. pp. 21–2, 41ff., D. McRoberts, 'The Manse of Stobo in 1542', *Innes Rev.* xxii (1971), 19–31, 101–9.

cheiz' weighing twenty-two pounds (the grandeur of this item makes us think of yet another of Henryson's *Fables*).

Dunfermline now, though a pleasant town, is hardly one of Scotland's showplaces. The spirit of one of its later sons, Andrew Carnegie, is perhaps more in evidence than that of Robert Henryson. It still enjoys its fine situation, and is still dominated by the abbey (whose great Romanesque nave and columns are among the finest ecclesiastical remains of the country) and by the vast ruins of the palace ('a delicate and princely mansion' at the time of the visit of John Taylor the Water Poet in the early seventeenth century).[19] Our illustration (Plate 1) from Slezer's *Theatrum Scotiae*, an impression of the very late seventeenth century, gives us perhaps a better idea of what it might have looked like in Henryson's time. It was not only an impressive and important burgh, but it was—with Stirling and Edinburgh—a favoured residence of the king. The great abbey, the burial place of kings and the object of pilgrimage,[20] was one of the most powerful in Scotland, and its mitred abbot one of the leading prelates of the land. Its privileges were considerable—and sometimes curious. It was entitled to tithes of the gold and the wild mares of Fife and Forthriff, to every seventh seal caught at Kinghorn after the tithe (in addition to large fishing rights, the abbot had his own boat), and to a part of the coal which was later to become so important a product in the area.[21]

The burgh records which survive from the latter part of the fifteenth century[22] are of some interest to the student of Henryson, not because his works are crammed with local allusions (nineteenth-century scholars, convinced that they were, saw in the 'secreit yet' out of which Cresseid went a reference to a postern gate in the south wall of the monastery, in the 'village half ane myle thairby' a reference to the Nethertoun, and the 'spittaill hous' as the Hospital of St. Leonard),[23] but rather because they give us a sense of a particular and local *milieu*, and

[19] *The Pennilesse Pilgrimage* (London, 1618), f. E i.

[20] It contained the shrine of St. Margaret, Queen of Scotland (d. 1093).

[21] P. Chalmers, *Historical and Statistical Account of Dunfermline* (Edinburgh, London, 1844), pp. 211–12, E. Henderson, *The Annals of Dunfermline* (Glasgow, 1879), pp. 156–9.

[22] Erskine Beveridge ed., *The Burgh Records of Dunfermline 1488–1584* (Edinburgh, 1917).

[23] Cf. Henderson, pp. 169–70; on St Leonard's, see D. E. Easson, *Medieval Religious Houses. Scotland* (2nd ed. Ian B. Cowan and D. E. Easson, London, 1976), p. 175.

bring us close to the unpoetic details of ordinary life which he made into poetry in the *Fables*. It is something of a delight to find the names of the streets of the old town—both the main thoroughfares (or 'gates') and the lesser streets, the 'wynds', and 'vennels', and 'closes' which no doubt in every Scottish town 'tended to be narrow, steep and nasty, like the wynds of Southey's day "into which no English nose would willingly venture, for stinks older than the union are to be found there"'[24]—Colyeraw, Newraw, Causagate (or Calsaygate), the Maygate, the common vennel, Crosswynd, 'the commone gait extendand to the gramour scull'—and the names of the citizens—David Couper (Provost in 1488), David Litster and William of Balloune baillies, Thome Murray, Agnes Mawer, Agnes Bell, Marian Simson, Jamy Spens, Andro Braidwod and Margaret his spous, Effe Malcum, Johne Frog, and many others. In the records, everyone (even the most eminent) is referred to by his first name—Jamie, Wat, Sandie, etc.—just as when in 'The Sheep and the Dog' Henryson refers to the wicked practices of false 'crownars' who change the records he says that they 'scraip out Johne and wryte in Will or Wat'. Among the officials, besides the provost and the baillies, we find flesh-pricers, ale-tasters (larger towns like Aberdeen had tasters of wine), measurers of tenements. Among the traders are bakers, brewers, weavers, websters, walcars, litsters (references to *linget* 'flax seed' and *lynt* 'flax' may remind us of a famous passage in 'The Preaching of the Swallow'), and the cadgers who brought fish to the town, as in yet another fable. In Dunfermline in 1494 they had to bring six loads of fish to the town each week (on Wednesdays, Fridays and Saturdays) and remain with their wares at the Mercat Cross for two hours at the least.

It is obviously unfair to the good folk of the town that our picture of their life should be drawn from legal records, but the student of Henryson cannot forbear noticing with pleasure that a certain number of 'misdoars' among his fellow-citizens emerge with a touch of the vividness of some of the characters in his *Fables*. The punishments imposed are usually fines, sometimes 'sentens of cursing' (excommunication for non-payment of debt) and sometimes take a more public form—there are references to 'the stokis', 'the gowe', 'the cuk stuyll' (all apparently the same thing), and the 'lear stane' (possibly also the stocks, for the fraudulent). Generally the simple and bald records suggest a more orderly course of justice than is found in the *Fables*,

24 J. G. Dunbar, *Historic Architecture*, p. 172.

but there is a splendid moment in 1488 when one John of Murra angrily appeals against a fine pronounced by the dempster (the officer who pronounced the sentence of the court), Adam Man:

> And than incontinent Johne of Murra falsit the doym sayand that o this wis I Johne of Murra sais to ye Adam Man dempstar that the doym that ye has gyffyn is ewyl fals and rottyn in the self...[25]

The offences are generally 'strublans' (breach of the peace)—to which one of the cadgers, John Burne, seems to have been particularly prone during the years 1489–1491—and 'wrangus withhaldin', which seems to cover various forms of non-payment and debt: 'the qwhilk day Davy Burne wes maid quit of the wrangwis haldyn of John Thomsonis pot', or (1489) 'Mege Hutone in amerciament for the wrangwis haldyn a cheir fra George of Kynros' (in the same year this lady was fined several times, and also accused of 'wrangwisly' occupying the house of Andro Archbald). Sometimes a small dramatic scene clearly lies behind the entries—Johne of Burne eldar accuses James Gray 'tveching the vranguis strublyn of his child and riffyn of his bonet', but the court in its wisdom finds otherwise, 'the sade child wes funde the caus of the sade strublans'; Madde Vilson accuses Michell Jhonson 'for the vrangvis trublyn of hir in the gait and castyn of hir dublar to the Cros', and he responds with an accusation 'for the vrangvis bladyn (damaging) and castyn awaye of his fische and thai unpayit for' (he was unsuccessful, but the last phrase seems to preserve the tone of his voice from the ravages of the centuries).[26] Occasionally, there were offences slightly more picturesque than the 'wrangus withhalding of ane pot' or the 'wrangvis avay takyne...of ane leg of beiff'. There is 'the wrangus brekkyn of ane sex qwart pitschar and the done castyn of the aill that wes contenit in it', and 'the vrangvis dounecasting of ane brig made betuix his lyme pottis and the incasting of erde and filtht in the same'. In 1496, Adam Mane (apparently the dempster of 1488) is said to have 'held unlefull opyne wyndois wid and large in the sidwall of his hous one the bak half liand at the northt end of the yard of the said Johnis at the quhilkis he and his familiaris maid commone ische (exit) and entre witht furth casting of water and utheris filthis abhominable in gret hurt skaitht and dampnage to the said John', and finally is told to 'upclois' the windows.

The barely subdued chaos of ordinary life cannot be fitted easily into

[25] Beveridge, 5. [26] Beveridge, 134.

the neat periodization of popular history, and it is somehow reassuring to find that in 1492, a year not without significance for Western Europe, the inhabitants of Dunfermline were about their usual occupations. Jamy Sytheson was fined twice 'for strublans of Andro Cristisone and of Lanse'. Fined also for 'strublans' were Toppe Neis, Pate Morton, and John Illis. Jamy Malcom was 'in amerciament for a gris' (pig), Rob Gibsone 'for he cuttit a tre', and Cristiane Hasty 'for ail'. The court was still struggling with the problems of Meg Hutton and her occupation of the house of Andro Archbald. She appeared, with the consent of her husband, and 'deponit the grete aitht' that 'schow suld of fre will ich and dewod (remove) hir self and hir gudis owt of the hows of Andro Archbald incontinent the qwhilk scho occupiit and grantis hir nevir to haff no clame tharto in tyme to cum na nevyr tribill the nychtburris in tyme to cum'.

It is time, however, for us to raise our eyes from the streets of Dunfermline to larger vistas. We have already seen enough to suggest that the conventional foreign stereotype of Scotland as a wretched and backward land was far from the whole truth. Enough has remained to show that in the cultural history of Scotland the fifteenth century was a splendid and creative period. It is sadly true, however, that we must have recourse to a phrase like 'enough has remained', for it is largely from ruins and fragments that we have to construct our picture. The art and architecture of the period has suffered grievously not only from the rigours of the climate, but also from Englishmen, Reformers and developers. Dunfermline itself had its tribulations; at the beginning of the eighteenth century Defoe speaks of the 'full perfection of decay' of the place.[27] The fifteenth century was, however, clearly a period of extensive building. The Scottish landscape is still dotted with castles wholly or partly from that time. The choir and nave of Dunkeld Cathedral were begun in this century. In Perth (once a walled town full of religious houses) St. John's still survives, restored as a war memorial. At St. Andrews, Holy Trinity Church (1412) survives, though much altered. The College of St. Salvator (1450) founded by Bishop Kennedy has disappeared, except for the church of St. Salvator with the remains of Kennedy's fine tomb. In Edinburgh,[28] St. Giles

[27] *A Tour through the Whole Island of Great Britain*, intro. G. D. H. Cole and D. C. Browning (London, 1974), p. 364.

[28] Royal Commission on the Ancient Monuments of Scotland, *Edinburgh* (Edinburgh, 1951), pp. 25–30, 144–53, 36–40.

was completed with its distinctive tower (storks were building in the superstructure in 1416; the crown of the tower apparently dates from *c.* 1500), and Holyrood Palace was begun by James IV in 1501, but little of the original work survives. The Somerset Herald (present for the king's wedding with Margaret Tudor) describes several of the apartments; some were hung with tapestries depicting the deeds of Hercules and 'the ystory of Troy towne'. Trinity College Church, founded in 1460 by Mary of Gueldres, the widow of James II, was taken down in 1848—in spite of protests—to make room for Waverley Station. In Stirling[29] we still have the fifteenth-century church of the Holy Rude, and the splendid and original Great Hall, 'the finest achievement of late-Gothic architecture in Scotland'. Tradition has it that the Hall was designed by Cochrane, in later legend one of James III's most resented favourites; the larger part, however, seems to have been constructed during the reign of James IV (*c.* 1500).

The architectural landscape of Henryson's time must have been one of striking contrasts. At Carnock, a few miles west of Dunfermline, he could have seen a small and very humble church, built many years previously (c. 1200), which would have had a roof of heather. It is the kind of church that Dunbar, in one of the wittiest of his pleas for preferment, says that he would be content with—'Greit abbais grayth I nill to gather, / Bot ane kirk scant coverit with hadder'.[30] Probably there was not much money available to embellish or extend (as would have been done in many English rural parishes) these small, older country churches. Things could be very different, however, where a wealthy burgh or a powerful patron was involved. Just outside of Edinburgh, in a most beautiful setting, stands Rosslyn Chapel, one of the most extraordinary buildings of the time. It was begun in 1446 by William Sinclair, the Earl of Orkney, and is thought to have taken about forty years to complete; according to a later tradition, 'that it might be done with greater glory and splendor, he caused artificers to be brought from other regions and foraigne kingdoms'.[31] Certainly

[29] R.C.A.H.M.S., *Stirlingshire*, pp. 129–40, 205–11, 42.

[30] *Poems* ed. W. M. Mackenzie (London, 1932), p. 31. Cf. J. M. Webster, *History of Carnock* (London, Edinburgh, 1938).

[31] Full description in R.C.A.H.M.S., *Midlothian and West Lothian* (Edinburgh, 1929), pp. 98–106. The quotation is from the seventeenth-century antiquary, Fr. Richard Augustin Hay, *Genealogie of the Sainteclaires of Rosslyn* (pr. Edinburgh, 1835), p. 27. Hay also says that the Earl 'caused the draughts to be drawn upon

the richness of the decoration is so overwhelming that the visitor might be forgiven for thinking that he was in a church in Spain or Portugal. 'The architecture within,' says Dorothy Wordsworth, who visited it in 1803 with her brother, 'is exquisitely beautiful...The stone both of the roof and walls is sculptured with leaves and flowers, so delicately wrought that I could have admired them for hours.'[32] The compartments of the barrel vault are divided by curved ribs of differing design, and each is powdered with stars and roses and other shapes. The surfaces and the columns are decorated with an exuberant profusion. Grotesques peep out through the foliage. On the window-corbels the subjects include a fox preaching to the geese, a goose saved from the fox, butting lambs, a camel, and an angel with a trumpet. Sculptured scenes and schemes—seven works of mercy, seven deadly sins, scenes from the *Dance of Death*—are tucked everywhere, and make up a most amazing pattern of decoration. And in Henryson's day it would also have been filled with images and hangings and altars. Anyone who remains for any time in this fifteenth-century interior has no difficulty in understanding the taste of the poets for aureate diction.

These two buildings, Carnock and Rosslyn, may be taken to illustrate two extremes which co-exist in the Scottish culture of Henryson's day, and to which he seems deeply responsive. One is an unobtrusive example of the simple, the humble and the austere, the other displays a taste for elaboration and decoration which borders on the fantastic. In one building, the visitor's thoughts would be of local and Scottish crafts and skills, in the other they would begin to stray to other regions and foreign kingdoms, to Scotland's connections with the world beyond, and the way in which foreign sources of inspiration were received and adapted. The same contrasts may be found in other areas. Besides the remains of the local and humble arts of the wood-carver or the stone carver,[33] there are (though lamentably few survive) those splendid works of art commissioned from European masters by

Eastland boords and made the carpenters to carve them according to the draughts thereon, and then gave them for patterns to the massons, that they might therby cut the like in stone.'

[32] *Journals of Dorothy Wordsworth* ed. E. de Selincourt (London, 1941), I, p. 387 (cf. II, p. 41). Cf. also William's sonnet, *Poetical Works*, ed. E. de Selincourt (2nd ed., Oxford, 1954), III, pp. 266–7.

[33] Cf. J. S. Richardson, *The Medieval Stone Carver in Scotland* (Edinburgh, 1964).

wealthy patrons.[34] The painting by Hugo van der Goes (dated *c.* 1478–9 by Panofsky, after 1479–80 by Whinney)[35] which now hangs in the National Gallery of Scotland was done for Sir Edward Bonkill, the Provost of Trinity College, whose brother was a merchant and a naturalized citizen of Bruges. It was probably designed to be used as organ-shutters. The exterior shows the Trinity of the Broken Body with a mourning figure of God the Father, while on the right Bonkill (the realism of whose face suggests that he sat for the artist in the Low Countries) kneels in front of a magnificent organ, with a hymnal in which one can see the first stanza of the hymn to the Trinity 'O lux beata Trinitas'. An angel of exquisite beauty plays the organ, assisted by another working the bellows. The stiff depictions of James III and his son seem to have been added later, possibly in Scotland. Besides a few examples of unpretentious Scottish illuminated manuscripts, the fine 'Hours of James IV', now in Vienna, is a surviving example of those richly decorated Flemish manuscripts made for noble patrons abroad. It was probably done at Ghent for the marriage of James IV and Mary Tudor in 1503; one of the illuminators was probably Gerhart Horenbaut, who later became court painter to Henry VIII.[36]

In literature, remains are rather more extensive, although it is clear that a great deal has been lost. It is a sombre exercise to read through Dunbar's list of 'makars' and find so many of whom nothing is known. It is, no doubt, unlikely that they were all excellent poets, but the fact that Dunbar thought them worth recording is of some importance. We need also to remind ourselves that Scotland was a country of two languages—or, more precisely, from the marriage of James III, of three, for we should include the Norse dialects of Orkney and Shetland. 'The language of the savages who dwell in some parts of Scotland and on the islands' had its own distinctive literature, as its speakers had their

[34] Cf. D. McRoberts, 'Notes on Scoto-Flemish Artistic Contacts', *Innes Rev.* x (1959), 91–6.

[35] E. Panofsky, *Early Netherlandish Painting* (Cambridge, Mass., 1953), I, pp. 335–6, figs. 467–9, M. Whinney, *Early Flemish Painting* (London, 1968). Cf. C. Thompson and L. Campbell, *Hugo van der Goes and the Trinity panels in Edinburgh* (H.M.S.O., Edinburgh, 1974).

[36] Cf. F. Unterkircher, *European Illuminated MSS. in the Austrian National Library* (tr. J. M. Brownjohn, London, 1967), pp. 230–3, L. Macfarlane, 'The Book of Hours of James IV and Margaret Tudor', *Innes Rev.* xi (1960), 3–21. D. McRoberts, *Innes Rev.* xix (1968), 144–67 describes a late 15th century book done (probably in Flanders) for the Dean of Aberdeen. For a Scottish MS., see W. J. Anderson, 'Andrew Lundy's Primer', *Innes Rev.* xi (1960), 39–51.

own culture and social structure. Gaelic literature was mainly, but not exclusively, oral. Beside the Ossianic lays, there are apparently fragments of translations of the *Thebaid* and the *Pharsalia*.[37] The way of life of the Highlanders remained probably almost without change until their 'discovery' by eighteenth-century English travellers. It is difficult to say what, if any, Gaelic influence there was on the Lowland culture. There was, of course, plenty of hostile contact—and Dunbar uses 'Irish' as a term of abuse.[38] Rather movingly, Henryson gives his Cresseid a Gaelic cry of lament—'Ochane'—but this may very well have been one of the few Gaelic loanwords in Middle Scots. There is no firm evidence that either he or Dunbar knew Gaelic, and the linguistic as well as the social and cultural barriers must have been considerable. As for 'Inglis', as most of the Middle Scots poets call their language (a living vernacular marked by variety of usage, not an artificially created 'literary' language),[39] it is important for the modern reader (whether English or Scottish) to realize that the writers who use it use it as the accepted vernacular language of an independent kingdom, do not regard it as an outlandish dialect, and do not feel any need to be defensive or self-conscious about it.

It was Henryson himself, and his successors Dunbar and Douglas, who brought literary distinction to Middle Scots, and ensured that it would be read and studied outside the confines of Scottish antiquarian circles. It was not, however, an achievement *ex nihilo*. What remains of the Scottish literature before and during Henryson's time suggests a

[37] Cf., e.g., D. S. Thomson, 'Gaelic Learned Orders and Literati in Medieval Scotland', *Scottish Studies* xii (1968), 57–78, W. J. Watson, *Scottish Verse from the Book of the Dean of Lismore* (Edinburgh, 1947) (among the Middle Scots pieces in this commonplace book is a single stanza of *The Testament of Cresseid* (pr. Fox, *Testament*, p. 132)). On the Highlands, cf. I. F. Grant, *The Lordship of the Isles* (Edinburgh, 1935); there is a 16th-century account in Monro's *Western Isles of Scotland and Genealogies of the Clans*, ed. R. W. Munrow (Edinburgh, London, 1961). For the 18th-century English discovery, see A. J. Youngson, *Beyond the Highland Line* (London, 1974).

[38] Mackenzie ed., pp. 7, 123, 173. Cf. the insulting treatment of the Lowland Bishop Lauder (A. I. Dunlop, *The Life and Times of James Kennedy, Bishop of St, Andrews* (Edinburgh, London, 1950), p. 370). J. MacInnes, 'The Oral Tradition in Scottish Gaelic Poetry', *Scottish Studies* xii (1968), 40, suggests a possible connection with Middle Scots 'flyting'.

[39] See A. J. Aitken, 'Variation and variety in written Middle Scots' in *Edinburgh Studies in English and Scots* ed. A. J. Aitken, A. McIntosh, H. Pálsson (London, 1971), pp. 177–209.

tradition of some distinction and much variety. The prose, whether translation—as *The Buke of the Laws of Armys*, the version of Bonet's *Arbre des Batailles* made by Gilbert of the Hay in 1456 in Rosslyn Castle[40]—or original—as John of Ireland's *Meroure of Wyssdome* (1490)[41]—is competent rather than exciting. In the verse, however, we can find premonitions of some of the qualities of Henryson's style. Already in Barbour's *Bruce* (1375), a fine celebration of the heroic virtues of fortitude and loyalty, we find a work which, although it has nothing of Henryson's complexity, can combine an exciting narrative with an eloquent seriousness, and can handle dialogue and direct speech and a simple grim irony. Some of its lines have the concision and strength of the later makars—after the battle of Loudon Hill

> The feld wes weill neir coverit all
> Bath with slayn hors and with men.[42]

The same vigour and forcefulness occasionally appear in Hary's *Wallace*[43] in the fifteenth century, where at some moments we feel uncomfortably close to the cruelty and vindictiveness of the Scottish medieval wars. At one point, Wallace burns the barns of Ayr in retribution, and watches the red blaze:

> 'Forsuth,' he said, 'this is a plessand sycht;
> Till our hartis it suld be sum radres.' (VII, 430–1)

Here again we find—though much less frequently than in the *Bruce*—a tough, strong line that will make us think, however remotely, of Henryson. In an incident which could almost have appeared in *Havelok*, Wallace fights with a churl, and breaks his back:

> The carll was dede: of him I spek no mar (II, 45).

In another, a woman utters a fine, simple lament over Wallace's dead uncle:

> 'Out off yon bern,' scho said, 'I saw him born,
> Nakit, laid law on cald erd me beforn.
> His frosty mouth I kissit in that sted,
> Rycht now manlik, now bar, and brocht to ded!'
> (VII, 277–80)

[40] Ed. J. H. Stevenson, STS xliv, lxii (1901, 1914).

[41] Available in part in STS ed. C. Macpherson, NS xix (1926), and (Books III–IV) ed. F. Quinn, 4th ser. ii (1965).

[42] VIII, ll. 332–3, ed. W. M. Mackenzie (London, 1909), p. 142.

[43] Ed. M. P. McDiarmid, STS 4th ser., iv, v (1968–9).

The mention of these two verse chronicles may also serve to remind us that the conventional label of 'Scottish Chaucerian' so often applied to Henryson and his successors can be dangerously misleading if we interpret it in too limited a manner. Henryson was indeed profoundly moulded by his reading of the great English poet. He also knew something of the work of his disciples Lydgate, and James I, whose *Kingis Quair*[44] is pre-eminent among the works of the earlier Scottish literature. But he was also sensitive to others of the various strands of the Scottish literary tradition. Alliterative poetry, for instance, lived on longer in the north,[45] and Henryson uses its emphatic combinations and formulae much more readily than any English contemporary learned poet would have done. We may also note topics and forms close to those of Henryson. We have a lively parliament of birds in Holland's *Buke of the Howlat*,[46] and besides romances, a number of anonymous tales of uncertain date, which sometimes show distinct narrative skill (as *Rauf Coilyear* or *The Thre Preistis of Peblis*) and sometimes a bawdy and lively fantasy (as *Colkelbie Sow*, the story of the fate of the three pennies for which a merry man sold his sow).

Early sixteenth-century references suggest that the entertainment of royal circles had a typical variety. Alongside performers from Italy and France, and the 'Spaniards who danced before the king on the causeway of Edinburgh' (we hear also of 'gentil Johne the Inglis fule' and of the king's 'litill lutare') are more homely figures—'Widderspune the foulare, that tald talis and brocht foules to the king' or 'Watschod the tale tellare' or the 'tua fithelaris that sang Graysteil to the king'. The populace at large had a variety of dramatic or semi-dramatic entertainment ranging from cycles of mystery plays to folk plays and folk festivals. The texts have vanished, but the many references collected by Anna J. Mill[47]—often from the records of a

[44] Ed. W. M. Mackenzie (London, 1939), J. R. Simon (Paris, 1967), J. Norton-Smith (Oxford, 1971), M. P. McDiarmid (London, 1973).

[45] See Sir William Craigie, 'The Scottish Alliterative Poems', *Proceedings of the British Academy* xviii (1942), 217–36.

[46] *The Buke of the Howlat*, ed. D. Laing (Bannatyne Club, 1823), A. Diebler (Chemnitz, 1893) (cf. M. P. McDiarmid, *MÆ* xxxviii (1967), 277–99, Nicholson, p. 467); *Rauf Coilyear* ed. S. J. Herrtage, EETS ES xxxix (1882), facs. of Lekpreuik print, with intro. W. Beattie (Edinburgh, 1966); *Thre Preistis* ed. T. D. Robb, STS NS viii (1920); *Colkelbie Sow* in *Ancient Popular and Romance Poetry of Scotland* (D. Laing, ed. J. Small, Edinburgh, 1885), pp. 234–65.

[47] *Medieval Plays in Scotland* (Edinburgh, 1927). The examples quoted are on

later and hostile Kirk—show how deeply rooted all this was in the life of medieval Scotland. One Reformer laments (1546) that at Haddington, where two or three thousand people would have been at 'ane vane Clerk play', now the audience of 'the messinger of the Eternall God' barely musters a hundred. Aberdeen in 1580 and 1581 had trouble with the 'enormities' committed by the 'disordourit barnis and scholaris of the grammer schuill' who took over the school at Christmas, 'fosterand the ald ceremonie and rite of preuilege'. They were continuing a practice which was widespread; many references in our period speak of the 'king of the bean' (at Epiphany), 'saint Innocentis beschop', the abbot of Unreason—the 'Abbot of Bonacord', and the like. There are references to plays of Robin Hood, to May games, and various kinds of 'guising'. What was insisted on before the Reformation—(Aberdeen, 1508) 'all personis burges nichbouris and inhabitaris burges sonnys habill to rid to decor and honour the towne in thar array conveniant tharto sall rid with Robert huyd and litile Johne quhilk was callit in yeris bipast Abbot and priour of Bonacord one every Sanct Nicholas day throw the towne as wse and wont has bene...'—was later denounced—in Elgin, at the end of the century, Tiberius Winchester was accused several times, e.g. for a 'gysing' on 27 December 1593/4 'accompaneit with a pyper and certaine utheris ryotous pepill efter nyn houris of the nicht', and the splendid reprobate was at it still in 1604, when he was 'obseruit be sum superstitiouslie and prophanelie for having a bedcod on his heid and ryding thairwith throuche the town...', to which he confessed, and also 'for uttering uncomlie speaches the nycht the minister catecheized'. One cannot but suspect that even in the more relaxed atmosphere of earlier times, some of these activities may not be unconnected with the prevalence of 'strublans'. Other old practices included pilgrimages to holy wells, the ringing of vessels on Uphaly day, midsummer bonfires, harvest festivals (later described as 'pastymes in the grange upon the sabboth quhilk lattis the meting of the pople to the preiching'), the playing of football in the churchyard or (as is still practised in Kirkwall) through the town. The people of Perth were still in 1580 going in procession to the 'Dragon Hole' 'with pyping streking drummeis'.

No doubt what was described in 1574 as 'plaing, dansin and singin

pp. 74n. (Wishart on Haddington), 156 (Aberdeen, 1580), 137 (Aberdeen, 1508), 238, 240–1 (T. Winchester), 244 ('pastymes in the grange'), 162 ('fylthe carrolles').

off fylthe carrolles on Yeull Day' was also common earlier. *The Complaynt of Scotlande* (1549) gives a long list of dances and songs current at the time—including 'the breir byndis me soir', 'brume brume on hil', 'trolee lolee lemmen dou', 'the frog cam to the myl dur', 'Sal I go vitht you to rumbelo fayr', 'the huntis of cheuet', 'the perssee and the montgumrye met', and many others.[48] A body of oral songs and ballads certainly formed part of the popular literature of Henryson's time. This popular literature is rather more than a picturesque backdrop to his sophisticated poetry. Not only does he allude to it—the cadger sings 'huntis up, up' as he drives along, and Sprutok sings 'wes never wedow sa gay'—or adapt it (*The Bludy Serk* has the ring of a popular romance), but, since it is part of the fabric of ordinary life, it is important to him in a more fundamental way. This has been somewhat obscured in recent criticism in a well-meaning attempt to refute the erroneous view that Henryson was a simple rustic bard. As Kynaston saw, he was 'questionles a learned and witty man', but besides his undoubted learning and his skill in rhetoric, he has an ear for colloquial talk, and knows how to use popular idioms and forms. As with his master Chaucer, one reason for his distinction as a poet is that he understands both 'learned' and 'popular' tradition.

We know something, though not enough, about the intellectual life of Henryson's Scotland. As in England, this was a period of educational expansion. In Scotland there were abbey schools, burgh schools, 'sang schools' and the forerunners of the 'dame school' of later centuries; by the end of the fifteenth century, it has been estimated that every town of any size had its grammar school.[49] The function of such a school was to teach the boys to read, write and speak Latin; an Edinburgh master, Adam Mure, had to promise, in 1531, 'to maik the bairnis perfyte grammariarris within thre yeiris'. At Aberdeen in the sixteenth century only the 'elementarians' of the first year were allowed to use the vernacular. The life of the pupils was very severe, but that of their master can hardly have been easy. He was on duty for a long day (from 7 a.m. to 6 p.m. approximately) and, it seems,

48 Ed. J. A. H. Murray, EETS ES xvii (1872), pp. 64–5.

49 See J. Durkan, 'Education in the Century of the Reformation' in *Essays on the Scottish Reformation* ed. D. McRoberts (Glasgow, 1962), J. Scotland, *The History of Scottish Education* I (London, 1969), J. Grant, *History of the Burgh and Parish Schools of Scotland* I (London, Glasgow, 1876), Cosmo Innes, pp. 270ff. Cf. also N. Orme, *English Schools in the Middle Ages* (London, 1973), C. P. McMahon, *Education in Fifteenth-Century England* (1947, repr. New York, 1968).

accompanied them to church on Sundays. An entertaining case concerns the schoolmaster of Linlithgow in 1538–1539, James Brown, who complains that he and his children are terrorized by the curate, Schir Hendrie Louk, who makes them go to church twice a day on Sundays and on festal days as well, 'and settis doun in the said kirk on cauld stanis, quhen tha migcht have dune gret proffit and steed to thaimselves to have levit in the schull, tynand thair tyme.'[50] The schoolmasters in burghs were often Masters of Arts, and seem, sometimes at least, to have been of some dignity and importance. They were clerics, though possibly in minor orders, and occasionally married men; chaplains formed the commonest group. The abbot of Dunfermline in 1468 provided a house for the town schoolmaster (perhaps Henryson) and lands and rents to the annual value of eleven marks.[51]

Three of the four oldest Scottish universities are fifteenth-century foundations: St. Andrews (1411), Glasgow (1451), and Aberdeen (1494). Student life[52] seems to have had the usual medieval characteristics of poverty and violence (in 1457 St. Andrews students were forbidden to carry arms); the curriculum was traditional (a fifteenth-century controversy at St. Andrews concerned the relative merits of the doctrines of Buridan, the fourteenth-century French schoolman, and Albert the Great). No doubt, as in England, one would have found in intellectual life a great deal of continuity with the past as well as a rather cautious receptiveness to the new. For the literary historian, by far the most significant of the new tendencies was the growth of Scottish humanism. The development of humanism in England in the fifteenth century has been ably charted by Roberto Weiss; the Scottish records are more scanty, but Dr. John Durkan, Professor MacQueen and Mrs. Bawcutt have been able to piece together something of the story.[53] The currents of the new learning were certainly beginning to

[50] Sir James Balfour Paul, 'Clerical Life in the Sixteenth Century', *SHR* xvii (1919), 181–2.

[51] See Durkan, *art. cit.*, and D. E. Easson, 'The Medieval Church in Scotland and Education', *Scottish Church History Society Records* vi (1936–8), 13–26.

[52] See J. Robb, 'Student Life in St. Andrews before 1450 A.D.'. *SHR* ix (1911–12), 347–360, A. I. Dunlop, 'Scottish Student Life in the Fifteenth Century', *SHR* xxvi (1947), 47–63, R. G. Cant, *The University of St. Andrews* (rev. ed. Edinburgh, London, 1970), pp. 17–22.

[53] R. Weiss, *Humanism in England during the Fifteenth Century* (2nd ed., Oxford, 1957); J. Durkan, 'The Beginnings of Humanism in Scotland', *Innes Rev.* iv (1953), 5–25, J. MacQueen, 'Some Aspects of the Early Renaissance in Scotland',

move in the time of Henryson, but just how much impact they made on Scottish intellectual life is hard to ascertain. It would be wildly over-enthusiastic to claim anything like the English flowering at the end of the fifteenth century; before the great Buchanan (1506–1582), there is no one who could be placed beside Erasmus or More. There are, however, a number of scholars who were humanists or who may well have been influenced by the new learning. As a safeguard against the perils of enthusiasm let us arm ourselves with Weiss's definition of a 'humanist' *stricto sensu* as 'the scholar who studied the writings of ancient authors without fear of supernatural anticiceronian warnings, searched for manuscripts of lost or rare classical texts, collected the works of classical writers, and attempted to learn Greek, and to write like the ancient authors of Rome' (and who—it might be added—was often led on to an interest of a special kind in the letters, life and civilization of antiquity).[54] A number of Scots have some claim to be included in this category. William Turnbull[55] (d. 1454), the Bishop of Glasgow and the founder of Glasgow University (which was modelled on Bologna), spent some time at the court of Eugenius IV, and in 1439 took a doctorate in Canon Law at Pavia (where two very well known humanists, Lorenzo Valla and Maffeo Vegio, were teaching). Archibald Whitelaw, tutor and secretary to James III, taught at Cologne and St. Andrews, and delivered a fine Latin oration in 1484. He collected Italian books and MSS. We know that he possessed Lucan's *Pharsalia*, Horace, Sallust, the commentary of Asconius on Cicero, Appian, and—a more traditional book, perhaps—Albert, *De Animalibus*. All except the Lucan were printed in Italy. He seems clearly a 'humanist' in the strict sense.[56] William Elphinstone (d. 1514), Bishop of Aberdeen and founder of King's College, Aberdeen, was a graduate of Glasgow, and went on to Paris and Orleans. He possessed a copy of that important and influential humanist work, Valla's *Elegantiae Latinae Linguae*, which he copied himself, possibly when at Paris in the late 1460s—and

Forum for Modern Language Studies iii (1967), 201–22, and *Robert Henryson* (Oxford, 1967), chapter 1, Priscilla Bawcutt, *Gavin Douglas* (Edinburgh, 1976), esp. pp. 23–46.

[54] Weiss, p. 1. On the word, see A. Campana, 'The Origin of the Word Humanist', *JWCI* ix (1946), 60–73, G. Billanovich, 'Auctorista, humanista, orator', *Rivista di cultura classica e medioevale* vii (1965), 143–63.

[55] Cf. J. Durkan, *William Turnbull, Bishop of Glasgow* (Glasgow, 1951; first pr. *Innes Rev.* ii).

[56] See J. Durkan and A. Ross, *Early Scottish Libraries* (Glasgow, 1961), p. 159.

also solid works by Augustine and Ockham, Bartholomew the Englishman's *De Proprietatibus Rerum* and the *Glossa Ordinaria*.[57] Other names include Paniter, Latin Secretary of James IV and James V, Alexander Stewart, the natural son of James IV, who studied at Padua for a time with Erasmus, James Foullis of Edinburgh (c. 1485–1549), a poet.[58] And, as we move further into the sixteenth century, the names become more familiar—Hector Boece (*c.* 1465–1536), a contemporary of Erasmus at Paris, and the first principal of Aberdeen, which became a centre of humanistic studies, and George Buchanan himself (1506–1582), of whom Dr. Johnson made the unforgettable remark:

> However unfavourable to Scotland, he uniformly gave liberal praise to George Buchanan, as a writer. In a conversation concerning the literary merits of the two countries, in which Buchanan was introduced, a Scotchman, imagining that on this ground he should have an undoubted triumph over him, exclaimed, 'Ah, Dr. Johnson, what would you have said of Buchanan, had he been an Englishman?' 'Why, Sir, (said Johnson, after a little pause) I should *not* have said of Buchanan, had he been an *Englishman*, what I will now say of him as a *Scotchman*,—that he was the only man of genius his country ever produced.'[59]

One or two remarks in the foregoing account of the pioneers of Scottish humanism have already suggested that what was old, accepted and well-tried continued to exist and to flourish at the same time. The same picture emerges clearly from the lists of surviving books of the period.[60] Alongside the few classical texts stand many commentaries which reveal a deep interest in late scholasticism—even Boece, who had a copy of Ficino's *De triplici vita*, also had Duns Scotus on the Sentences. The same is true of a number of figures of whose biography we know something. Beside Turnbull, Elphinstone and Whitelaw, we might set James Kennedy (d. 1468), the Bishop of St. Andrews and the founder of St. Salvator's College, a great prelate interested in learning and

57 Cf. L. J. Macfarlane, 'William Elphinstone, Founder of the University of Aberdeen', *Aberdeen University Review* xxxix (1961), 1–18, 'William Elphinstone's Library', *ib.* xxxvii (1958), 253–71, Durkan and Ross, pp. 31–4.

58 See J. IJsewijn and D. F. S. Thomson, 'The Latin Poems of Jacobus Follisius or James Foullis of Edinburgh', *Humanistica Lovaniensia* xxiv (1975), 102–60.

59 *Life of Johnson*, ed. R. W. Chapman (new ed. corr. J. D. Fleeman, Oxford, 1970), p. 1209.

60 See Durkan and Ross; cf. A. Ross, 'Libraries of the Scottish Blackfriars: 1481–1560', *Innes Rev.* xx (1969), 3–36.

morality, but not, it seems, in humanistic studies,[61] William Schevez (or Schives) (d. 1497), a later Bishop of St. Andrews, a favourite of James III, and a very political churchman, deeply interested in astronomy and astrology as well as medicine and theology (besides Peter Lombard, Alexander of Hales and D'Ailly, he possessed a copy of Martial's *Epigrams* printed at Venice in 1482),[62] or, among the scholars, John Major (Mair) (1479–1550), theologian, friend of Wolsey, a good historian, and a successful teacher at Paris, Glasgow and St. Andrews, traditional in doctrine and learning, and later rather unfairly labelled 'the last of the schoolmen'. Although not a humanist like Erasmus, he seems to have had a wide knowledge of classical and neo-Latin literature, and his works are of importance in the history of law and science.[63]

It is very difficult to say with certainty whether or not Henryson himself was in any way affected by the new learning. It is certainly possible (especially if he studied abroad) that he had come into contact with it. He has been acclaimed as an early Northern humanist, and even enthusiastically called 'the first of the University Wits'.[64] There is, however, no evidence which can be regarded as conclusive. We have no idea what his Latin style was like, or what he thought of Valla or Pico or Ficino (or indeed whether he had even heard of them), any more than we know what his views on the rival claims of Buridan and Albert were. Imaginary biography is sometimes pressed into service—but there is no firm evidence that he studied at Rome or at Bologna. Nor can we be happy with arguments which imply a kind of 'virtue by contagion'; the fact that he lived at the same time as Poliziano or Ficino does not therefore make him into what Erasmus would have recognized as a 'humanist'. Internal evidence from his poetry is equally inconclusive. He quotes Aristotle and uses Trivet's commentary on Boethius, but so might any learned Scottish writer of his day. It has not yet been convincingly shown that he used the work of any humanistic writer, and it seems very likely that he did not know anything of contemporary Italian humanist work on Aesop. His apparent belief that the fabulist's 'native land is Rome' would undoubtedly have

[61] Dunlop, *Kennedy*, p. 301. [62] Durkan and Ross, pp. 47–9.

[63] Cf. C. M. MacDonald, 'John Major and Humanism', *SHR* xiii (1915–16), 149–58, J. Durkan, 'John Major: After 400 Years', *Innes Rev.* i (1950), 131–47, and 'The Cultural Background in Sixteenth-Century Scotland', *ib.* x (1959), 389–92, J. Burns, 'The Scotland of John Major', *ib.* ii (1951), 65–77, 'New Light on John Major', *ib.* v (1954), 83–100.

[64] MacQueen, *Henryson*, p. 23.

startled Valla or Erasmus. It may be simply a matter of a few crucial years. His younger Scottish contemporary Gavin Douglas was certainly in touch with the new learning; at about the time of Henryson's death he was—it seems likely—completing a humanist education in Paris.[65] But if there is nothing which clearly shows Henryson was a humanist of the new style, there is a good deal to suggest that he may be related to an older (and wider) tradition marked by an interest in classical antiquity, literature and mythography which is not at all uncharacteristic of the latter Middle Ages. Perhaps we might here compare him with such enthusiasts for the stories of antiquity as Chaucer, or the English 'classicizing' friars of the fourteenth century.[66] He certainly shares with Chaucer a *humanitas* which may well owe something to the study of classical authors.

Edwin Muir, in the passage quoted at the beginning of this chapter, remarked that Henryson 'inherited the medieval completeness and harmony'. That something like 'completeness and harmony' does emerge from his poetry may well be argued, although contradictions, paradoxes, ironies and ambiguities are fully present. Perhaps the word 'inherited' suggests that this 'completeness and harmony' came to him rather more straightforwardly than is likely to have been the case. Everything suggests that such an ideal was not one which was easily achieved by a writer of the second half of the fifteenth century. While we should be chary of over-dramatic or simplified views of the period as nothing but a 'waning' or a 'ferment', there is much to suggest that it was one of tension and urgent questioning. In the spiritual landscape of the time there are, beside examples of humane piety of the Henrysonian kind, examples of an enthusiasm which is very far from any 'power to see life whole'. At one extreme we have a highly sophisticated theology, still attempting, with varying degrees of conviction, to support the truths of the Christian religion by rational argument, while at the other there is an intense and fervid popular piety which shades almost imperceptibly into folklore and magic. The first church in Scotland, apparently, to have the distinction of suffering from the Reformation was the parish church of Restalrig near Edinburgh, which had been rebuilt in 1487. In 1560 it was ordered to be destroyed 'as a

[65] Bawcutt, *Douglas*, pp. 27ff.

[66] See B. Smalley, *English Friars and Antiquity in the Early Fourteenth Century* (Oxford, 1960). Cf. also the essays in A. Fournier, *L'humanisme médiéval dans les littératures romanes du xiie au xive siècle* (Paris, 1964).

monument of idolatrie'. It had attached to it the well of St. Triduana, with a chapel (the upper chapel was endowed by James III), which was a 'balm-well' to which pilgrims resorted for cures of the diseases of the eyes.[67] On the practices of popular religion and superstition, John Major is more tolerant than the Reformers: 'country women are guilty of little or no sin in many vain superstitious practices: for they are not taught any better...they make St. Bridget's Bed on her feast day [for any passing stranger]. On the feast of the Purification, they singe the hair of their menfolk and oxen with a blessed candle. On Hallowe'en they put bundles on the points of spears and set fire to them...They believe that two brothers should not be allowed to eat of the same kidneys...', etc. Among the practices of divination (of which he strongly disapproves) he describes how 'the faces of those suspected of a theft are painted on a wall. If the painted face of the man who took the article is touched with iron, his own face will be wounded, and his eyes will first shed tears and eventually be blinded if he does not confess the truth'.[68] For centuries after the Reformation the 'Great Bell' of St. Giles (originally cast in Flanders in 1460) rang out across the city, bearing—like some other Scottish bells—an unnoticed inscription from Popish times, and one which at its end has a reference to yet another popular practice—the ringing of bells for protection against storms and thunder: '...defunctos plango: vivos voco: fulmina frango' (I toll the knell of the dead, I call the living to prayer, I break the force of the lightning).[69]

One merchant's book from the late Middle Ages which has survived[70] has in it, along with elaborate commercial instructions for Scottish traders in the Low Countries, a long prayer-charm of a kind common all over Europe, said to be efficacious for journeys, quelling

[67] *Acts and Proceedings of the General Assemblies of the Kirk of Scotland from the Year M.D.LX* (Maitland Club, Edinburgh, 1839), I, p. 5. Cf. Lindsay, *Monarche* 2366 (*Works* ed. D. Hamer, STS 3rd ser., I, p. 269), R.C.A.M.S., *Edinburgh*, p. 253. Nearby was St. Margaret's Well (*ib.*, p. 239); cf. also St. Vildrin's (R.C.A.H.M.S., *Stirlingshire*, p. 436). (On Saints Triduana and Vildrin, see A. P. Forbes, *Kalendars of Scottish Saints* (Edinburgh, 1872), pp. 453–4, 458.)

[68] Tr. Burns, 'The Scotland of John Major', pp. 71, 72.

[69] R.C.A.M.S., *Edinburgh*, p. 33. Bells with 'Popish' inscriptions seem sometimes to have escaped the Reformers; cf. (Holy Rude, Stirling) R.C.A.H.M.S., *Stirlingshire*, p. 138, *Fife*, p. 94, *SHR* x (1910–11), 327–8. For the practice of ringing bells against storms, cf. Gray, *Themes and Images in the Medieval English Religious Lyric* (London, 1972), p. 241.

[70] A. Hanham, 'A Scots Merchant's Handbook', *SHR* l (1971), 107–20.

storms, for all kinds of pain and for childbirth. 'Quicumque oracionem sequentem dixerit cottidie, remissionem omnium peccatorum habebit et nunquam mala morte morietur': this is that 'suddand deith' (*Fables* 2157) so dreaded in the Middle Ages, a death for which one was not prepared, and had to 'dye as beistis without confessioun'. The fear of death and judgement found expression sometimes in grimly macabre images, as in the Dance of Death or as in Henryson's *The Thre Deid Pollis*, and—although these are not as omnipresent as is sometimes alleged—a sense of the imminence and the terror of death is found again and again. We may instance Dürer's 'Der Spaziergang' or 'Young Couple threatened by Death' (*c*. 1497/8), where the two lovers walk through a beautiful countryside covered with flowers, while Death with his hour-glass hides behind a tree. With a typical eye for detail, Dürer accompanies the portrait of his mother made in the year she died with an account of her death: 'she greatly feared death, but she said she did not fear to appear before God. She had a hard death, and I noticed that she saw a frightening vision...I saw also how death dealt two great blows to her heart and how she closed mouth and eyes and died in agony...'.[71]

More than any other artist of the time, Dürer catches a mood of apocalyptic doom, the way in which the deep fears of the age could express themselves in chiliastic fantasies (cf. especially, 'The Artist's Dream', 1525). But in the late fifteenth century even in subjects which are far from macabre, and under surfaces which seem calm and tranquil, we may feel a sense of strain and tension or the suggestion of darker currents. A case in point is the Bonkill painting of Hugo van der Goes. Panofsky says perceptively that here even where we find Hugo's style 'in perfect purity', we may detect 'an increase of inward excitability combined with a kind of outward assuagement', that beneath the apparent calm there lurks a tendency—still controlled—to 'abolish rationality altogether', and remarks on the strangely unreal effect produced by the recurring modulations of one colour, red.[72] The painting certainly has uneasy and tense undertones. At the height of a spectacularly successful career, Hugo had decided (by November 1475)

[71] Quoted by M. Levey, 'Dürer and the Renaissance' in C. R. Dodwell, *Essays on Dürer* (Manchester, Toronto, 1973), pp. 17–18. For 'Der Spaziergang', see E. Panofsky, *The Life and Art of Albrecht Dürer* (4th ed., Princeton, 1955), plate 99.

[72] Panofsky, *Early Netherlandish Painting*, p. 336.

to retire from the world to the Roode Kloster near Brussels. He continued to paint and to see clients, but in 1481 suffered a terrible crisis, a major attack of suicidal melancholy, in which he 'incessantly said that he was damned and judged to eternal damnation', and wished to take his life. In spite of attempts to assuage his melancholy by music 'et alia spectacula recreativa', he continued to 'talk wildly and say that he was a son of perdition'. He recovered, but survived only for a year. One of the monks gives us a detailed account of the illness;[73] he thinks that it was not (as some said) demonic possession, but rather melancholy coming from the passions of the mind. Hugo worried deeply, it seems, about how he could complete the paintings which he had to do ('...ut tunc dicebatur vix novem annis perficere potuisset'). Another rumour recorded in 1495 attributes his breakdown to the inability to reach the perfection of the great Ghent altarpiece. The problems of creation of the sensitive artist must have been exacerbated by an intense religious enthusiasm. Gaspar Ofhuys, the monastic chronicler, says somewhat mysteriously that Hugo was always deeply immersed in a Flemish book. The drinking of wine because of his guests, he also says, aggravated the condition. With more than a touch of self-righteousness he concludes that the attack was an act of Providence to humble the pride of Hugo and to give an example to the other brothers.

The great majority of ordinary folk, less talented and less intense than the great Flemish artist, probably managed to cope with the problems of life by the help of simple faith and trust in the Church; like Dürer's mother, many of them probably feared death but did not fear to appear before God. 'Our Lord, our life, our faith, our sicht, leid ws, feid ws, and speid ws, in the pilgramage of this mortalite...Fra suddane and unprovidit ded preserve ws...Mak ws joyfull to tak tribulacioun for the lufe of the' run some phrases from a prayer from MS. Arundel 285, a collection of Scottish devotional verse and prose compiled in the early sixteenth century, and marked by an intense and loving relationship of man with Christ;[74] *The Contemplacioun of Synnaris* in the same MS. concludes with the injunction 'Quhat euer God send, blis him ay blythly'. Order and harmony in society and in the created world are important themes in *The Meroure of Wyssdome*

[73] Ed. H. G. Sandar, 'Beiträge zur Biographie Hugos van der Goes', *Repertorium für Kunstwissenschaft* xxxv (1912), 519–45.

[74] Ed. J. A. W. Bennett, *Devotional Pieces in Verse and Prose*, STS 3rd ser. (1955).

of John of Ireland, a 'mirror for a prince', dedicated to James IV.[75] His argument is philosophical and learned, 'starklie fundin in haly writt', and with examples from antiquity. Ireland insists on the need for authority, for justice tempered with mercy, for a true wisdom that is achieved through humility and grace: 'Souverane wissdome is a gift of the haly spreit, and ane of the hiest and maist nobile of the divinite and hevinly thingis...Bot waurldly wissdome is accumilacioune of honoris, digniteis, riches, gud fortoune and happines, and it is oftymes na wissdome bot foly...' Ireland makes Peace, the heavenly lady, pleading for man, speak with some lyrical feeling: 'exile pess, and than distroyit is for evir the hevinly realme, and the eternall habitacioune without pess may nocht indure. The hevinly melody and concord of the speris and planetis abuf without pess and concord may nocht stand; stabilite amang the elementis without pess may nocht indure, na lif in man nore beist; for the contrariete of the foure humoris and fyrst qualite is in concord, and in armony standis all the wertu of musik, sueit notis and sangis...'. Yet he is aware of the presence of ignorance and of 'errors against the faith'. And indeed, throughout the century, a number of Lollards and Hussites were burnt, or driven out.[76] Old patterns of belief were beginning to be questioned, older allegiances strained by growing tensions over the need for reform, and the manner in which it could be achieved. Probably the 'practical disorder of life' often seemed to call into question the ideals of secular society also. Although embodiments of the noble and chivalric ideals like Bernard Stewart or Bayard could still be admired, some at least of the manifestations of chivalry's 'Indian summer' must have seemed outmoded. It is perhaps worthy of note that this aspect of medieval life plays no significant part in Henryson's poetry—except for a religious adaptation in *The Bludy Serk* and for a brief moment in *The Testament of Cresseid* where we catch a glimpse of the noble Troilus.

A harmonious vision of the world, we may suspect, no longer came easily to a sensitive poet of the later Middle Ages. He was faced, moreover, by urgent problems of artistic form. In contradiction to Muir's age of the 'long calm of story-telling', when the 'imagination could

[75] Cf. J. Burns, 'John Ireland and the Meroure of Wyssdome', *Innes Rev.* vi (1955), 77–98, Brother Bonaventure, 'The Popular Theology of John Ireland', *ib.* xiii (1962), 130–46. The quotations later in the paragraph are from Macpherson, pp. 12, 119.

[76] See the *Scotichronicon* ed. W. Goodall (Edinburgh, 1759), II, pp. 495–8.

attain harmony and tranquility', we might set the view of a German historian, Peuckert, that the fifteenth century lacked the power to master and to order 'the chaos of things and of life', that the prevailing tendency to collect, to accumulate without discrimination, as if the material itself will give aesthetic satisfaction, leads in the end to the dissolution of form.[77] We might recall the strictures of the classically-minded Michelangelo on the lack of symmetry and proportion in the landscapes of some Northern painters.[78] In literature, too, there are examples of encyclopaedic, didactic, baggy monsters, of stylistic experiments losing themselves in ornate 'babuinerie', of a concern for the 'thisness' of things sitting uneasily with a passion for greater and greater abstraction. The writer had to struggle with the problems of art itself, with the relationship of fiction to truth. The old fear that words and matter would be lost in oblivion was reinforced by the problems of finding an aesthetic order for the 'chaos of things' in some 'authentic' manner, without 'lying'. This was probably exacerbated by the way in which beneath the familiar surface of life patterns of thought and belief were shifting. It is, for instance, often notoriously difficult in the later Middle Ages to decide where 'earnest' ceases and 'game' begins. This is especially so with attempts to play out dreams. 'One might ask...,' says Huizinga,[79] '...whether the princes and nobles really took seriously all the bizarre fantasies and the play-acting with which they embroidered their plans of campaign and their vows. It is extremely difficult within the realm of medieval thought to arrive at a neat distinction between what is play and what is earnest, between honest conviction and that attitude of mind which the English call pretending.' That there is no such neat distinction might suggest to a bold writer the exploitation of complex intermediate states, of delicately shifting relationships. It is certainly not surprising that in a period when past certainties were being undermined we should find in literature a liking for enigmas, contradictions, and ironies. 'Completeness and harmony' were still ideals, but no longer a straightforward inheritance. To achieve them was a challenge.

[77] Will-Erich Peuckert, *Die Grosse Wende, Das apokalyptische Saeculum und Luther* (Hamburg, 1948), pp. 54–5.

[78] *Four Dialogues on Painting*, tr. A. F. G. Bell (London, 1928), pp. 15–16.

[79] J. Huizinga, *Herfsttij der Middeleeuwen*, *Verzamelde Werken* iii, p. 196, tr. E. H. Gombrich, 'Huizinga and Homo Ludens', *TLS* Oct. 4, 1974, p. 1085 (the equivalent passage in the abbreviated English version, *The Waning of the Middle Ages* (1948 repr.) is on p. 217).

CHAPTER TWO

Beasts and Wisdom:
(i:) Feigned Fables of Old Poetry

Fables have delighted listeners and readers—old as well as young, kings as well as slaves—for many centuries. Among those who have written or used them we must number teachers and preachers, satirists and humorists, friars, monks, and Protestant Reformers, humanists, and rationalists of the Enlightenment. The remarkable way in which this simple and humble form has unfailingly maintained its popularity suggests that it has some qualities which appeal to something deeply rooted in the human consciousness. Besides pleasing the common reader 'uncorrupted with literary prejudices', it has also fascinated the learned: scholars have argued about its origins, critics about its nature. Above all, throughout its long history, the fable has challenged the creative imagination of writers. It will be the contention of this and the following two chapters that in the period between the great fabulists of antiquity and the greatest fabulist of all, La Fontaine, whose first collection appeared in 1668, the most original, ambitious and successful fables are those of Henryson—*The Morall Fabillis of Esope the Phrygian*, as the early prints describe them—and that his little masterpiece is not only 'one of the most delightful books in Scottish literature', but must also have an honoured place in the history of the European fable.

Henryson's collection of thirteen fables is surrounded by a number of unsolved mysteries and problems. He undertook the work, he says in his Prologue

> Nocht of my self, for vane presumptioun,
> Bot be requeist and precept of ane lord,
> Of quhome the name it neidis not record.

The name of the 'lord'—if he existed—has remained hidden ever since. We do not have any certain indication of the date of the *Fables*. It has been claimed that Henryson knew and used Caxton's *Aesop* of 1484, but this has not been conclusively proved. Nor is it certain that he knew Caxton's *Reynard* of 1481. Supposed historical allusions in one or two fables are also far from certain. Moreover, the text of the *Fables* presents grave problems for the editor. The surviving complete, or more or less complete, versions come from a time long after the work was written, and we would not be justified in assuming that any single one preserves in every reading the *ipsissima verba* of the poet.[1] There are further questions about the order of the *Fables*, the completeness of the collection, and the possibility of revision. We do not know if Henryson had completed his work. Did he propose to turn into Scots yet more of the many fables available? Certainly the ending of the last fable in the Bassandyne/Harley/Charteris order sounds very like a farewell:

> Adew, my freind!...
> Now Christ for us that deit on the rude,
> Of saull and lyfe as thow art salviour,
> Grant us till pas intill ane blissit hour

and the first fable, 'The Cock and the Jasp', corresponds to the first fable in the particular Aesopic collection which Henryson used, and the whole version presents what seems to be a unified and complete work.[2] The Bannatyne MS., however, has a different order—and one which has been claimed to be superior—beginning with 'The Preaching of the Swallow', and ending with 'The Lion and the Mouse', with the Prologue and other fables and tales coming between them. As it stands, this hardly seems a coherent order, and may represent a re-ordering by Bannatyne or by some predecessor. To complicate matters, the title-page of the Asloan MS. suggests a different order, beginning this time with 'The Paddock and the Mouse', and ending with 'The Two Mice' (which is the only fable whose text survives in this version)

[1] The Bassandyne print (1571), which is the basis of Wood's and Elliott's editions, has inaccuracies and shows signs of Protestant revision, but although an editor might often prefer the readings of the Bannatyne MS. (1568), it is hard to agree with Professor MacQueen (*Henryson*, Appendix I (and *Innes Rev.* xiv)) that it is 'so much superior to any of the others that it must necessarily form the basis of a satisfactory edition'. Cf. Denton Fox, *NQ* ccxii (1967), 348–9, and see his forthcoming edition. On Caxton, see Fox, 'Henryson and Caxton', *JEGP* lxvii (1968), 586–93. On historical allusions, see pp. 142–44 below.

[2] Strongly argued by H. H. Roerecke, *The Integrity and Symmetry of Robert Henryson's Moral Fables*, unpub. Ph.D. dissertation, Pennsylvania State University, 1969 (I am indebted to Professor Denton Fox for this reference).

Again, it is possible that we are dealing with a selection. Elaborate theories of revision have been based on these differences of order—that, for instance, the Bannatyne is derived from an 'early version' which did not include 'additions made after 1485'.[3] This is not impossible, but far from certain. Attempts to date 'revisions' on the dates of supposed sources remain highly speculative.

Fortunately, rather less mystery surrounds the kind of work that Henryson chose (or was asked) to write. With conventional modesty, he presents his *Fables* as a 'translatioun' from his author Aesop:

> In mother toung of Latyng I wald preif
> To mak ane maner of translatioun.

It is in a very special sense '*ane maner* of translatioun', for his version is far more ambitious than he makes it sound. The story-material which he used was, however, quite traditional, coming from Aesopic fables, fables associated with the Aesopic collections, and stories from the beast-epic of Reynard the Fox. In the Middle Ages, there was a vast mass of fable-material, much of it reaching far back into antiquity. It is beyond the scope of this study to attempt any comprehensive account of this *corpus* and its extremely complicated historical relationships. This chapter, deliberately selective and deliberately discursive, attempts simply to illustrate the development of the Aesopic fable tradition and that of Reynard into the forms in which it may have been available to Henryson, to uncover something of the nature of the beast-fable, and to isolate some of the possibilities it would offer to his poetic imagination.[4] The tradition in which he consciously placed himself was not only heterogeneous and varied, and fascinating in its paradoxes, but also of considerable antiquity. He seems to recognize this in the phrase he uses in his opening line, 'feinyeit fabils of ald poetre', and, like the learned poet he is, to relish it. It is unlikely, though, that he knew just how ancient the tradition was.

The Aesopic animal-fable is a very distinctive and particular form of the much larger category of animal stories, which are found in many

[3] MacQueen, *Henryson*, p. 193.

[4] On fables in general, cf. (among many studies) B. E. Perry, 'Fable', *Studium Generale* xii (1959), 17–37, J. Jacobs, *The Fables of Aesop* (London, 1889) I, K. Doderer, *Fabeln* (Zürich, 1970), E. Leibfried, *Fabel* (Stuttgart, 1958), A. Schirokauer, 'Die Stellung Äsops in der Literatur des Mittelalters' in *Festschrift für Wolfgang Stammler* (Berlin, 1953), G. C. Keidel, *A Manual of Aesopic Fable Literature* in *Romance and Other Studies* (Baltimore, 1895).

cultures. In 'traditional' societies, men live in a closer and more intimate relationship with animals and the animal world than is usually the case in the urbanized and industrial societies of the Western world. It is not, however, a Romantic 'nearness to nature'. The complexities of the relationship are well illustrated in a recent comparative study of animal-symbolism in three African cultures by Dr. Roy Willis.[5] Animals may be used as religious, magical, psychological and social symbols, having a significance within the cosmos of the people involved. They are not only 'good to eat', but, in Lévi-Strauss's phrase, 'good to think', forming part of the symbolic structure of a conception of the universe,—and Dr. Willis would add, 'good to feel' and 'good to imagine' as well. He finds that animals are especially apt for a symbolic rôle because they can be used to express opposites and hold them in tension, being at once close to man and yet unalterably different. The symbolism of his three tribes presents some revealing variations. The Nuer, herders of the southern Sudan, venerate the ox. They conceive of animals as organized in an analogous way to their own community, and their attitude to them is that of detached observers. They take little interest in the world of wild animals, and regard hunting as an unworthy occupation. But their relations with the ox are very intimate—the 'soulful ox' provides inspiration for poetry, each man has an 'ox-name', and all social processes and relationships are defined in terms of cattle. Balanced oppositions, as that of man against nature, are characteristic of the Nuer world view. The ox symbolizes for them the identity and continuity of their society, representing 'a transcendent individual, the inmost, essential being denuded of all external, specific attributes of time or place'. The Lele, living on the edge of the rain-forest of the Congo, venerate the pangolin. For them the forest (sharply contrasted with the village) has great prestige and religious significance. It is the source of all good things, and the proper habitat of animals (domestic animals are regarded as essentially anomalous). Hunting for them is the one great communal activity, and success in it is controlled by the spirits. The pangolin, an anomalous creature of the forest, of peculiar behaviour and characteristics, is a spirit animal, and mediates between the opposed spheres of village and forest, and the demands of individual and community. The Fipa, who live on the shore of Lake Tanganyika, have a much more utilitarian

[5] *Man and Beast* (London, 1974) (for the Nuer and the Lele, he draws on the work of Evans-Pritchard and Douglas).

relationship with domestic animals, which they regard simply as different forms of wealth, and a neutral attitude to the world of wild animals (for them, hunting is a solitary and utilitarian activity). In general they do not attach symbolic significance to animals, except for the sacred python. Their conception of the universe is not one of opposed contraries, but is unitary and dynamic. They see human society as superior to wild nature, and the business of men to extend their control over it. Dr. Willis argues that in their search to transcend plurality and diversity they find the image of ultimate value in the python, 'the wild creature of the earth whose domestication by man symbolizes the central life-process by which the strange and unknown is brought into the light and order of human understanding'.

Many of the animal stories which have been recorded from societies such as these during the last two centuries are strikingly similar in nature to those of Western Europe, even though, in most cases, they are apparently quite independent. In Africa, for instance, where animal stories form part of a rich oral literature, one early collector called his series of Hottentot stories *Reynard the Fox in South Africa* to underline the likeness.[6] Students of African animal tales have often been struck by the importance and the number of 'small, wily and tricky animals who cheat and outdo the larger and more powerful beasts',[7] animals who belong to that type known to folklorists as 'tricksters', of whom the medieval Reynard is a notorious and lively example. In some parts of Africa the animal in question is the little hare (possibly the antecedent of a transported Brer Rabbit); in West Africa it is the spider Inanse, and elsewhere the tortoise or some other animal. As in European stories, the trickster, though he is usually successful, is sometimes himself tricked; he is wily, but also sometimes stupid, gluttonous and ineffective. The animals are shown speaking, thinking, and acting like humans, and in a human setting. As in Europe, they sometimes have traditional attributes and rôles. In Angola, apparently, it is the elephant who is the supreme beast: 'in the fables, the elephant is equally supreme in strength and wisdom; the lion is strong, but not morally noble....The hyena is the type of brutal force united with stupidity; the leopard that of vicious power combined with inferior wits. The fox or jackal is famous for astuteness; the monkey for shrewdness and

[6] W. H. I. Bleek, *Reynard the Fox in South Africa* (London, 1864).
[7] Ruth Finnegan, *Oral Literature in Africa* (Oxford, 1970), p. 344.

nimbleness; the hare or rabbit for prudence and agility...'[8] The animals act like humans, yet the fact that they are also animals is not forgotten, and this incongruity becomes a source of humour and wit. The stories are entertaining, sometimes light-hearted, sometimes satirical. Some of them, like Aesopic fables, are designed to teach a lesson, and may even end with a moral, sometimes in proverbial form.[9]

Like the animal symbolism discussed by Dr. Willis, these traditional stories are more complex in their rôle and their nature than is at first apparent. They are simple, but at the same time—and here we come upon a paradox which we shall find again in the history of the European fable—they have a curious sophistication of their own. They are, as Ruth Finnegan in her study of African oral literature says, 'a medium through which in a subtle and complex way, the social and literary experience of narrators and listeners can be presented... Doubly removed from reality in being set among animals, the animal tales reflect, mould, and interpret the social and literary experience of which they form part.' They also make use of a quite sophisticated method of transference, of metaphorical thought, fundamental to the animal tale, and capable of the most delicate variations, which is also, clearly, of immense importance in the development of literature and of human culture. Sir Ernst Gombrich (defining *metapherein* as 'transference') remarks:

> The possibility of metaphor springs from the infinite elasticity of the human mind; it testifies to its capacity to perceive and assimilate new experiences as modifications of earlier ones, of finding equivalences in the most disparate phenomena, and of substituting one for another. Without this constant process of substitution, neither language nor art, nor indeed civilised life, would be possible.[10]

It would, of course, be dangerous to assume, without further evidence, that animal stories of this type collected in 'traditional' societies in modern times (and of which the true date cannot possibly be known) are exact replicas of their supposed antecedents in antiquity. There is, however, some evidence which suggests the existence of

[8] H. Chatelain, *Folk Tales of Angola* (Memoirs of the American Folklore Society I, 1894), p. 22.

[9] Finnegan, p. 346.

[10] E. H. Gombrich, *Meditations on a Hobby Horse* (London, 1963), p. 14.

animal-tales of a not dissimilar kind. From Babylonia there survives in fragmentary form a kind of beast-epic which has as its hero a fox who has something in common with Reynard. Professor Perry summarizes the story: 'the fox conspires successfully with the wolf to outwit the shepherd-dog and to prey upon his sheep. The dog is put on trial before Shamash for neglect of duty and is vigorously accused by the fox...in the next fragment the dog, who has apparently been acquitted, is successfully prosecuting the fox and the wolf, while the fox by tears and entreaties is trying to beg off from his sentence. In the last fragment the fox is in the proximity of a lion who is threatening to eat him, and here again Reynard is resorting to tears.'[11] It seems reasonable, therefore, to see animal stories of the traditional type as part of the background of the European fable. Quite possibly the wise and grateful animals and the tricksters of some classical fables come from folk-literature of this sort. The tradition of the European fable has generally a rather literary cast, but examples of Aesopic fables occur in oral tradition,[12] and the fable was always liable to melt back into the larger and less didactic background of the animal story, 'out of which', as Perry says, 'as fable, it had been moulded, curtailed and disciplined by the intellectual culture of the ancient world.'[13]

In earlier times, when the question of the origins of European fables was hotly disputed, students were impressed by similarities with fables in the large collections of Indian stories. In the *Jātakas* or stories of the Buddha's former births (a version in Pali dates from *c.* 430 A.D.), where animal fables are given a spiritual meaning, there are parallels with Aesopic examples (e.g. the Wolf and the Lamb). Others (e.g. the Lion and the Mouse) are found in the versions of the *Panchatantra*, composed originally at some time during the first five centuries of the Christian era. Animal stories are here used as part of a 'mirror for princes'—a wise man teaches, in an entertaining and realistic way, the principles of statecraft and of everyday morality. The first book, which has for its framework the story of two jackals (later appearing as

[11] Perry, 'Fable', p. 26n.

[12] Cf. G. Pitrè, *Fiabe, Novelle e Racconti popolari siciliani* IV (Palermo, 1875), pp. 162ff. Possibly 'The Wedding of the Frog and Mouse' mentioned in *The Complaynte of Scotlande*, and popular later (cf. A. H. Tolman and M. O. Eddy, 'Traditional Texts and Tunes', *Journal of American Folklore* XXXV (1922), 393–399, A. Williams, *Folksongs of the Upper Thames* (London, 1923), p. 133, etc.), is related to the fable of the Frog and the Mouse.

[13] Perry, 'Fable', p. 37.

Kalilah and Dimnah) is the original of the 'fables of Bidpai' which come into the European fable-tradition by a complicated route.[14] La Fontaine certainly knew the fables of Bidpai, but Henryson shows no sign of having done so.

More recently, however, students of the classical fable have investigated its relationship with another, and earlier, form of literature, the 'Wisdom literature' of the Middle East. This is certainly the other most important part of the background of the European fable. Wisdom literature is most familiar to modern Western readers in a book such as the Old Testament book of *Proverbs*, which is in fact a number of collections of the teachings of 'wise men', sayings and maxims which relate to various forms of wisdom, ethical and practical as well as religious. Maxims of practical everyday prudence—*Lebensklugheiten*—in which considerations of self-interest are by no means negligible, and which show how to survive, or how to live with success, coexist with advice on how to live virtuously, and with ideas (thought by some scholars to be later) of a divine wisdom and providence made manifest in creation ('the Lord by wisdom hath founded the earth; by understanding hath he established the heavens')—ideas which we can recognize centuries later in the opening of Henryson's 'Preaching of the Swallow'. Old Testament Wisdom literature includes such books as *Ecclesiastes*, *Job*, *Ecclesiasticus*, *Wisdom*; behind it lies an older background of closely related works from Egypt, Assyria, Babylonia and Sumer.[15] It is of some interest to find that this Wisdom literature, in the prototypes of the story of Job, makes a very early attempt to deal with those questions of suffering and of justice which are often so prominent in later fables. A Babylonian poem about a righteous man who suffers unjustly at the hands of providence gives vehement expression to (as well as a reply to) the sentiments of disbelieving sceptics.

Proverbs and fables are closely related (the same word is used for both in various Middle Eastern languages), and this literature contains many examples (some from Sumer going back to the opening centuries

[14] Cf. Jacobs, *Fables of Aesop*, I, pp. 52ff. The fables of Bidpai arrive finally in a thirteenth-century translation by Giovanni da Capua, *Directorium humanae vitae alias parabole antiquorum sapientum*, and find their way into printed books and vernacular versions (cf. J. Jacobs, *The Earliest English Version of the Fables of Bidpai* (London, Edinburgh, 1888)).

[15] Cf., e.g., W. McKane, *Proverbs* (London, 1970), R. H. Pfeiffer, *Introduction to the Old Testament* (revised ed., 1948), pp. 645–59, S. Langdon, *Babylonian Wisdom* (London, Paris, 1923).

of the second millennium B.C.) of animal proverbs, short proverb-fables, as 'He did not yet catch the fox, but he is making a neck-stock for it' (cf. 'Don't count your chickens...'), and some which are extended to little narratives of a kind very similar to the later Aesopic tales.[16] The Sumerian fox, 'a small creature who is full of conceit', and prone to exaggeration, sounds not unlike the fox of Aesop's 'Sour Grapes'. A fable from the *Book of Ahikar* has a confrontation of a familiar sort, when a leopard meets a goat and says 'Come, I will cover thee with my hide'—'the goat answered and said to the leopard, "What need have I for it, my lord? Take not my skin from me."...' Besides the dramatic encounter and the dialogue, we recognize the honeyed and ironic words of a dissembling villain, and the notion that intelligence and foresight may protect the innocent and the weaker from the villainous and the stronger. We are not concerned here with questions of origins; I need simply underline the importance of this early connection of the fable and Wisdom literature, for it is a relationship which, as we shall see, has some interesting suggestions for the student of later fables.

The tradition of fable in Western Europe which Henryson knew came directly from the Latin fable of late antiquity, and the impulse for this came from Greece. 'Aesop', whose name is always associated with this tradition, is a shadowy figure. Herodotus says that he was a slave on the island of Samos in the sixth century B.C., which may well be true, and records the fact—or legend—that he was a Thracian. The universal later belief that he was a Phrygian may be due to an analogy with the Phrygian Marsyas, as 'the spokesman of a homely rural culture'.[17] There is a 'Life', but it is certainly not contemporary and probably dates from the first century A.D.[18] In this Aesop appears as

[16] Edmund I. Gordon, *Sumerian Proverbs* (Philadelphia, 1959); cf. S. N. Kramer, *From the Tables of Sumer* (Indian Hills, Colorado, 1956). On the *Book of Ahikar*, cf. McKane, pp. 156ff. (There are one or two fables in the Old Testament, and, apparently, about three dozen more in the Talmud and Midrash; cf. D. Daube, *Ancient Hebrew Fables* (Oxford, 1973)).

[17] *Babrius and Phaedrus* ed. B. E. Perry (Loeb Classical Library, 1965), pp. xl–xli. Cf. also Perry, 'Fable', pp. 28ff. My remarks on the ancient fable are deeply indebted to the studies of Perry, M. Nøjgaard, *La Fable antique* (Copenhagen, 1964, 1967), A. La Penna, 'La morale della favola esopica', *Società* xvii (1961), 459–537, and M. Pugliarello, *Le origini della favolistica classica* (Brescia, 1973).

[18] It is associated later with the thirteenth-century scholar, Maximus Planudes (described by Bentley as 'that idiot of a monk').

a clever slave, famous for wise counsels and witty proverbs. He outwits his master; he wins his freedom by interpreting an omen; he writes fables for King Croesus, and solves riddles for King Lycurgus; finally, because of a trumped-up charge of sacrilege, he is thrown by the Delphians over a cliff. This romantic 'Life' was translated into Latin by Rinuccio d'Arezzo in 1474, whence it passed into the late fifteenth-century fable collections of Steinhöwel and Caxton. Steinhöwel's frontispiece (which is copied in Caxton) shows Aesop surrounded by illustrations of fables and episodes from his 'Life'. He is shown as a short, deformed, hunch-backed and ugly man, in conformity with the description in the Life: 'for he had a grete hede, large vysage, longe jowes, sharp eyen, a short necke, corbe backed, grete bely, grete legges, and large feet, and yet that whiche was werse he was dombe, and coude not speke...'. This image of the fabulist lived on even after Bentley had demolished the claims of the 'Life', and for centuries Aesop was 'one of the stock illustrations of the law of compensation': 'Aesope was crooked: Socrates purblinde, long-legged, hairy...Horace a little blear-eyed contemptible fellow, yet who so sententious and wise?'[19]

The Aesop who appears to Henryson in a dream (ll. 1348ff.) does not look like this at all. He is a 'poet laureate', and is treated with great reverence. 'Now my winning is in hevin for ay' he says (he has apparently joined the ranks of the righteous heathen); he is 'off gentill blude', and his 'native land is Rome withoutin nay'.[20] He is dressed like a university graduate, and he appears to the poet to be 'the fairest man that ever befoir I saw', with white beard, eyes that are 'grit and gray', and 'off stature large'. It sounds as if Henryson's own imagination has created a handsome visual image appropriate to an 'auctor'. There is no hint in the text of any deliberate reversal of the description of the ugly slave of the 'Life' or of the representations which are so

[19] Burton, *Anatomy of Melancholy*, quoted by M. Ellwood Smith, 'Aesop, a Decayed Celebrity', *PMLA* xlvi (1931), 228. Small ugly figures of Aesop among animals occur quite late; cf. *Æsop's Fables with Instructive Morals and Reflections* (London, 1740), or the polyglot *Hundert Fabeln* (Berlin, 1830) reproduced in Doderer, *Fabeln*.

[20] So too in Lydgate, he 'dyd hym occupy / Whylom in Rome to plese the senate / Fonde out fables...'. Professor Norton-Smith suggests to me the possibility that Henryson's idealized portrait borrows some of its details from the facts known about the Roman tragic actor Aesop, a friend of Cicero's, and of good family, a Claudian. His style of speaking was grave and passionate ('gravis', 'gravior', Horace, *Epist.* 2.1.82, Quintilian, *Inst. Orat.* 11.3.111).

prominent in Steinhöwel and Caxton; we are left with the strong suspicion that Henryson was unaware of the image of Aesop as an ugly, wise slave, and consequently that he probably had not read either Steinhöwel or Caxton. So powerful, however, was the tradition of the 'ugly Aesop' from these sources in later times that the Bassandyne print of the *Fables* has a version of Steinhöwel's portrait on its title-page, in spite of what Henryson himself says!

Individual Greek Aesopic fables are attested from quite early times, but they seem to have been brought together only in the late fourth century B.C. In the Augustana collection of prose fables (probably derived from a compilation of the second century A.D.) on which modern editions are based, we can find many of the favourites of later ages—'The Fox and the Grapes', 'The Ass in the Lion's Skin', etc.—and some of the remote antecedents of Henryson's fables—'The Wolf and the Lamb' (showing us that 'when a man is determined to get his knife into someone, he will turn a deaf ear to any plea, however just'),[21] 'The Lion and the Mouse' ('a change of fortune can make the strongest man need a weaker man's help'), 'The Two Mice' ('a simple life with peace and quiet is better than faring luxuriously and being tortured by fear'), or 'The Rat, Frog and Kite', which is Henryson's 'Paddock and Mouse'.

From 'Aesop', the later tradition received not only lively stories, but also lively protagonists, a series of animal actors with distinctive characteristics—the cunning and wicked fox, who tries to profit from every situation (though he is sometimes foolish and stupid, and like the tricksters of oral animal tales often 'out-foxed' at the end), the wolf who is voracious, violent, and faithless, and the lion, the king of the animals, noted both for his generosity and for his cruelty. These animals are largely those of popular lore, but they also have some relation to the scientific observation of the 'nature of things'.[22] The Aesopic animal world—in which foxes yearn for grapes or for cheese, can hardly be called 'scientific', but it is not irrational. We are a long way from the magical or religious animals of primitive myths, and there is something in 'Aesop' of the rational outlook which lay behind

[21] Translations from Aesop are those of S. A. Handford, *Fables of Aesop* (London, Penguin Books, 1954).

[22] Cf. F. Klingender, *Animals in Art and Thought to the end of the Middle Ages* (London, 1971); the translations from Aristotle are those of D'A. W. Thompson, quoted by Klingender, pp. 88–9.

the very real achievements of Greek zoology. Aristotle was interested in the signs of rational intelligence in animals and in their physical qualities: 'so in a number of animals we observe gentleness and fierceness, mildness or cross temper, courage or timidity, fear or confidence, high spirit or low cunning, and, with regard to intelligence, something equivalent to sagacity...'. His careful distinctions were easily blurred in later and more popular science, and, indeed, some of his own material seems to be drawn from popular lore (he makes use of traditional moral characteristics: 'cautious and watchful as the goose' (cf. Chaucer's 'waker goos'), 'jealous and self-conceited as the peacock', etc.). A body of stereotyped 'characters', opposed categories of sympathy and antipathy, and examples of animal sagacity was eventually bequeathed to the popular science of the Middle Ages; some of it, filtered through the science and medicine of late antiquity with its love for mystical harmonic correspondences, was to provide a rich store for medieval moralists. But this was still to come. In the rational, dispassionate world of the Aesopic fable, this material was moulded into a flexible symbolic language. As Francis Klingender says, 'in Aesop's use of the fable the transition from beast-magic to beast-symbol was already completed. By evoking childhood memories of animal fairy-tales, and, to some extent also, every-day observations, these new symbols could gain a powerful hold on the imagination'.[23]

The moral world of Aesop is not a sunny place. We are presented with a series of particular case-histories rather than with a coherent philosophical system, and such morality as emerges seems often to have self-interest as the main, if not the only motive. As in the older Wisdom literature, the maxims are often utilitarian and pragmatic, concerned largely with the value of prudence in an unjust, or at least arbitrary, world, and with the craft of survival. There is a strong sense that any change in man's condition is unlikely, that people should make the best of their lot, and that they may indeed be safer if they are poor and obscure—the fisherman catches the big fish in his net, but the smaller ones escape through the meshes—a sentiment which was not forgotten in the moral fables of the Middle Ages.

The corpus of Aesopic fables became known to Western Europe through the collection of Phaedrus (first century A.D.), who like Aesop was a slave (and later a freedman of Augustus). His fables are a trans-

[23] Klingender, p. 86.

lation into Latin verse of some earlier Greek 'Aesop' collection. He begins with the name of his 'auctor'—

> Aesopus auctor quam materiam repperit,
> Hanc ego polivi versibus senariis

('Aesop is my source. He invented the substance of these fables, but I have put them into finished form in senarian verse' (Perry)), and makes constant reference to him, sometimes representing him, rather like the sage in the *Jātakas*, as responding to a particular situation with some apt doctrine—'Aesop told them this little tale...', 'Aesop saw a large crowd at the wedding of his neighbour, a thief, and at once began this fable...'. It is not hard to see the beginnings of the development which led ultimately to the 'poet laureate' whom Henryson met in his dream. Phaedrus carries the Aesopic concision to extremes, and something of that brevity of style which was his ideal is preserved in the medieval versions deriving from him (La Fontaine, who makes it into high art, says with self-conscious modesty that he cannot match 'l'élégance, ni l'extrême brèveté qui rendent Phèdre recommandable'). Phaedrus is also very self-consciously plebeian—it is he who in the Prologue to Book III claims that the fable was invented by slaves who could thereby voice thoughts that were not otherwise permitted.

Another strand of Aesopic tradition comes into Western Europe through the Latin verse fables of Avianus (? *c.* 400) which are adaptations from the Greek verse fables of Babrius (? first century A.D.), themselves based on Aesopic material, gentler in tone and with a greater interest in psychology and sentiment. However, the central Western tradition is, as Joseph Jacobs says, 'Phaedrus with trimmings'.[24] The trimmings are considerable. Of the prose paraphrases of Phaedrus, the most important is a collection of about eighty fables known as 'Romulus' (one of the various explanations with which it is prefaced says that an emperor called Romulus translated Aesop for his son Tiberinus). Its origins are mysterious; it may date from *c.* A.D. 350–500. This was turned into verse again by an unknown author, probably in the twelfth century. This collection has been attributed to Gualterus Anglicus or Walter the Englishman, to Salone of Parma and to

[24] Jacobs, *Fables of Aesop*, p. 1. Texts of the later Latin versions in L. Hervieux, *Les Fabulistes latins*, 5 vols. (Paris, 1893–99); 'Romulus' ed. G. Thiele, *Der Lateinische Aesop des Romulus und die Prosafassungen des Phaedrus* (Heidelberg, 1910) and Hervieux, II.

others;[25] it is sometimes called the 'Anonymus Neveleti' because it found its way into a compendium edited by Nevelet in 1610, but since this is such a cumbersome title I shall refer to it as 'Walter'. Whoever wrote it did his work with brevity and polish, and the collection remained deservedly popular throughout the Middle Ages.

The twelfth century is a period of especial importance in the history of the fable. It produces a number of well-known animal stories—Nigel Wireker's *Speculum Stultorum*, the early versions of the *Roman de Renart* (see below, pp. 63–9), and, possibly, the lively debate-poem *The Owl and the Nightingale*—and a number of fabulists besides 'Walter'. The scholar Alexander Neckham (d. 1217) wrote a *Novus Aesopus* and a *Novus Avianus*. Marie de France produced at the request of a certain 'count William' an elegant series of fables in French verse, which she says are translated from the English of 'King Alfred'.[26] In fact, most of them come, ultimately at least, from 'Romulus', some from the stories of Renard, and some probably from oral tradition. She adapts the morals to the interests of a knightly patron; now, among the animals, *leialté* and *felunie* appear, and the figure of the *vilain*. Like Henryson later, she begins to expand the narrative material of the fables. Another interesting vernacular version is the Hebrew *Mishle Shu'alim*, or 'Fox Fables', by Berechiah ha-Naqdan. His fables are marked by a gentle satire, and—if one may judge from the lively translation of Moses Hadas[27]—by vivid detail. Thus in his version of the Paddock and the Mouse, the eagle holds both mouse and frog tied together, 'but when he saw that he could not reach the mouse because of the thick hide drawn tight over his back and the black hairs that sprouted from it, he turned his attention to the frog, which he found goodly to behold and pleasant to eat, and swallowed her down at a single gulp'. Berechiah's country mouse, after all its tribulations, takes a distinctly Biblical farewell: 'All thy life is vexation and wrath; but bread in secret is sweet. Why hast thou slandered the forest? Better a dry crust and tranquility therewith than a house filled with the

[25] Cf. Hervieux, I, pp. 475–95; doubts concerning Walter's authorship are expressed by G. Paris (*Journal des Savants* (1885), p. 39). Cf. S. Rossi, *Robert Henryson* (Milan, 1955), p. 16. Text of 'Walter' ed. Hervieux, II, pp. 316ff., and J. Bastin, *Recueil général des Isopets* (Paris, 1929).

[26] Ed. K. Warnke, *Die Fabeln der Marie de France* (1898); cf. the selection by A. Ewert and R. C. Johnston (Oxford, 1942). Cf. E. Mall, 'Zur Geschichte der mittelalterlichen Fabelliteratur', *Zeitschrift für Romanische Philologie* ix (1885), 161–203, H. R. Jauss, *Untersuchungen zur mittelalterlichen Tierdichtung* (Tübingen, 1959), chapter 1.

[27] *Fables of a Jewish Aesop* (New York, 1967).

sacrifices of contention. From every man that approaches thou fleest in panic and in breathlessness takest refuge in one tent and another. In my place I shall find song and joyful shouting, the beauty of Carmel and Sharon.'

Fables proliferate throughout the rest of the Middle Ages. They may be found in sermons, or in collections of stories intended for use in sermons, for Christian preachers, like their Buddhist counterparts, obviously found them useful. Odo of Cheriton (d. 1247) for instance, in his 'Parables'[28] uses material from Aesop, from the *Physiologus*, and from *Renart*. He tells how Isengrim the wolf enters a monastery, and when he is asked to repeat the Pater Noster, responds always with *Agnus* (lamb) and *Aries* (ram). Or they may appear in separate fable-collections, like the French 'Isopets'[29]—*Isopet I* and the *Isopet de Lyon* are versions of 'Walter', *Isopet II de Paris* and the *Isopet de Chartres* of Neckham's *Novus Aesopus*. A number of the fables of the Romulus redaction appear in the French translation of the *Speculum Historiale* of Vincent of Beauvais by Jehan de Vignay (1333).[30] The fifteenth century shows, if anything, even greater interest and activity.[31] MS. copies of 'Walter' and other early versions continue to be made. In England, Lydgate has a short collection, *Isopes Fabules*. In Italy, besides the older versions, there appear products of a humanist interest in fables. The text of Phaedrus was rediscovered and transcribed by Perotti. Greek texts of Aesop became known, and found their way eventually into print (e.g. at Milan, *c.* 1480); versions from the Greek were made by Rinuccio d'Arezzo and Lorenzo Valla. The early printers found a market for books of fables. Steinhöwel's collection (first printed by Zainer at Ulm, *c.* 1478) includes Romulus with a trans-

[28] Hervieux, IV; see A. C. Friend, 'Master Odo of Cheriton', *Speculum* xxiii (1948), 641–58. Cf. also the stories of Bozon, *Les contes moralisés de Nicole Bozon*, ed. P. Meyer (Paris, 1889).

[29] See Bastin, *Recueil*, K. McKenzie and W. A. Oldfather, *Ysopet-Avionnet: The Latin and French Texts* (Urbana, 1919).

[30] Cf. G. E. Snavely, *The Aesopic Fables in the Mireoir historial of Jehan de Vignay* (Baltimore, 1908), and 'The Ysopet of Jehan de Vignay' in *Studies in Honor of A. Marshall Elliott* (Baltimore, 1911) I, pp. 347–74. Another popular fourteenth-century collection is that of the Swiss, Ulrich Boner, *Der Edelstein* (ed. F. Pfeiffer, Leipzig, 1844).

[31] For Lydgate, see *Minor Poems*, ed. H. N. McCracken (EETS cxcii, 1934), II, pp. 566–99; for Perotti, cf. Perry, *Babrius and Phaedrus*, p. xcviii. Valla was translated into French by Tardif for King Charles VIII (cf. H. Guy, *Histoire de la poésie française au 16e siècle*, Paris, 1910).

lation into German, fables from other sources—'Walter', Avianus, miscellaneous fables which he called *extravagantes*, some of Poggio's *facetiae*, and some stories from the *Disciplina Clericalis* of Petrus Alphonsus. Steinhöwel's book, adorned with numerous woodcuts, proved very popular; it was produced in various forms and languages at least twenty-seven times before 1500. From a French translation of it by Macho came Caxton's *Book of the subtyl historyes and Fables of Esope* of 1484, which made available to English readers an extensive and attractive anthology of fables in prose.[32]

Henryson's *Fables* is the earliest known vernacular collection in Scotland, although there is evidence not only of a knowledge of fables in and before his time, but also of a general interest in animal stories.[33] In spite of much devoted scholarly endeavour, it is still not easy to say exactly how much of the mass of medieval fable-material was available to him. It is certain that he used the verse fables of 'Walter', and probable that he knew a French version or versions of them, the *Isopet de Lyon* or something similar. He knew Chaucer's *Nun's Priest's Tale*, and probably Lydgate's fables and Odo of Cheriton's parables.[34] Beyond this, all is uncertain. The sheer excellence and individuality of Henryson's treatment of the traditional matter is the main reason for our difficulty in ascertaining his precise sources, but another is that Aesopic fables belonged to that category of well-known stories which would be held and transformed in the individual memory and passed on in oral as well as literary form. In the case of 'The Two Mice', for instance, it seems that 'Walter' is his immediate source, but there are differences—Henryson's version, for instance, has two moments of danger for the mice—which may come from unrecorded oral versions, whether from the lips of preachers or from the Scottish equivalents of Wyatt's 'mothers maydes' who 'sang sometyme a song of the feld mowse...'. Professor Fox draws our attention to an early sixteenth-century fragment of just such a song in the notebook of a Danish

[32] Ed. R. T. Lenaghan, *Caxton's Aesop* (Cambridge, Mass., 1967), Jacobs, *Fables of Aesop*.

[33] Cf. I. W. A. Jamieson, 'The Beast Tale in Middle Scots', *Parergon* ii (1972), 26–36; R. J. Lyall, 'Dunbar's Beast Fable', *Scottish Literary Journal* i (1974), 17–28.

[34] See A. R. Diebler, *Henrisones Fabeldichtungen* (Halle, 1885), and especially, I. W. A. Jamieson, *The Poetry of Robert Henryson: A Study of the Use of Source Material*, unpub. Ph.D. thesis, University of Edinburgh, 1964; cf. also Jamieson, 'A Further Source for Henryson's "Fabillis"', *NQ* ccxii (1967), 403–5.

humanist ('It was twa mousis, biggit in twa housis...') and rightly cautions us against imagining our poet working away surrounded by 'a litter of variant versions of a fable', selecting now this detail, now that.[35]

The inherent liveliness of fables was not the only reason for their enormous popularity in the Middle Ages. It may well owe something to a widespread and genuine interest in animals throughout the period, an interest not only in the prodigious and exotic beasts which we see arriving to participate in Henryson's 'parliament', but also a curiosity about the habits and properties of more homely creatures—'I hadde wonder at whom and where the pye lerned / To legge the stykkes in whiche she leyeth and bredeth'.[36] Such curiosity could, and did, become scientific. Something at least of ancient zoology was recovered in the twelfth century, and medieval scientists show some independent observation. A delight in the plenitude and variety of natural species is reflected in the thousands of insects, birds and animals which are scattered over the margins of medieval illuminated manuscripts, in the menagerie of creatures which inhabit the capitals, bosses, misericords and bench-ends of churches, in the crowds of birds who surround the goddess Nature in Chaucer's *Parlement of Foules* and the animals who fill the forest in his *Book of the Duchess*.

This interest in animals was intensified by the belief that one might learn from them. They were part of a symbolic universe, which was a 'mirror' or a 'book written with the finger of God', or an enigma (the 'Aenigma Dei' which was to exercise the wit of the seventeenth century),[37] at which one looked with wonder and from which one received illumination. Wonder at the strange and instructive witnesses of God's wisdom—'who gave the hedghogge prickes, and taught it to wallow it self in apples shaken downe with the winde, with the which being loden, and going, it maketh a noyse like a carte. And the ante which foreseeing winter to come, fylleth her barnes with corne...'—leads easily to delight at the perception of *multum in parvo*—'a little body made with great wysedome. Great wisdom in which there is no oversight, but hath geven them eyes, which the eye can scantely spye,

[35] D. Fox, 'A Scoto-Danish Stanza, Wyatt, Henryson, and the Two Mice', *NQ* ccxvi (1971), 203–7; cf. R. Bauman, 'The Folktale and Oral Tradition in the Fables of Robert Henryson', *Fabula* vi (1964), 108–24.

[36] *Piers Plowman* ed. W. W. Skeat, B xi. 339–40. Cf. also J. A. W. Bennett, *The Parlement of Foules* (Oxford, 1957).

[37] See Kitty Scoular, *Natural Magic* (Oxford, 1965).

and in so little bodyes, all the partes be so fitly, and fully fynished, that there wanteth nothing in the least of all the same thinges, wherwith nature hath bewtifyed the greatest.'[38] In mystical philosophers and allegorists, the metaphorical transference of primitive animal stories may appear in complex and ambitious schemes or in extraordinary analogies and similitudes, as in the 'divine emblems' of the *Physiologus*, that curious blend of Christian allegory and the mystical science of late antiquity, where under the veil of the properties of creatures the author sees the pilgrimage of the life of man constantly threatened by the wiles and wickedness of the devil: 'as the woodpecker, when he finds a hollow tree, builds his nest in it, so also does the devil with man; for when he finds one faint-hearted in the path of virtue, therein he takes up his abode...'.[39] The 'wonder' of this symbolic universe may range from fantastic lore to a philosophical wonder at the mysterious *discordia concors* of creation in which opposites such as fire and water, body and soul are held together through the wisdom of God.

As for centuries, animals were thought of as having an intimate relationship with men. In its extreme forms the relationship may still be a magical or a mystical one—on the one hand moralists are continually rebuking popular superstitions—'Beleve nought yn the pyys chetreyng, / Hyt is no trouthe but fals beleving'[40]—while on the other there are the well-known stories of saints (most notably St. Francis) who find a spiritual union with the animal world. More typically, perhaps, moralists were fond of seeing the animality in man's nature, while writers of popular science found it easy to project human emotions and moral characteristics on to animals—'of all domestic animals', we still read in an eighteenth-century encyclopaedia, 'the character of the cat is the most equivocal and suspicious'.[41] This kind of transference may appear in a charmingly witty form—in one medieval window the owl is shown ringing a bell, with the inscription 'we must pray for the fox', and the tit as cellarer, with 'who blameth this ale'—or in a more philosophical awareness of similarities and links: 'God

[38] Hugh of St. Victor, *PL* clxxvi, 820 (tr. Richard Coortesse (Curteys), 1577), ff. E i^v^, E i (the latter quoted by Scoular, p. 82).

[39] *Physiologus* tr. J. Carlill, in *The Epic of the Beast* intro. W. Rose (London, 1924), p. 209. Cf. Klingender, pp. 92–4.

[40] *Handlyng Synne* ed. F. J. Furnivall, EETS cxix (1901), p. 13. Cf. G. R. Owst, 'Sortilegium in English Homiletic Literature of the Fourteenth Century', in *Studies Presented to Sir Hilary Jenkinson*, ed. J. Conway Davies (London, 1955).

[41] *Encyclopaedia Britannica* (London, 1773), II, p. 586.

made man...creature resonable, and he made nevyr in beste othir than is founden in man. For a man is hardy as a lyone, ferd as an hare...harde and sharpe as ravene or crowe. Meek as a turtille... malicious and angry as a foxe, lowe as a lambe...hevy and slowe as a bere...Resonabille and chast as aungille, lecherous as swyne, fowle as an owle...and shortly to say that ther is no condicioun in best, ne in planet of hevene, ne in erthe that it ne is founden in man, and therfore the philesofre callith man the litille world.'[42] The natural world had of course been created for the use of man, and over it, before the Fall, he had exercised his rule or *imperium*. Bartholomew the Englishman explains in his *De Proprietatibus Rerum* (*c.* 1230) that 'alle kynde of bestes, wilde and tame, goynge and crepynge is ymade and yordeigned for the beste use of mankynde'—whether for food or for 'servyce'. Some are made to help men by providing medicines—an adder's skin boiled in oil 'abateth ache of eeren', while the 'longe tieth of a wolf heleth lunatyke men'. Some are created 'for mannes merthe, as apes and marmusettes and popyngayes', and some 'for man schulde knowe his owne infirmite and the myght of God. And therefore beeth ymade flees and luys.' Man, the 'little world', is the 'worthiest of creatures', a 'best iliche to God'. Other animals look downward to the earth, but God gave man a face which looks upward to the stars.[43]

There was another reason for the great popularity of fables. They were familiar because of a humble but important social rôle they had in the medieval world—their use as vehicles of instruction in the pulpit and in schools. Many medieval preachers liked to mingle entertainment with their doctrine, and found a rich store of *exempla* from animal life and bestiary lore (the crow is forever singing 'cras, cras' (tomorrow) like a reluctant penitent, etc.).[44] Naturally, enough, fables form an

[42] *Three Prose Versions of the Secreia Secretorum*, ed. R. Steele, EETS ES lxxiv (1898), p. 35. The window referred to on p. 48 (probably originally from a secular hall) is now in Yarnton Church, Oxfordshire (J. D. Le Couteur, *English Medieval Painted Glass* (London, 1926), p. 152, fig. 51).

[43] *On the Properties of Things* (Trevisa's translation), ed. M. C. Seymour and others (Oxford, 1975), pp. 1110–11, 90–1.

[44] G. R. Owst, *Literature and Pulpit in Medieval England* (Cambridge, 1933, 2nd ed. Oxford, 1961), discusses pulpit moralizations of natural history. On *exempla* cf. J. A. Mosher, *The Exemplum in the Early Religious and Didactic Literature of England* (New York, 1911), J. Th. Welter, *L'Exemplum dans la littérature religieuse et didactique du moyen âge* (Paris, Toulouse, 1927). On animal symbolism, cf. also B. Rowland, *Blind Beasts* (Kent, Ohio, 1971), *Animals with Human Faces* (Knoxville, 1973).

important part of their repertory of 'tales olde'. Bromyard adapts the old Aesopic advice of being content with one's lot to the benefit of honest and simple peasants confronted with sinners boasting of their riches, and counsels them to say in their heart with the country mouse 'I prefer my rustic poverty, with security and happiness, to those splendid banquets and robes with remorse of conscience...and the fear of punishments in hell'.[45] The over-enthusiastic use of stories by preachers was often criticized,[46] sometimes because of the crudity and popular character of what was passed off as doctrine, but sometimes because of a distrust of fiction itself. Wyclif says that friars 'maken hem besi on the holy day to preche fablis and lesyngis to the peple and not the gospel', and frequently returns to the theme, linking 'fablis' with 'lesyngis', 'gabbyngis' and 'poises'. Chaucer's Parson, with the fine austerity we should expect of him, refuses to indulge his hearers: 'thou getest fable noon ytold for me', quoting St. Paul's reproof of those that 'weyven soothfastnesse / And tellen fables and swich wrecchednesse'. The careful defence of 'feigned fables' in Henryson's Prologue may well suggest an awareness of such attacks on fabulous stories.

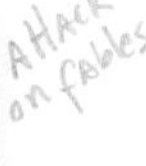

The much older connection of the fable with elementary education was possibly an even more significant reason for its popularity. Throughout the Middle Ages the Latin 'Aesop' formed part of the elementary curriculum.[47] Aesop was one of the 'minor authors' along

45 *Summa Praedicantium*, s.v. ministratio (ed. Venice, 1586, f. 33), quoted by Owst, p. 296.

46 Cf., e.g., Mosher, p. 18, Welter, pp. 102–7, Smalley, *English Friars*, pp. 299–300; *The English Works of Wyclif*, ed. F. D. Matthew, EETS lxxiv (1880), p. 8 (cf. pp. 50, 59, 73, 105–6, 153, 175).

47 Cf. E. R. Curtius, *European Literature and the Latin Middle Ages* (tr. W. R. Trask, London, 1953), pp. 49ff., 57–8, 464. In antiquity, Quintilian (*Inst. Orat.* I. ix. 2, tr. H. E. Butler (Loeb)) says '...pupils should learn to paraphrase Aesop's fables, the natural successors of the fairy stories of the nursery (*fabulis nutricularum*), in simple and restrained language and subsequently to set down this paraphrase in writing with the same simplicity of style: they should begin by analysing each verse, then give its meaning in different language, and finally proceed to a free paraphrase in which they will be permitted now to abridge (*breviare*) and now to embellish (*exornare*) the original, so far as this may be done without losing the poet's meaning...'. At Winchester in 1530, the first form studied a fable of Aesop on Sundays, the second form fables for 'constructions' throughout the week, except for Saturday mornings, when they did Cato, and the third form studied them on Mondays and Wednesdays (C. P. McMahon, *Education in Fifteenth-Century England*, p. 106).

with Donatus, Avianus and 'Cato', the reputed author of the sententious *Distichs*, and venerated as an *auctor*, a fund of wisdom and philosophical 'sentence'. Sometimes the surviving copies of the Latin Aesop are well-thumbed and heavily annotated, and seem to have been pored over by master or pupil. Even in the seventeenth century the young La Fontaine would probably have begun his study of Latin with Phaedrus, and of Greek with Aesop.[48] John Locke is still recommending (1693) the Fables of Aesop as children's reading: 'which being stories apt to delight and entertain a child, may yet afford useful reflections to a grown man.'[49] Outside the schoolroom, children probably were delighted and entertained by fables, which were perhaps the nearest thing they had to a 'children's literature'. In the *Dialogue of Comfort*, More in the person of Anthony recalles a 'Mother Maud' who used to tell the children stories when she sat by the fire; among her 'fond childish tales' was the fable telling how 'the Ass and the Wolf came on a time to confession to the Fox'.[50]

This profound and early familiarity means that in these centuries allusions to Aesop come almost as easily as allusions to the scriptures. Dante, describing the grotesque pursuit of Ciampolo by the devils (*Inferno* xxiii), thinks instantly of the fable of the frog, the mouse and the kite. In *The White Devil* (IV. i) Monticelso alludes to others as *exempla*:

> ...undermining more prevails
> Than doth the cannon. Bear your wrongs concealed,
> And, patient as the tortoise, let this camel
> Stalk o'er your back unbruis'd: sleep with the lion,
> And let this brood of secure foolish mice
> Play with your nostrils, till the time be ripe
> For the bloody audit and the fatal gripe...

From this hasty historical survey something of the nature of the Aesopic fable has already emerged. It is a form which is full of curious

48 G. Couton, 'Du Pensum aux *Fables*', *La poétique de La Fontaine* (Paris, 1957).

49 *Some Thoughts concerning Education* (London, 1693), pp. 183–4.

50 *A Dialogue of Comfort Against Tribulation*, ed. Leland Miles (Bloomington, London, 1965), pp. 92–8. On the place of fables in children's literature, see F. J. Harvey Darton, *Children's Books in England* (2nd ed., Cambridge, 1958). Among the hundreds of later 'Aesops' are some nice oddities, e.g. Mary Godolphin, *Aesop's Fables in Words of One Syllable* (of which one edition is in Isaac Pitman's phonetic shorthand).

and suggestive contrasts and paradoxes. We have seen that it is both learned and popular, written for kings and yet known to the very humble and the very young. It has traditionally been associated with children and with elementary school, yet it has constantly attracted highly literate and sophisticated authors. To our list of names (which is by no means complete)—'Walter', Neckham, Marie de France, Lydgate, Valla, Henryson—may be added another from antiquity. According to the *Phaedo*, Socrates spent his last few days in prison putting a few Aesopic fables into verse, and constructing a new one. He has been struck by what an unaccountable thing pleasure is, and how wonderfully it is related to its apparent contrary, pain—'and it seems to me...that if Aesop had observed this he would have made a fable from it, how the deity, wishing to reconcile these warring principles...united their heads together, and from hence whomsoever the one visits, the other attends immediately afterwards' (tr. Cary).

This strange form, humble and sometimes despised, and yet at the same time respected as the vehicle of wisdom, 'those fables of Aesope, and other apologies invented for doctrine sake by wise and grave men',[51] finds itself, interestingly, in the forefront of the defence of poetry, in support of a rather different paradox, that poetry, though it is 'feigned' is yet true. The 'pretty allegories' of Aesop, according to Sidney, give good proof that the poet is 'the right popular philosopher'—'so think I none so simple would say that Aesope lied in the tales of his beasts: for who thinks that Aesop writ it for actually true were well worthy to have his name chronicled among the beastes he writeth of'.[52] In medieval discussions of poetic fiction, too, Aesop's

[51] Puttenham, *The Arte of English Poesie* (1589), ed. E. Arber (London, 1869), p. 252. Quintilian (V. xi. 19) says that Aesopic fables are 'specially attractive to rude and uneducated minds, which are less suspicious than others in their reception of fictions and, when pleased, readily agree with the arguments from which their pleasure is derived' (tr. Butler), mentions Livy's story of Menenius Agrippa reconciling the plebs to the patricians, and remarks that Horace did not regard the use of fables as beneath the dignity of poetry. Cf. Erasmus, *De Copia* (tr. D. B. King and H. D. Rix, Marquette University Press, Milwaukee, 1963), pp. 84–5): fables captivate 'country people, the uneducated, and anyone else whose ways have a flavour of the golden age'; Wilson (*Arte of Rhetorique* (1553), ff. 105^{v}–106): 'not onely they delite the rude and ignoraunt, but also they helpe much for perswasion'. Henryson remarks once that Aesop wrote a fable when he 'waikit from mair autentik werk' (l. 1890).

[52] *An Apology for Poetry*, ed. G. Shepherd (London, 1965), pp. 109, 114. Cf. Elyot's defence of 'Histories', *The Governour* III, ch. xxv: 'I suppose no man

tales appear as examples of 'impossible' fiction: 'by Aesop's fables we are brought to some insight into behaviour, and yet they signify nothing true'.[53] Henryson's own remarks on 'feigned fables' are part of these discussions.

Because of its considerable variety, it is difficult to find a wholly satisfactory definition of the fable. Dr. Johnson, in reproving Gay, sets up a clear criterion:

> Of this kind of Fables, the authors do not appear to have formed any distinct or settled notion. Phaedrus evidently confounds them with Tales, and Gay both with Tales and Allegorical Prosopopoeias. A Fable, or Apologue. . . seems to be, in its genuine state, a narrative in which beings irrational, and sometimes inanimate, 'arbores loquuntur, non tantum ferae', are for the purpose of moral instruction, feigned to act and speak with human interests and passions.[54]

Johnson's definition would in fact suit Henryson's *Fables* perfectly, since there we find only 'irrational' beings as protagonists, but so many fabulists besides Phaedrus and Gay have confounded fables with tales that we are probably forced into allowing some more generous definition, though it remains true that it is usual for animals (or trees, etc.) to play the major rôles. 'The purpose of moral instruction', however attenuated or bizarre it may become, probably is a necessary part of any adequate description.[55] In what Professor Perry calls the

thinketh that Esope wrate gospelles, yet who doughteth but that in his fables the foxe, the hare, and the wolfe, though they never spake, do teache many good wysedomes?' See M. Ellwood Smith, 'The Fable as Poetry in English Criticism', *MLN* xxxii (1917), 466–70.

[53] William of Conches, quoted by Peter Dronke, *Fabula* (Leiden, 1974), p. 18. Aesopic fables are defended by St. Augustine, *Contra Mendacium*, *PL* xl. 538. On the discussion, cf. Dronke, *passim*, Curtius, Excursus VI, D. Fox, 'Henryson's Fables', *ELH* xxix (1962), 339ff., K. Doderer, 'Über das "betriegen zur Wahrheit", Die Fabelbearbeitungen Martin Luthers', *Wirkendes Wort* xiv (1964), 379–88.

[54] *Lives of the English Poets* ed. G. B. Hill (Oxford, 1905), II, p. 283.

[55] Cf. Lessing ('Von dem Wesen der Fabel'): 'when we are desirous of illustrating a general moral precept by a particular instance, and in order to bestow upon that particular instance a real existence, we invent a story in which the general moral is intuitively perceptible—such invention is called a fable' (*Fables and Epigrams with Essays on Fable and Epigram*, from the German of Lessing, London, 1825). See also the studies of Perry, 'Fable', and M. Ellwood Smith, *JEGP* xiv (1915), 519–29, *MP* xv (1917–18), 93–105.

'best definition of Greek Aesopic fable', a Greek rhetorician, Theon, simply says that it is 'a fictitious story picturing a truth'.[56] His word *logos* reminds us of the essentially narrative nature of the fable, that it is a story, even if (as for example in 'The Cock and the Jasp') a story in miniature. It is not surprising therefore to find that in the Middle Ages words like *fabula* or *fable* are used of a variety of forms, and that fables in their 'genuine state' are often associated with (and not necessarily differentiated from) other related types of 'tale', the beast tale, the anecdote, the novella, the parable, the exemplum.[57] In the sixteenth century, Bannatyne groups Henryson's fables with other stories of different kinds.

Most readers would probably agree in finding certain recurrent and important characteristics. Fables are usually short, and simple (although their simplicity may be more apparent than real). They are usually vivid, and memorable—one excellent reason for their popularity with orators and preachers, and for their longevity. (Most readers of this book will be surprised at the number of Aesopic fables they are able to remember and to hand on to the next generation.) It is a commonplace of the fabulist that he means to please as well as to instruct (this is Luther's view as well as Henryson's and La Fontaine's), and the fable can still entertain even serious children (the first thing George Eliot remembered laughing at, according to Cross, was one of Aesop's fables). Whether or not fabulists have been equally successful in their attempts to improve mankind is beyond the judgement of a mere mortal. Certainly, one aspect of the fable has proved especially attractive to writers from Aesop to Orwell—its power for sharp correction, for social and political satire.

There are, however, less obvious characteristics of the fable which deserve examination. We have already noticed the close historical connection between the fable and the Wisdom literature of the Middle East. Metaphorical proverbs, such as 'the mountain laboured and gave forth a mouse' or 'still waters run deep' are sometimes almost fables in miniature,[58] and some later proverbs—'sour grapes', 'a dog in the

[56] Perry, 'Fable', p. 22.

[57] Cf. Curtius, p. 452, H. de Boor, *Über Fabel und Bispêl* (Bayerische Akad. der Wissenschaften, Phil.-Hist. Kl., Sitzungsberichte, 1966, Heft 1).

[58] Quintilian (V. xi. 21) notes the similarity of fables with 'that class of proverb which may be regarded as an abridged fable and is understood allegorically'. The Semitic words which are used for both forms mean 'likeness' (cf. Perry, 'Fable').

manger' come from fables. There are resemblances between fables and even the more general types of wise sayings. Like the fable, the proverb unites the particular and the general. In 'traditional' societies this is an important intellectual function. One collector working among the Jabo of Liberia found that in verbal expression proverbs 'furnish almost exclusively the means by which generalizations are made explicit'.[59] Similarly the *whakatauki* or proverbial maxims of the Maori, analysed by Professor Firth,[60] provided a 'convenient phraseology in which to sum up an occurrence of daily life, or a fact of experience'. Like fables, proverbs are brief, concise, and memorable. Like fables, they 'picture the truth', and have an important rôle in the transmission of inherited wisdom. Among the Jabo, the function of a proverb was 'to cope with a situation...by regarding it in the light of something that has occurred before'; they were important in oratory, and in legal discussions, and had the social function of reducing friction and dissatisfaction, of helping the individual in adjusting himself to his fate or to his status (in the manner of some fables of Aesop). Similarly, the Maori *whakatauki* represented the crystallized wisdom of past generations; they were 'sayings of the ancestors', and were sometimes associated with some dead chief of great renown, rather in the way in which proverbs in Europe, with an equal veneration for the past, were often associated with the names of great sages of former days—'Solomon' or 'Cato' or 'Alfred'—as fables were with 'Aesop'. The *auctoritas* of the maxim is sometimes indicated by formulae such as 'an old said saw', 'it is known from old', 'as say these clerks'. In traditional societies the sanctions of proverbial lore are especially powerful because it is acquired—like that of fables—in childhood, from elders.

The Maori proverbs recommend norms of behaviour, and correct deviations from them. This social use of proverbs to reprove, or rebuke, implies, of course, a recognition of the difference between ideals of conduct and actual behaviour, a contrast which the more extended narrative form of the fable allows it to make explicit or to explore. But there is a striking similarity with the traditional 'truth' of fables in that the principles of conduct recommended by these

[59] G. Herzog, *Jabo Proverbs from Liberia* (London, 1936), p. 2 (The Jabo also apparently use the same word for proverb and fable.)

[60] Raymond F. Firth, 'Proverbs in Native Life, with special reference to those of the Maori', *Folklore* xxxvii (1926), 134–53, 245–70.

proverbs do not form a logical or a self-consistent scheme. Like the morals of most Aesopic fables, they are usually empirical observations, and often imply opposed ideals of conduct. There are, for instance, sayings both in favour of hospitality and generosity and against them, recommending one not to be too lavish in giving and to eat the food oneself, or to give hospitality from a motive of self-interest, in the expectation of receiving something in return. As Professor Firth shows, there emerge two diametrically opposed principles of conduct, one advocating the sacrifice of personal interest to the benefit of society, the other, 'really contrary to the expressed morality of the social group, but professed, tolerated, and widely acted upon because it was so deeply rooted in human nature', advocating the achievement of the individual's immediate advantage, in constant and—for a society made up of individuals—fruitful conflict. It is not hard to see parallels to this in European wisdom-lore, where maxims of self-interest ('charity begins at home', etc.) co-exist with more altruistic ethical ideas, or in the moral world of Aesop.

There is, therefore, greater ambiguity and relativity in proverbial lore than is sometimes thought. Among the Jabo, 'the same proverb can be used in two senses which directly contradict each other; a person may condemn or praise the same behaviour with the very same proverb...the wide range of applicability and the ease with which the meaning of the proverb can at times shade into its opposite, suggest that in Africa the use of proverbs may become an intricate and artistic intellectual exercise...'.[61] They can be adapted to circumstances as easily and as skilfully as fables. In Europe, too, it is possible to give varying interpretations of the same proverb, and to find pairs of proverbs which recommend opposed courses of action—'look before you leap' / 'he who hesitates is lost', etc.[62] 'Wisdom' is relative to particular situations in which one course of action may be better than another. Henryson who, like many fabulists, is a great user of proverbs, sets side by side in 'The Paddock and the Mouse' just such a pair of opposed proverbs with a nice dramatic skill and irony (showing us, incidentally, the difficulties of applying 'wisdom' to particular situations). The mouse is worried by the ugly appearance of the frog who offers a passage across the river, and muses on the lore of physiognomy, capping her reflections with a proverb:

61 Herzog, p. 6. Cf. *The Study of Folklore* ed. A. Dundes (1965), p. 294 n.
62 Cf. also *Proverbs* xxvi, verses 4 and 5.

The auld proverb is witnes off this lorum—
Distortum vultum sequitur distortio morum (2831–2)

'That proverb is not true,' says the frog, and produces in refutation a series of exempla, and a contrary maxim—'thow suld not juge ane man efter his face'. In this case, the mouse would have done better to trust the lore of physiognomy.

When fables picture a truth, they normally do so under a veil. Socrates embodied his general truth of the relationship of pleasure and pain in a symbolic story, producing what would have been called in early Wisdom literature a 'likeness' or 'similitude', a sophisticated example of the human mind's 'capacity...of finding equivalences in the most disparate phenomena'. In fact, Socrates 'fell into an allegory'—if we may use the word in its most general and ancient sense, of 'speaking otherwise than one seems to speak'; Quintilian defines it thus: '*allegory*, which is translated in Latin by *inversio*, either presents one thing in words and another in meaning, or else something absolutely opposed to the meaning of the words.'[63] It is similar to the parable, a particular form of the similitudes which were used in rhetorical argument to exhibit and prove a point, an illuminating 'juxtaposition', or in Puttenham's words, a 'resemblance misticall'.[64] Associated with allegory are other more arcane forms of analogy or similitude, such as the enigma or riddle, where the reader is invited to search for a hidden solution, or to perform a more fundamental exercise of 'translation', and in some forms of allegory there may be a considerable gap between the surface meaning and the hidden meaning...*ac etiam interim contrarium*. Some medieval fabulists sometimes like to plunge, rather than to fall, into an allegory which can be in its most arcane forms, literally 'the other utterance in public', a kind of coded message whose purport is only apparent to those who have been taught how to search for it. We shall need to return to this in a later section; here it is sufficient to remark that, traditionally, fables contain 'hidden wisdom', and though apparently lucid, may be teasingly enigmatic. A seventeenth-century fabulist, L'Estrange (*Fables of Æsop and other Mythologists*, 1692), likens their 'symbolical way of moralizing' to the Egyptian 'Hieroglyphicks', an 'agreeable vehicle found out for conveying to us the truth and reason of things, through the medium of images and shadows'. It is also worth pointing out that

63 VIII. vi. 44 (tr. Butler).

64 Ed. Arber, p. 251.

since many, if not most forms of allegory are 'open-ended', it should not surprise us to find that an individual fable may be given different interpretations. The interpretations of even simple allegories may vary, and the critic of fables would be well advised to remember the dictum, 'les fables n'ont jamais un sens définitivement arrêté'[65]—fables never have a definitive meaning. An awareness of this helps us to understand their notorious adaptability—they appear as happily in the labyrinth of Versailles under the aegis of the God of Love (or, rather, in alliance with him, for the ugly figure of Aesop stood on one side of the entrance, and Cupid on the other), as with the twentieth-century interpretations of Thurber, for whom the moral of 'The Mouse who went to the country' is 'Stay where you are, you're sitting pretty'.

One final, and especially interesting, aspect of fable deserves consideration. Some of the characteristics we have been discussing may already have begun to suggest images or pictures, and it is indeed not without difficulty that I have refrained from using the term 'speaking picture'. For fables quite literally picture the truth. In the Middle Ages, they are associated with images in a number of ways.[66] There are many representations of individual fables on the capitals of churches, and in the borders and the initials of manuscripts. A series of fable-illustrations, accompanied by verse *tituli*, was formerly in eleventh-century frescoes in the abbey of Fleury. Another, also from the eleventh century, is to be found in the border (said to be imitating an ancient frieze) of the famous Bayeux tapestry. In all, nine fables have been identified with certainty.[67] When Harold sets sail from Bosham, we can clearly see the fox and the crow, with the cheese falling, and the wolf and the lamb on opposite sides of their stream. Under the scene of Harold arriving at the French coast, we can see the kite swooping down on the frog and the mouse, and beneath the messengers of William coming to Harold and his captor Guy, we have what looks like the swallow and the other birds. It has been suggested that the *geste* cele-

[65] Couton, *Poétique*, p. 21.

[66] For the following section, see A. Goldschmidt, *An Early MS. of the Aesop Fables of Avianus and related Manuscripts* (Studies in Manuscript Illumination, I, Princeton, 1947), G. Thiele, *Der illustrierte lateinische Aesop in der Handschrift des Ademar* (Leiden, 1905).

[67] H. Chefneux, 'Les fables dans la tapisserie de Bayeux', *Romania* lx (1934), 1–35, 153–94. L. Hermann, *ib.*, lxv (1939), 376–82, attempts to increase the number to 26. The similarity with the *chanson de geste* is suggested by C. R. Dodwell, *The Observer*, 31 October 1965.

brated in the tapestry is like that of the Old French epics, and that like the 'editorial aside' of the poems, the fables on the border are being used to foretell the theme of betrayal and treachery. A large number of copies of the various medieval versions of Aesop are illustrated. It seems quite likely, although no example has survived, that ancient copies of Phaedrus, Babrius, 'Romulus' and Avianus were illustrated with cycles of pictures. The two earliest medieval illustrated Aesops—an Avianus from the end of the ninth or the beginning of the tenth century and a Romulus from *c.* 1030—have been related by art historians to lost earlier models from late antiquity. In Ademar's Romulus we can see for the first time some of the fables known to Henryson appearing as illustrated poems, the texts accompanied by vivid drawings of the wolf and the lamb drinking from the stream, the dog accusing the sheep, the lion and the mouse. In the following centuries there are illustrated copies[68] of the various Latin versions, including 'Walter', and of their vernacular adaptations—Boner's *Edelstein*, Marie de France, the French *Isopets* (cf. Plates 4 (a), 4 (b) from the fourteenth-century MS. Add. 33781 in the British Library), the fables in Jehan de Vignay's *Mireoir historial*, the Italian version of Accio Zucco (cf. Plates 5 (*b*), 6 from MS. Add. 10389 (1462) in the British Library)—and this well-established tradition passed into the early printed books of the fifteenth and sixteenth centuries. The collection of Steinhöwel, and its derivatives, Macho and Caxton, are elaborate and fully illustrated books (Plate 5 (*a*) shows a typical page from a Zainer Steinhöwel).[69] Our plates of pages from one of the fifteenth-century Italian editions of 'Walter' with the translation by Accio Zucco will

[68] On these, cf. Goldschmidt, pp. 50ff. (MS. Add. 33781 was formerly Grenville 13). On the MSS. of the *Isopets*, see McKenzie and Oldfather, *Ysopet-Avionnet*, pp. 35–41. The illustrations of the *Isopet de Lyon* are reproduced in *Bibliothèque de la Ville de Lyon. Documents paléographiques, typographiques, iconographiques* II (November, 1923). MS. Add. 10389 (the illustrations are Venetian, according to Goldschmidt) is the unique MS. of Zucco; cf. M. P. Bush, 'Esopo Zuccarino' in *Studies in Honor of A. Marshall Elliott*, I, pp. 375–450.

[69] On Steinhöwel, cf. E. Weil, *Der Ulmer Holzschnitt im 15. Jahrhundert* (Berlin, 1923), pp. 34–8, 108–13; on the later copies see Lenaghan, *Caxton's Aesop*, pp. 23–4. There is a facsimile of Caxton in Scholars' Facsimiles and Reprints (Delmar, New York, 1975). Tardif's Valla was printed by Vérard with woodcuts. The Fables of Bidpai, in the guise of the *Directorium*, also appear as an illustrated book (according to Jacobs there was a connection of illustration and text already in Arabic and Hebrew).

give some idea of the elegance which is sometimes reached in early fable-woodcuts.[70]

It would be wrong to give the impression that all MS. or early printed versions of Aesop are illustrated. There are plenty of plain texts. But so many are illustrated that it seems most likely that a fabulist of Henryson's time would have seen one or more examples. It is perhaps significant that the unique MS. of the *Isopet de Lyon*, a work which he may have known, is illustrated. Plates 2–6 give some idea of the nature and the variety of late medieval illustrated fables. It will be noticed that there is a certain similarity in the iconography, with differences of detail. As early as Ademar's Romulus there is a liking for a compositional scheme involving two opposing figures or groups facing each other over the object of dispute or concern (which corresponds to a fundamental dramatic pattern in the structure of many Aesopic fables). The wolf and the lamb face each other across or beside the stream, the dog and the lamb over the disputed loaf. Sometimes the solitary cock of the cock and the jasp is given a pair of companions on the other side of the central jewel (as in the Zucco print). Sometimes, in the manner of medieval narrative painting, two or more moments of the story are united in one picture (as in Ademar's lion and the mouse, or our Zucco illustration of the frog and the mouse or the *Isopet*'s 'Two Mice'). The fact that the simplest fables (such as 'The Cock and the Jasp' or 'The Fox and the Grapes') have an inherently emblematic quality which makes the task of visual representation easier than it is with those which have a more complicated narrative structure, or which (like 'The Two Mice') are highly verbal and depend on contrasts of social behaviour or of tone does not seem to deter the illustrators. They try to catch a significant scene, and to express that fleeting moment in such a way that it is fixed in the memory. The technique is elegantly adapted, centuries later, in the fountains of Versailles,[71] where, for instance, a cock was represented in the middle of the basin, gripping 'a large piece of chrystall, cut in imitation of a diamond' and ejecting 'a perpetual stream as high as possible, by way of murmur against Fortune for putting him in possession of such a gaudy trifle, instead of a substantial grain of corn'. In books, the

[70] Outstanding among the several excellent Italian Aesops is that of 1479 from Verona (see 'A Renaissance Book Reborn', *TLS*, 7 December 1973, p. 1515).

[71] An English description with illustrations is found in 'Aesop at Court' in *Ethnic Amusements* by Mr. Bellamy (London, 1768).

illustration is usually placed at the head of the fable, and is clearly intended to complement the effect of the words with a concrete image.

These illustrated Aesops, where the text is accompanied by a visual representation of the 'speaking scene' which is in turn expounded and explained in the text, sometimes begin to approach the later emblems of the Renaissance. The more general definitions of the emblem, such as 'a sweet and morall symbole, which consists of picture and words, by which some weighty sentence is declared' could be directly applied to the late medieval illustrated fable. The format is very similar. The fable has the two essential parts which Menestrier finds in the emblem: 'les deux parties essentielles de ce beau composé sont les figures, et leur signification, ou leur sens moral.'[72] Fables, although they share the moral intention of emblems, are not usually so self-consciously arcane. Yet they have, as we have seen, a sufficiently enigmatic quality for L'Estrange to compare them with 'Ægyptian Hieroglyphicks'. The medieval illustrated fable is not—like the 'Hieroglyphics' of Horapollo—a *direct* progenitor of the emblem, but it is certainly part of the corpus of 'illustrated poems' which form its background.[73] By the time of La Fontaine, the two forms had grown very close together in appearance[74] (Menestrier indeed refers to Aesop's fables as emblems). Modern readers are often surprised to discover that in almost all of the early editions of La Fontaine the fables are accompanied by woodcuts, and that they should—as with Blake—be reading the texts along with their illustrations. If we were to think of the pictures as in any way competing with the texts, it would certainly be true that the demands made upon the illustrator by the delicate ambiguities of a La Fontaine fable would be too great. One of the poet's most sensitive modern critics, Mme Odette de Mourgues, has expressed her dislike of the illustrations: 'comment fixer sur le papier les formes protéennes et transparentes de ces êtres dont toute la réalité n'existe que par un art

[72] *L'Art des Emblemes* (Lyon, 1662), p. 50.

[73] On Horapollo cf. G. Boas, *The Hieroglyphics of Horapollo* (New York, 1950); on illustrated poems, cf. J. Evans, *Pattern* (Oxford, 1931), I, iv, Gray, *Themes and Images in the Medieval English Religious Lyric* (London, 1972), pp. 45–55, 240–5.

[74] Cf. Margaret M. McGowan, 'Moral Intention in the Fables of La Fontaine', *JWCI* xxix (1966), 264–81, G. Couton, 'La Fontaine et l'Art des Emblèmes' in *La Poétique de La Fontaine*. McGowan finds only one seventeenth-century edition of the *Fables* without illustrations. (Menestrier's description of Aesop's Fables as emblems is in the revised edition of 1684.)

sans équivalence dans les autres arts.'[75] Our plate 7, taken from the *Fables Choisies* of 1678–1694, seems to indicate, however, a different, and less hopeless purpose. In the manner of the old illustrated Aesops, the eye of the reader is given a visual speaking picture to complement that given to his mind's eye by the words of the fable, a memorable image, and an object for meditation. The illustrations of these editions have a slightly old-fashioned look; they are—we might say with a touch of condescension—rather charming. They are perhaps touching delicately on the humble, slightly childish, slightly primitive air of the fable form itself, and adding a piquant contrast to the words on the page, where a simple surface conceals art of the highest degree of sophistication. We might suspect that their effect would be perhaps like that of the deliberately simple and naïve quatrains which begin each canto of *The Faerie Queene*. It seems clear, certainly, that La Fontaine himself wanted pictures, and it has been demonstrated that he knew the emblem books and seems to have directed his engraver to follow that tradition. The fashion for emblem books declined and disappeared, but the desire for illustrated Aesops continued unabated, helped no doubt by the fable's traditional connection with children. Like many others, Gay's collection has the picture set at the head of each fable in the old way. And, of course, the illustration of fables attracted artists of real talent: in England, for example, Hollar, Bewick, Tenniel; in France, Oudry, Grandville, Doré. One suspects that even now a modern parent looking for a book of fables for a child will still expect it to contain pictures.

All this is, of course, a long way from the *Fables* of Robert Henryson, and our conclusions in respect of that work must be carefully put. It seems reasonable to suppose that Henryson may well have seen illustrated copies of Aesop, but since we have such fragmentary evidence for the early stages of his text, it is impossible to say that he intended his fables to be illustrated, or that they were illustrated in his own day. Of the later copies, the Bassandyne print has pictures of Aesop and of 'The Cock and the Jasp' and the Harley MS. (copied from a printed book) has 'The Cock and the Jasp' and 'The Preaching of the Swallow'.[76] I would, however, wish to emphasize the essentially emblematic nature of the fable, and to suggest that it is useful to regard

[75] *O muse, fuyante proie...Essai sur la poésie de La Fontaine* (Paris, 1962), p. 165.

[76] Reproduction of illustrations from Bassandyne are in Wood, from MS. Harley 3865 in Gregory Smith, II.

Henryson's fables as 'speaking pictures' created in the mind. This will be treated in more detail in the following chapter; here it is sufficient to indicate something of the literary potential of the fable as 'speaking picture'. It will picture truth allegorically, in a vivid, memorable and exemplary image; thus Menestrier:

> ...quand nous voyons une troupe de Fourmis, qui travaillent à ramasser du grain, tandis que les Cigales chantent sur les arbres; il n'est personne de ceux, qui ont lu Esope, qui ne comprenne aussi tot que c'est l'image de ceux qui travaillent durant leur jeunesse pour avoir dequoy s'entretenir dans la vieillesse, et de ceux, qui ayant passé leur vie dans les delices se trouvent dans la necessité sur le declin de leurs jours.[77]

It is indeed remarkable how memorable some of the crucial scenes from fables are—most readers, no doubt, will have their own fairly exact visual image of such favourites as the Fox and the Grapes or the Fox and the Stork. Some fables—like the Cock and the Jasp—give us what is almost a static scene, a frozen moment in which we seem taken out of time; others present a series of such scenes or moments, or a series of images in action. But even in the most dynamic of narratives, the scenes of the fable seem to have a curiously emblematic quality. Some lines from a French emblem book—whose motto 'Cognoy toy mesme' is one of which Henryson would certainly have approved—could almost serve as a description of his collection of fables:

> Celuy doncques qui est de vertu curieux
> Prenne un peu le loisir de courir de ses yeux
> Ces tableaux, ou se void la naifve peinture
> Des humaines actions, afin d'y remarquer
> Tant le bien que le mal, pour au bien s'appliquer
> Et corriger le mal qu'il trouve en sa nature.[78]

The material which Henryson took from the stories of Reynard the Fox spectacularly increases the variety of plot and tone in his collection. With this we are recalled to the world of animal stories that lay behind the fables, to the splendours and miseries of animal tricksters.

The *Roman de Renart* was begun about 1175, and finished about 1200, and there are evident signs of its popularity from the thirteenth century

[77] Menestrier (1662), p. 51.
[78] *Le Microcosme* (Amsterdam, n.d.), quoted by McGowan, p. 270 n. 23.

on.[79] It is hardly a 'roman' in any usual sense of the word, but rather a collection of separate stories (or 'branches') written by different authors at different times, linked by the central figure of Renart. Its origins have been the subject of much discussion. The immediate background seems to be Latin poems like the *Ecbasis cuiusdam captivi* (tenth/eleventh century), the tale of the fate of a calf which escapes from its stall and falls into the power of a wolf (with an 'inner fable' of the sick lion from the Aesopic tradition), and the *Ysengrimus* (1149) of Nivardus of Ghent, where for the first time we find the feud between the fox (Reinardus) and the wolf (Ysengrimus). Beyond these lie the written Aesopic collections, and probably—though the question of 'literary' as against 'oral' origins is fiercely debated—oral beast-tales from earlier times.[80] The development from *c.* 1175 is fairly clear. The quarrel between the fox and the wolf is taken up and elaborated by Pierre de St. Cloud. He tells the story of Renart's adultery with Isengrim's fickle wife Hersent, his summoning before King Noble, and his escape to his castle and safety. Later authors imitated and continued the stories of the great feud. Other enemies of Reynard, such as Tibert the cat, are introduced, and the whole becomes a series of tales about the fox and his adventures—Renart and Isengrim in the well (branche IV), the trial of Renart (I), Renart the minstrel (Ib). More are added in a later group: Renart the physician (X), Renart's duel with Isengrim (VI), Renart's pilgrimage (VIII), Renart's death and funeral procession (XVII). Later still (*c.* 1205–1250) comes a final group of nine branches, with stories such as Renart the magician (XXIII) and Renart's childhood (XXIV). From the thirteenth century the matter of Renart becomes 'a vast collection of continuations, imitations and translations'.[81] His adventures were read by the French as far away as Cyprus, where one Philippe de Novare (thirteenth century) uses the material for satire. We have such works as Rutebeuf's *Renard le bestourné* (1260–1270), the *Couronnement de Renart* (1263–1270), in which Renard succeeds Noble and begins a reign of wickedness and injustice, *Renart le Nouvel* (Jacquemard Gelée, 1288/9), an allegorical poem in which Noble (Virtue) wars against Renart (Vice), and, from

[79] Cf. J. Flinn, *Le Roman de Renart dans la littérature française et dans les littératures étrangères au moyen âge* (Toronto, 1963), R. Bossuat, *Le Roman de Renard* (Paris, 1957).

[80] Cf. Jauss, *Tierdichtung*, pp. 12ff.

[81] Flinn, p. 5.

the early fourteenth century, *Renart le Contrefait*. Stories of Renart begin to appear in other languages, Italian, German (in the late twelfth-century *Reinhart Fuchs*, where the adventures are made into a unified whole), and there are similar versions in Middle Dutch, from one of which came Caxton's English book of 1481[82] (separate stories are represented earlier in England by *The Fox and the Wolf* and *The Nun's Priest's Tale*).

The *Roman de Renart* is a brilliant expression of the comic spirit, and an extraordinary celebration of the shifts and ruses of its hero. Among the targets of its caustic satire are several aspects of feudal society, notably the trickery and flattery found in courts. Noble the lion, invested with all the majesty of a medieval king, holds court like a Charlemagne or an Arthur, surrounded by his barons and counsellors. It is the traditional function of the king to concern himself with the governance of the realm, to hear the complaints of his subjects, to judge conflicts, to right wrongs, and to maintain peace and order. The wrongs done by Renart, however, prove a rather difficult matter... At Noble's court, all is trickery and flattery; under the façade of courtliness there is nothing but brutality and cruelty. It is a world in which the weaker are mercilessly crushed, and in which only the most intelligent villain can survive. In the *Couronnement*, when Renart becomes king, he gives splendid gifts to the rich, but nothing to the poor. When the hedgehog and the sheep complain of this, he says that he has simply treated them according to their condition, and that he cannot make them what God did not create them to be. They are responsible for their own misfortune, and should be content. The behaviour of the clergy—priests and their ways with women, and monks in and out of their cloisters—affords another rich field for satire. Renart himself flouts, adapts, or cynically misuses the rules of religion with gay abandon. He performs his hypocritical confessions with enormous zest, taking particular delight in the recital of his misdeeds. *Renardie* soon became almost synonymous with hypocrisy, and especially with religious hypocrisy.

The stories are full of memorable characters—Isengrim the wolf, Grymbart the badger, Cuwart the hare, Bellyn the ram—but dominating everything is the protean character of Renart himself, devious and cunning, deceitful, cruel, gluttonous, proud, and totally cynical. He is the supreme 'anti-hero' of medieval fiction, the successful rogue whose destructive genius makes society look foolish, and who destroys

[82] *The History of Reynard the Fox* ed. N. F. Blake, EETS cclxiii (1970).

all accepted standards of moral behaviour. His trickery is the expression of a kind of genius. It is trickery taken to the highest pitch of art, at once the natural reaction of a cunning animal determined to survive, and the artfulness of a self-conscious ironist. As Edwin Muir says in a thoughtful essay on Reynard,[83] 'this mean creature...extracts from us somewhat the same liking and admiration as...he wins from his unhappy victims before they find him out. It is as if the whole human race had an inherited predisposition or even an active wish, to be deceived to its own undoing, and at the same time vicariously identified itself with the deceiver.' The extraordinary thing is not his cunning, but that even though everyone expects deceit from him he still succeeds in deceiving. Muir suggests that the admiration we feel for a villain like Reynard has its source in 'parts of our nature of which we are less conscious than our ancestors were: in the fact that all active human qualities are rooted in animal virtues'. The tricksters of traditional animal-tales share many of Reynard's qualities—such as his irrepressible gift for turning any situation to his own advantage—and seem, like him, to represent a spirit of disorder in opposition to society's normal values.[84] According to Robin Horton, Ikaki, a tortoise trickster among the Kalabari, appears as 'the amoral, psychopathic confidence trickster...the intelligent plausible psychopath, that universal threat to the fabric of the community'. The stories about him help to deal with society's fears by showing the trickster outwitted, or by exaggerating him until he becomes absurd, and is thus in a sense 'tamed'. Another trickster, Ture of the Azande (in the Sudan) is described by Evans-Pritchard as 'a monster of depravity: liar, cheat, lecher, murderer; vain, greedy, treacherous, ungrateful, a poltroon, a braggart...utterly selfish...everything against which the Azande warn their children most strongly'. He is an engaging rogue (and, unlike Reynard, is not malicious); Evans-Pritchard thinks of him as a kind of 'mirror-opposite': 'it is as if we were looking into a distorting mirror, except that they are not distortions. We really are like that. What we see is the obverse of the appearance we like to present...What Ture

[83] *The New Statesman*, 1 November 1930, pp. 112–13.

[84] Cf. Finnegan, *Oral Literature*, pp. 352ff., R. Horton, 'Ikaki—the Tortoise masquerade', *Nigeria Magazine* cxiv (September 1967), p. 237, E. E. Evans-Pritchard, *The Zande Trickster* (Oxford, 1967), p. 30; P. H. Radin, *The Trickster. A Study in American Indian Mythology* (London, 1956 (with commentaries by Kerényi and Jung)).

does is the opposite of all that is moral; and it is all of us who are Ture. He is really ourselves. Behind the image convention bids us present, in desire, in feeling, in imagination, and beneath the layer of consciousness we act as Ture does.' Or as Reynard does? The tricksters of North American Indians present similar satirical and parodic reversals of accepted moral values. Reynard is not, like them, a culture-hero (both a divine being and buffoon)...and yet, he seems to have appealed to something deep in the consciousness of medieval audiences. He is certainly not one of the rationally conceived, 'demythologized' animal characters from the classical Aesop. Perhaps he is a kind of Jungian 'shadow' figure; perhaps he recalls us to an earlier period in cultural history when there was a closer, more magical interrelationship of animal and man. 'Car sur Regnart poeult on gloser, / penser, estudier, muser / Plus que toute rien qui soit';[85] his elusive character refuses to be neatly labelled and filed away. A powerful and primitive destructive force often seems to take hold of the stories about him, turning an already virulent satire into something much more nihilistic, which defies attempts to exorcize or to tame it.

Even in Caxton's late and more moral version, where Reynard and his doings are held up as an example—there are many among lords spiritual and temporal 'that crepe after his waye and his hole'; '...ther is in the world moche seed left of the foxe, whiche now overal groweth and cometh sore up, though they have no rede berdes...now clerkes goon to Rome, to Parys, and to many other place for to lerne Reynardis crafte'—the old unregenerate Reynard emerges with a triumphant hypocrisy. His gallows speech (ch. 32), in which he confesses his misdeeds, but saves himself by playing on the king's cupidity, is still a masterpiece of irony. Caxton preserves the crude comedy and burlesque of the tournament with the wolf—which Reynard wins by distinctly unchivalric means. Reynard shows no mercy to the weak or the stupid. His cruel irony becomes apparent early in the book. Bruin, in pursuit of honey, finds himself, thanks to Reynard's wiles, stuck in a tree, and is attacked and cruelly beaten by the villagers. He manages to extricate himself, leaving his skin and his ears behind, so that 'never man sawe fowller ne lothlyer beest, for the blode ran over his eyen'. Reynard meanwhile has slipped off to remove a hen from the house of Lantfert the carpenter, who has taken a leading part in the attack on

[85] *Le Roman de Renart le Contrefait* ed. G. Raynaud and H. Lemaître (Paris, 1914), Br. I, 105–7, quoted by Jauss, p. 12.

Bruin. When he finds that the bear has escaped, he is furious with Lantfert, and poor Bruin gets no sympathy. Echoing the words he spoke as he left the bear stuck in the tree ('Is that hony good? how is it now? Ete not to moche it shold do you harme') he addresses the bear 'sore wounded, bebled, and right seke':

> Have ye ought forgoten at Lantferts? Have ye also payd hym for the hony combes that ye stale fro hym? If ye have not, it were a grete shame and not honeste. I wyl rather be the messager my self for to goo and paye hym. Was the hony not good? I knowe yet more of the same prys. Dere eme, telle me er I goo hens in to what ordre wille ye goo, that were this newe hode? Were be ye a monke or an abbot? He that shoef your crowne hath nyped of youre eeris. Ye have lost your toppe, and don of your gloves.[86]

Henryson manages to put just this same cruel irony into the gloating speech of one of his foxes at the expense of a wolf in 'The Trial of the Fox'.

Stories of Reynard seem to have been known to everyone in the Middle Ages, and allusions to them come, if not as frequently as to Aesopic fables, almost as easily. In the English prose *Pilgrimage of the Life of Man*, Orguill (Pride) tells the pilgrim about her mantle, Ypocrysie, which she often wears to church: 'I do it on also whan I am al put out and deposed, and make the Sanctificetur to recovere sum hap. I do as Renard dide, that made him ded in the wey for to be cast in to the carte, and thanne have of the heringe.'[87] They were the special favourites of the artists, who show Reynard on bench-ends, misericords, capitals, and on the pages of manuscripts. The pages of Dr. Varty's *Reynard the Fox*[88] give ample evidence of the richness of the material. The fox making off with a cock (or some other domestic bird), and the pursuit of the fox by the wife with her distaff are found again and again. Reynard is shown as a holy hypocrite with a cowl, or

[86] Ed. Blake, p. 18.

[87] *The Pilgrimage of the Lyf of the Manhode*, ed. W. A. Wright (Roxburghe Club, London, 1869), II. cxxiii, p. 12. Cf. Bromyard's adaptation to 'foxy' hypocrites who wish to be set in offices but pretend to be modest and humble (*Summa Praedicantium* s.v. *humilitas* (Venice ed., 1586, f. 364^{v})) quoted by Owst, *Literature and Pulpit*, p. 257 (but *alecia* is not 'poultry' but 'herrings' (see Du Cange, *Glossarium Mediae...Latinitatis*, s.v. *allecium*)).

[88] K. Varty, *Reynard the Fox. A Study of the Fox in Medieval English Art* (Leicester University Press, 1967).

as an enthroned bishop, or preaching to geese, ducks or hens ('when the fox preaches, beware the geese' ran a popular proverb). He appears as a pilgrim, as a physician, as a minstrel or musician. There are scenes of his trial, his death, funeral and resurrection. Our illustration (Plate 8 from MS. Douce 360, a copy (1339) of the French *Roman*), shows one scene from this mass of material which has an equivalent in Henryson): we see the crafty fox making off with the fish from the cart.

The lineaments of Reynard are clear to see in the various members of Henryson's 'skulke of foxis'. One very striking effect of the Reynard material on medieval fables was to encourage the fabulist to use a more extended narrative, and to make more use of vivid scenes and scene-settings. This can be seen in *Isopet I* (where the author has sometimes used names from the *Roman de Renart*) and in some of Steinhöwel's *Fabulae Extravagantes*, but to a much greater and more interesting extent in Henryson. The Reynard fables increase the variety of his collection by providing stories which are close to fabliaux. But it is especially the figure of Reynard which he finds most useful and imaginatively exciting. This trickster, this spirit of disorder, roguery and cynicism adds a new level and a new ambiguity to the moral world of the fables. He may be glossed and allegorized, but there is something about him that defies the moralist. The essential Reynard is indestructible. At the end of Caxton's book, he returns home, tells of his adventures, and lives defiantly and happily on: 'and the foxe lyved forthon wyth his wyf and his chyldren in grete joye and gladnes.'

CHAPTER THREE

Beasts and Wisdom:
(ii) The Unbent Bow

Thocht feinyeit fabils of ald poetre
Be not al grunded upon truth, yit than
Thair polite termes of sweit rhetore
Richt plesand ar unto the eir of man...

Henryson's Prologue is based upon that of 'Walter', but it is far more ambitious and extensive in its scope. It offers in miniature a defence of poetic fiction, and of the fable in particular, in terms which are not entirely dissimilar from those used later by Sidney.[1] The tone, however, is rather more defensive. Later in the *Fables*, even Aesop himself, when Henryson meets him, is so saddened by the sin of the world and its deafness to truth, that he wonders 'quhat is it worth to tell ane fenyeit taill / Quhen haly preiching may nathing availl?', and has to be urged on by his disciple with the thought that he at least may derive some benefit from it. His earlier remarks to his author (ll. 1379–80, 1386–7) echo his Prologue in balancing fiction and moral weight. He has an underlying confidence in 'feigned fables'—at the end of the final fable in the Bassandyne order, he neatly and wittily alludes for the last time to the question of feigned truth: 'Giff this be trew speir ye at thame that saw.' Fables instruct and improve—and were invented to reprove man's 'misleving' 'be figure of ane uther thing'—but in the course of his defence, Henryson states very firmly the traditional doctrine that poetry should please as well as instruct. 'Ernist', he says, should be mixed with 'sport', in words which almost remind us of La Fontaine's 'une morale nue apporte de l'ennui',[2] and he drives the point home with a vivid image:

[1] Cf. p. 52 above; on Henryson's poetics, see I. W. A. Jamieson, 'To preue thare preching be a poesye', *Parergon* viii (April, 1974), 24–36. Cf. also S. Manning, 'The Nun's Priest's Morality and the Medieval Attitude toward Fables', *JEGP* lix (1960), 403–16.

[2] *Fables*, VI. i.

...ane bow that is ay bent
Worthis unsmart and dullis on the string;
Sa dois the mynd that is ay diligent
In ernistfull thochtis and in studying:
With sad materis sum merines to ming
Accordis weill: thus Esope said, iwis:
'*Dulcius arrident seria picta iocis.*'

The image of the bow is referred in the Middle Ages to a story of St. Anthony, who gave a practical demonstration by means of a bow to an archer who was displeased to find him 'syttand emang his brethir makand merie with thaim', and as a proverbial figure of man's need for 'game', becomes, in Professor Kolve's words, 'one of the central images by which the Middle Ages understood the human psyche.'[3]

It is Walter, rather than Aesop (though the spirit of the remark is certainly Aesopic), who says that 'serious things please more sweetly when painted with jests'; he goes on to offer his readers a choice, if they wish to make it, between the fruit and the flowers in his 'little garden':

si fructus plus flore placet, fructum lege; si flos
plus fructu, florem; si duo, carpe duo.

Henryson does not offer this choice to his readers, but most of them—at least in modern times—have made it, and made it emphatically for the 'flowers' rather than the 'fruit'. The relationship of 'game' and 'earnest' in Henryson's *Fables* is more complicated, more delicate, and more interesting than such an abrupt and exclusive choice can allow, and my decision to postpone fuller consideration of the *moralitates* and the moral themes which emerge from the *Fables* until the next chapter is not intended to endorse it, but is done simply for reasons of convenience. We must certainly 'gather the two'. The 'somwhat of lust, somwhat of lore' that Gower promised his readers is found both in the fables and in their *moralitates*. In this chapter I shall concentrate on those features which make them into such pleasing examples of narrative art.

The way in which Henryson treats his animal protagonists is of fundamental importance. We turn again to the Prologue:

[3] V. A. Kolve, *The Play called Corpus Christi* (London, 1966), pp. 128–9. Cf. Whiting B 478, and see G. Olson, 'The Medieval Theory of Literature for Refreshment and its Use in the Fabliau Tradition', *SP* lxxi (1974), 219–313.

My author in his fabillis tellis how
That brutal beistis spak, and understude
Into gude purpois dispute and argow,
Ane sillogisme propone, and eik conclude...

This is a traditional statement of the nature of the beast-fable—'beings irrational...are for the purpose of moral instruction feigned to act and speak with human interests and passions'. Since Henryson is here defending the form, it is not surprising that it should be 'the purpose of moral instruction' that he proceeds to emphasize—Aesop 'put in exempill and similitude' how many men 'ar like to beistis in conditioun'. Sinful men, he continues, become so fixed in their sin that they are transformed into brutal beasts. This, of course, is a traditional moral attitude, but Henryson probably has more than a preacher's point in mind. It is curious that when, centuries later, La Fontaine is stressing the moral and useful aspects of fables he should recall the old doctrine that man is the 'little world' made up of all the characteristics of animals—'nous sommes l'abrégé de ce qu'il a y de bon et de mauvais dans les créatures irraisonnables'. The intimacy and mystery of the relationship of man with the larger world of animal nature (brought back sharply to the attention of modern readers by recent work on animal behaviour) is fundamental for both moralist and artist. The very choice of animal protagonists in fables is already an implied judgement on human nature and behaviour. The animal world is a mirror-image of the world of men. In later centuries, students of physiognomy were sometimes led to recognize resemblances to animals in human faces. In one startling moment in the modern cinema, in Eisenstein's *Strike*, the faces of the human actors are suddenly transformed into their animal 'equivalents'. Later illustrators of fables sometimes like to exploit the grotesque possibilities given to them by the techniques of visual metaphor developed in the new art of caricature.[4]

The art of Henryson's *Fables*—and of La Fontaine's—is, however, not that of bold caricature or grotesque. The animal protagonists exist in full autonomy; their relationship with human life and manners is a

[4] As, e.g., *The Fables of Aesop and Others translated into Human Nature* (London, 1857), with illustrations by Bennett, where the title-page shows a man looking into his mirror and seeing a fox. Cf. the illustrations of faces in G. B. Porta, *Physiognomiae coelestis libri vi* (Naples, 1603). See E. H. Gombrich and E. Kris, *Caricature* (London, 1940).

shifting and delicate one. It is also a relationship which contains, beside the 'earnest' of instruction, a great deal of 'game'. The fabulist endows his creatures with human characteristics and patterns of behaviour—they speak, dispute and argue—but at the same time makes them retain the observable characteristics of their own animal kind. His art lies in the careful manipulation of this curious balance, which is the source not only of moral satire (with the animals showing in an especially ridiculous light the foibles and follies of their 'betters'), but also of comedy, when the protagonists are kept hovering subtly and unpredictably between animal and man. In *The Nun's Priest's Tale*, for instance, Chauntecleer quotes Boethius and other authors to good purpose; he also summons his hens with a 'chuck', 'for he hadde founde a corn lay in the yard'. One eighteenth-century French theorist of the fable singles out the practice of giving the animals human titles (Maître Corbeau, etc.) as a 'mascarade ingénieuse qui ne va pas à les faire méconnaître, mais seulement à nous mieux représenter en eux, et qui offre tout à la fois à l'imagination, et l'Animal, et l'Homme joué sous son nom.'[5] There is something of this in Henryson, though it is less self-consciously 'ingénieuse'. The names he gives to his creatures sound like good folk names, which reflect the closeness of animals and men rather than the ingenious playfulness of poets—Pertok, Sprutok, Toppok, Lawrie, Russell, Corbie Raven, Perrie Doig, Gib Hunter—and the effect is rather like the homeliness of the Dunfermline Burgh Register, where good and bad appear as Davy or Wat or Megge.

The balance of animal and human kinds in the protagonists is an artful one, which, mingling fantasy and realism, creates an odd yet coherent world, which is sometimes recognizably that of real animals, and sometimes that of fabulous natural history. It is a revealing fact that the earlier critics of La Fontaine tended to fall into two opposed camps, one of which praised his realistic observation of the animal world, while the other maintained with equal vehemence that he was an atrocious zoologist. Mme Odette de Mourgues is surely right to sweep away this absurd argument, and to insist that what is important is that the fabulist presents us with the 'poetic reality' of animals. A fine passage in which she expounds this[6] can be applied almost exactly to the world of Henryson's *Fables*:

[5] La Motte, *Discours sur la Fable*, quoted by S. Blavier-Paquot, *La Fontaine. Vues sur l'Art du Moraliste dans les Fables de 1668* (Paris, 1961), p. 62.

[6] *O muse, fuyante proie...*, pp. 163–5.

> Cette réalité est d'abord complexe. Dans une certaine mesure ces animaux sont des symboles traditionnels et le lecteur reconnaît sans peine dans le renard la personnification de la ruse et dans l'agneau celle de l'innocence. Mais ces masques de bêtes ont bien plus qu'une valeur héraldique; ils ne sont pas simplement destinés à symboliser une qualité abstraite; ils sont si intimement moulés sur les traits changeants et vivants des hommes que l'on ne peut plus distinguer entre le visage et le masque. L'homme et l'animal ont la même nature, nous a dit La Fontaine dans sa préface; aussi pour qui sait les entendre parlent-ils le même langage et ont-ils les mêmes gestes de brutalité, de convoitise ou de frayeur. De l'homme et du singe, quel est celui qui singe l'autre? Le symbole de l'ingratitude, est-ce serpent ou l'être humain? Ainsi les animaux des *Fables* peuvent-ils jouer tous les actes de la comédie humaine sans cesser d'être des animaux; il n'y a qu'un théâtre et qu'une pièce....

It is a changing world, which is often ambiguous; 'le caractère indéfinissable des personnages créés par le poète tient à de constantes variations d'éclairage...L'univers des *Fables* est un univers de métamorphoses évanescentes'.

The hovering and equivocal relationship, the masks, the constant changes of lighting or of perspective are characteristic of Henryson's technique. In 'The Lion and the Mouse', the lion lies sleeping, 'beikand his breist and belly at the sun', and a whole troop of mice runs across him and dances on him with rash abandon ('Sum tirlit at the campis off his beird, / Sum spairit not to claw him on the face...'). When the lion catches with his paw 'the maister mous', this unfortunate creature makes a little formal *planctus* or lament ('Now am I tane ane wofull presonair...') as it faces the wrath of the regal lion:

> 'Thow cative wretche and vile unworthie thing,
> Ouer-malapart and eik presumpteous
> Thow wes, to mak out ouer me thy tripping.
> Knew thow not weill I wes baith lord and king
> Off beistis all?' 'Yes', quod the mous, 'I knaw;
> Bot I misknew because ye lay so law.' (1427–30)

The contrasting pronouns of address indicate emotion as well as difference in social rank. The disparity in size as well as in status, which is the basis of the comedy of the scene, has already been deftly established. The comedy coexists with a real threat of violent and summary execution. The lion's language—'my noble persoun thus to vilipend'—suggests that he takes his authority very seriously; the mouse's attempt to excuse itself by saying that they had thought him dead provokes the haughty rejoinder that even if he had been dead, and his skin 'stoppit full off stra', the mouse should still have fallen on its knees 'because it bare the prent of my persoun'. Execution seems imminent, and the lion's particularity of detail emphasizes both the threat and the comedy of the situation:

> Thairfoir thow suffer sall ane schamefull end
> And deith sic as to tressoun is decreit—
> Onto the gallous harlit be the feit. (1458–60)[7]

At the same time, a teasing moral relativity has been suggested by the mouse's plea that it did not act from negligence, malice or presumption, but simply from joy at the 'sweit sesoun', 'sic mirth as nature to us leird...', implying that its action was determined by 'kind'.

The mouse now launches into a long and eloquent plea for mercy, which extends over forty lines (1461–1502; the equivalent in 'Walter' is about ten). Its diction rises to match the status of the recipient—words like *coronate, collateral, honour triumphall, your celsitude, contagious,* have more than a suggestion of that 'heigh style, as whan that men to kynges write'—and the whole speech, with its 'polite termes', is in its own right a fine piece of rhetorical pleading. The mouse asks for mercy on four points: (1) it appeals to the lion's *gentrice*, and the mercy which is traditionally proper to a good ruler; (2) the 'honour triumphall' of every victor depends upon the 'strength' of his conquest, and there is no honour in slaying a defenceless mouse; (3) for one used to 'meittis delitious' and 'wont till be fed with gentill vennesoun' a mouse's flesh and blood would be unwholesome; (4) neither the life nor the death of a mouse is of any worth, but if it were allowed to live, it might happen that it could be of use to the lion later. This final appeal to self-interest is delivered with an easy allusion to the world of men: 'ane man of small stature' has often rescued 'ane lord off hie honour'—'sic cace may be your awin'.

The flickering comedy of the scene comes very close to the mock-heroic, but because of the shifting border between real and fantastic,

[7] In l. 1460, I follow Fox in preferring Bannatyne *onto*.

and between animal and man, it defies any simple categorization. The speech is both serious and comic at the same time, and this is very appropriate to the fable as a whole, for it both engages the emotional sympathy of the reader and demands rational detachment. The fable turns on a moral and ethical action, which at one level resolves itself into a solemn question of justice and mercy in those who have power over others, and at another, more popular level, of quitting 'ane gude turne for ane uther'. We are not allowed to forget that this skilful pleader is a captive mouse. When the lion finally grants 'remissioun', the mouse expresses its gratitude with a splendidly human gesture:

> . . . and scho on kneis fell doun
> And baith hir handis unto the hevin upheild.

'Mus abit et grates reddit' says Walter succinctly; Henryson has caught the 'poetic reality' of a liberated mouse.[8]

In 'The Two Mice', we can see the technique being used to differentiate the two characters. The ancient opposition of town and country has been neatly adapted to late medieval Scotland: the country mouse lives 'uponland', 'soliter, quhyle under busk, quhyle under breir', and suffers distress in winter in her 'sober wane' made of moss and fern, whereas the other lives in splendour as 'gild brother' and 'fre burges'. The fact that in this version of the fable the two mice are sisters is important for the comedy. The town mouse is the elder, and throughout the tale she is the confident worldly-wise one who takes the lead ('the eldest wes the gyde and went beforne / The younger to hir wayis tuke gude keip'). Thanks largely to their social situations, the two sisters have become very different. The town mouse longs to hear of her sister's welfare—but the thought comes to her when 'scho wes full and unfutesair', and when she goes to visit her, 'to se quhat

[8] Henryson has the gift of finding a significant detail to act as an imaginative focus for a whole scene. These are often gestures or other physical reactions (cf. the excitement of the reunion of the mice, 192–3), sometimes those directly appropriate to animals (cf. 467–8), but more usually distinctively human gestures. Thus his animals will kneel (as here, or as the fox before Chantecleir (432–6) in a dissimulating parody of feudal practice (cf. the ironic repetition in 572–5)) or even laugh (sometimes in pure delight (193), more usually with irony of various kinds in the background (e.g. 446, 1741, 2331)). See especially the fox fables (cf. e.g. 2338, 2371). Cf. W. Habicht, *Die Gebärde in englischen Dichtungen des Mittelalters* (Bayer. Akad. der Wiss., Phil.-Hist. Kl., Abhandlungen, N.F., xlvi, Munich, 1959).

lyfe scho had under the wand', there is perhaps a touch of patronizing self-righteousness in that she goes 'bairfute, allone, with pykestaf in hir hand / As pure pylgryme'. One suspects that the manner of this native's return is not motivated so much by the search for holiness as by the expectation of finding a disagreeable poverty. The country mouse recognizes the voice of her sister, 'as kinnisman will do / Be verray kynd', and there is a touching scene of reunion—'grit kyndnes was schawin thame betwene'. But from this point on, the differences—produced by 'nurture' rather than 'kynd'—become painfully apparent. The burgess mouse has become something of a gourmet, and her aversion to the 'rude dyat' she is served ('thir wydderit peis and nuttis... Wil brek my teith' (219–23)) is delightfully comic. The difference in their style of food is not only the source of social comedy, but of moral comment, for in Henryson's version the emphasis on the food makes it into a symbol of their differing ways of life and of the difference of 'nurture' and 'nature'. The younger mouse, who is the hostess, and is perhaps upset at not having lived up to her sister's expectations, has become defensive. With some irony, she calls her sister 'madame', and refers her to their mother's practice:

> 'Madame,' quod scho, 'ye be the mair to blame;
> My mother sayd, sister, quhen we wer borne,
> That I and ye lay baith within ane wame:
> I keip the rate and custume off my dame...' (212–15)

Unfortunately, recalling that they once lay in the same womb simply emphasizes how different they have become. The rural mouse reads her sister a little lecture on the importance of 'ane gentill hert', 'gude will', etc., but to no avail. In a nicely human way, the burgess mouse 'hevilie...kest hir browis doun'. Her snobbery becomes quite explicit—this might (she says, 'halff in hething') be good enough for 'ane rurall beist' (her easy use of the word 'beast' shows how beautifully the technique of the 'hovering' relationship is working), but 'lat be this hole', and come and see how things can be. And so throughout the rest of the fable the two sisters continue in comic opposition, the proudly ostentatious older mouse who has 'made it' in the world, and the younger mouse, worried and uncertain, and easily reduced to abject terror. In the description of their feast at the home of the town mouse, which is done with great gusto and much local detail (it includes groats and oatmeal-cakes), the narrator takes care to remind us that they are real mice. They cry 'Haill, Yule! Haill!', but in their 'subcharge' (extra course) they have 'mane' (fine white bread) instead of jelly, and white candle instead of spice, 'to gust thair mouth withall'. (The alert reader will notice that this is precisely what the rural mouse had offered her sister (l. 206), but with the vital difference that this candle is of the highest quality—'ane quhyte candill owt off ane coffer stall'.) Most delightfully—and with a touch of delicate satire—they 'counterfeit' 'ane lordis fair'

> Except ane thing—they drank the watter cleir
> Insteid off wyne; bot yit thay maid gude cheir.

There is surely no need to labour the obvious point that this technique is of fundamental importance throughout the *Fables*. However, Henryson's 'univers de métamorphoses évanescentes' sometimes produces effects which are surprisingly subtle or complex. In 'The Trial of the Fox', the lion, who has called a parliament, sits in regal splendour:

> And in that throne thair sat ane wild lyoun,
> In rob royall, with sceptour, swerd and croun. (878–9)

The single adjective 'wild' gives us the necessary hint, and by reminding us of the animality of the king forces a sudden change of perspective upon us, so that we do not quite know what to expect from the story, or what sort of justice is likely to emanate from such a ruler. The whole of this fable is especially interesting in the ways it uses the shifting relationship of man and beast, and changes from shades of fantasy to shades of realism while always remaining totally coherent. The villain of the piece, Tod Lowrie, is introduced in the first episode, which plays ironically with the 'kind' and 'kindness' of animals and men. It is strongly suggested (ll. 803ff.) that this fox, because of his lineage and the manner of his begetting, is certain to prove wicked—'off verray kynde behuifit to be fals'. We are instantly given an example. He comes upon the body of his father (the fox who was killed at the end of the preceding fable), 'nakit, new slane', and going to him, 'tuke up his heid, and on his kne fell down'. But in this attitude of filial piety what he says ('thankand grit God off that conclusion') is cynical in the extreme: 'Now sall I bruke, sen I am air, / The boundis quhair thow wes wont for to repair.' The outraged voice of the narrator elaborates on his wickedness; yet, nevertheless, he says, the fox

throw naturall pietie
The carioun upon his bak he tais.

This is a scene which might perhaps momentarily suggest to the more learned of Henryson's readers that celebrated instance of 'piety' when Aeneas carried off his old (and still living) father from the destruction of Troy. Whether Henryson meant us to think of this or not, there is irony in his voice, for all that is in the fox's mind is the simple question of disposal:

Syne with the corps unto ane peitpoit gais,
Off watter full, and kest him in the deip,
And to the devill he gaif his banis to keip. (828–30)

It is this fox who hears with some trepidation the summons of the unicorn, whose 'buisteous bugill', it seemed to him, 'maid all the warld to waig' (does Tod Lowrie remember enough Christian doctrine for this 'bugill' to have an apocalyptic sound in his guilty ear?). The great assembly of animals begins, and the solemn day is marked with a formal *chronographia*, in which Henryson carefully sets hints of an almost heraldic scene side by side with words which suggest the fertility and plenitude of nature: 'The ground wes grene and als as gold it glemis', the grass 'growand gudelie'. Birds sing sweetly, 'trippand fra tre to tre', while beneath them come three heraldic leopards bearing a crown of gold, who set up the pavilion in which we see the king, the 'wild lyoun'.[9]

The poet takes an obvious delight in the resounding catalogue of four-footed beasts who now assemble. 'I sall reheirs ane part off everilk kynd' he says with some determination, and lists them for the following five stanzas. It is clearly something of a *tour de force*, but the excitement is not exclusively rhetorical. The list of animals is a dramatic exhibition of the richness of nature, and of the infinite diversity and individuality of her species ('unknawin to man, and sa infinite, / In kynd havand sa fell diversiteis' as Henryson remarks elsewhere (397–407)). It contains over sixty species, and some rather inclusive items, such as 'the hors of everilk kynd', 'doggis all divers and different', and the unspecified number of unidentified beasts who bring up the rear, after the 'lytill mous', suggest further regiments. Creatures mythological—the minotaur 'ane monster mervelous', etc.—lead a procession of beasts

[9] Wittily, Henryson makes the three leopards of England pitch the tent of the Scottish lion (B. Dickins, *TLS*, 21 February 1924, p. 112).

ranging from the exotic—the elephant, the dromedary, the camel—to those more familiar in fifteenth-century Scotland. The passage generates a most curious sense of wonder and exhilaration. This comes partly from the brilliant display of Middle Scots vocabulary, partly from the changing rhythms ('the da, the ra, the hornit hart, the hynd') partly from the insistent alliterative patterns ('the quhrynand quhitret with the quhasill went', etc.). But most of all it is caused by the jostling of bizarre and commonplace, fantastic and homely. Sometimes an epithet applied to a creature will be traditional and decorative—'the peyntit pantheir'—sometimes, one suspects, a popular or folk epithet—'the gukit gait'—sometimes startlingly precise—'the hirpland hair'. Sometimes the alliterative patterns rather than any zoological order determine the grouping of animals, so that the reader's imagination is pulled hither and thither, and he is unable to decide whether the grouping is pure alliterative fantasy or whether it is the expression of some arcane and mysterious order of the poetic imagination: 'baith otter and aip, and pennit porcupyne' or, most brilliantly,

> The marmisset the mowdewart couth leid,
> Because that nature denyit had hir sicht.

It is to this wonderful parliament that Tod Lowrie, sorrowfully, decides that he must come. His arrival is a memorable scene, in which he becomes more 'human' than ever—tearing his hair and quaking for dread:

> His hude he drew laich attour his ene,
> And winkand with ane eye furth he wend;
> Clinschand he come, that he micht not be kend,
> And for dreddour that he suld thoill arreist,
> He playit bukhude behind, fra beist to beist. (966–70)[10]

At the end of the fable, when he is summarily punished, it is a cruel irony that he has to meet his end naked like his father—but before this happens he has provided us with much entertainment.

When, occasionally, men enter the fables, their world is often in conflict with that of the animals. There is one case where the dominion of man is secure: the kindly widow attempts to rescue her 'gentill Chantecleir' from the crafty fox. More usually, men bring death or the threat of death. This is the case in 'The Preaching of the Swallow',

[10] In 967, I follow Fox in preferring Bann. *thoill*.

'The Confession of the Fox', and 'The Lion and the Mouse', and (in the arrival of the spencer) in 'The Two Mice'. There are two 'merry tales', however, in which clever foxes outwit men—'The Fox, Wolf and Cadger' and 'The Fox, the Wolf and Husbandman'. 'The Fox, Wolf and Husbandman' opens with a realistic rural scene of ploughing, of the kind one might find represented in a late medieval Book of Hours.[11] It is a scene that might perfectly express the orderly dominion of man over nature. But the oxen are young, and spoil the furrow, whereupon in his anger the ploughman utters a rash oath—'may the wolf have you!' Immediately, we move into the more fantastic world of the beast story, for all unknown to him '... the wolff wes neirar nor he wend', accompanied by Laurence the fox. The wolf emerges from a bush, confronts the 'carl', and claims the oxen:

> The husband hamewart with his cattell past.
> Than sone the wolff come hirpilland in his gait,
> Befoir the oxin, and schupe to mak debait.
> The husband saw him and worthit sumdeill agast,
> And bakwart with his beistis wald haif past. (2254–8)

In the ensuing debate the wolf urges his claim vigorously, even quoting from *Proverbs*: 'But lawte / All uther vertewis ar nocht worth ane fle' (a sentiment around which Henryson, in his usual way, wreathes some strands of irony before the fable is done). When the carl claims that there was no witness to his rash oath, Laurence appears 'lourand, for he lufit never licht' and presides over the dispute. The element of 'game' is totally dominant here, and the mock trial that he conducts comes closer than anything else in the *Fables* to burlesque. 'Now I am ane juge amycabill' he says gleefully, and calls on them to swear to stand at his 'decreit':

> The wolff braid furth his fute, the man his hand,
> And on the toddis taill sworne thay ar to stand

[11] Henryson is rightly praised for the evident delight he takes in such scenes (cf. especially 'The Preaching of the Swallow'). It is also appropriate to the humble genre that they should be those of the country. 'The dog to bark on nicht and keip the hows' is significantly placed among the examples of the 'inclinations' of animals (403); cf. the expansion of the image of man's soul as the bat's eye (1638–9). The landscape is an inhabited one, with towns, cadgers, a manor house, etc. Beyond is the 'wildernes' (1951), in which the 'revand wolff' of 'The Fox, the Wolf and the Cadger' lives.

—a scene which must surely be one of the high points of the animal fable. The 'juge amycabill' takes the husbandman aside and gives him a cynical lesson in legal practice, in particular on the value of 'gifts', and does not have much difficulty in extracting the promise of six or seven fat hens. Into the comedy, a new tone of sharp satire has imperceptibly entered. Laurence now goes off to the wolf, 'privily plucks him by the sleeve', and begins to persuade him to give up his claim to the oxen in favour of a (quite imaginary) cheese of immense proportions. 'Realism' (in Laurence's desire for hens), and 'fantasy' (in the wolf's desire for the cheese) are beautifully fused. In the end, after further japes, the unfortunate wolf is left at the bottom of a well, persuaded that the shadow of the moon 'pennyfull' is the great 'cabok' he so much desired, while Laurence is left triumphant, 'blyith as ony bell'. It is remarkable in this fable how effortlessly Henryson makes us accept all the shifts of perspective, all the 'métamorphoses évanescentes'. We feel no more surprised when the wolf accosts the husbandman—'Quhether dryvis thou this pray?'—than we do in the ballad when Thomas the Rhymer meets the Queen of fair Elfland. This is the result of a confident and consummate skill in narrative art.

'Une morale nue apporte de l'ennui...'. The success of the fabulist (though he is working with inherited material) depends pre-eminently on his narrative skill. Even in an age which excelled in narrative poetry, Henryson's *Fables* stand out as a masterpiece; all the story-teller's arts and techniques work together to produce a unified and pleasing whole, from which the poet's attitudes, 'sentence' and sympathy[12] emerge. Henryson has adapted the traditional form of the medieval Aesopic fables. Perhaps encouraged by his knowledge of a French *Isopet* and of the *Roman de Renart*, he has expanded them, and transformed them into *contes* or miniature short stories. Even his 'Cock and the Jasp', the shortest fable and the one closest to the traditional form, contains *in toto* 98 lines (in the *Isopet de Lyon* it has 34, in 'Walter' only 10 (with, sometimes, an *additio* of 4 lines)). Walter's 'Two Mice' has 32 lines +4), the *Isopet de Lyon*'s 94, Henryson's 235. The two fables to which Henryson has added a prologue—'The Lion and the Mouse' and 'The Preaching of the Swallow'—are even longer (301 and 329 lines respectively). Walter's fables are, like the majority of medieval fables, extremely short, and his verses manage to catch the polished brevity of

[12] Cf. Gregory Smith, I, pp. xiv–xv.

the Phaedrian Latin fable. Among the vernacular fables, those of Marie de France have something of the old elegant, epigrammatic quality, but for a completely successful and sophisticated imitation of the lapidary form of the ancient fable we have to wait for La Fontaine (who, quite apart from his exceptional gifts, could benefit from a tradition of humanistic education, and from a knowledge of classical epigram, of the text of Phaedrus, and of the practice of the emblem-books). Henryson chose the safer path for a medieval poet, allowing himself a greater narrative scope, and yet keeping his fables tight and concise in structure and style.[13]

The most obviously 'emblematic' of Henryson's fables is 'The Cock and the Jasp', which gives us a simple 'speaking picture', with a single character and a single episode. The conflict is an interior one; details of the outside world, or of character or of motivation are of lesser importance. At the other extreme we have a fable like 'The Trial of the Fox', where there is a series of episodes, considerable interest in characterization and motivation, and narrative techniques which are quite elaborate. It would be too simple, however, to conclude that Henryson had abandoned, or was in process of abandoning the emblem for the story. We have come upon yet another paradox of the fable. 'Emblem' and 'story' are simply the two extremes of the same form. The fable looks toward emblem-books, and aspires to the condition of an image, a speaking picture, static, with simultaneous layers of significance, while at the same time it also looks towards the tale or the

[13] His apology (36ff.) for his 'hamelie language', etc., is of course a traditional assertion of modesty (cf. Curtius, pp. 83–5)—as he wittily demonstrates in the next lines, when in asking for correction he uses a cluster of words which are far from homely. In fact, he achieves a style which is neither too 'deminute' nor too 'superfluous'. 'Qui brevis et bonus est, ille poeta placet' (on brevity as an ideal of style, see Curtius, Excursus XIII). Cf. 'In breif sermone ane pregnant sentence wryte' (*Testament* 270). Brevity of style is not necessarily the same thing as shortness. The fables of Phaedrus, which always give the impression of brevity, are sometimes as long as those of Babrius, which do not (Nøjgaard, *La Fable antique*, II, pp. 22–3, and cf. ch. 12). This is exactly the case with Henryson's 'amplified' fables, which remain succinct and pointed. Moreover, as Erasmus says (*De Copia*, I, ch. v, tr. King and Rix), 'who could speak more tersely than he who has ready at hand an extensive array of words and figures from which he can immediately select what is most suitable for conciseness.' The concision of Henryson's style is made possible by the copiousness of his vocabulary, which ranges from the local and humble (*slonkis*, *bollis*, *fowmart*, etc., etc.) to the clerkly (*vilipend*, *contumax*, etc.).

anecdote and demands a story with a consecutive and linear[14] motion (even in 'The Cock and the Jasp' something happens). Although the effect of Henryson's expansions and elaborations is to move his fables towards the pole of the 'story', he still preserves much of their emblematic aspect. In spite of their length, his fables have a notable brevity of style, and in all of them he shows his fondness for the 'speaking picture', the scene which shows forth the 'soul' of the situation. Some of his scenes are, in miniature, rather like those of a later allegorical poet, Spenser, in that they are at the same time static, visual, expressive and memorable and also dynamic, suggesting both a past and a future. They are always visual, whether full of movement as when the troop of mice release the lion (picturing the truth that one good deed deserves another) or with the suggestion of movement to come, as when Chantecleir is poised on his toes just before the fox pounces, or of the more static Aesopic sort—the wolf and the lamb beside their stream, the cock confronted by its jasp.[15]

Some characteristics of his short verse tales are immediately obvious. He takes full advantage of the fact that his stories are traditional and 'often told' (he reminds us of this again and again by referring to his author, 'Esope ane taill puttis in memorie', etc.). This gives them (like popular tales) a certain air of inevitability, and a certain naturalness. We know that the two mice will act in their different ways, that the cock will always spurn the jasp, that the birds will never take heed of the preaching of the swallow, yet no matter how many times we read the fables we are always surprised. His tales have a unity and a completeness, a concentrated and inner coherence that sometimes reminds us of the later prose short story. There are significant moments, when 'the veil is lifted'. They are at the same time brief and complete, achieving a curious sort of 'transparent density'.

[14] Cf. A. Walton Litz, *The Art of James Joyce* (Oxford, 1961), pp. 56–7.

[15] It may be that Henryson's love of detail, so often singled out for praise, arises from a 'delight in the world of the senses'. Characteristically, however, he uses details rhetorically to create vivid scenes and to give them a sense of solidity and particularity. Even in 'The Cock and the Jasp', his nearest approach to the bare setting of the ancient fable, the dunghill has ash, and is close to a house. A detail carefully used will suddenly bring home the grimness of a situation (cf. 1085, 1878–80, 2891). Cf. also the fabliau-like particularity of the description of the fox lying down to feign death (2049–55), repeated with comic zest and irony in 2161–4. He also uses details to instruct as well as to please: the precise legal terms of some fables are weapons in a satirist's armoury.

Henryson has made the humble form into a coherent and finished work, but in the traditional matter he allows much of the original simplicity to survive. Here we are far from the intricate *entrelacement* of French courtly romance; the episodes follow in plain and simple linearity. He preserves the fable's fondness for simple oppositions, encounters between two characters, for simple episodes and motifs, for simple functions of the *dramatis personae* (cf. 'The Wolf and the Lamb'), which he then develops to his own artistic ends. At the heart of the matter of 'The Paddock and the Mouse' is the simple and popular episode of a chance meeting with a stranger. The journey with another person, which has offered a surprising range of literary possibilities to generations of story-tellers, can be found in 'The Trial of the Fox'.[16] In their combination of the humble and popular with learning and high art Henryson's tales are a true expression of the paradoxical form of the fable. We may perhaps illustrate this briefly by considering his methods of opening the tales, and his variations upon the traditional opening formulas, the most famous of which—'once upon a time', 'es kam einmal' etc.—establishes at once a familiarity with the teller and a significance and a timelessness for the tale. Twice he uses the traditional formula or something close to it, adapting it to his fable—(no. 1 in the Bassandyne order) 'Ane cok, sumtyme,...fleu furth', (no. 12) 'Ane cruell wolff...Upon ane tyme past to ane reveir'. Or, he will use the traditional formula and in addition make a reference to his 'auctor' (thus producing in miniature a nice combination of humble folk-tale technique and of learning): Nos. 9 ('Qwhylum thair wynnit in ane wilderness— / As myne authour expreslie can declair'), 10 ('In elderis dayis, as Esope can declair'), 11 ('Qwhylum thair wes, as Esope can report'), and 13. Sometimes he uses more literary openings. In two he simply makes an authenticating reference to Aesop (No. 2, 'Esope, myne authour, makis mentioun / Of twa myis' and 6 'Esope ane taill puttis in memorie'). Two fables are explicitly linked to their predecessors (Nos. 4 and 5). Three others have more elaborate openings. No. 7, 'The Lion and the Mouse' has a prologue with a *chronographia* and a kind of *chanson d'aventure* with the poet meeting

[16] Cf. Bauman, 'The Folktale and Oral Tradition', *passim*, von Sydow, 'Kategorien der Prosa-Volksdichtung' in *Volkskundliche Gaben*, ed. H. Schewe (Berlin, Leipzig, 1934), p. 256, Mia I. Gerhardt, *Two Wayfarers. Some Medieval Stories on the Theme of Good and Evil* (Utrecht, 1964) (from whom I have taken the phrase 'transparent density'.)

Aesop (though the fable Aesop tells begins simply 'Ane lyoun at his pray...'). 'The Preaching of the Swallow' (No. 8) begins with a *sententia* ('The hie prudence...') and a philosophical prologue. It also recalls the *chanson d'aventure* in that the poet is present throughout. 'The Cock and the Fox' (No. 3) begins with a general *sententia*—'Thocht brutall beistis be irrationall...'—and moves to 'ane cas'—'Ane wedow dwelt...'.

One of the most striking features of Henryson's skill is his control—of pace, of mood, of the turns and climaxes of the story, and of the audience's emotions. In this an important part is played by the distinctive voice and presence of the narrator. Henryson has the supremely dramatic gift of being able to 'submerge the teller's egoism in the tale'[17] when he wishes, but at other points the 'teller' is brought very prominently before the eyes of the audience. This is done much more consistently than in other medieval fable collections, and it seems most likely that he has learnt from Chaucer's extensive use of self-conscious narrators. In the Prologue there is scarcely a hint (as there certainly would have been in Chaucer) that the narrator is to emerge so distinctively. There his 'I' is only found in the second half, with a *captatio benevolentiae* and a statement of his purpose. He offers us the first fable very firmly as that of his author—'first of ane cok *he* wrate'. The narrator allows us to see the scene, but even here he gives us a little digression (for which perhaps the reservation in line 2, 'albeit he was bot pure', should prepare us). He stops the scene, and devotes one stanza to reflecting on the careless way in which some girls sweep out houses (ll. 71–7), thus holding up, in a rather Chaucerian way, the flow of the narrative in order to increase the dramatic effect, and introducing the narrator's presence and personality. At first we are tempted to take this as simply a chatty expression of his prejudices, but it soon becomes clear that there is more to it. He adds a little mystification—'peradventure, sa wes the samin stone'—and he is, I think, teasing his audience, leading us to suppose that the cock is being more prudent and wise than these 'damisellis wantoun and insolent'. The rest of the fable is presented quite dramatically: we simply overhear the cock's speech—until the end, when the 'I' of the narrator appears again with another little mystification—'But quhen or how or quhome be it wes found, / As now I set to hald na argument...'—and becomes the 'I' of the moralist ('of the inward...I sall reheirs'). Similarly in

[17] Gregory Smith, I, p. xv.

'The Two Mice' we have a dramatic presentation of the scenes with the occasional aside from the narrator—'as I hard say' (197), 'as I suppose' (295)—and again at the end, professing ignorance, 'I can not tell how weill thairefter scho fure...Bot I hard say', leading on to the more vehement and personal 'I' of the *moralitas*. These are the remarks of an authenticating narrator, giving a sense of solidity to the story, confirming the reader's conviction that he is being told the truth. At the same time, they elegantly set up a shifting relationship between the narrator and his story, suggesting both his interest in it and his detachment from it—a hint that it has a separate existence independent of its teller. This fable has an interesting variation on the technique in an apparently chance word—'Quhen in come Gib Hunter, *our* jolie cat...'. This is rather like a narrative adaptation of the syntactic 'ethic dative' which was still found in contemporary English, but it suggests more than a narrator's interest in the story, rather an involvement which, momentarily at least, seems total, a kind of complicity. Henryson uses a similar device in two other fables, where he claims knowledge from one of his creatures—in each case the leading villain! In 'The Confession of the Fox' he speaks (634) 'as Lowrence leirnit me' about the stars, for two stanzas. The effect of the remark here is both a delicately comic undermining of his own rhetoric and learning, and the suggestion of an intimacy, which, because it is unexplained, remains mysterious, with his decidedly shifty astronomer. In 'The Trial of the Fox', when we are given the splendid catalogue of the four-footed beasts, Henryson introduces a startling shift in perspective by claiming that he knows of this on the authority of Lawrence the fox himself: 'And quhat thay wer, to me as Lowrence leird, / I sall reheirs...'. The suggestion is that the villain has the ear of the poet.

There are some fables where the narrator does not remind us so explicitly of his presence. The story of 'The Wolf and the Wether' unfolds before us without a single 'I' from the narrator. In others, the narrator's 'I' appears only at the end of the fable, as 'The Fox, the Wolf and the Cadger', 'The Fox, the Wolf and the Husbandman' (where the 'I' appears in a final question 'Quha haillit him out, I wait not, off the well'), 'The Wolf and the Lamb' (where the audience is included in a question, 'Off his murther quhat sall we say, allace?'), and 'The Paddock and the Mouse' (where a remark which suggests that he has been present at the scene—'Off thair debait thus quhen I hard outred...' is followed by a witty invitation to the audience, 'Giff this be trew speir ye at thame that saw'). 'The Cock and the Fox' has a rather literary beginning—'I purpose for to wryte'; the following remark 'Ane cais I fand' suggests the use of an example from experience which will prove the authority of the doctrines propounded. The illustrative fable is told without an 'I'; almost at the end the audience is included: 'Now juge ye all quhairat Schir Lowrence lewch'.

There are many variations. The grim Aesopic tale of 'The Sheep and the Dog' is presented to us dramatically, except that from time to time the narrator's feelings seem to burst out in exclamations of irony and outrage—'I beschrew thame ay that leis' (1222), 'On clerkis I do it, gif this sentence wes leill' (1229), 'Off this sentence, allace, quhat sall I say' (1248). Finally in the *moralitas* he overhears the 'cairfull cry' of the oppressed sheep:

as I passit by
Quhair that he lay, on cais I lukit doun,
And hard him mak sair lamentatioun...

This is an interesting extension of the technique (of which we have seen a hint in 'The Paddock and the Mouse') of the narrator suggesting that he is overhearing or taking part in the scene he has himself invented. 'The Confession of the Fox' has another example (694): 'Quhen I this saw, I drew ane lytill by...'. In 'The Sheep and the Dog' the alternation between extremes of authority ('Esope ane taill puttis in memorie'), a dramatic mode of narration, and of the experience provoking a subjective and impassioned response on the part of the narrator is particularly successful. In 'The Trial of the Fox', however, we find the narrator in a much more loquacious and moralizing mood. The first example of behaviour proving the lore of 'like father like son' produces an abrupt *exclamatio*: 'Fy! Covetice unkynd and venemous: / The sone wes fane he fand his father deid...'. He tells us what we should think of the fraudful fox, and warns us against a too simple faith in our heirs. When the fox is worried and perplexed, the narrator addresses him directly—'O fylit spreit, and cankerit conscience!'...'Thy cheir changis, Lowrence...'—and he draws in his audience with him, instructing them at the same time

Luke to this tod, how he wes in effray,
And fle the filth of falset, I the reid. (982–3)

(For all the art, it is hard to avoid the suspicion that in this part of the fable the sympathy the narrator has for his particularly scandalous anti-hero seems to provoke a rather more vehement moralization in the body of the tale than is usual.) Then, with considerable dramatic effect, this very active narrator withdraws, and swiftly presents the vivid scenes which follow to the end.

'The Lion and the Mouse' presents yet another variation, in that there the fabulist meets his 'author' in a dream—and like other meetings of poets with 'auctores' in medieval literature it is a very emotional and significant event.[18] Aesop obligingly tells a fable, so that here we have the 'narrator' listening to another voice. Finally, in 'The Preaching of the Swallow', the fabulist tells us that he goes out into the wood, where he sees (at various times) the action of the whole fable.[19] He is a philosophical observer, yet full of *pite* for the foolish birds (cf. ll. 1874–6). At the end, when the swallow flies off, the narrator makes what we now recognize as a characteristic remark 'bot I hir saw no moir'.

Henryson has built up a curiously intimate relationship between the narrator and the audience. He is still close enough to oral poetry to be able to sound quite unselfconscious (even if it is not quite so simple

[18] See, for instance, Dante, *Inf.* i, 79–90, iv, 83ff., Petrarch, *Secretum*, ed. E. Carrara (in *Prose*, ed. G. Martellotti, P. G. Ricci, E. Carrara, E. Bianchi (Milan, Naples, 1935)), p. 25, (tr. W. H. Draper (London, 1911), p. 3); cf. Lydgate's version of Boccaccio's meetings (*Fall of Princes*, VIII, 50ff., IX, 2511) (in contrast, Douglas's encounter with Maffeo Vegio, the continuator of Virgil, in Prol. *Eneados* XIII, is a lively affair). The *locus amoenus* (cf. Curtius, pp. 195ff., N. B. Hansen, *That Pleasant Place* (Copenhagen, 1973)) so enthusiastically described (cf. 1340–1) is an appropriate setting for such an event, a kind of sacred place in which one might meet a representative of ancient wisdom.

[19] Possibly a recollection of another literary topic, 'the poet in the wood', that idea of writing poetry in solitude under trees which has been traced back to Hellenistic literature (cf. Curtius, pp. 187, 207–8). Here however the wood seems to be, as it often is in medieval literature, a place of mystery. When Henryson rests 'under ane hawthorne grene' he does not, as in 'The Lion and the Mouse' (or as the poet of *Wynnere and Wastoure*), dream a wonderful dream, but experiences something even more remarkable, for the action takes place before his waking eyes. It is on this very tree that the swallow sits (1735), and near it is 'ane *ferlie* flicht' of small birds, 'rycht *mervellous*...'. That we are to think of the magical reputation of the tree and of its connection with fairyland (cf. L. C. Wimberly, *Folklore in the English and Scottish Ballads* (Chicago, 1928), pp. 123–4, 319, Stith Thompson, *Motif-Index of Folk-Literature* (Bloomington, 1934), D 950.13, D 958) is suggested by the remark made as the poet returns home, 'swa ferliand as I had sene ane farie', and by the fact that when he comes back to the spot in June, he finds 'be aventure and cace' those very same birds.

in fact) in the direct way he speaks—(190) 'The hartlie joy, God! geve ye had sene', (365) 'Freindis, ye may find, and ye will tak heid', (586) 'Now, worthie folk, suppose this be ane fabill'.[20] His narrative voice plays a part in creating something like La Fontaine's 'ironie poétique'—'une vision double et contrastée des choses'[21]—and in controlling the constant changes of perspective. It has been said of fabulists that they themselves are the chief characters in their fables. Henryson, like Aesop in the later illustrations, sometimes walks among and talks with his own creations. His voice is constantly present in the whole of every fable, so that when at the end he takes his leave with the words 'Adew my freind', his readers feel that it is farewell from a narrator whom they know.

'Cette joie de conter', a splendid phrase once used of La Fontaine,[22] could certainly be applied to Henryson, whose *Fables* invariably show not only a complete and consummate control but also a delight in the exercise of the art of story-telling. Walter's 'Cock and the Jasp', for instance, has much of the austere timelessness of one of Aesop's fables. The action takes place against an empty background; the finding of the jasp is related only to the cock's attempt to find food: Dum... fodit...dum quaeritat...Dum stupet inventa jaspide Gallus, ait... It has the 'absolute time' of Aesop: 'son action ne semble pas demander du temps: elle paraît momentanée...la composition vise à concentrer la fable autour d'une situation qui ne contient qu'une seule action: l'action de choix.'[23] There is still something of this in Henryson's version, but he treats it rather differently. His has a rather more leisurely introduction, made into a scene in its own right,[24] with some

[20] Henryson's 'suppose', 'as I suppois', etc., have something of the effect of La Fontaine's conversational phrases—'quant à moi', etc.,—and although he does not share quite the same notions of 'studied ease', he achieves something not altogether unlike La Fontaine's familiar style, which 'suggests the actual presence of the public and gives the fable the liveliness and freedom one associates with improvised story-telling' (J. D. Biard, *The Style of La Fontaine's Fables* (Oxford, 1966), p. 80).

[21] Odette de Mourgues, p. 132.

[22] F. Gohin, *L'Art de La Fontaine dans ses fables* (Paris, 1929), p. 134.

[23] Nøjgaard, I, p. 216.

[24] It is an example in miniature of the way in which Henryson amplifies 'Walter'. Erasmus, *De Copia*, II, suggests methods of varying and embellishing apologues—by descriptions, fuller narration, *sermones*, *sententiae*, and especially by 'circumstances' (cf. Wilson, 'Who, what and where, by what helpe and by whose, / why, how and when, do many things disclose'). So Henryson gives the circumstances of time, place and of the persons, the cause of the cock's action, its

chronological indications. It happened 'sum tyme'. The cock flies on to the scene ('fleu furth upon ane dunghill') at a certain time ('sone be day'); we know something not only of his appearance but also of his nature, and his intentions ('to get his dennar set was al his cure'). There is the glimpse of an action—'scraipand...he fand'. Then there is the digression on 'wantoun' damsels. But in the climax, time is concentrated and seems to stand still. This is achieved by the central monologue of the cock (much expanded by Henryson) in which it reveals his innermost thoughts. This *sermocinatio* is a very eloquent speech, which shows Henryson's awareness of the art of persuasion. It opens with an emphatic exclamation: 'O gentill jasp! O riche and nobill thing!' and vehemently insists on two things: (*a*) the splendour of the stone, and (*b*) the fact that it is of no use. The control of register is admirable—when the cock speaks of himself, and not of the jasp, he uses a humbler style:

> 'I had lever ga scra[ip] heir with my naillis
> Amangis this mow, and luke my lifys fude,
> As draf or corne, small wormis or snaillis...

and he quotes (as part of his pattern of self-persuasion) a popular proverb 'For wyfis sayis, lukand werkis ar licht'—an onlooker's work is easily done. After his praise of 'glad poverty' he turns finally to the splendid jewel, and his address rises to a climax with rhetorical questions, anaphora, and, with the nice conceit of a personification, he brings his argument to a triumphant conclusion:

> 'Quhar suld thow mak thy habitatioun?
> Quhar suld thow dwell bot in ane royall tour?
> Quhar suld thow sit bot on ane kingis croun,
> Exaltit in worschip and in grit honour?
> Rise, gentill jasp, of all stanis the flour,
> Out of this midding, and pas quhar thow suld be;
> Thow ganis not for me, nor I for the.' (106–12)

appearance, and means of livelihood, and what La Fontaine's teachers called *ethopoeia* (the cock is 'richt cant and crous'). For instructions on amplification in La Fontaine's day, cf. Pomey, *Novus Candidatus Rhetoricae*, who gives 'The Wolf and the Lamb' in two versions, *stylo simplici* and *stylo ornatiore* (with the rhetorical figures indicated in the margin).

After the moment of choice, we are brought back into time: the cock leaves the scene ('his wayis went')—whereas the cock in 'Walter' does not go anywhere—and the stone (now transformed into an object of mystery) is left lying 'law upon the ground'.

In 'The Two Mice' the burgess mouse quickly leads her country sister to her 'worthie wane' and the promised feast (ll. 260ff.). There is some particularity in the chronological and geographical setting—they arrive at the town 'in the morning, or the laverok sang', and the sister's dwelling is 'not fer fra thyne'. They hasten to make themselves at home, and when they are ready to eat, they address themselves to it with indecent haste: 'Withowtin grace thay wesche and went to meit'. As they are enjoying their banquet their happiness seems complete, and the tempo of the narrative slows down. The burgess mouse proudly asks her sister if she notices any difference 'betuix that chalmer and hir sarie nest'. The sister's typically worried and timorous reply—'Ye, dame,' quod scho, 'how lang will this lest?'—gives the audience a hint of unease, which is intensified by the other's over-quick reaction—'For evermair, I wait, and langer to.' Two more stanzas elaborate their fine fare and high spirits; then, signalled by a gravely portentous *sententia* from the narrator—'Yit efter joy oftymes cummis cair, / And troubill efter grit prosperitie'—there is a sudden emergency. The spencer comes in with his keys, no doubt to open up for the morning, and 'thame at denner fand'. Henryson's version is unusual in having two climaxes, two interruptions to the dinner,[25] and they are faultlessly differentiated. Here the scattering of the mice is observed with wry humour:

> Thay taryit not to wesche, as I suppose,
> Bot on to ga quha that micht formest win

—and the unfortunate country mouse is so alarmed that she 'fell in ane swoun neir deid'. But the danger passes—'Bot as God wald,' remarks the narrator dryly, 'it fell ane happie cace'—and the spencer goes out (leaving the door open, conveniently, for the next source of danger). The pace changes again, and we are given an elaboration of the plight of the distraught country mouse which is both comic and pathetic at the same time:

[25] Cf. p. 46 above (unusual among medieval versions—Aesop (Handford, 41) has two interruptions, Babrius two surprises).

This rurall mous lay flatling on the ground,
And for the deith scho wes full sair dredand,
For till hir hart straik mony wofull stound;
As in ane fever scho trimbillit fute and hand...

and of her sister's attempts to get her to return to the feast. She is scarcely settled when there is an even greater emergency, and the cat seizes her by the back. The tempo becomes a flurry of excitement:

...the burges up with that
And till hir hole scho went as fyre on flint;
Bawdronis the uther be the bak hes hint. (327–9)

Henryson has emphasized the speed by omitting the verb of motion in line 327, and he has transformed a conventional simile into a brilliant image of a mouse streaking for its hole. The irony of the cat's greeting, 'bad God speid', is continued in the next stanza in the simile 'als cant as ony kid' used to describe the way in which it tosses the unfortunate mouse up and down, and in the game 'buk heid' (blindman's bluff) it plays with her. The pace slows, and the grimly playful motions are expressed through the rhythm:

Fra fute to fute he kest hir to and fra,
Quhylis up, quhylis doun, als cant as ony kid;
Quhylis wald he lat hir rin under the stra,
Quhylis wald he wink, and play with hir buk heid...

The central episode of 'The Cock and the Fox' (ll. 432ff.) shows how cleverly he can manipulate the timing of a climax. At the culmination of a scene in which time seems to stand still, the cunning fox tricks the vainglorious cock into standing on his toes and crowing loudly. We are quite certain that the moment has arrived for the fox to pounce. This, in fact, is what he does in Chaucer's version, but Henryson has his own variation. He makes the most of the suspense, and of the fox's cunning, for his fox takes a sadistic delight in demonstrating his psychological power. This fox does not pounce, but simply says to the cock, 'very good, you really are your father's son'. There is just one thing, he continues, 'bot off his cunning yit ye want ane slicht'—your father used to 'wink and crow and turne him thryis about'. The vain bird is now completely in the fox's power, and when, 'inflate with wind and fals vanegloir'[26] ('that mony puttis unto con-

[26] Line 474 (I follow Fox in preferring Bann. *inflate*).

fusion' adds the narrator, to tease our anticipation) he tries again, we have at last the expected sudden movement: 'And suddandlie... The foxe wes war and hint him be the throte.' This incident alone would be a convincing demonstration of the *joie de conter*, but there is still more to come, for it is followed by a hilariously comic interlude, which sounds very much like Henryson's own invention. There is a scene of consternation as the fox makes off with Chantecleir. The hens cry out, while the widow is in a positive frenzy—

> scho sichit and gaif ane schout:
> 'How, murther, reylok!—with ane hiddeous beir—
> 'Allace, now lost is gentill Chantecleir!' (485–7)[27]

—and after tearing of hair and beating of breast she falls down 'half in ane extasy'. She is left lying there, and the hens, leaving their food (the poet slyly remarks) fall into a 'disputation'. All the while, Chantecleir is being carried away, and his spouses assume that he is gone for good. The disputation begins to build up larger ironies extending beyond the vanishing form of the unfortunate Chantecleir to wider questions of husbands and hypocrisy. It is a masterly change of perspective. Pertok begins with a rhetorical *planctus*.[28] Her lament is in its own right a fine lyric; it handles the stock topics of the lament for the dead—the exclamation, the rhetorical questions, and the praise of the deceased's virtues—with heightened style. It is designed to influence the emotions, as Cicero says panegyric should do.[29] Unfortunately, if we were to expose her eloquence to the cold light of reason—as we

[27] For the Bann. *reylok* ('robbery') see B. Dickins, *TLS* 21 February 1924, p. 112 (Fox).

[28] That Henryson is a master of the formal rhetorical *planctus* is evident from the examples in *The Testament of Cresseid* and *Orpheus and Eurydice*. (On English laments for the dead (usually marked by simple rhetorical features such as exclamation, balanced or parallel phrases, repetition), see V. B. Richmond, *Laments for the Dead in Medieval Narrative* (Duquesne University Press, 1966).) The humbler genre shows some interesting variations. Cf. the sheep's 'sair lamentatioun' (1286ff.), or that of the captive lion (1530–41), who, as befits a fallen prince, draws attention to the sad reversal of his might with some dignity (his first rhetorical question is an echo of the common 'Ubi Sunt' formula). Less straightforward is the *planctus* in question here, and that of the shepherd over the dead dog (2471–5), where the hyperbole perhaps hints that the grief, real though it is, is a shade more intense than the context requires.

[29] *De Oratore* III, quoted by Richmond, p. 86.

are soon to be encouraged to do—Chantecleir's past actions might appear somewhat less than heroic, consisting as they do of (1) waking them up, and providing (2) food and (3) sex. With a delicate touch of the mock-heroic (which Henryson learnt, no doubt, from *The Nun's Priest's Tale*) she is made to speak 'with teiris grit attour hir cheikis', and with an eloquence that is just a shade too elevated—

> Quha sall our lemman be? Quha sall us leid?
> Quhen we are sad, quha sall unto us sing?... (502–3)

Sprutok, however, is less worried about their fate. She is already a merry widow, and has a proverb to match—'Als gude lufe cummis as gais', as well as a gay snatch of song, 'Wes never wedow sa gay!' He had his faults, she points out—he was 'angry' and jealous, and he was not much good any more at 'chalmerglew'. She concludes with another proverb, 'Let quik to quik, and deid ga to the deid'. His nearest and dearest have not yet done with Chantecleir, for Toppok joins in, speaking 'lyke ane curate'. 'Yone wes ane verray vengeance from the hevin', she says; he had more than seven 'kittokis', and he was 'prydefull' and 'joyit of his sin':

> Thairfoir it is the verray hand off God
> That causit him be werryit with the tod.

At this—the conjunction must prove something—the widow recovers, starts up and urgently calls her dogs

> 'How, Birkye, Berrie, Bell, Bawsie Broun,
> Rype Schaw, Rin Weil, Curtes, Nuttie Clyde!—
> Togidder all but grunching furth ye glyde!
> Reskew my nobill cok or he be slane... (546–9)[30]

and the pace is on again with a fine pursuit, with galloping alliteration, and with that formulaic simile once again marvellously revivified:

> With that, but baid thay braidet ouer the bent;
> As fyre off flint thay ouer the feildis flaw,
> Full wichtlie thay throw wood and wateris went...[31]

[30] In l. 546, I follow Fox's reading.

[31] In 'hamelie' mood, Henryson is content to use proverbial similes of the type 'pure as Job', 'the hart is hard as stane'. Sometimes such comparisons are vivid in themselves (cf. 2168, 2395, 2421). For other examples of a proverbial simile being given new life, cf. 359, 2046, 2242. The ugly paddock produces a nicely

'The Sheep and the Dog' is different again. It has an inevitable movement—there is no escape for the sheep. The fable is not set in time, but time is used within it; it is significant that the false court sits in the evening (a point which is not lost on the intelligent sheep (l. 1201)). The rhythm of this fable cleverly suggests two quite separate movements—the convolutions and slowness of the law's delays (cf., e.g., ll. 1173–1242) and the sudden speed of wicked injustice (the sheep is summoned 'peremtourlie, within twa dayis or thre' and at the end is charged to pay without delay). 'The Lion and the Mouse' on the other hand turns on free choice, and the moments of decision are made into extended scenes. The climax of that in which the mice respond to the 'maister' mouse's request 'Cum help to quite ane gude turne for ane uther' is one of Henryson's best descriptions of busy activity:

> Thay tuke na knyfe, thair teith wes scharpe anewch.
> To se that sicht, forsuith it wes grit wounder—
> How that thay ran amang the rapis tewch;
> Befoir, behind, sum yeid about, sum under... (1559–62)

The hurried rhythms remind us of those of earlier scenes in the fable—of the mice dancing on the lion (ll. 1412–16), and of the lion's frenzied attempts to free itself from the net (ll. 1542–8).

Henryson is skilful in his handling of sudden turns and climaxes, or sudden changes of atmosphere. There is a good example in 'The Trial of the Fox' where Lawrence, who has just murdered a lamb, is back before the parliament and is enjoying the humiliation of the wolf, when suddenly everything changes:

> As thay wer carpand in this cais, with knakis,
> And al the court in merines and in gam,
> Swa come the yow, the mother off the lam. (1066–8)

Especially impressive are the abrupt and grim endings of some of the fables—the sudden dive of the kite at the end of 'The Paddock and the Mouse', or the precisely described death of the Wether:

inappropriate simile—'wer I als fair als jolie Absolon'. Others, less proverbial, are almost speaking pictures, as the irate wolf's 'white as a friar' (2550), or (of the joy of the cadger) (2062) 'as he had hard ane pyper play he gais', or the fox entrancing the wolf with the 'nekhering' (2127): 'callour, pypand lyke ane pertrik ee'.

> Than be the crag bane smertlie he him tuke
> Or ever he ceissit, and it in schunder schuke (2586–7)

and that of the Lamb:

> The selie lamb culd do na thing bot bleit:
> Sone wes he deid: the wolff wald do na grace,
> Syne drank his blude, and off his flesche can eit
> Quhill he wes full, and went his way on pace. (2700–3)

The deaths are there in the traditional matter of the fables, but their grimness is Henryson's.

It is not surprising that a poet with such a vivid, dramatic imagination should show a great fondness for direct speech and dialogue. Again, this is unusual as well as distinctive. There is a great deal of racy dialogue in the Renart cycle, but the traditional Aesopic fable uses direct speech sparingly. Walter's fable *De Mure et Rana*, for instance, goes its way without any direct speech at all. His *De Mure rustico et urbano* has a little more, but this consists largely of the final speech of the country mouse. Henryson vastly extends it. In his 'Two Mice', seven of the twenty-nine stanzas are completely in dialogue, and seven others contain some direct speech. It is only very occasionally that Henryson will use indirect speech.[32] He much prefers the dramatic impact of direct speech, even if it means externalizing an interior monologue or discourse. Characters may express themselves by speaking 'in mynd'.[33] In 'The Fox, the Wolf and the Cadger', when the Cadger finds what he takes to be the dead fox

> he wes fane,
> And till himself thus softlie can he say:
> 'At the nixt bait, in faith, ye sall be flane,
> And off your skyn I sall mak mittennis tway.' (2056–9)

The adverb 'softlie' brilliantly captures the tone of his musings. The fox in this fable when he sees the wolf discomfited, 'said to himself': 'Thir hering sall be myne'. In 'The Sheep and the Dog' the brutal tempo is emphasized by a sudden, unannounced switch into direct speech: [the apparitour]

[32] Cf. 988ff., 1202ff., 1224ff., 1245ff., 1422, 1763.

[33] Cf. 556 (where the fox has to speak 'in mynd', or he would have dropped his victim).

> Summonit the scheip befoir the wolff, that he
> . . . Compeir under the panis in this bill,
> 'To heir quhat Perrie Doig will say the till'. (1163–6)

Dialogue in the *Fables* is both frequent and lively. At the beginning of 'The Fox, the Wolf and the Cadger' the two villains meet and greet each other ceremoniously:

> 'Welcum to me,' quod he, 'thow Russell gray.'
> Syne loutit doun and tuke him be the hand:
> 'Ryse up, Lowrence! I leif the for to stand.' (1962–4)

'Quhair hes thow beene this sesoun fra my sicht', he continues, and they go on conversing for nine stanzas, the wolf voicing his (well-founded) suspicions, the fox blandly denying all thought of deceit, and protesting his own disabilities for the post of 'steward' to the wolf. The exchange is cleverly and ironically brought to a close when the fox swears an oath of allegiance to the wolf. Later in the fable, the fox plays on the wolf's immense and gluttonous passion for 'nekhering' in another brilliant scene conducted entirely in dialogue. A snatch will give something of its flavour:

> 'Bot quhat wes yone the carll cryit on hie,
> And schuke his hand?' quod he. 'Hes thou no feill?'
> 'Schir,' said the foxe, 'that I can tell trewlie;
> He said the nekhering wes intill the creill.'
> 'Kennis thou that hering?' 'Ye, schir, I ken it weill,
> And at the creill mouth I had it thryis but dout;
> The wecht off it neir tit my tuskis out.
>
> 'Now suithlie, schir, micht we that hering fang
> It wald be fische to us thir fourtie dayis.'
> Than said the wolff: 'Now God nor that I hang,
> Bot to be thair I wald gif all my clays
> To se gif that my wappinnis mycht it rais.'
> 'Schir,' said the foxe, 'God wait, I wischit you oft
> Quhen that my pith micht not beir it on loft.' (2112–25)

Once again, there are many variations. In 'The Paddock and the Mouse', where Henryson makes his 'brutal beistis' 'dispute and argow', the suspicions of the mouse are allayed by smooth talk and a false oath. At the end, when the tragic course is set, and the paddock in the middle of the river 'preissit doun' so as to drown the mouse, the mouse is given a single anguished cry:

> Persavand this, the mous on hir can cry:
> 'Tratour to God, and manesworne unto me!
> Thow swore the murthour aith richt now that I
> But hurt or harme sul ferryit be and fre!' (2882–5)

They struggle 'till at the last scho cryit for ane preist'. The kite who appears instead does not speak but (we are back in the cruel world of animals) carries them off, 'pyipand with mony pew'. In 'The Wolf and the Lamb' we can see how Henryson uses dialogue (which is there in the traditional fable) to build up a whole scene. From 'Aesop' through the centuries, this has been a very committed fable, sharply opposing vice and virtue, set in isolation (except for the one essential property, the river) and moving to its climax with a strange and terrible logic. The version of 'Walter' has a splendid concision:

> Est Lupus, est Agnus; sitit hic, sitit ille; fluentem
> Limite non aequo quaerit uterque viam.
> In summo bibit amne Lupus, bibit Agnus in imo...[34]

The French versions extend this taut scene. The *Isopet de Lyon* gives a slightly more detailed setting:

> Au dessus boit de la fontaigne
> Li Lous, de pansee mal sainne;
> Li Aigneax de simple coraige
> Bevoit au desoz dou rivaige...[35]

and Henryson makes us see the scene even more precisely—there is 'ane reveir / Descending from ane rotche unto ane well' (2617–18), and he remarks—quite incidentally it seems at first—on the clearness of the water ('drank of the water cleir'), and insists more strongly on the threatening nature of the wolf (using his favourite emphatic device of alliteration—'the wolfis thocht wes all on wickitnes'), and on the innocence of the lamb (of whom he repeatedly uses the adjective *selie*). In 'Walter' and the *Isopet de Lyon* the lamb's fear simply arises when the wolf threatens him. Henryson, however, recasts the scene to build up the opposition of the two before anything has happened. The *selie* lamb (who 'of his fa the wolff nathing he wist') drinks at the

34 Bastin, *Recueil*, II, pp. 8–9.

35 *Ib.*, p. 87.

stream to cool his thirst (it is noteworthy that here the contrast between the two in the manner of drinking is done with a verbal elegance worthy of La Fontaine—the ravenous wolf 'to *slaik* his thirst *drank* of the watter cleir', whereas the lamb 'in the streme *laipit* to *cule* his thrist'). Henryson (ll. 2623–8) insists on the difference in intent in the two creatures. Then, finally, the wolf sees the lamb, and finds an object for his 'wickedness' ('The wolff him saw and rampand come him till. / With girnand teith and awful angrie luke') and here we begin the traditional dialogue, now set in a much more dramatic scene. The *Isopet de Lyon* makes the wolf 'thunder' in a slightly more impassioned manner than 'Walter' does:

> 'Mavais Agneax,' dit li traites,
> A la fontaigne mar venites!
> Vos m'avez corrociez sanz dote,
> L'aigue m'avez troblee tote'

but this sounds very pale beside the dramatic truculence of Henryson's wolf:

> ...'Thow cative wretchit thing!
> How durst thow be so bald to fyle and bruke,
> Quhar I suld drink, with thy foull slavering?
> It wer almous the for to draw and hing,
> That suld presume, with thy foull lippis wyle,
> To glar my drink, and this fair watter fyle!' (2630–6)

This speech shows Henryson's powers of emphasis at their best. We should note how the wolf immediately uses the scornful 'thow'... 'thy' forms of address, and how its vehemence (the lamb's 'lapping' has become 'slavering') rises to a climax in the last line, with its strong balanced rhythm, and its splendid Scots word 'glar' (= to make muddy). Henryson also cleverly suggests that the wolf has already decided on the lamb's fate ('it wer almous the for to draw and hing'). The lamb, as in the French fable, 'se deffent per raison', but in Henryson this is preceded by a physical reaction of fear—'quaikand for verray dreid, / On kneis fell...'. The tone of its reply is quiet, humble and deferential. It calls the wolf 'schir', and uses the polite forms of address throughout. Its language has a distinctly legal cast (cf. 'ye can nocht preif,' 'ergo'). Later in the fable (2679–92) it makes a direct appeal for legal justice, and that Henryson was thinking of legal injustice as one very distinctive part of the 'morality' already begins to emerge. The lamb's speech is highly rational. Almost with a touch of pedantry, it picks up the only two 'points' that can be found in the wolf's tirade, and refutes them: (a) since 'all hevie thing man off the selff discend', the river cannot run backwards; I was below you, *ergo* 'for me your bruke wes never the war', and (b) my lips have not touched anything 'contagious'. And so the argument continues, with the lamb clearly having everything that is rational and civilized on its side. Its urgent and fearful innocence is well expressed by a vehement ejaculation, marked by neither 'quod' nor 'said':

> 'Schir, it is wrang that for the fatheris gilt
> The saikles sone suld punist be or spilt!...' (2663–4)

But even its apposite quotation of scripture is met by the jeers of the stupid and wicked wolf:

> 'Yaa!' quod the wolff, 'Yit pleyis thow agane?'

Henryson's interest in the characters and personalities of his creatures is very notable. Such an interest is rarely, if ever, found in earlier fables, where 'character' is usually no more than a function of the narrative. In the Greek Aesop the protagonists are the embodiment of forces, motivated, almost always, solely by self-interest. Something of this comes through to Henryson's *Fables*, but more often the question that springs to his reader's mind is 'How will this particular animal react to this situation?' In the fable we have just considered, for instance, the pitiless Aesopic logic of conflict is still central, but a new interest in the emotions of the protagonists has been added, so that the fable has been turned into an expression of the conflict of two opposed characters—the wicked wolf and the *selie* lamb—and from it various aspects of their personalities emerge—the deferential niceness of the lamb, and the truculence of the wolf. Here personality—expressed in public behaviour—and character—their actual sentiments—accord, and this gives each of them a kind of integrity.[36] The lamb is admirable, but ill-fated, the wolf reprehensible, but successful. The two are notably separate, however, in the case of Henryson's dissimulating animals, especially his foxes. In 'The Cock and the Fox', the 'wylie' tod 'dissimuland' finds a weakness in the character of the cock, which

[36] On 'character' and 'personality', cf. A. Quinton, 'The Continuity of Persons', *TLS* 27 July 1973, 873–4.

is 'inflate with wind and fals vanegloir'. Here Henryson (like Theophrastus) has a moral view of character. The remarks at the beginning of the fable, however, about the 'inclination' of beasts ('ilk ane in thair kynd naturall / Hes mony divers inclinatioun')—so that the bear is 'busteous', the fox 'fenyeit'—suggest a scientific and determinist view. So the fox in 'The Trial of the Fox' 'off verray kinde behuifit to be fals'. There is no attempt to reconcile these two points of view, which are, one suspects, poetic rather than philosophical; we are left with a mirror of the world, shifting and uncertain. We can immediately recognize the problem which some of Henryson's protagonists have of trying to estimate the true character of those whom they meet. This is obviously—and comically—the case with the victims of his various foxes, but it is also the problem of the little mouse confronted by an ugly toad. When she attempts to apply the scientific criteria of physiognomy ('Giff I can ony skill of phisnomy, / Thow hes sumpart off falset and invy' (2824–5)), it is not just smooth talk that deflects her. She is also in the grip of an obsession, a passionate desire for the food on the other side of the river. Henryson is always shrewdly aware of the power of obsessive desire—the wolf in 'The Fox, the Wolf and the Cadger' thinks only of the wondrous 'nekhering' ('Bot ever upon the nekhering he thinkis, / And quyte forgettis the foxe and all his wrinkis' (2166–7)).[37]

In 'The Two Mice', where we are given in the burgess mouse a comic example of personality determined by social status, we are never certain how far this represents the true character. Near the end there is a flash of emotion when she is moved to pity by her sister's terror:

> For verray pietie scho began to greit,
> Syne confort her with wordis hunny sweit. (314–15)

But the adjective 'hunny sweit' perhaps suggests that her social personality is quickly taking over again. These sudden moments of revelation or near-revelation are very distinctive. We do not find (and in this succinct form would not expect) those elaborate analyses of behaviour and thought so characteristic of the courtly romances. Henryson prefers to show character or personality expressing itself through speech or gesture, or through a scene, with the narrator's more general indicators—adjectives like 'fals', 'wylie', etc.—forming a background. We have already seen an example of sudden flash of

37 Cf. also 'The Cock and the Jasp', l. 67.

self-revelation in the speeches of the hens in 'The Cock and the Fox'. There is another revealing moment in 'The Paddock and the Mouse' where the little mouse's obsessive desire grows restive during the Paddock's lengthy and learned speech of self-justification—'"Let be thy preiching!" quod the hungrie mous'. Another appears in a suggestive visual detail in 'The Fox, the Wolf and the Husbandman' (2378ff.) where the fox at last thinks of a solution to the problem of producing the 'cabok' he has promised the wolf:

> Yit at the last he findis furth ane wyle,
> Than at him selff softlie couth he smyle.

'The Wolf and the Wether' has a very subtle example. It is worth looking at this in the context of the whole fable, in order to appreciate its full dramatic impact. The closest traditional fable to it so far noticed is one in Steinhöwel's 'Extravagantes', of which I quote Caxton's version for comparison:

> Grete folye is to a fool that hath no myght that wulle begyle another stronger than hym self, as reherceth this fable of a fader of famylle whiche had a grete herd or flock of sheep, and had a grete dogge for to kepe them, which was wel stronge, and of his voys all the wolves were aferd, wherfore the sheepherd slepte more surely. But it happed that this dogge for his grete age deyde, wherfore the sheepherdes were sore troubled and wrothe, and sayd one to other, 'We shall no more slepe at oure ease by cause that our dogge is dede, for the wulves shall now come and ete our sheep.' And thenne a grete wether fyers and prowd, whiche herd alle these wordes came to them and sayd, 'I shalle gyve yow good counceylle–shave me, and put on me the skynne of the dogge, and whanne the wolves shalle see me, they shalle have grete fere of me.' And whanne the wolves came and sawe the wether clothed with the skynne of the dogge, they beganne all to flee, and ranne awey. It happed on a day that a wulf whiche was sore hongry came and toke a lambe, and after ran awaye therwith. And thenne the sayd wether ranne after hym. And the wulf whiche supposed that it had ben the dogge shote thryes by the waye for the grete fere that he had, and ranne ever as fast as he coude, and the wether also ranne after hym withoute cesse, tyl that he ranne thurgh a bushe full of sharp thornes, the whiche thornes rente and brake

> all the dogges skynne whiche was on hym. And as the wulf loked and sawe behynde hym, beynge moche doubtous of his dethe, sawe and perceyved all the decepcion and falshede of the wether, and forthwith retorned ageynste hym, and demaunded of hym, 'What beest arte thow?' And the wether ansuerd to hym in this maner, 'My lord, I am a wether whiche playeth with the.' And the wulf sayd, 'Ha, mayster, ought ye to playe with your mayster and with your lord? Thow hast made me so sore aferd that by the weye as I ranne before the I dyde shyte thre grete toordes.' And thenne the wulf ledde hym unto the place where as he had shyte, sayenge thus to hym, 'Loke hyther—callest thow this a playe? I take hit not for playe, for now I shalle shewe to the how thou oughtest not to playe so with thy lord.' And thenne the wulf took and kylled hym, and devoured and ete hym. And therfore he that is wyse muste take good hede how he playeth with hym whiche is wyser, more sage, and more stronge than hym self is.[38]

After reading Henryson, this seems like just so much raw material awaiting the artist's hand. A number of differences are immediately obvious (I need only mention those which have a bearing on our present concern)[39]—Henryson's fable appears to have only one shepherd (thus suggesting that the death of the dog is an even greater disaster); the dog dies rather mysteriously 'off suddand seiknes'; the catastrophe is unexpected, and the shepherd is moved to give a little *planctus*. The rhythm of the narrative has already become very different. It is at this point that the wether offers itself. We are not prejudiced against it, as we are in Caxton by the label 'a grete wether fyers and prowd'. Henryson brings out the incongruity more subtly. The wether advances 'wichtlie',[40] and speaks with an air of great confidence: 'Maister', quod he, 'mak merie and be blyith...' and his speech rises to a defiant vaunt:

> 'Than will the wolff trow that I am he,
> For I sall follow him fast quhar ever he fair...
> And he persew, be God, I sall not spair

[38] Lenaghan, *Caxton's Aesop*, pp. 160–1 (punctuation and spellings of u/v, etc., modernized).

[39] Cf. I. W. A. Jamieson, 'Henryson's *Taill of the Wolf and the Wedder*', *SSL* vi (1969), 248–57.

[40] The emendation suggested by T. W. Craik, *NQ* ccxiv (1969), 88–9.

To follow him as fast as did your doig,
Swa that I warrand ye sall not want ane hoig.' (2483–9)

This seems the answer to the shepherd's prayer, and Henryson carefully starts to build up a potential pattern or irony (though it is still submerged):

Than said the scheipheird: 'This come of ane gude wit;
Thy counsall is baith sicker, leill and trew;
Quha sayis ane scheip is daft, thay lieit of it.'

The characteristic balance of fantasy and realism proceeds; here it does seem that 'clothes' may 'make the man', for the wether's personality has undoubtedly changed: 'Than worth the wedder wantoun off his weid: / "Now off the wolff," quod he, "I have no dreid."' He has assumed not only the skin and the duties of the dog, but—it seems—its character as well. The rational part of the reader's mind ought to find this ludicrous and worrying, for this total faith in the disguise implies a progressive self-delusion. But Henryson's art makes us sympathize with the wether. Its confidence is infectious: we begin to wonder if, by some strange power of the imagination, its belief that it will become the dog may not in fact be brought about. We are also made to respond with delight to the element of 'game'. It will be a merry sport, and we want the wether to win. The fable's narrative action, and its psychological action—the growth of illusion—proceed side by side. It seems that the deception is hilariously successful: 'in all thingis he counterfait the dog'. Henryson, with his sure sense of narrative rhythm, pauses here, with the wether at the summit of success:

Was nowther wolff, wildcat nor yit tod
Durst cum within thay boundis all about,
Bot he wald chase thame baith throw rouch and snod;
Thay bailful beistis had of their lyvis sic dout,
For he wes mekill and semit to be stout... (2504–8)

'Semit' is a carefully chosen word. A hungry wolf (it is not just 'sore hongry'; it expresses its desperation in a speech) summons up the courage to steal a lamb and risk the wrath of the 'dog'. His headlong flight from the enraged guardian of the flock is described with a comic zest which makes Caxton's 'chase' look pathetic:

Went never hound mair haistelie fra the hand
Quhen he wes rynnand maist raklie at the ra
Nor went this wedder baith over mois and strand,
And stoppit nouther at bank, busk nor bra,
Bot followit ay sa ferslie on his fa...
And maid ane vow to God that he suld have him.
(2518–24)

The pursuit continues, enlivened not only by alliteration but also by carefully chosen visual details—'with that the wolff let out his taill on lenth'. The wolf is so terrified that he throws away the lamb, but even this will not satisfy the wether's assumed personality. In a moment of acute psychological observation, Henryson makes him reveal by a remark that he has been deceived by his own deceit: 'Na', quod the wedder, 'in faith we part not swa: / It is not the lamb, bot the, that I desyre.' This instant of self-revelation is very like a Joycean epiphany,[41] a sudden spiritual manifestation in which the interior psychological action of the fable, the progressive growth of illusion reaches its public climax. The familiar 'thee' with which the wether addresses its victim seems to hover between the threateningly hostile and the caressingly erotic. The 'game' has now really become 'earnest'—the wether is determined to deliver a *coup de grâce* and his pursuit is inexorable. When, suddenly, and by chance, a bush rips off the wether's skin, there is an instant change of atmosphere and tone; in a vivid scene we are shown the suppressed wrath of the wolf:

'Na,' quod he, 'is this ye that is sa neir?
Richt now ane hound, and now quhyte as ane freir.
I fled ouer fer, and I had kennit the cais:
To God I vow that ye sall rew this rais!' (2549–52)

The true, rather feeble, character of the wether is now revealed. It can only offer the weak excuse that it was really all a game; it now speaks with a new deference, as a servant (cf. 2580), addressing the wolf as 'Maister' and politely as 'yow'. The wolf is (with some justification) vindictive and is determined to put an end to this game—'Is this your bourding in ernist than?'—but he still finds it difficult to believe the

[41] 'A sudden spiritual manifestation, whether in the vulgarity of speech or of gesture or in a memorable phase of the mind itself' (*Stephen Hero*). Cf. the discussion by M. Beja, *Epiphany in the Modern Novel* (London, 1971).

evidence of his eyes ('Now is this ye?') and his tone becomes ironic: 'Na, bot ane hound I wene! / Me think your teith over schort to be sa kene.' The ironic pattern, now a sinister one, culminates in a typically violent and abrupt end. 'Sikkerlie' says the wolf, grimly echoing the wether, 'now shall we not dissever', and breaks its neck.

The balance of sympathy and detachment characteristic of this fable is maintained throughout. That it is so is remarkable, for Henryson's irony is consistent and pervasive and often very grim. Irony of course comes easily to a fabulist concerned to exploit the shifting relationship of animal to man; also, since it implies evaluation, it is a natural and effective weapon for a moralist. Henryson, like La Fontaine, contrives to maintain 'les deux sourires du moraliste, de l'intelligence et de la tendresse'.[42] He has often—and justly—been praised for his sympathy, and for his unfailing humour. It has less often been noticed how sensitively he controls his tone, and how, under the moralist's two smiles, different levels of comedy and irony coexist, giving new perspectives and 'constantes variations d'éclairage'. The dominant tone of a fable may range from the urbanity of 'The Two Mice' to the sharp satire of 'The Sheep and the Dog', where there is no gentle detachment or suggestion of moral relativity. Usually, each fable will contain a variety of tones and perspectives within itself. This is most obviously the case with those longer fabliau-type tales turning on 'renardie'. Tod Lowrie in 'The Trial of the Fox', for all his moral shortcomings, has that supreme quality of the fabliau hero—intelligence. His quick-wittedness never deserts him—even at the end when he is confronted with the mother of the lamb he has killed, he has no difficulty in thinking up an excuse:

> 'Aa, soverane lord, saif your mercie!' quod he.
> 'My purpois wes with him for to haif plaid;
> Causles he fled, as he had bene effraid;
> For dreid of deith, he duschit ouer ane dyke,
> And brak his nek.' (1078–82)

There is something brilliant in the effortless way he produces this explanation. Its dramatic effect is the greater because throughout the fable our attention has been carefully directed to the methods by which the fox defends himself—'throw falset how he micht himself defend'. He dominates the scenes of the fable, from the moment when

[42] Odette de Mourgues, p. 138.

he begins his defence at the parliament by a comic disguise. His cunning is a source of power, and he cleverly involves another much more stupid villain in the taking of the message to the mare. He begins to set up an ironic pattern at the expense of the wolf: 'The wolff is better in ambassatry, / And mair cunning in clergie fer than I' (997–8) which he ruthlessly maintains when the unfortunate wolf, tricked even by the mare, has its head kicked, and exploits to the full in his moment of triumph before the king:

> 'Quhair is yone meir, Schir Tod, wes contumax?'
> Than Lowrence said: 'My lord, speir not at me!
> Speir at your Doctor off Divinitie,
> With his reid cap can tell yow weill aneuch.'
> With that the lyoun and all the laif thay leuch. (1050–4)

And with much sarcasm he describes how 'this wittie wolf', 'this clerk off age' came by his 'reid bonat'. The laughter of the court, 'in merines and gam' is a little more hearty than it would be today, for the audience of the Middle Ages (and the Renaissance, as readers of Rabelais will not need to be reminded) had a stronger stomach for the comedy of pain. Such cruelty, which is here elaborated (the wolf has lost the crown of his head; he has 'brokin skap and bludie cheikis reid'), is unusual in the fable, but is common enough in the fabliau.

There is another ironic pattern running through this fable which has yet to take effect. There are a number of proverbs, statements of wisdom which, as we saw in the last chapter, may be very relative and ambiguous, and easily take their colour from circumstances. With an additional irony these are first introduced by the fox himself, who says 'Ay rinnis the foxe als lang as he fute hais' when he carries his father's body off. Rather smugly, he quotes a Latin proverb to the mare, knowing that she will not understand it: *Felix quem faciunt aliena pericula cautum* ('He is happy whom other mens perilles maketh ware').[43]

[43] Richard Taverner (tr.), *Proverbes or Adagies gathered out of the Chiliades of Erasmus* (1545), f. iii^v. Henryson's proverbs are as numerous, and certainly more various, than those of the Wife of Bath's Jankin, who 'knew of mo proverbes / Than in this world ther growen gras or herbes' (cf. the lists in B. J. Whiting, 'Proverbs and Proverbial Sayings from Scottish Writings before 1600', *Medieval Studies* xi (1949), 123–205, xiii (1951), 87–164). He is aware of their ambiguities, but at the same time seems to love their homely vigour; he uses them himself as narrator or moralist (cf. 375, 2608), and his language often has a proverbial cast ('nocht worth ane fle', 'of this mater to speik it wer bot wind', etc.).

The spectacle of that unfortunate 'clerk', the wolf, standing before the ridicule of the court inspires the king to quote another well-known saying—'the greitest clerkis are not the wysest men'—and he continues, more appropriately than he knows, to echo the fox's own remark—'the hurt of ane happie the uther makis'. The sudden ending of the fox's successful career of cunning by the evidence of his own bloody snout has the effect of a *peripeteia*, which makes all this proverbial lore dramatically ironic. Finally, the narrator joins in with an irony of his own at the expense of his hero destined for the gallows—'the wolff, that new-maid Doctour, couth him schrif'. 'And thus he maid his end'—but one is left feeling that 'ay rinnis the foxe als lang as he fute hais' would be an appropriate epitaph for son as well as father.

A similar ironic adaptation of proverbs may be seen in other fables. For a villain like the wolf in 'The Fox, the Wolf and the Husbandman' to cite the book of *Proverbs* in order to make off with the man's oxen on a verbal quibble is transparently hypocritical, but in the light of what his comrade the fox does to him later in the fable it is even more richly ironic. That fox finally takes leave of his victim with a proverb which is a favourite of medieval moralists,[44] in a nice 'speaking picture'—the stupid wolf is in one bucket going down to the bottom of the well, where he is to be abandoned, and Lowrence in another going upwards to the ground:

> Than angerlie the wolff upon him cryis:
> 'I cummand thus dounwart, quhy thow upwart hyis?'
> 'Schir,' quod the foxe, 'thus fairis it off Fortoun:
> As ane cummis up, scho quheillis ane uther doun!'
>
> (2416–19)

There are some complicated ironic uses of proverbs in 'The Fox, the Wolf and the Cadger'. This is much crueller—the wolf is battered by the cadger so that he is nearly blind (much to the amusement of his companion the fox), and in the brisk and amoral ending, is left with his blood 'rynnand over his heillis'. The play on 'nekhering' (= blow on the neck), which the wolf is led to believe is a gigantic herring, is a broad jape, appropriate to the stupidity of the wolf, and to the rough and popular core of this sophisticated fable. The wolf, who is aware—

[44] Cf. the examples in Whiting (*Proverbs, Sentences and Proverbial Phrases*), B 575, N 179. There is a delicious irony here, for the wolf's reverse is not at all due to any blind working of Fortune, but to the fox's Machiavellian scheming.

though not sufficiently so—of the cunning of the fox, has a proverb for it, 'for everie wrink forsuith thow hes ane wyle', which turns out to be truer than he imagines. In the following stanza (1993–9) he waxes sententious, using no less than three proverbs, of which one—'falset will failye ay at the latter end'—is destined to be proved true of him, but not of the fox! This wolf has some ironic perception—he neatly adapts the traditional heroic formula of *fortitudo et sapientia* to his fox: 'Thow art ane berne full bald / And wyse at will' (2110–11)—but he is up against a master not only of 'wrink' and 'wyle' but of irony. We should guess this from the witty and detached way the fox applies a stock (and nicely inappropriate) simile to himself: 'I think to work als besie as ane be; / And ye sall follow ane lytill efterwart / And gadder hering...' (2046–8). His supreme moment comes when he sends off the wolf to attempt to deceive the cadger once more:

> I sall say *In Principio* upon yow,
> And crose your corps from the top to tay;
> Wend quhen ye will, I dar be warrand now
> That ye shall de na suddand deith this day! (2154–7)

The first two words of the Gospel of St. John were widely regarded—mostly by those of the level of theological awareness of this wolf—as of powerful if not magical virtue.[45] Others, however, might have associated them with friars, which—at least in the eyes of satirists—might have rendered them suspect. The magical blessing of this pseudo-friar will ensure that there is no 'sudden death' (cf. p. 27), for, we suspect, he is looking forward sadistically to the spectacle of the wolf finding a lingering and painful death at the hands of the cadger.

When Henryson's irony is grim, it is very grim indeed. Perhaps before we attribute this to some deep-seated part of his imagination or his personality, we should pause to remember that it would not have been hard to find even more cruel examples in fifteenth-century life. Atholl, the murderer of James I, was put to death brutally—part of his torment, according to Major, was that 'a red-hot iron crown was placed upon his head, whereby they would signify the fulfilment of that prediction of the witch that he should one day wear a crown, or, as Monstrelet observes, he was in this way declared to be a king among traitors'.[46] Two fables in particular are suggestive here. Henryson

[45] Cf. M. W. Bloomfield, 'The Magic of In Principio', *MLN* lxx (1955), 559–65.
[46] Major, *A History of Greater Britain*, tr. A. Constable (Edinburgh, 1892), p. 369.

expands considerably Walter's austere version of 'The Preaching of the Swallow'. After his stately opening,[47] he takes great trouble to establish in the succession of warnings and their reception an ironic rhythm. The first (ll. 1734ff.) is greeted by the lark with laughter (ironically calling the bird 'Schir Swallow'); even when the swallow explains the nature of the danger, the lark laughs again. Henryson here makes especially effective use of the ambiguities of proverbs. The lark in her scorn quotes a string of proverbs to dispose of the swallow's clerkly warning that to be forewarned is to be forearmed—(*Nam levius laedit quicquid praevidimus ante*):

> The lark, lauchand, the swallow thus couth scorne,
> And said scho fischit lang befoir the net—
> 'The barne is eith to busk that is unborne;
> All growis nocht that in the ground is set;
> The nek to stoup quhen it the straik sall get
> Is sone aneuch; deith on the fayest fall.'
> Thus scornit thay the swallow ane and all. (1762–8)

The last three lines are to be proved true, but in a way the birds do not expect, for they themselves are 'fey'. The swallow warns them again in June. This time 'thay cryit all and bad the swallow ceis', and, despite her patient argument, refuse to pull up the flax before it ripens—for 'linget (linseed) is to lytill birdis fude'. The final warning is in winter, and the birds have been driven to shelter in the barn and corn-stack, to the anger of the fowler. The tempo of this scene is carefully handled. The swallow, sitting on 'ane lytill branche neir by' is moved (like Cassandra, to whom La Fontaine compares her) to a last impassioned speech (1853–66). Henryson does not make his birds reply to this, but still holds back the moment of climax. He adds a solemn descant of his own to the folly of those that have 'na thing in thocht / Bot thing present' (and with a sombre anaphora he repeats the phrase 'grit fule

47 The description of the seasons is one of Henryson's famous set pieces. Traditional details are filled with new vitality (e.g. Summer's 'jolie mantill of grene' is 'furrit' with flowers, on every 'fent' (= opening in garment). It has been 'lent' (a precisely chosen word) to him by Flora—and we have a nice play on her name: 'Flora Goddes off the flouris quene'). At the same time, the descriptions are fitted to the philosophical opening and to the rhythms of the following fable. The visible world declares the glory and Providence of God; the succession of seasons expresses the orderly movement of time, and forms an ironic background to the grim succession of foolish choices that follows.

is he' three times). He gives us a brief but pathetic glimpse of the hungry birds scraping for food, and then the swallow flies up into a tree, and the gruesome conclusion follows:

Sum with ane staf he straik to eirth on swoun,
Off sum the heid he straik, off sum he brak the crag,
Sum half on lyfe he stoppit in his bag. (1878–80)

The development of the ironic pattern is admirably done in this fable, but a slight sense of unease left by the ending makes one wonder if it is quite so totally under control as it seems. We are reminded, just before their end, of the undoubted fact that the birds are foolish, but the brutality of their killing seems to go beyond what even harsh justice would demand. We begin to wonder if the 'bludie bowcheour' has not overstepped the limits of man's dominion over the beasts (though his brutality is consistent with his rôle in the allegorical *moralitas*). After such a vivid scene, the concluding remarks of the swallow cannot but sound a little smug ('Lo...thus it happinnis mony syis...'). The fable has been called 'a tragedy within a larger comedy', but the terrible violence of the ending almost begins to call in question the providential framework. Even grimmer, in some ways, is the final touch of irony in 'The Paddock and the Mouse'. When the kite swoops down because it has noticed the struggle (which is put in a new perspective by the phrase 'this wretchit battell'), he disposes of them quickly and efficiently:

And with ane wisk, or owthir off thame wist,
He claucht his cluke betuix thame in the threid;
Syne to the land he flew with thame gude speid,
Fane off that fang, pyipand with mony pew;
Syne lowsit thame, and baith but pietie slew.

Syne bowellit thame that boucheour with his bill,
And belliflaucht full fettislie thame fled... (2898–904)[48]

but then we are told (with a sudden shift to the kite's point of view) that 'all their flesh' would hardly be half a meal:

Bot all thair flesche wald scant be half ane fill—
And guttis als—unto that gredie gled.

[48] I follow Fox in preferring Bann. *owthir* (2898), and in the suggested reading *fettislie* in 2904.

He hardly seems to notice it, and flies off across the fields. The grim relativity of this seems to suggest that less controlled irony that Professor Wayne Booth calls 'unstable',[49] so that the apparently tightly controlled form of the fable sets up disturbing resonances and ambiguities which go beyond its text, raising questions beyond those posed by the narrator. This is often the case with the destructive 'renardie'[50] of the fox anti-heroes (all of whom are themselves ironists). Yet the larger ironic vision of the fabulist contrives to make a coherent whole from the conflicts and contradictions. As Mme de Mourgues says of La Fontaine, poetic irony achieves 'un équilibre très savant entre des éléments fondamentalement discordants'.[51] The art of the fabulist consists in finding a balance of opposites—sympathy and detachment, comedy and tragedy, in creating his constantly shifting world.

Finally, a brief consideration of 'The Confession of the Fox' may enable us to see how these various narrative techniques work together to create a finished whole. This fable is clearly linked to its predecessor; it promises to tell us 'the subtell aventure and destenie' that befell the fox that carried off Chantecleir. It opens with the fox lurking and 'bydand nicht'. Night comes, and we are given what begins as a rather elaborate rhetorical *chronographia*—

> Quhill that Thetes the Goddess off the flude
> Phebus had callit to the harbery,
> And Hesperous put up his cluddie hude,
> Schawand his lustie visage in the sky (621–4)[52]

but ends with a characteristic change of register:

> Than Lourence luikit up, quhair he couth ly,
> And kest his hand upon his ee on hicht,
> Merie and glad that cummit wes the nicht.

[49] Wayne C. Booth, *A Rhetoric of Irony* (Chicago, 1974).
[50] Cf. K. Ranke, 'Schwank und Witz als Schwundstufe', *Festschrift für W.-E. Peuckert* (Munich, 1955), pp. 41–59, J. Beyer, *Schwank und Ernst* (Heidelberg, 1969), pp. 11ff. Huizinga remarks, 'play is a category which can devour everything, just as folly, once it had taken hold of the mind of Erasmus, had to become the queen of the whole world' (*Verzamelde Werken* V, p. 23, tr. Gombrich, *TLS* 4 October 1974, p. 1089).
[51] *O muse...*, p. 140.
[52] In l. 621, I follow Elliott and Fox in preferring Bann.

'Kest his hand...' is one of those nice gestures which exploit the hovering relationship between animal and human. His mood changes quickly. From the top of a hill Lowrence looks at the stars. We are given a precise account of the disposition of the planets for almost three stanzas—'as Lowrence leirnit me' says the narrator (with a hint of a profession of his own limitations as an astronomer, and a not too serious gesture of admiration towards his hero). Lowrence is perhaps a credulous astrologer, but his learning comes from nature and not from human science:

> But astrolab, quadrant or almanak,
> Teichit off nature be instruction...

The disposition is malevolent, and in the stars Lowrence sees his destiny. (We may already sense that a potential ironic pattern is beginning to form.) He thinks upon his end, decides that he should find a confessor to shrive him, and is moved to deliver a formal *planctus* on the sad lot of 'us thieves' in which his self-pity nicely blends with the narrator's irony:

> 'Allace,' quod he, 'richt waryit ar we thevis!
> Our lyif is set ilk nicht in aventure;
> Our cursit craft full mony man mischevis;
> For ever we steill and ever ar lyke pure;
> In dreid and schame our dayis we indure;
> Syne "Widdi-nek" and "Craik-raip" callit als,
> And till our hyre ar hangit be the hals.'[53] (656–62)

His easy use of what are presumably slang terms for 'gallows-bird' perhaps suggests a greater familiarity with the underworld than with the world of the confessional. However, 'accusand thus his cankerit conscience', as the narrator blandly puts it, he spies a likely looking confessor. He sees coming 'ane lytill than frome hence'

> Ane worthie Doctour in Divinitie;
> Freir Wolff Waitskaith, in science wonder sle,
> To preiche and pray wes new cummit fra the closter,
> With beidis in hand, sayand his pater noster. (666–9)

('With beidis in hand' is a nicely chosen detail.) There follows a delicious scene between the two, which is full of sustained irony, and

53 I follow Fox in preferring Bann. 'lyif is' (657) and 'ar hangit' (662).

is a hilarious mixture of straight and double talk. Each of them is a villain, each of them knows himself to be a villain, and each of them knows the other to be a villain. After an elaborate opening paraphernalia of flattery and dissimulation, we move into a glorious parody of a confession. The irony is maintained by the protagonists:

> 'Your bair feit and your russet coull of gray,
> Your lene cheik, your paill, pietious face,
> Schawis to me your perfite halines'

says the fox, realizing what a 'hap' it will be to have this 'gostlie father' shrive him—and also by the narrator, who, when the confession begins, remarks with a mixture of complicity and tact:

> Quhen I this saw, I drew ane lytill by,
> For it effeiris nouther to heir, nor spy,
> Nor to reveill thing said under that seill (694–6)

—which, of course, he immediately does. The fox makes a very bad showing in the confession. (He fails in each of the three traditional parts—contrition, confession, satisfaction.) It is one of Henryson's inspired dialogues, and from it the character emerges very clearly and comically—he is false, weak, full of self-pity and altogether cynical:

> 'Art thow contrite and sorie in thy spreit
> For thy trespas?' 'Na, schir, I can not duid:
> Me think that hennis ar sa honie sweit,
> And lambes flesche that new ar lettin bluid;
> For to repent my mynd can not concluid
> Bot off this thing—that I haif slane sa few.' (698–703)

He imputes his stealing to 'neid'. Turning to the question of penance, they settle, after some difficulty, for something fairly light—the fox ought to refrain from meat except twice a week ('for', according to popular wisdom, if not official doctrine, 'neid may haif na law'). There is of course a barbed satire here against easy confessions, and in particular against the easy confessions allegedly given by the members of the mendicant orders (Chaucer's Huberd was 'esy...to yeve penaunce'), and their reputation for hypocrisy. But it would be wrong to limit the fable simply to this.[54] The satire is directed even more closely

[54] So Rossi, *Henryson*, p. 34 (J. B. Friedman, 'Henryson, the Friars and the *Confessio Reynardi*', *JEGP* lxvi (1967), 550–61, claims that the entire fable is

against the fox, the 'penitent' (it is slowness in repentance which is singled out in the *moralitas*) and the fable as a whole obviously has a much wider scope.

There follows a fine scene. The fox goes off, apparently really meaning to carry out his confessor's instructions, and comes to the 'flude', intending to catch fish. But the sight of the water and the waves throws him into a comic desolation; he says 'Better that I had hidden at hame / Nor bene ane fischar in the devillis name'. There is an enormous sense of relief when 'under ane tre' he sees 'ane trip off gait'. The wise saying 'neid may haif na law' is now proved true. He catches a kid, takes it down to the 'see', and then in a marvellous sacramental parody:

> ...in the watter outher twyis or thryis
> He dowkit him, and till him can he sayne:
> 'Ga doun, Schir Kid, cum up Schir Salmond again!'
> Quhill he wes deid; syne to the land him drewch,
> And off that new maid salmond eit anewch. (749–53)

This splendid folk-motif[55] suits Henryson's purposes beautifully. Similar stories are told as real miracles in saint's lives—to avoid eating meat (St. Patrick, for instance, immerses the meat in water: Mira res! carnes illae aquis immersae ac extractae statim in pisces sunt conversae), or as a defence against detractors (according to the *Golden Legend*, when Becket's accuser took a leg of chicken to the Pope to prove his wickedness, and unwrapped it, a fish fell out)—and survive as merry tales (when Cardinal Wiseman's hostess had forgotten the Friday fast, he stretched out his hands in benediction, and said 'I pronounce all this to

organized as an argument against the mendicants). On the questions to be asked of penitents, see Myrc's *Instructions for Parish Priests*, ed. Peacock, EETS xxxi (1868), pp. 28ff.

[55] There are similar incidents in written fables; cf. *De Lupo et Mutone* (Hervieux, II, pp. 365, 557—and in the French versions (Bastin, *Receuil*, II, pp. 289–90, 419)) (Jamieson, *Poetry of Henryson*). The examples quoted are from *Acta Sanctorum* March II, 545/1 (Jocelin of Furness, ch. 3), *Golden Legend* ed. F. S. Ellis (Temple Classics, 1900), ii, p. 191. Cf. also C. Plummer, *Vitae Sanctorum Hiberniae* (Oxford, 1910), I, 43 (Aedus), II, 219 (Molua), C. Grant Loomis, *White Magic* (Cambridge, Mass., 1948), pp. 79, 110, K. Jackson, *The International Popular Tale and Early Welsh Tradition* (Cardiff, 1961), pp. 7–8, 134, Poggio, *Facetiae* (London, 1798), I, pp. 222–3, Jakob Frey's *Gartengesellschaft* (1556) ed. J. Bolte (Tübingen, 1896), pp. 100–1. For Wiseman, see *TLS* 1 May 1953, p. 277 (review of Augustus Hare); for recent converts, *ib.* 1937, p. 512, 15 May 1953, p. 317.

be fish'). Such tales are recorded of recent converts (e.g. a Turk, an Aborigine) caught eating meat on forbidden days, who say in reply 'you threw water on me and told me I was a new creature. I have simply done the same thing with this—I put water on it and said "you are fish"'. Here (as in Henryson) the story is double-edged. It illustrates the ignorance (or in Laurence's case the hypocrisy) of the 'convert', but at the same time, the 'savage answers back' in a way which brings the taboo itself into question. The fox reclines on his back in the sun, full of 'young tender meit'. The sense of contentment and ease which envelops him is quite unlike the worry and unease of the beginning of the fable. He has now forgotten all about his destiny in the stars. Then—'rekleslie' says the narrator—he makes a jest, 'straikand his wame aganis the sonis heit': 'my full belly would be a good target for an arrow now' ('Upon this wame set wer ane bolt full meit'). His destiny is nearer than he thinks, for the goatherd pins him to the ground with an arrow. But this ironic *peripeteia* is not quite the end. The fox's 'game' has been cruelly turned to 'earnest', but there is a sudden last change of perspective. This delightful villain has the last word, with a bitter jest in the face of death:

> ...Me think na man may speik ane word in play,
> Bot now on dayis in ernist it is tane' (770–1)

and in a way which is quite different from its leisurely opening, the tale is brought to an abrupt and grim conclusion by the actions of the goatherd:

> He harlit him, and out he drew his flane;
> And for his kid and uther violence,
> He tuke his skyn, and maid ane recompence

—so that the fox's 'satisfaction' turns out to be crudely commercial. The *moralitas* follows quickly and easily.

CHAPTER FOUR

Beasts and Wisdom: (iii) Figure of an other thing

Each fable has a *moralitas*, which follows quickly. Whether it follows easily is perhaps a more debatable question. The majority of Henryson's modern readers have admired the tales, but been less than enthusiastic about the moralities. A fairly representative view is that of Professor Bauman: 'Henryson's emphasis seems to have been as much upon the entertainment value of the stories themselves as upon their moral messages, which are confined for the most part to the end of each tale where they could not interfere with the entertainment',[1] or this from a recent editor, Mr. Elliott:

> The over-all method shows a dichotomy...The dichotomy is due to the unfailing *moralitas*. Henryson exploits the narrative potential of his material so that it becomes independent and satisfying in 'literary' terms. From this the *sentence* is deliberately detached. The direct and blatant 'teaching' has no counterpart in Chaucer...Henryson accepts, and assumes in his audience, the medieval ethos. The paths of right and wrong, towards bliss or bale, are clear and distinct.[2]

To such views there has recently been a small, but powerful reaction, in studies which stress the importance of the moral and didactic purpose in Henryson's *Fables*, and argue that it can be seen in the disposition and in the telling of the tales themselves as well as in the moralities.[3] There is a danger, however, that if this is presented in an extreme form, readers are left with the impression that there is nothing much else in the fables apart from teaching, the *moralitates* being

[1] 'The Folktale and Oral Tradition', *Fabula* vi (1964), p. 117.

[2] *Robert Henryson, Poems* (2nd ed., Oxford, 1974), pp. xi, xii.

[3] For example, D. Fox 'Henryson's *Fables*', *ELH* xxix (1962), 337–56, J. MacQueen, *Robert Henryson*.

nothing but a triumphant Q.E.D., or that allegories unheard of on the banks of the Nile will climb out and devour the creatures of the poet's imagination, leaving no trace.

The extremes of both positions are inadequate, for the question is a more complicated one. The fable is a moral and didactic form of literature and there is no doubt at all that a *moralitas* (whether an *epimythium* or a *promythium*) is traditionally a part of its form. We still expect a fable to conclude with a morality, and still find it, even in Thurber's *Fables for Our Time*. When Henryson meets Aesop he asks him for 'ane prettie fabill / Concludand with ane gude moralitie' (1386–7) (making, it will be noticed, a value-judgement on both), and when Aesop has ended his tale of the 'Lion and the Mouse', the poet asks him:

> 'Maister, is thair ane moralitie
> In this fabill?' 'Yea, sone,' he said, 'richt gude.'
> 'I pray yow, schir,' quod I, 'ye wald conclude'
>
> (1570–2)

and he brings it to its conclusion with a morality. Other fabulists have always insisted on the importance of the morality. Marie de France thought that there was no fable without 'philosophie', La Fontaine that 'conter pour conter me semble peu d'affaire'.[4] He, indeed, in his *Préface* uses a striking image: 'L'apologue est composé de deux parties, dont on peut appeler l'une le corps, l'autre l'âme. Le corps est la fable; l'âme, la moralité.' Henryson not only expects a morality as conclusion to a fable; he also devotes himself to the task of moralizing with a certain enthusiasm. If he expands the fables of 'Walter', he expands the moralities even more. His 'joie de conter' is certainly matched by a 'joie de moraliser'.

The Prologue shows how seriously he took the *moralitates*. He explains that the means by which the old fables reproved 'the haill misleving' of man was 'be figure of ane uther thing'—in other words, that they were allegories. 'Figure' is one of his favourite words; at the end of the Prologue he uses it again—Aesop 'be figure wrait his buke'—and several times throughout the fables (the 'selie scheip may

[4] Marie de France, *Fables*, Prol., ll. 23–4 (cf. H. R. Jauss, *Untersuchungen zur mittelalterlichen Tierdichtung* (Tübingen, 1959), pp. 29–30, L. Spitzer, 'The Prologue to the *Lais* of Marie de France and Medieval Poetics', *MP* xli (1943–45), 96–102); La Fontaine, VI. 1.

present the figure / Of pure commounis' (1258–9); Aesop is asked (1400–1) for 'ane morall fabill' 'under the figure of ane brutall beist'). He speaks of 'similitude of figuris', 'typis figurall', 'ane fabill figural', or uses the word 'figurate'. Behind such words lie those notions of *figura* which were of such far-reaching and rich consequence for medieval literature.[5] It should immediately be stressed that such allegorical or figurative interpretations do not imply any dissolution of the literal senses—the brutal beast remains unharmed. As C. S. Lewis says, warning us not to throw aside the allegorical imagery for the abstract significance, 'allegory, after all, is simile seen from the other end; and when we have seen the point of simile we do not throw it away'.[6] The various senses coexist.

Especially relevant to a consideration of Henryson's technique in the *moralitates* are two images in the Prologue, which both illustrate aspects of his idea of 'figure'. Firstly, he uses an organic simile—just as flowers and corn spring out of the earth (if it is 'laubourit with grit diligence')

> Sa springis thair ane morall sweit sentence
> Oute of the subtell dyte of poetry (12–13)[7]

and this may be useful ('to gude purpois'), for whoever—he adds cautiously—'quha culd it weill apply'. We should note, as well as the significant verb 'spring', the serious and elevated view of poetry (cf. the word *subtell*, etc.) and the conjunction of 'morall' and 'sweit'. His second image is slightly different. It is that of the nut, whose shell, 'thocht it be hard and teuch', contains the kernel which is 'delectabill':

> Sa lyis thair ane doctrine wyse aneuch
> And full of frute under ane fenyeit fabill (17–18).

This is a traditional image of medieval exegesis.[8] Immediately, by means of a saying from the *Distichs* of Cato, he moves on to the image of the bow and the question of delight which we considered at the beginning of the last chapter. The speed of this transition, and the use

5 Cf. Fox, 'Henryson's *Fables*', p. 314, E. Auerbach, *Mimesis* (tr. W. Trask, Princeton, 1953), and 'Figura' (tr. R. Manheim) in *Scenes from the Drama of European Literature* (New York, 1959), P. Dronke, *Fabula* (Leiden, Cologne, 1974).

6 *The Allegory of Love* (Oxford, 1936), p. 125.

7 In l. 12, I follow Fox in preferring the reading *springis*.

8 Cf. 'Walter', 'ut nucleum celat arida testa bonum'. See D. W. Robertson, Jr., *A Preface to Chaucer* (Princeton, 1962), pp. 32, 344ff.

of those words 'sweit' and 'delectabill', suggest that we should expect to find delight in the midst of instruction and morality, and, perhaps, that we should not be surprised to find some 'merie sport' in the moralities as well as in the fables.

The fable is an allegorical form, and, as we saw in chapter 2, it is open-ended. It may generate many significances. Of these, the *moralitas* which concludes it will single out one or more for our special attention and instruction. In a number of Henryson's fables the morality which is thus crystallized does arise quite naturally from the tale itself (springing from it like the flowers and corn from the earth). These are the moralities which have already presented themselves to the mind of the reader. Thus in 'The Two Mice', although the fable suggests much more, it is perfectly reasonable and natural for the *moralitas* to point out that life is full of adversity, and particularly for those who 'climb up high', and are not content with 'small possessioun'. The notion 'blissid be sempill lyfe withoutin dreid' is in fact implicit in the fable. So it is with 'The Cock and the Fox', where the story turns on the moral questions of pride and vainglory and the dangers of flattery. And so, reasonably enough, 'The Confession of the Fox' (although, as we have seen, it shows forth truth in many other ways) may be taken as an 'exempill', 'exhortand folk to amend'. So it is with 'The Sheep and the Dog', 'The Wolf and the Lamb', and 'The Lion and the Mouse', where the *moralitates* give the fables a wider, or a more precise political or legal scope. In all, about seven or eight of the Fables have *moralitates* of this kind, which, though they may strike a modern reader as limited, and possibly limiting, arise easily enough from the tales. These may be called 'clear' moralities: the fables are allegorical, but the allegories are based on a more or less straightforward perception of similitude.

In other cases, however, the *moralitas* comes as a distinct surprise. The first fable of Bassandyne, 'The Cock and the Jasp', presents a striking example. The cock, it will be remembered, finds the precious stone on the dunghill, and after due consideration, leaves it to go on looking for corn. After Henryson's careful staging of the scene and the cock's eloquent speech, most readers will think that the cock is showing a wise disregard for a useless jewel. He is right, surely, to concentrate on finding his own proper food. The jewel is part of the paraphernalia of royalty. He is not deluded by pride or vain self-seeking, but is simply accepting his humble lot. The moral we expect is something like the 'sickernes with small possessioun' of 'The Two Mice'. But the *moralitas* tells us that the 'inward sentence and intent' is quite other than we had supposed. The Jasp in fact betokens 'perfite prudence and cunning'; it is wisdom, eternal food for man's soul. The cock 'may till ane fule be peir' who scorns wisdom; he does not understand the depths of things, and now the priceless jewel is lost. After surprise, the next reaction of the modern reader is likely to be irritation. He feels tricked. It is as if the moralist is a 'spoilsport' who has stopped the game. It is small consolation to know that it is a traditional morality (it is in fact Walter's, greatly expanded) found in many places—Romulus, La Fontaine and others—but perhaps a little more comforting to find that some earlier readers also had difficulty with it. L'Estrange says: 'The moralists will have wisdom and virtue to be meant by the Diamond: the World and the Pleasures of it by the Dunghill; and by the cock a Voluptuous Man...Now with the favour of the Ancients, this Fable seems to me, rather to hold forth an Emblem of Industry and Moderation. The Cock lives by his honest Labor, and maintains his family out of it....The precious stone is only a gaudy Temptation that Fortune throws in his way to divert him from his Business and his Duty....'[9] There is in fact a 'sensible' interpretation of the fable along these lines, and something like it is found in the fifteenth-century version of Lydgate, where the cock is a virtuous man who avoids 'all ydelnesse' and is content with 'suffisaunse'. We are obviously dealing with a problem of the open-endedness of allegory.

Some have attempted to show that this *moralitas* should not come as a total surprise, but that the poet has placed hints which we should have picked up and therefore should have taken a more critical view of the cock. On reflection, we might agree that we had not noticed a hint of the motivation of the cock in his desire for food in the apparently offhand remark 'to get his dennar set was al his cure', but the significance of such details does not strike us until we look back after reading the *moralitas*. It is very hard to believe that on first reading a medieval reader would think that, as the cock is speaking, we are being given 'a defence of natural man, common sense and materialism'.[10] It seems rather that Henryson has been leading us on, carefully deluding us into

[9] So Bewick (1818), 'the most obvious meaning of the fable is surely to shew, that men who weigh well their own real wants...', etc.

[10] Fox, 'Henryson's *Fables*', p. 344. Cf. MacQueen, *Robert Henryson*, pp. 100–10, and see the discussion in *TLS* 1967, pp. 726, 781, 824.

accepting the cock's point of view. He has teased us, for example, by his digression on the wanton damsels (cf. p. 86), which we read as implying that the cock has a higher estimation of the jewel than they), by an apparently apologetic aside 'albeit he wes bot pure' (which we took to imply virtue and good sense) and by little bits of mystification—'peradventure sa wes the samin stone', or the remark at the end that he will not tell us 'as now' 'quhen or how or quhome be it wes found'.

In fact, once we have got over our initial shock, this arcane morality proves more interesting than the more obvious and sensible one. We suddenly realize that the fable has an enigmatic surface (the tough skin of the nut in Henryson's image). This speaking picture turns out to be a little like one of those trick pictures discussed by Professor Gombrich where a rabbit may be a duck, depending on how we interpret the signs.[11] The poet has been indulging in 'merie sport' at our expense, for we, as well as the cock, have been deluded by the appearances of things. In the light of the techniques we examined in the last chapter, what has happened is perhaps less surprising. In his favourite manner he has set up a careful, hidden pattern of irony at the expense of the cock, and surreptitiously and wittily has operated the same pattern against us, his readers. This is an extreme example of the allegory which says one thing but means another, made into a large ironic pattern; it is also an example of those characteristic changes of perspective which we have seen operating in the fables themselves. One of its implications is rather chastening—that we humans are no better at seeking and finding hidden wisdom than this brutal beast. Yet it is also intended to be a sudden moment of enlightenment, a moment of spiritual insight, in which we see the picture in a completely new way. The effect is both witty—demonstrating to us that we need to use mental agility in the reading of the succeeding fables—and grave—sharply reminding us at the beginning of the collection that wisdom is not easily found, nor its value realized, and urging us to the quest: 'Ga seik the jasp, quha will, for thair it lay.'

Other fables have these surprising arcane 'dark' moralities. Who would have guessed the reading offered of 'The Trial of the Fox' (which obviously omits a great deal!), in which the Lion 'is the warld be liknes', the mare 'men of contemplatioun',[12] while the wolf can

[11] E. H. Gombrich, *Art and Illusion* (London, 1960).
[12] So Bannatyne; Bassandyne's 'of gude conditioun' sounds like a Protestant revision (cf. MacQueen, p. 151).

be likened to sensuality, the mare's hoof to the thought of death, and the fox to temptations? Similarly, in 'The Preaching of the Swallow', the carl is the fiend sowing poison in man's soul, the birds 'we may call' wretches 'greddie to gadder gudis temporall', and, of course, the swallow is the holy preacher—a reading which largely ignores the function of the philosophical prologue and of the succession of the seasons. In 'The Fox, the Wolf and the Cadger', the fox can be likened to the world, the wolf to a man, the cadger to death, and the herring to gold, and the likenesses suggested for 'The Fox, the Wolf and the Husbandman' are equally selective and arbitrary.

It is clear that with these esoteric or dark moralities we are dealing with a tradition of allegorical exegesis, with allegory of the type which Rosemond Tuve calls 'imposed'[13]—although one suspects that Henryson might not have welcomed such a word, for he speaks in traditional manner of searching for hidden truth under the surface. He begins the *moralitas* of 'The Trial of the Fox' with a simile from metallurgy:

> Richt as the mynour in his minorall
> Fair gold with fyre may fra the leid weill wyn,
> Richt so under ane fabill figurall
> Sad sentence men may seik, and efter fyne—
> As daylie dois the Doctouris of Devyne,
> That to our leving full weill can apply
> And paynt thair mater furth be poetry. (1097–1104)[14]

The Doctors of Divinity do indeed work great wonders on the words of Holy Writ, but the modern reader is usually startled when he finds this technique, or something like it, employed outside the exegesis of scripture. He is stopped dead in his tracks when in Malory's tale of the Sankgreal he comes upon the first 'old monk' who explains to Galahad the significance of the events which have just been described—Sir Melyas's decision to take the left-hand road, and to pick up a crown of gold.[15] Malory is adapting the French *Queste del Saint Graal*, a romance which consistently uses this kind of dark allegory.

It is less surprising when we recall its background. It arises from a symbolic view of the universe, which is created by God as a book:

[13] Rosemond Tuve, *Allegorical Imagery* (Princeton, 1966), chapter 4.

[14] In l. 1100, I follow Fox in preferring the reading *fyne*.

[15] Ed. Vinaver, II, p. 886.

'For the whole world which is knowne by sence is as it were a booke written with the fynger of God...and every the creatures be as it were certaine letters...ordeyned by the judgement of God, to make knowne, and as it were after a certaine maner to signify the invysible wisdome of God'[16] or as a picture ('wherein, as in a pourtraict, things are not truely, but in equivocal shapes'), which affords a multiplicity of 'symbolic images'[17] to the contemplation of man. Under the enigmatic veil of the properties of things divine wisdom lay hidden, as it did under the dark words of Scripture, and under the words of the fables of the Gentiles, from where it might be quarried to good purpose, to enrich the Hebrews with the spoils of the Egyptians. Perhaps it goes some way towards an apology for the extravagances of the exegetes to recall that the world itself, the Aenigma Dei, was thought to be full of paradox, and that the moralizers were attempting to 'find equivalences in the most disparate phenomena'. This manner of dark allegory is not inconsistent with the nature of the fable, a vehicle 'for Conveying to us the Truth and Reason of Things through the Medium of Images and Shadows', and it would no doubt have a special attraction for a fabulist so sensitive to changes of perspective and to irony.

Henryson was not unique, nor was he the first, in finding dark allegories in fables. Odo of Cheriton in his moralized fables for preachers was doing much the same thing, and there was also a tradition of 'Aesops' with commentaries and moralizations. These are commonly found in early printed books of the late fifteenth and early sixteenth centuries, but also occur in earlier MS. copies of 'Walter', and it seems very likely that Henryson had seen one or more of them. In the annotated copies (often, no doubt, used in schools) of 'Walter' we find notes on the constructions and glosses. This is the scholastic 'expositio ad litteram'. Some have also an 'expositio ad sensum'—the narrative meaning—and 'ad sententiam'—the spiritual or philosophical meaning—with 'moralities' additional to those in 'Walter', which are sometimes allegorical. These may be in the form of marginal

[16] Hugh of St. Victor, *PL* clxxvi, 810, tr. R. Coortesse (1577), *An Exposition of certayne words of S. Paule to the Romaynes*, f. B iv. The following quotation is from Browne's *Religio Medici* ('the severe schools shall never laugh me out of the philosophy of Hermes...').

[17] Cf. E. H. Gombrich, '*Icones Symbolicae*' in *Symbolic Images. Studies in the Art of the Renaissance* (London, 1972), pp. 123–91.

notes, or set out in the formal manner of a 'gloss'. Some of them find many more dark allegories than Henryson ever did. One *Aesopus cum commento*[18] allegorizes fables such as 'The Wolf and the Lamb' ('per agnum debemus intelligere deum creatorem nostrum'), 'The Sheep and the Dog', 'The Two Mice', as well as 'The Frog and the Mouse'. In another early sixteenth-century edition[19] notes at the side give us a clear morality for 'The Wolf and the Lamb': 'per lupum allegorice impios intellige, per agnum innocentes' but a darker one for 'The Two Mice': 'allegorice per murem urbanum voluptatibus plenum intelligimus. Per rusticum spirituales qui nullo modo formidant'. There is an elaborate Italian example of this in Zucco's *Esopo historiado*, mentioned in chapter 2 (cf. Plates 2, 3, 5(*b*), 6). Here, as may be seen from our illustrations, each fable consists of four items—the illustration, the Latin text of 'Walter', and two sonnets in Italian, of which the first, a 'sonetto materiale', is a translation of the Latin fable and its morality, and the second a 'sonetto morale' which gives a further moral meaning.

If Henryson had ever seen a copy of this, he did not make use of it for his *Fables*. There are, however, some Latin copies of 'Walter' with commentaries containing readings which are closer to Henryson's allegories. One such commentary, which is commonly found in early printed books, gives a kind of *expositio ad sensum*, a short prose retelling of the Latin verse fable (making it sometimes into a little *conte*) and a further extended moral explanation. Plate 9, from a printed book of 1492, shows the typical arrangement of the text with interlinear glosses and commentary. (The pages reproduced contain the end of *De Mure et Rana* and the beginning of *De Cane et Ove*.)[20] In 'The Cock and the Jasp', for instance, the *doctrina* is explained 'dicens quod per gallum intelligere stultum, per lapidem preciosum scientiam et sapientiam. Unde sicut gallus spernit lapidem preciosum tanquam sibi non valentem neque utilem, sic etiam stultus spernit sapientiam eo quod non reputat eam necessarium neque utilem.' At the beginning of 'The Two Mice' the moral point about 'sickerness' is stressed: 'hic ponit documentum quod melius est possidere pauca cum securitate et libere

[18] *Fabularum Liber cum glosa* (Paris, ? *c.* 1492), Bodleian Library, Auct. 2. Q inf. II 75, f. I iii^{v}.

[19] *Autores octo morales* (Lyon, 1538), notes on pp. 131, 135.

[20] *Esopus moralisatus cum bono commento* (1492), Bodleian Library, Auct. 5 Q VI. 80. Cf. Douce 60 (1488), Douce A 256 (1510), Douce 58 (1495); the commentary appears also with variations elsewhere.

quam multa cum servitute et timore.' Very interestingly, this commentary gives an allegorical reading for precisely those two Aesopic fables which in Henryson's selection have dark moralities. On *De Lino et Hirundine* it says at the beginning 'Hic autor ponit aliam fabulam cuius documentum est quod nullus debet contemnere consilium alterius quia accidit multotiens quod respuentes consilium aliorum inutiles fiunt unde frequenter eis malum evenit'. After telling his *conte* it continues 'allegorice per aves intelligere possumus peccatores, per hyrundinem vero spirituales homines qui sepe ammonent peccatores ut desistant et abstineant a peccatis, sed peccatores ammonitionem et doctrinam spiritualium contemnentes tandem per retia dyaboli capiuntur et eterno igni traduntur.' This is very close indeed to Henryson. (Another commentary, in a fourteenth-century MS.,[21] says explicitly that the 'agricola' is the devil, the swallow the 'spiritualem predicatorem', and refers to 'consuetude' in sin, 'in consuetudinem peccandi'). In *De Mure et Rana* we are told, 'Allegorice per ranam potest intelligi caro humana, per murem autem intelligitur anima quae adversus carnem semper militat: caro concupiscit adversus spiritum, et spiritus adversus carnem. Caro enim nititur trahere animam ad terrena et carnales delectationes, anima vero resilit ad bona opera, et istis sic litigantibus venit miluus .i. diabolus quasi bolus .i. morsus duorum, scilicet corporis et anime et rapit ambo' (which again is close to Henryson, except that for him the kite does not signify the devil,[22] but death). 'Vel aliter', it continues, '...per ranam intelliguntur deceptores bonum dicentes sed deceptionem intendentes...'.

'Vel aliter'...There is an interesting similarity with Henryson here too, for he gives a double *moralitas* to this fable, and in so doing gives us a valuable insight into his technique of moralization. He begins by drawing out a clear implicit 'sentence' of the fable—the need for prudence, and the danger of 'ane wickit mynd with wordis fair and sle' (2913) and he warns his 'brother' of the dangers of binding oneself 'quhair thow wes frank and fre', concluding 'this simpill counsaill' with a proverb: 'Better but stryfe to leif allane in le / Than to be matchit with ane wickit marrow' (2932–3). Then he pauses, with the words 'This hald in mynde', and continues, giving an alternative dark morality ('rycht more I sall the tell / Quhair by thir beistis may be

[21] British Library, MS. Add. 11,897, f. 8v.

[22] The Berne Romulus (Hervieux, *Les Fabulistes Latins*, ii, p. 758) also takes the kite as the devil (Jamieson, *Poetry of Robert Henryson*).

figurate'): the paddock is man's body, while the mouse is the soul bound to the body, the water is the world, and the kite is death that comes suddenly.

The giving of a double morality is not unlike the technique of the *Ovide moralisé*, where a single episode will have added to it various allegories and moral explanations. There is no reason to be surprised at this multiplicity of readings: 'the multiplicity of significant associations evoked by a single image', says Klingender of twelfth-century animal imagery, 'which caused the symbolic approach to the outer world to be rejected in the scientific revolution of the seventeenth century, was precisely what recommended it to medieval contemplatives in search of the hidden connections between things.'[23] Allegorists delighted in the profusion of possible interpretations. One scriptural commentary gives eight significances for the lion—and they include both Christ and Antichrist.[24] The exegete was not afraid of contradictions. As a near contemporary of Henryson, Bishop Fisher, puts it in a sermon (explaining how the lion may signify both Christ and the Devil, and Jonah both Christ and a sinner), 'for one and the same thynge by a dyvers consdyeracyon may be taken fyguratyvely for two contrarys'. In other words allegory is open-ended, and alternative interpretations may be selected according to context 'by a dyvers consyderacyon', or 'held in mind' at the same time as two different perspectives, or as ironic alternatives. These alternative readings should remind us also of another fundamental point, that the *moralitas* does not purport to give the final and exclusive meaning of the fable. It is not '*the* moral message', but *one* possible and useful significance of it; it hardly gives an adequate account of the rich intentions of the fable and is obviously not intended to do so.[25]

The 'dark' moralities are therefore rather more complicated and interesting than they seem at first. They involve the reader in the difficult but pleasing search for significances under the enigmatic surface, and in the teasing out of moral implications. By making him work, they both instruct and please him. Nor are the moralities them-

[23] *Animals in Art and Thought* (London, 1971), p. 328.

[24] *PL* cxii, 983, quoted by B. Rowland, *Blind Beasts* (Kent, Ohio, 1971), pp. 4–5. The following quotation is from Fisher, *English Works*, ed. J. E. B. Mayor, EETS ES xxvii (1876), p. 201.

[25] M. McGowan, 'Moral Intention in the Fables of La Fontaine', *JWCI* xxix (1966), p. 278.

selves without wit. They remind us of the title Caxton gave his Aesop, 'The Subtyl historyes and fables'. When a medieval moralist becomes enraptured by his task of allegorical exegesis his enthusiasm sometimes begins to generate a curious sense of exhilaration. There is something of this in the *moralitas* to 'The Fox, the Wolf and the Husbandman'. The cheese is accounted for with exegetical glee: 'the cabok may be callit covetyce...' (as it is handled in the fable, it *is* a magnificent symbolic image of *covetyce*) and it is hard to think that there is not conscious humour as well as allegorical enthusiasm in the remark 'the hennis ar warkis that fra ferme faith proceidis'.[26] There is a nice touch of wit in the *moralitas* of 'The Two Mice', when Henryson addresses the wanton man who makes his belly into a god: 'Luke to thy self, I warne the weill but dreid/The cat cummis, and to the mous hes ee' (383–4). And at the end of the *moralitas* of the last fable in Bassandyne, 'The Paddock and the Mouse', he makes a joke at the expense of the friars, so justly famed for their skill at extracting moral significances. It is slipped in immediately after a solemn warning of the coming of death and immediately before an equally solemn final prayer:

> Adew my freind! And gif that ony speiris
> Of this fabill, sa schortlie I conclude,
> Say thow, I left the laif unto the freiris
> To mak exempill and ane similitude... (2969–72)

The word 'schortlie' alerts us to an irony at his own expense, for this is the only fable for which he has provided two *moralitates*! Had Erasmus and More known his work, they might have forgiven allegories delivered with such a blend of piety and wit. There is also, quite explicitly, a suggestion of tentativeness about most of the *moralitates*. They are not presented as inevitable or all-inclusive 'messages'. Henryson significantly uses the word 'may', not 'must', again and again: (588) Yit may ye find ane sentence richt agreabill, (600) This fenyeit foxe may weill be figurate, (1100) Sad sentence men may seik, and efter fyne, (1258) This selie scheip may present the figure, (1573–4) ...this mychtie gay lyoun / May signifie... (and cf. 1891, 1916, 1923–4, 2205, 2425, 2434, 2449, 2707 and 2934–5). This apparently deliberate stressing of the limited nature of the moral interpretations supports, I think, the suggestion of relativism which one or two

[26] Unless it is the product of later earnest Protestant revision (suggested to me by Dr I. W. A. Jamieson).

perceptive critics of the *Fables* have discerned,[27] a relativism which is intelligent and subtle. There are tensions in the world of the *Fables* which strain the balance of sympathy and detachment, but the humble tentativeness of these phrases strongly suggests that we are not dealing with an inflexible moralist.

Although no modern reader will ever be persuaded to prefer the *moralitas* to the fable—and there is no reason why he should—he should be aware that Henryson practises an 'art of moralizing' as well as of telling stories. There is wisdom in what Montaigne says: 'most of Esopes fables have divers senses, and severall interpretations. Those which mithologize them, chuse some kind of colour well-suting with the fable, but for the most part, it is no other then the first and superficiall glosse: there are others more quicke, more sinnowie, more essentiall, and more internall, into which they could never penetrate.'[28] The *moralitas* of 'The Fox and the Grapes' from *The Fables of Aesop and Others translated into Human Nature* (1857) runs:

> It is natural that we should affect to despise what we cannot obtain. In the ballroom of life, the unfortunate 'wall-flower', who has wearied herself out with jumping up in the vain hope of catching a partner, will be found, towards the close of the entertainment, expressing herself in the severest terms on the folly and impropriety of Dancing.

There obviously is a challenge in creating a *moralitas* which goes beyond the pithy one or two line *sententia* (Aesop, Phaedrus and 'Walter' would have been content with the first sentence of the above), and in achieving a correct balance with the 'speaking picture'. This example fails because, among other reasons, it simply appends another exemplum, which is a rival 'speaking picture' but of too limited and particular a kind for the fable, which is genuinely universal, and has such mnemonic power that it has become a proverb.

It is not quite true to say of Henryson's *Fables* that 'the *sentence* is deliberately detached'. A number of fables would sound rather odd if they were not accompanied by some sort of comment or explanatory *titulus*, and this alone would suggest that they were written with a

[27] Cf. Jamieson, 'The Beast Tale in Middle Scots', *Parergon* ii (1972), p. 29, H. E. Toliver, 'Robert Henryson: from *Moralitas* to Irony', *English Studies* xlvi (1965), p. 302.

[28] *Essayes*, tr. Florio (1603), II, x.

moralitas in mind. A number seem to work up to a narrative *pointe* (as the sheep which 'naikit and bair syne to the feild couth pas') which invites the voice of the moralist to continue. Furthermore the voice of the moralist is quite discernibly the voice of the narrator who has told the fable. Sometimes indeed the two are linked by his own 'I'. In 'The Cock and the Jasp', I, says the narrator, do not intend to tell you how and when the jewel was found, but I shall tell you the 'inward sentence', and in the *moralitas* he answers his own rhetorical questions:

> Quha may be hardie, riche, and gratious?
> Quha can eschew perrell and aventure?
> Quha can governe ane realme, cietie, or hous
> Without science? No man, I yow assure. (134–7)

He ends in the same direct manner:

> Thairfore I ceis and will na forther say:
> Ga seik the jasp, quha will, for thair it lay. (160–1)

Exactly the same thing is found in 'The Fox, the Wolf and the Husbandman', where it is especially effective with a surprise *moralitas*. The narrator ends his story:

> ...And left the wolff in watter to the waist:
> Quha haillit him out, I wait not, off the well. (2422–3)

and continues immediately:

> Heir endis the text; thair is na mair to tell.
> Yit men may find ane gude moralitie
> In this sentence, thocht it ane fabill be.
>
> This wolf I likkin to ane wickit man
> Quhilk dois the pure oppres in everie place...
> ...The foxe the feind I call into this cais.

This is the narrator speaking, the narrator who, as we have seen, has been constantly guiding and controlling the movement of the fable, developing the complex moral levels, the contrasts and gradations, controlling our sympathies and judgements, and, from time to time, explicitly drawing our attention to one or more of the significances of the fable.

Henryson has something of the skill and delicacy of La Fontaine in the way he is present as a moral commentator throughout the fable. The narrator's moral comments range from asides—'for comonly sic pykeris luffis not lycht'—and digressions, as on the 'wanton damsels', to proverbial reflections carefully set in his narrative ('Yit efter joy oftymes cummis cair, / And troubill efter grit prosperitie' (290–1). He will sometimes 'place' a character with a strongly evaluative adjective—'craftie and cawtelows', 'selie' etc.—or give an explicitly moral interpretation of its behaviour (cf. ll. 474–6), or begin to participate in the story either as an observer in 'The Preaching of the Swallow', or, as in 'The Trial of the Fox' with moral exclamations:

> O fulische man! plungit in warldlynes,
> To conqueis warldlie gude, and gold, and rent,
> To put thy saull in pane or hevines
> To riche thy air... (831–4)

Sometimes he will put a moral speech in the mouth of the characters themselves. He gives the rural mouse an eloquent, though ineffective, praise of simplicity:

> 'Quhat plesure is in the feistis delicate,
> The quhilkis ar gevin with ane glowmand brow?
> Ane gentill hart is better recreate
> With blyith curage, than seith to him ane kow.
> Ane modicum is mair for till allow,
> Swa that gude will be kerver at the dais,
> Than thrawin vult and mony spycit mais' (232–8)

which he calls approvingly a 'mery exhortatioun'. At the end of the story of 'The Preaching of the Swallow', it is the swallow who puts the clear morality:

> 'Lo,' quod scho, 'thus it happinnis mony syis
> On thame that will not tak counsall nor reid
> Off prudent men or clerkis that ar wyis... (1882–4)

which is then supplemented by (and certainly not displaced by) the dark *moralitas* that follows. And, of course, throughout the *Fables* the moral presence of the narrator is felt to be present indirectly in the way in which he controls our sympathy, detachment and judgement, now committing us firmly to one view of right and wrong (in 'The Sheep and the Dog' or 'The Wolf and the Lamb'), now holding our sympathy and judgement in balance (in 'The Wolf and the Wether'), now with a different perspective allowing a self-confessed villain in one of Reynard's manifestations to exist and prosper with an autonomy which is almost complete.

The *moralitates* in themselves, mostly in the straightforward and clear manner of medieval didactic poetry, are obviously not as complex or as interesting as their fables. But they should not be dismissed too lightly. They show some variety, not only in length (the abrupt end of 'The Confession of the Fox' is appropriately followed by a succinct moral coda of three stanzas, while other *moralitates* extend over as many as nine or ten stanzas), but in form. The *moralitas* of 'The Two Mice' is in a different metrical pattern from the rest of the fable, consisting of four 8-line stanzas, the final line of each being an almost identical refrain which emphasizes the 'sickernes' or the 'blyithnes in hart' that comes 'with small possessioun'. The first two lines connect it closely to its fable ('into this fabill'), but it immediately becomes what could almost be a separate moral lyric of some eloquence. In 'The Lion and the Mouse' the *moralitas* as well as the fable is within the framework of the poet's dream. 'The Sheep and the Dog' is different again. The *moralitas* begins by making the application to legal injustice inescapably clear. This it does with the precision and the care for detail that we have seen so often in the *Fables* (cf. the reference to 'scraip out Johne and wryte in Will or Wat'). Then there is quite a new turn, for the poet steps into the scene in the way he does elsewhere, and describes how he overhears the sheep's lamentation. The setting is done with the detail and the significant gestures of the tales: the sheep 'Quaikand for cauld, sair murnand ay amang / Kest up his ee unto the hevinnis hicht' (1293–4). If we follow Dr. Jamieson's suggestion[29] that his lament continues to the end of the *moralitas*, he becomes in the course of it the representative of the 'pure pepill':

> 'We pure pepill as now may do no moir
> Bot pray to The; sen that we are opprest
> Into this eirth, grant us in hevin gude rest!' (1318–20)

There is also something at least of the variety of tone which we found in the fables. The narrator still has a fondness for proverbial wisdom, and beside the enthusiastic tones of the allegorical exegete, we find the urbane Horatian tone of the end of the *moralitas* of 'The Two Mice':

[29] 'Henryson's "Fabillis"', *Words* ii (1966), p. 30 (following Laing).

Thy awin fyre, my freind, sa it be bot ane gleid,
It warmis weill, and is worth gold to the... (389–90)

His voice will unite the audience with him in a prayer (cf. 1139–45, 2973–5)—at the end of 'The Preaching of the Swallow' in a prayer which sounds like the conclusion of a meditation:

Pray we thairfoir quhill we ar in this lyfe
For four thingis: the first, fra sin remufe;
The secund is fra all weir and stryfe;
The thrid is perfite cheritie and lufe;
The feird thing is, and maist for oure behufe,
That is in blis with angellis to be fallow.
And thus endis the preiching of the swallow. (1944–50)

Or he will use the preacher's tone, and his characteristically popular and vivid style:

Allace, quhat cair, quhat weiping is and wo,
Quhen saull and bodie departit ar in twane!
The bodie to the wormis keitching go,
The saull to fyre, to everlestand pane.
Quhat helpis than this calf, thir gudis vane,
Quhen thow art put in Luceferis bag,
And brocht to hell and hangit be the crag? (1930–6)

(cf. the splendid line 'deith cummis behind and nippis thame be the nek' (2223)). The moralist's voice can speak with impressive urgency (cf. e.g. ll. 789–95), or authority—'Thir twa sinnis, flatterie and vaneglore, / Ar vennomous; gude folk, fle thame thairfoir!' (612–13). In clarity and vividness, the eloquence is at least reminiscent of that of the tales:

The gled is deith, that cummis suddandlie
As dois ane theif, and cuttis sone the battall:
Be vigilant thairfoir and ay reddie,
For mannis lyfe is brukill and ay mortall:
My freind, thairfoir mak the ane strang castell
Of gud deidis; for deith will the assay
Thow wait not quhen—evin, morrow or midday.
(2962–8)[30]

[30] In l. 2967, I follow Fox in preferring Bann. *gud deidis*.

The *moralitates*, therefore, are more than a simple statement, *fabula docet*. Their relationship with the fables has something of the intimate bond of soul and body; the two complement and illuminate each other.

From the whole work, fables and moralities, there emerges what is in effect a 'Mirror of Human Life'. It is presented dramatically; it is not a coherently argued and organized philosophical system. Different, and sometimes opposed, ideas and attitudes jostle each other in what is a more limited version of La Fontaine's 'une ample comédie à cent actes divers'.[31] In it, through the figures of his fables Henryson explores and illuminates the moral characteristics of man, the 'little world', as an individual with passions, vices and virtues, in his relationship with himself and with other men, in his relationship with society, and, since he is 'l'abrégé de ce qu'il y a de bon et de mauvais dans les créatures irraisonnables', his relationship with the rest of the universe. Henryson is, of course, more concerned than the La Fontaine of the *Fables* with the spiritual and transcendent world which lies behind the world in which his characters move. Any reading of his *moralitates* shows that he had a deeply religious view of the world. But it must be stressed that it is a view which is concerned not with abstract theology, but with the spiritual life of man. It is most obviously seen in the dark moralities, but it is by no means confined to them. In 'The Cock and the Fox', flattery and vainglory are sins—and 'vennomous'—and the pride of Chantecleir reminds the moralist of the 'puft up pryde' which led to the fall of the angels. The emphasis is always firmly on the spiritual struggles of man's life on earth. In 'The Confession of the Fox' the suddenness of death is an 'exempill...exhortand folk to amend'; the 'perfite prudence and cunning' of the jasp is full of wonderful 'virtue' for life in this world.

The dark moralities reveal the familiar spiritual landscape of late medieval religion. The world is flattering and deceitful, full of temptations to sins—pride, covetousness, sensuality—and the fiend 'apostata' sows poison in men's souls. For all its pleasures and joys, it will not last: in the *moralitas* of 'The Lion and the Mouse' the landscape is moralized, by means of a traditional image, with a blend of sadness and joy:

> The fair forest with levis lowne and le,
> With foulis sang and flouris ferlie sweit,

[31] V. i.

Is bot the warld and his prosperitie,
As fals plesance myngit with cair repleit.
Richt as the rois with froist and wynter weit
Faidis, swa dois the warld, and thame desavis
Quhilk in thair lustis maist confidence havis. (1580–6)

The transience of life and the sudden, unexpected coming of death is strongly felt. Death comes suddenly, like the cat, the cadger, the kite, or the arrow—and there is no defence. The thought of this sudden death should lead man to think on his end: 'wilt thow remember, man, that thow mon de'. Nothing is permanent in this world:

For in this warld thair is na thing lestand;
Is na man wait how lang his stait will stand,
His lyfe will lest, nor how that he sall end
Efter his deith, nor quhidder he sall wend. (1940–3)

Man's body is as uncertain as the rest:

The paddok, usand in the flude to duell,
Is mannis bodie, swymand air and lait
In to this warld, with cairis implicate—
Now hie, now law, quhylis plungit up, quhylis doun,
Ay in perrell and reddie for to droun. (2936–40)

Since man's life is 'brukill and ay mortall' it is best to make 'ane strang castell' in good deeds and faith. And yet this religious view is not essentially an ascetic or an otherworldly one. The mirror of the life of man's soul becomes the mirror of man's life in this world. Man, with his passions and his failings, is very firmly in the centre.

'Mannis lyfe is brukill and ay mortall'—Death hovers in the background of the fables (about half end with a death; another four have a threat of death). Fortune is false and changeful, 'quhilk of all variance / Is haill maistres, and leidar of the dance / Till injust men' (1604–6); destiny unavoidable. The 'sikernes' that man seeks is hard to find. The world of the *Fables* is grim and realistic. Henryson shows the world as it is; where there is a vision of harmony it is an ideal one which is contrasted with cruel and blind actuality. 'The Preaching of the Swallow', for instance, sharply opposes the wisdom and providence of God and the stubborn blindness of man.[32] The prologue stresses the

[32] On this fable, see J. A. Burrow, 'Henryson: *The Preaching of the Swallow*', *Essays in Criticism* xxv (1975), 25–37.

blindness of man in a way which is characteristic of late medieval religious writing, with its acute sense of the limitations of reason—we cannot clearly understand nor see God as he is, and since man is so weak of understanding,

> Nane suld presume be ressoun naturall
> To seirche the secreitis off the Trinitie,
> Bot trow fermelie and lat all ressoun be. (1647–9)

Nevertheless, says Henryson, we can have 'knawlegeing' of God through his creatures, and the prologue moves into an eloquent hymn in praise of God's harmony. His wisdom may be seen in the cosmic order of the created universe:

> The firmament payntit with sternis cleir,
> From eist to west rolland in cirkill round,
> And everilk planet in his proper spheir,
> In moving makand harmonie and sound;
> The fyre, the air, the watter and the ground—
> Till understand it is aneuch, iwis,
> That God in all His werkis wittie is.
>
> Luke weill the fische that swimmis in the se;
> Luke weill in eirth all kynd off bestiall;
> The foulis fair sa forcelie thay fle,
> Scheddand the air with pennis grit and small;
> Syne luke to man, that he maid last of all,
> Lyke to His image and His similitude;
> Be thir we knaw that God is fair and gude. (1657–70)

The protagonists of the bloody tragedy that is to ensue are themselves 'foulis fair' and man 'lyke to His image', and the blindness and violence of the fable are far removed from this harmonious vision. In addition to this controlled irony, the fable sets up further tensions and ambiguities (cf. pp. 111–2). The 'carl' may be figured as the treacherous fiend, and this fits well with his final act when 'that bludie bowcheour beit thay birdis doun' as well as with the care that he takes over the preparation of his snares. But other questions suggested by the fable remain unexorcized. Is he a very human fowler, provoked by the birds, or a tyrant? Or is it that what seems from the birds' point of view 'fals intentioun' may also be seen as the actions of a man carrying on his normal and orderly duties of sowing, reaping and hunting? Is destruction and death in some mysterious way part of the harmonious order? It seems that in this fable Henryson is allowing unresolved tensions to stand.

Questions of harmony and order are raised also in 'The Trial of the Fox'. The splendid pageant of the fourfooted beasts is a demonstration, among other things, of Nature's ordered variety. But again it is not straightforward; it is not quite the realization of an ideal order. The procession itself, as we see it, with human eyes in a fallen world, seems in fact unnatural, and this is emphasized by the poet's touches of fantastic detail—'the marmisset the mowdewart couth leid'. Why should all these creatures come together? One answer introduces a nice double-edged irony, in that these 'brutall beistis and irrationall' are making a political attempt to live according to reason in a way in which men conspicuously do not. We are also reminded (if we needed reminding) that some of the animals arriving are far from virtuous. They will have to be kept in order, and the king commands peace for twenty miles around:

> 'Se neir be twentie mylis quhair I am
> The kid ga saiflie be the gaittis syde,
> The tod Lowrie luke not to the lam,
> Na revand beistis nouther ryn nor ryde.' (943–6)

The tod Lowrie does indeed prove to be a handful, and his villainous exploits bring us back with a vengeance to the world as it is. The vision of peace proves here to be a fleeting one. The ancient theme, however, is a powerful expression of an ideal—the recovery of a lost 'golden world'. Skilfully Henryson makes it coexist (before it fades) with its opposite, the ironic realization that things are not like this in the world nowadays. This fable, we may recall, begins with a startling display of disharmony and 'unkindness' by the fox. Moreover, there is a hint of irony in the background of the 'vision of peace' itself, since it is established by 'ane wild lyoun' of a distinctly autocratic animal nature.

Dr. Schwarzbaum has shown that the vision of peace in the animal kingdom is usually treated ironically in fables.[33] It is quite often pressed into service by the fox himself. In one fable of Berechiah, the fox offers himself to the fish as king and suggests that they should live in peace

[33] H. Schwarzbaum, 'The Vision of Eternal Peace in the Animal Kingdom', *Fabula* x (1969), 107–31. Cf. Isaiah ii, 4, xi, 6–9. Babrius, No. 102, is remarkable for a gentle and optimistic treatment.

with him on the land. In another, the fox tries to beguile the cock by reporting to him a new law establishing peace among the animals. When he is chased away by some dogs, he says that the dogs have not yet heard of the new law. The folk wisdom behind these stories (of the need for caution in accepting offers of help from strangers, or believing those in authority when they proclaim that the ideal state is already here) is very ancient—Dr. Schwarzbaum reminds us of the fable of the leopard and the goat in the *Book of Ahikar* (cf. p. 39 above). Interestingly, in Henryson's 'Cock and Fox' there is a hint of just this theme, when the fox describes to the gullible Chantecleir how his father, 'the sweit', died in his arms:

> 'Yea, my fair sone, I held up his heid
> Quhen that he deit under ane birkin beuch,
> Syne said the Dirigie quhen that he wes deid.
> Betuix us twa how suld thair be ane feid? (447–50)

Animals in their infinite diversity have varying inclinations and antipathies, for as Chaucer's Nun's Priest says, a beast will naturally desire to flee from his 'contrary' even if he has never seen it before. Among such 'contraries' are cocks and foxes, mice and cats (still enshrined in the matter of Tom and Jerry) and, apparently, frogs and mice. Conflict seems to be built into the world of nature. It would be wrong to try to force Henryson into a completely self-consistent philosophical position here. One could easily arrive at a determinist position, or on the other hand one could argue (as was sometimes done in discussions of planetary influence) that 'inclination' does not necessarily determine choice. Henryson avails himself of the poet's liberty. Foxes in the *Fables* are invariably crafty and 'cawtelous'. The two sister mice, however, although they are from the same 'wame' have been made by circumstances into very different creatures. On the animal side of the animal–human relationship there is a good deal of determinism—the creatures as animals tend to act according to their 'kind' (the cock wants its dinner, and the little mouse is desperate to reach the food on the other side of the water), but in their more human rôles they make rational or irrational choices (Chantecleir decides to sing in the way the fox wants him to, and the wether decides to forsake its 'kind' and become a dog). That Henryson was aware of these questions is evident from the exchange in 'The Paddock and the Mouse', where the mouse using its 'skill of Phisnomy' remarks

For clerkis sayis the inclinatioun
Of mannis thocht proceidis commounly
Efter the corporall complexioun
To gude or evill, as nature will apply... (2826–9)

to which the Paddock quickly rejoins that 'this difference in forme and qualitie' is simply 'printed and set' by Nature in every creature, and that appearance is no guide to behaviour or character. In this case the mouse is apparently proved right, but it would be rash to suppose that this represents Henryson's considered view of the matter.

The vision of ordered Nature that emerges from the *Fables* is one which is complex, mysterious, and not easily 'harmonious'—and in this it is a 'shadow' of the world of men. It is a world of conflict, where cruelty, treachery and violence are kept in check with difficulty, if at all. Henryson's *Fables* are clearsighted almost to the point of pessimism. Justice is not always done, and the innocent suffer. Sometimes the deceivers are themselves deceived, and right triumphs, but this is far from inevitable. In this world, appearance and reality are not the same. The stupid are sometimes deceived by appearance or by 'false seeming', and sometimes—as in 'The Paddock and the Mouse'—the not so stupid are deceived as well. It is a world of threat and violence, of cynical deception and cruel irony. In many of its features we can recognize the world of the old 'Aesop', that world which appears again even more vividly in the *Fables* of La Fontaine: 'a tragic picture, with death and murder in the centre. Wickedness, stupidity, or just chance kill and destroy without the slightest regard for age or virtue...There is no pity, no security anywhere...This book which is supposed to be intended for children denies at every page the existence of the most elementary forms of justice and loyalty.'[34]

Of those fables which bear on men's relations with their fellows in society, the most important is 'The Lion and the Mouse'. The fact that it alone is told to Henryson by his *auctour* and spiritual guide in a vision gives it a special significance.[35] It concerns itself with good governance, with the relationship of the classes of society, and with the duties and obligations of a ruler, notably the balance he has to keep between mercy and justice. The fable's combination of sympathy and

[34] Odette de Mourgues, *La Fontaine: Fables* (London, 1960), p. 22.

[35] Cf. N. von Kreisler, 'Henryson's Visionary Fable: Tradition and Craftsmanship in *The Lyoun and the Mous*', *Texas Studies in Literature and Language* xv (1973–74), 391–403.

detachment finds a parallel in the varying demands of altruism and self-interest advanced in the argument. Already in the plea which the captive mouse makes, there is some sound doctrine on the need to temper justice with mercy, delivered with specific legal detail:

In everie juge mercy and reuth suld be,
As assessouris and collaterall;
Without mercie justice is crueltie,
As said is in the lawis speciall:
Quhen rigour sittis in the tribunall
The equitie off law quha may sustene? (1468–73)

Since there is a less philosophical and political side to the mouse's argument, an appeal in the manner of traditional fable-morality to self-interest—'sic cace may be your awin'—Henryson delicately refrains from telling us precisely which points of the argument succeeded in convincing the lion, who 'thocht according to ressoun, / And gart mercie his cruell ire asswage'. Before the second episode, the narrator carefully detaches some of our sympathy from the lion (rather in the way he had earlier emphasized the mischievous *hubris* of the mice) by insisting that he is 'this cruell lyoun' who hunts with an excess that hardly suggests an ideal ruler:

For he had nocht, bot levit on his pray,
And slew baith tayme and wyld, as he wes wont,
And in the cuntrie maid ane grit deray. (1511–13)

The resolution neatly illustrates the homely wisdome of the proverbial argument that one good turn deserves another; as La Fontaine succinctly puts it, 'on a souvent besoin d'un plus petit que soi'. On another level the fable is for Henryson an unusually optimistic statement of an ideal realized, an ideal of mutual help and order ('il faut s'entraider'). It suggests that one generous and magnanimous act will produce another, as is shown in those tales of Chaucer (such as *The Franklin's Tale*) which treat the virtue of *gentilesse*—

'Now were I fals and richt unkynd
Bot gif I quit sum part thy gentilnes
Thow did to me' (1547–9)[36]

—which implies a less pessimistic view of life, and the belief that

[36] In l. 1548, I follow Fox in preferring Bann.

goodness exists and may generate goodness. *Gentilesse* is always associated with *pite* and mercy, and it is explicitly stated at the end of the fable that the lion was rescued 'because he had pietie'. This point is expanded in the *moralitas* with Henryson's usual homely vigour and local precision:

> Be this fabill ye lordis of prudence
> May considder the vertew of pietie,
> And to remit sumtyme ane grit offence,
> And mitigate with mercy crueltie:
> Oftymis is sene ane man of small degre
> Hes quit ane kinbute baith of gude and ill,
> As lord hes done rigour or grace him till. (1594–1600)

On the political level, the fable wittily demonstrates the need for mutual dependence (it is perhaps a less mystically authoritarian fable than 'The Belly and the Members', in that if the *menu peuple* depend on the mercy of the ruler, the ruler also depends upon their help; there is an implication of need and of limitation). It is these aspects that are developed in the *moralitas*. Aesop says that the lion may signify a ruler ('ane prince or empriour, / Ane potestate, or yit ane king with croun') and a ruler who is careless, who does not 'take labour'

> To reule and steir the land, and justice keip,
> Bot lyis still in lustis, sleuth and sleip (1578–9)

and the mice are the 'commountie', 'wanton, unwyse, without correctioun', who, if their lords and princes do not enforce justice, 'dreid na thing to mak rebellioun'. Justice, when it is executed, should be tempered with mercy. Aesop goes on to consider the fate of the lion. Who can know, he asks, how soon 'ane lord of grit renoun, / Rolland in wardlie lust and vane plesance' may be cast down by fortune, who will blind the careless ruler so that he will lose prudence and foresight?

Commentators have often seen in this fable and its morality a particular reference to some event in fifteenth-century Scottish history.[37] It has been claimed, for instance, that the sleeping lion is

[37] Cf. Mary Rowlands, 'The Fables of Robert Henryson', *Dalhousie Review* xxxix (1959–60), esp. pp. 496–7, J. MacQueen, *Robert Henryson*, pp. 170–3, M. Stearns, *Robert Henryson*, pp. 15–25, R. Nicholson, *Scotland. The Later Middle Ages* (Edinburgh, 1974), p. 509. Strong reservations are expressed by I. W. A. Jamieson, *The Poetry of Robert Henryson*, and R. J. Lyall, 'Politics and Poetry in Fifteenth and Sixteenth Century Scotland', *Scottish Literary Journal* iii (1976), No. 2, pp. 7–10.

James III (whose rule was not always effective) and that the reference is to the Lauder Bridge rebellion of 1482, and that the rescuing mice are a figure of the release of the king from Edinburgh by Albany and the burgesses, or, alternatively, that the reference is to the rebellion of nobles in 1466 led by Sir Alexander Boyd. To these suggestions it may perhaps be objected that (*a*) not all the details (e.g. the mice as the 'commountie') seem to fit, (*b*) that a political 'morality' is an inseparable part of this traditional fable, and that even if there were some particular reference, the fable would still have a universal significance (Aesop, it should be noted, says 'Figure heirof oftymis hes bene sene', and lists different sorts of rulers) and (*c*) that the advice to princes is quite traditional.[38] But the matter is not easily decided. The fable as a 'speaking picture' is both universal and particular, and can be applied to many relevant particular situations. Fables have been used as a form of instruction for princes (cf. the Fables of Bidpai), and it may well be that Henryson is presenting his 'lord' with a miniature *Speculum principis*, a 'Mirror of Wisdom'. Assuredly, one remark of Aesop's strongly suggests a veiled reference to some well-known contemporary event: when he describes how 'thir rurall men'

> Waittit alway amendis for to get—
> For hurt men wrytis in the marbill stane.
> Mair till expound as now I lett allane,
> Bot king and lord may weill wit quhat I mene...
>
> (1610–13)

The fact that the next line has the generalizing 'oftymes hes bene sene' may suggest to some that it is a deliberate piece of mystification. Moreover, the fervour of Aesop's conclusion suggests that Henryson thought it an ideal that was not always realized, and that it was especially relevant to the contemporary state of Scotland ('this cuntrie'):

> That tressoun of this cuntrie be exyld,
> And justice regne, and lordis keip thair fay
> Unto thair soverane king baith nycht and day.
>
> (1617–19)

Whether there is a particular political reference or not, there can be no doubt that the fable was relevant to 'this cuntrie' in the late Middle

[38] Cf., e.g., Dunbar's 'The Thrissil and the Rois'.

Ages. It is not hard to find examples of mischievous commons, or powerful men who harboured grudges and took vengeance on their ruler—or of rulers who neglected government. There are constant complaints that the realm was 'nocht governit'. The complaint in the Register of Moray (1398) echoes through the fifteenth century:

> In those days there was no law in Scotland, but the strong oppressed the weak, and the whole kingdom was one den of thieves. Homicides, robberies, fire-raisings and other evil deeds went unpunished, and justice, outlawed, was in exile, beyond the bounds of the kingdom.[39]

James III was advised (1473) that he should

> tak part of labor apon his persone and travel throw his Realme, and put sic Justice and polycy in his awne realme, that the brute and the fame of him mycht pas in utheris contreis, and that he mycht obtene the name of sa just a prince and sa vertewss and sa wele reuland his awne realme...that utheris princis mycht tak example of him.[40]

From the time of Babrius and Phaedrus the question of justice in this world has been an important one for the Western fable. In other fables of Henryson we are shown some clear cases where justice does not reign. The fable which in the Bassandyne order precedes Aesop's 'The Lion and the Mouse', 'The Sheep and the Dog', is a bitter tale of justice perverted, and of the suffering of the innocent. The wolf is a fraudulent judge, aided by villainous court officials. The innocence of the sheep is of no avail; here the proverbial dictum that 'falseness ever fails at the end' is patently not true. Henryson goes out of his way to show that even the sheep's knowledge of law, and its intelligent use of legal argument, is of no consequence. Naked might and fraud overcome innocence and intelligence. The situation is a traditional part of the fable, but Henryson has extended Walter's brief version, not padding it out, as one critic accuses him, 'with legal jargon',[41] but carefully

[39] Quoted by W. C. Dickinson, *Scotland from the Earliest Times to 1603* (Edinburgh, 1961), p. 200 (revised ed., pp. 200–1).

[40] *Acts of the Parliament of Scotland*, ed. T. Thomson (London, 1814), II, p. 104 (cf. also pp. 118, 122, 170).

[41] Bauman, 'Folktale and Oral Tradition', p. 118. On the details of legal procedure, see Mary Rowlands, 'Robert Henryson and the Scottish Courts of Law',

transforming it into a bitter and elaborate satire on consistory courts and civil law, which seem here to have nothing to do with true justice. The details are precise, and apparently accurate:

> ...ane doig, because that he wes pure,
> Callit ane scheip to the consistorie,
> Ane certane breid fra him for to recure. (1147–9)

(The ecclesiastical consistory courts, by the late Middle Ages, dealt mainly with suits which had no connection with worship or morality or ecclesiastical discipline. The majority of the cases which came before these tribunals were disputes over property and revenue, and it seems that in pre-Reformation Scotland they handled the bulk of the law business.) The judge, here 'ane fraudfull wolff', makes a citation against the sheep 'by the use and cours and commoun style' summoning him under pain of 'hie suspensioun' (*suspensio totalis*), 'grit cursing' (*excommunicatio major*), and 'interdictioun' (*interdictio*) to appear and answer the dog before him. The 'apparitour' is 'schir Corbie Ravin', 'quha pykit had full mony scheipis ee', who summons the sheep 'peremptourlie'. The writ is endorsed and delivered by the raven; the 'oure off cause' set is at evening, apparently a 'lawless hour'. The trial begins. The fox is clerk and notary; the dog's advocates are the kite and the vulture, who stand at the bar (the barrier marking the precinct of the judge's seat). The sheep answers the charge by 'declining' (objecting to) the judge, the time, and the place. The matter then goes to arbitration. The two arbitrators are the bear and the badger, who (of course), after much legal talk—

> Of civile law volumis full mony thay revolve,
> The codies and digestis new and ald;
> [Contra and pro], strait argumentis thay resolve,
> Sum objecting and sum can hald;
> For prayer or price trow ye that thay wald fald?
> Bot hald the glose and text of the decreis
> As trew jugis; I beschrew thame ay that leis (1216–22)—

Aberdeen University Review xxxix (1961–62), 219–26, and I. W. A. Jamieson, 'Henryson's "Fabillis"', pp. 21–8. On the background, cf. Cosmo Innes, *Lectures on Scotch Legal Antiquities* (Edinburgh, 1872), pp. 238–9, G. C. H. Patton in *An Introduction to Scottish Legal History* (The Stair Society xx, Edinburgh, 1958).

decide that the sheep must accept the court. He stands without an advocate, contests the dog's accusation, and the court proceeds to judgement:

> And thus the pley unto the end thay speid.
> This cursit court, corruptit all for meid,
> Aganis gude faith, law, and eik conscience,
> For this fals doig pronuncit the sentence. (1240–3)

The consistory courts were a favourite target of satirists.[42] In the early fourteenth-century MS. Harley 2253 there is an English verse attack on them. In sixteenth-century Scotland, in Lindsay's *Satire of the Three Estates*, Poverty complains of his experience trying to get recompense for a mare among 'ane gredie menyie'—over the years he got 'citandum...libellandum...opponendum...interloquendum... ad replicandum...concludendum...pronunciandum', 'bot I gat nevir my gud gra meir agane'. Lindsay's Poverty speaks openly of 'reform', and the abuses of the consistories with their 'polling Officials' and 'hell pestering rabble of sumners and apparitors' passed into anti-Catholic satire.[43] Whether they always deserved this reputation is another matter. A modern scholar who has investigated the history of the consistory court of Lincoln, Professor Colin Morris, is left with 'quite a favourable view of the efficiency and expedition of the court'.[44] It is probably the case that, as with other 'topics' of medieval satirists, one has to be extremely cautious in making historical generalizations. A lively tradition of anti-legal literature continued to flourish in both serious and lighthearted manifestations up to *Bleak House* and *Trial by Jury* and beyond. But even when one allows for exaggeration and poetic licence, the satires must reflect some dissatisfaction. Popular resentment (for which there are obvious reasons) is surely reflected in such cynical proverbs as 'nowadays...law goeth as it is favoured', 'Who will have law must have money', 'Laws are like lop-webs which take small flies and let great flies go', 'He that anoint the judge's hands often makes his ass lean', 'When a judge is wood it is hard to treat before him without loss of blood'. Like the remarks of satirists and preachers these show a

[42] For the Harley poem, cf. R. H. Robbins, *Historical Poems of the XIVth and XVth Centuries* (New York, 1959), No. 6; Lindsay, *Works* ed. D. Hamer, STS 3rd ser., ii, pp. 288–91.

[43] Cf. Googe's tr. of Naogeorgus, *The Popish Kingdome*, ed. R. C. Hope (London, 1880), ff. 15–15^{v}, *OED* s.v. 'apparitor'.

[44] 'A Consistory Court in the Middle Ages', *Journal of Ecclesiastical History* xiv (1963), p. 158.

sharp awareness of the difference between the ideal of justice and its practice among men.

In the *moralitas*, Henryson extends the scope of the legal satire. The wolf is likened to the sheriff, and the raven to the coroner, 'whose business it was to go before the Justice Ayre to arrest those whose names appeared on the Sheriff's roll of wrongdoers' (it is in this guise that he takes bribes for changing the names on the document). By making his readers think of both types of courts—the consistory and the sheriff's—Henryson is broadening his attack into one on legal injustice in general. There are other fables which contain satire on courts—'The Trial of the Fox' and 'The Fox, the Wolf and the Husbandman', where Lowrence plays the role of a 'juge amycabill':

> 'I am ane juge!' quod Lowrence than, and leuch;
> 'Thar is na buddis suld me beir by the rycht;
> I may tak hennis and caponis weill aneuch,
> For God is gane to sleip; as for this nycht,
> Sic small thingis ar not sene into His sicht... (2329–33)

The spirit here however is very different. Henryson (as medieval preachers had often done)[45] emphasizes the naked oppression of the poor. The sheep is the figure of the poor commons, 'that daylie ar opprest / Be tirrane men...' (1259–60). When the sheep begins his lament he uses that traditional image so cynically tossed off by Lowrence with the passion of outraged innocence:

> 'Lord God, quhy sleipis Thow sa lang?
> Walk, and discerne my cause, groundit on richt;
> Se how I am be fraud, maistrie, and slicht
> Peillit full bair!' (1295–8)

The feeling of the sheep's lament is close to that cry of the oppressed in *Ps.* xliv (A.V.): 'Awake, why sleepest thou, O lord? arise, cast us not off forever. Wherefore hidest thou thy face, and forgettest our affliction and our oppression'. The complaint gradually becomes more general, less concerned with his particular injustice, until it begins to sound like a 'complaint on the times', a favourite type of medieval poetic lament:

> Seis Thow not, Lord, this warld ouerturnit is,
> As quha wald change gude gold in leid or tyn;
> The pure is peillit, the lord may do na mis;

[45] Cf. G. R. Owst, *Literature and Pulpit in Medieval England* (2nd ed., Oxford, 1961), chapters v–vi.

And simonie is haldin for na syn;
Now he is blyith with okker maist may wyn;
Gentrice is slane and pietie is ago;
Allace, gude Lord, quhy tholis Thow it so? (1307–13)

'Gentrice is slane and pietie is ago' suggests a general disorder in the commonweal similar to that lurking in the background of 'The Lion and the Mouse'. Yet this *moralitas* in its passion and indignation goes much further than the usual poem of this type. The great questions posed in the complaint of Job and its predecessors in the ancient Wisdom literature of the justice of God, and the suffering of the innocent, begin to emerge in their full force—'Allace, gude lord, quhy tholis Thow it so?' It is a measure of Henryson's comprehensiveness of mind that he allows such questions to come through so strongly.

An answer is offered to the question which had exercised so many great thinkers of the Middle Ages from Boethius on. Few modern readers will find it satisfactory—'Thow tholis this evin for our grit offence...'. What was the sheep's great offence? But before we dismiss this final stanza, there are one or two things we need to remember. Firstly, there was in the Middle Ages a profound and almost primitive belief in immanent justice.[46] It finds its expression in a variety of ways—in the expectation that justice would be revealed or proved by ordeal, by duel, by battle, by holy war. The eye of faith hoped to see the justice of God revealed through the natural (i.e. spiritual) course of events. At the battle of Hastings, according to William of Poitiers, King Harold raised his eyes to heaven and prayed to God—'Dominus inter me et Willelmum hodie quod justum est decernat'. One may suspect that the discovery of a blatant injustice or an unmerited disaster produced greater tensions then than it does in an age which is prepared to see the universe as absurd, and does not expect order and justice from it. The pious response in the Middle Ages to catastrophe and disaster—whether war, plague, or personal mishap—is to explain it as allowed by God because of the sin of the victim. There is, perhaps, a sense of unresolved tension beneath the surface, emphasized by the very vehemence with which the sheep implicitly rejects any doubts

[46] Cf. P. Rousset, 'La Croyance en la justice immanente à l'époque féodale', *Le Moyen Age* liv (1948), 225–48. There are some interesting testimonies to the survival of this attitude in the notes of the late seventeenth-century antiquary, Richard Gough, on Myddle, near Shrewsbury (see D. G. Hey, *An English Rural Community. Myddle under the Tudors and Stuarts* (Leicester, 1974), pp. 185–6).

and questionings. Professor Rousset has pointed out that one primitive aspect of the medieval belief in immanent justice is a collective sense of the responsibility of the whole group.[47] This is certainly the case here. The sheep begins to speak as 'I' of its particular misfortune, but by the final stanza of the *moralitas*, the audience is included—'our grit offence', 'us', 'we pure pepill'.

Secondly, if we assume that the lament continues to the end of the *moralitas*, it would be the final part of a dramatic lament, by the sheep, not by the poet. It is also an outcry of the 'pure commounis'. Before the mystery of injustice and the absolute power of God, the sheep's humble response is perhaps a little like Job's 'Behold I am of small account, what shall I answer thee?...I know that thou canst do all things, and that no purpose of thine can be restrained...[I have] uttered that which I understood not, things too wonderful for me, which I knew not...'.[48] The resignation of the ancient Aesop has become the patience of popular Christianity. The sheep's words are an expression of simple faith—or of simple pietism—and they sum up a whole area of popular religious sentiment, and express in a most memorable form the sense of a great load of suffering, and of an almost desperate endurance:

> Thow tholis this euin for our grit offence;
> Thow sendis us troubill and plaigis soir,
> As hunger, derth, grit weir, or pestilence;
> Bot few amendis now thair lyfe thairfoir.
> We pure pepill as now may do no moir
> Bot pray to The, sen that we ar opprest
> Into this eirth, grant us in heuin gude rest! (1314–20)

Another fable of injustice, in which God seems to sleep, and which also demonstrates that 'la raison du plus fort est toujours la meilleure', is 'The Wolf and the Lamb'. As Phaedrus says, it was composed 'to fit those persons who invent false charges by which to oppress the innocent'. Henryson intensifies the bleakness and grimness of the traditional matter. It is useless for the lamb to say that the wolf's accusation 'failyeis fra treuth and contrair is to ressoun' (2643), for both of these qualities are irrelevant in this situation. 'Na' says the wolf, later in the fable, 'thou wald intruse ressoun / Quhair wrang and reif

[47] Rousset, p. 213. Cf. Hey, *An English Rural Community*, p. 243.
[48] *Job* xl, 4, xlii, 2–3 (R.V.).

suld duell in propertie'. It is just as useless to quote law or scripture. The world is upside down. Of all the fables, perhaps, this offers the sharpest clash between rational civilized values and violent injustice.

Henryson's extended *moralitas* takes the lamb to signify 'the pure pepill' and the wolf as 'fals extortioneris / And oppressouris of pure men'. It is again vehemently outspoken on the unjust treatment of the poor (defined here as 'maill-men (small tenant farmers), merchandis and all lauboureris / Of quhome the lyfe is half ane purgatorie'); the criticisms are given with some detail. There are three kinds of wolves in this world—false perverters of the laws (the poet is moved to an *exclamatio*:

> O man of law, let be thy subteltie,
> With nice gimpis and fraudis intricait!),

mighty rich men who are greedy and covetous and will not suffer the poor to live in peace:

> Suppois he and his houshald baith suld de
> For falt of fude, thairof thay gif na rak,
> Bot ouer his heid his mailling will thay tak

(these too are addressed directly: 'O man but mercie, quhat is in thy thocht? / War than ane wolf and thow culd understand!') and finally, 'men of heritage' (inherited possessions) who oppress poor tenants. This abuse is treated with considerable emotion and with very precise detail (*gressome*, for instance, is 'a fine paid by a tenant to his feudal superior on entering upon a holding...or...upon renewal of tenure'):

> ...Syne vexis him, or half his terme be gane
> With pykit querrellis for to mak him fane
> To flit or pay his gressome new agane.
>
> His hors, his meir, he man len to the laird,
> To drug and draw in court or in cariage;
> His servand or his self may not be spaird
> To swing and sweit withoutin meit or wage;
> Thus how he standis in labour and bondage,
> That scantlie may he purches by his maill
> To leve upon dry breid and watter caill... (2746–55)

It is an eloquent attack both on general injustice and on particular abuses. Insecurity of tenure was certainly a fact of late medieval

Scottish life. Major says of the country people that 'they have no permanent holdings, but hired only, or in lease for four or five years, at the pleasure of the lord of the soil; therefore do they not dare to build good houses, though stones abound'.[49]

This impressive passage has provoked some discussion. Professor Stearns, in his book on Henryson, rightly stresses the poet's humanity, but rather exaggerates his identification with the peasants (Henryson's favourite protagonist, he says, is 'a sturdily independent peasant')[50] and even suggests that his aversion to feudal lords is almost dangerous in its outspokenness. One should not, in reaction to this slightly romanticized view, try to reduce such a passage to a rhetorical rehearsal of commonplaces. The question of poets' 'feeling for the poor' in late medieval literature is an extremely difficult one. The wicked rich are a favourite subject of the pulpit,[51] and it is certainly dangerous to take such remarks *tout court* as accurately informed sociological views of late medieval society. As Miss Smalley has warned us: 'the interpretation of medieval moralists is such a tricky business that one can only consider the mind of the writer, while distrusting his picture of the state of society: this will normally be overdrawn and second-hand'.[52] It is also true that laments for the wretched state of the poor are far from unusual in late medieval literary works:

> Si fault de faim perir les innocens
> Dont les grans loups font chacun jour ventrée,
> Qui amassent a milliers et a cens
> Les faulx tresors; c'est le grain, c'est la blée,
> Le sang, les os qui ont la terre arée
> Des povres gens, dont leur esperit crie
> Vengence a Dieu, vé a la seignourie...

This stanza is quoted by Huizinga in a most interesting discussion of the topic in French and Burgundian writers.[53] His strictures on the material, though severe, are probably correct—the pity remains sterile,

[49] *A History of Greater Britain*, tr. A. Constable (Edinburgh, 1892), pp. 30–1.
[50] *Robert Henryson*, p. 117 (cf. also pp. 111, 124).
[51] Cf. G. R. Owst, *Literature and Pulpit*, esp. pp. 320–3.
[52] *English Friars and Antiquity in the Early Fourteenth Century* (Oxford, 1960), p. 199.
[53] *The Waning of the Middle Ages* (1948 repr.), pp. 49–53. The quotation is from Deschamps, No. 113, *Œuvres* ed. le Marquis de Queux de Saint-Hilaire (Paris, 1878), I, p. 230.

and produces no political action (though one may perhaps be permitted to wonder if any of the writers knew how to do anything about the plight of the poor), and much of it is 'theoretical and stereotyped commiseration' exhibiting nothing but a 'sentimental compassion for the miseries of the oppressed and defenceless people', having nothing to do with modern egalitarian sentiments. One suspects that strong feelings of guilt may sometimes lie beneath this kind of writing. However, even if it does not issue in practical action, and even if it does use traditional topics, the best of it is an impressively eloquent expression of the distress of that almost totally inarticulate class, which did strike a chord in the hearts of some people in the late Middle Ages. In *The Complaynt of Scotlande*[54] (1549) one of the three estates, 'Laubereris', utters 'ane lamentabil complaynt', which is an adaptation of a very eloquent lament which occurs in a work of the early fifteenth century from France, Alain Chartier's *Quadrilogue Invectif*; but even though it has been lifted from a source which is far removed in time and place, it is still not quite a conventional lament. Chartier's words were obviously felt to be still relevant to sixteenth-century, Scotland.

To return to the *moralitas* of 'The Wolf and the Lamb', one may perhaps venture to say that the 'picture of society' does not seem overdrawn and second-hand (the particularity of the detail distinguishes it from the vague generalities of some moralists). It sounds rather like a poet's intensification of what were felt to be real abuses. Finally, we are left with our own judgement of—in Miss Smalley's phrase—'the mind of the writer', and of his tone of voice. Although sentiments such as Henryson's are found elsewhere, they are not found in every late medieval poet—there is very little comparable in Dunbar, for example—and they are rarely so passionately expressed. If Henryson is not a modern democrat, he is not simply a conventional moralist either. The verses are traditional, rhetorical and heartfelt all at the same time. The *moralitas* is brought to its conclusion with a vehement injunction and a final prayer which reinforces the application to contemporary Scotland:

> God keip the lamb, quhilk is the innocent,
> From wolfis byit and fell extortioneris;
> God grant that wrangous men of fals intent
> Be manifestit, and punischit as effeiris;

[54] Ed. J. A. H. Murray, EETS ES xvii (1872), pp. 123ff.

And God, as thow all rychteous prayer heiris,
Mot saif our king and gif him hart and hand
All sic wolfis to banes out of the land. (2770–6)

The world of fables such as these is a violent place indeed—'there is no pity, no security anywhere'. We feel that we could well be in the grim world of the ancient fable where power and might and trickery rule. What—apart from hoping for salvation in the next world—can the inhabitants of this world do? They may be fortunate enough to escape through good luck, like the rural mouse, or they may be fortunate enough, as is the mouse in 'The Lion and the Mouse', to meet with a rare act of mercy. The great problem is survival, and the rate of success is not high. Sometimes a homely proverbial kind of morality, a morality of popular wisdom coming through from earlier times, offers some guide. As La Fontaine says,

Il est bon d'être charitable;
Mais envers qui, c'est là le point.[55]

In this world of 'seeming' it is hard to see clearly—'fair thingis oftymis ar fundin faikin' (2834—a proverb used, typically, by a deceiver). The protagonists have animal masks, but within their fables they assume other masks as well; greed, violence and egoism will present themselves as benevolence or justice. Ingratitude and unkindness are common, altruism is 'ane gude turn for ane uther'. In this perilous world, the worst vices or follies (as in *The Ship of Fools*, the two melt into each other) are those which involve an inability to see clearly—vainglory, especially if it is united with ignorance of one's own limitations, or obsessive greed as that of the wolf for the cabok or the herrings:

He that of ressoun can not be content
Bot covetis all, is abill all to tyne. (2189–90)

Cleverness may well be an asset in the task of survival (though innocent intelligence is not always, as we see in 'The Wolf and the Lamb' and 'The Sheep and the Dog'). It is sometimes possible for the physically weaker to defeat the stronger by means of wiles and stratagems. With self-interest as the dominant motive, there is an easy progression here from cleverness to sharpness to trickery. In Henryson's *Fables* an interest in trickery is constantly and often ambiguously

[55] VI, 13.

present. We watch his tricksters with admiration as well as with disapproval, even when they fail. If we take the *Fables* in the Bassandyne order, trickery first appears in 'The Cock and the Fox', with the wily fox and its dissimulating speech. There is a nice twist in this fable when the trickster is himself tricked. Chantecleir, previously so foolish, is inspired by 'sum gude spirit', and deceives his captor by astuteness. It is a mirror of the pattern of deception which led to his own downfall. In the midst of the hot pursuit he offers some counsel. He begins by reminding his captor how hungry and how hard-pressed he is. With unexpected cunning, he appeals to the fox's 'inclination' to dissimulation and lying—which, again unexpectedly, becomes his weak point: 'turn round and tell your pursuers that we have become friends "and fellowis for ane yeir"'. This is, of course, just the sort of 'wrink' that the fox himself in a less hectic moment would have used (and it is in fact a nice variation of the 'vision of peace in the animal kingdom' which the fox used earlier). The fox was indeed 'desavit be menis richt mervelous', for Henryson is thinking of the character of Chantecleir, and in the light of what we know of that, this sudden providential inspiration is comically unlikely. However, the fox *is* deceived, for 'falset failyeis ay at the latter end'—and yet like so many of Henryson's proverbs, this too is ambiguous, since the fox has been deceived by the application of his own technique. Here is a lesson on how to survive in a cruel world—be clever, and deceive your enemy—and it is one which pleases, 'car c'est double plaisir de tromper le trompeur'.[56] This is followed by two fables ('The Confession of the Fox', and 'The Trial of the Fox') in which trickery fails, but only at the very end, after many comic successes on the way. In two other fox fables, trickery is triumphant—and the fox carries away a good deal of our admiration along with his herrings and hens. Finally, in 'The Wolf and the Wether', we have an amateurish attempt at a cunning trick.

If one cannot win by a cunning trick, it is sometimes possible to keep out of trouble in other ways. That particular kind of prudence and forethought which consists in knowing and accepting one's status or capability is less dangerous than its opposite, as we see from 'The Wolf and the Wether'. Poverty and low station may have this advantage, that they make a man less exposed to the storms which fall upon the great. The fate of the wether shows that 'riches of array / Will cause

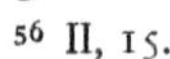

[56] II, 15.

pure men presumpteous for to be' and 'counterfeit' a lord, with dangerous results. Therefore, says the proverb quoted in the *moralitas*, 'Bewar in welth, for hall benkis ar rycht slidder' (2608). They were indeed, as the fate of Cochrane, Simnel and others in the fifteenth century shows. From most of the *Fables* it seems that 'sickernes' in this life is impossible to find. 'The Two Mice', however, suggests that one has more chance of finding it if one has 'small possessioun' and is contented with it—*tuta paupertas*, 'sickernes with small possessioun' is the dominant theme of the *moralitas*. In Aesop ('a simple life with peace and quiet is better than faring luxuriously and being tortured by fear') the superiority of the poor and tranquil life seems to be assumed on grounds which are largely utilitarian. It is safer—and there is a strong feeling in Aesop that any attempt to change one's state in society is likely to lead to ruin. This is still felt in Henryson's *moralitas*, where we are told that every estate has trouble and some vexation, but especially those 'quhilk clymmis up maist hie, / That ar not content with small possessioun' (371–2). But this fable is unusual in the Aesopic collection in that it turns on a choice of ways of life. The question is not simply that of contriving to stay alive, but of choosing the best way of living. Henryson's *moralitas* has, as well as a touch of Horatian urbanity, a proverbial insistence on moderation—'quha hes aneuch, of na mair hes he neid'. He urges a detachment from desires, especially desire for earthly wealth and earthly things, and there is a characteristic stress on the insecurity of the world ('swa interminglit is adversitie / With eirdlie joy'), so that his praise of the simple life has its reservation—'the sweitest lyfe...in this cuntre', 'best thing in eird...'. This caution is expressed again in his version of the piece of Old Testament wisdom by way of which the *moralitas* reaches its conclusion:

> ...And Solomon sayis, gif that thow will reid,
> 'Under the hevin thair can not better be
> Than ay be blyith and leif in honestie.'
> Quhairfoir I may conclude be this ressoun:
> Of eirthly joy it beiris maist degre,
> Blyithnes in hart, with small possessioun. (391–6)

As in the ancient fables, imprudence or lack of foresight is one of the most dangerous follies; there is a constant need for prudence, for clearsightedness and for knowledge: 'Wo is him can not bewar in tyme' (1789), 'Grit fule is he that will not glaidlie heir / Counsall in tyme' (1862–3), 'Best is bewar in maist prosperitie, / For in this warld thair is na thing lestand' (1939–40). As so often in Henryson the proverbial jostles and merges with the philosophical and the religious. The theme of wisdom (which lies behind the particular manifestation of it in prudence) is an important one, not only in 'The Preaching of the Swallow' from where the above proverbial remarks come, but throughout the *Fables* in a variety of contexts. It is firmly and centrally introduced in 'The Cock and the Jasp'. The Jasp betokens wisdom—'perfite prudence and cunning', 'science', 'science and cunning'—which is both an active virtue necessary for success in personal and political life, and a moral and spiritual force, which makes men able to win the victory over 'all vicis and spirituall enemie', and which is everlasting riches and everlasting meat for man's soul. It is man's duty to seek for it; only foolish ignorance opposes it:

> Quha is enemie to science and cunning
> Bot ignorants that understandis nocht?
> Quhilk is sa nobill, sa precious, and sa ding,
> That it may not with eirdlie thing be bocht?
> Weill wer that man ouer all uther, that mocht
> All his lyfe dayis in perfite studie wair
> To get science; for him neidis na mair. (148–54)

We are told to 'ga seik the jasp', for now it is 'tynt and hid':

> Haif we richis, na better lyfe we bid,
> Of science thocht the saull be bair and blind.

This last word is a hint of the series of images of 'seeing' and 'blindness' which run through the *Fables.* We have in fact already been presented with a speaking picture which illustrates this, for the cock thinks that it can 'see' the nature of the stone, but cannot. Wisdom is hidden, and not easy to find.

The idea of wisdom, whether in its manifestation as prudence or foresight in the face of a deceptive and dangerous world, or in its wider senses, is continued, explicitly and implicitly, throughout the work. There are examples of prudence or wisdom (or the lack of them) in individual, social, and political life. Some characters—like the country mouse—come to wisdom, but others—like the foolish birds in 'The Preaching of the Swallow'—will not heed the warning 'in tyme bewar'. In this fable, there is an especially interesting and elaborate treatment of wisdom, at various levels. There are the unwise birds, whose eyes the swallow desperately attempts to open—'O ye birdis... Ye sall weill knaw and wyislie understand', 'It is grit wisedome to provyde befoir'. She quotes a wise saying from the *Distichs* of Cato, *Nam levius laedit quicquid praevidimus ante*, and expands it for them:

For clerkis sayis it is nocht sufficient
To considder that is befoir thyne ee;
Bot prudence is ane inwart argument
That garris ane man provyde and foirse
Quhat gude, quhat evill is liklie for to be,
Off everilk thing behald the fynall end
And swa fra perrell the better him defend. (1755–61)

The swallow continues the idea of 'seeing' the truth in her later speech—'O blind birdis...Lift up your sicht and tak gude advertence! / Luke to the lint...'), and before the final disaster repeats her warning to 'be war'. The remarks of the narrator (1860–73) emphasize that prudence implies taking heed to the future as well as to the present moment ('where there is Prudence, there is no place for Fortune').[57]

The prologue to this fable gives an account of the cosmic aspect of divine wisdom:

The hie prudence and wirking mervelous,
The profound wit off God omnipotent,
Is sa perfyte and sa ingenious,
Excell[and] far all mannis jugement:
Forquhy to Him all thing is ay present,
Rycht as it is or ony tyme sall be,
Befoir the sicht off his Divinitie. (1622–8)

'Prudence', associated with God's 'profound wit' is here almost synonymous with wisdom.[58] It is the divine pattern of the human virtue of prudence, its shadow, but, whereas that depends on the consideration and interpretation of events in time, this is beyond time and encompasses it. (Prudence and providence are etymologically connected.) God can see everything. Mortals, however, cannot

[57] J. Cousin, *Livre de Fortune*, ed. L. Lalanne (Paris, London, 1883), pl. cix.

[58] *OED* sense 2. Cf. Wilson, *Arte of Rhetorique*, f. 17^{v}: 'Prudence or wisdom...is a vertue that is occupied evermore, in searchyng out the truthe...Under this vertue are comprehended Memorie, Understandyng, Foresight'.

'cleirlie understand nor se' God ('Our mirk and deidlie corps naturall / Blindis the spirituall operatioun'), and this is illustrated by the likening of man's soul to a bat's eye. We cannot comprehend the Creator; but His creation reveals His wisdom and providence ('that God in all his werkis wittie is'). In this fable, in short, we are shown the whole gamut of wisdom—from the Creator's wisdom to the counsels of prudence, 'bewar in tyme', from the metaphysical to the proverbial. The broad view of wisdom which emerges is a traditional one.[59] From antiquity the knowledge of the first causes and the principles of things blends with the Christian view of God as the embodiment of wisdom. God is wise, whereas man is a seeker who tries to become wise. Wisdom is also a moral, prudential and active virtue—'the learned man knows the truth, the wise man loves and does the good'.[60] There is also the proverbial wisdom of moderation and self-control—'fortified by wisdom, (man) is fundamentally committed to life, yet emotionally detached from it. He remembers the ineluctability of death, stands above the shifts of fortune, and submits to fate'.[61] In fables, as in the 'Wisdom literature' of antiquity, prudence operates at a humble level. If it is impossible to 'search the secrets of the Trinity', it is difficult in the flux of events and in the midst of deception to see the final end, to see beneath the surface. The birds are foolish because they ignore the counsel of the wise. Others—like the mouse in 'The Paddock and the Mouse'—do not even have the benefit of wise counsel.

One particular traditional application of Wisdom in the life of man has an important place—the ancient dictum of self-knowledge, 'Know thyself'. The Delphic maxim γνῶθι σεαυτόν came through to the Middle Ages, extended and adapted in various ways.[62] Perhaps the Stoic version, knowing oneself to be mortal, being aware of human limitations, helped the idea to pass into the religious literature of death:

> Knowe thi-self, that thow schalt dye,
> But what tyme thou nost never whenne[63]

[59] Cf. E. F. Rice, *The Renaissance Idea of Wisdom* (Cambridge, Mass., 1958).

[60] Rice, p. 2.

[61] Rice, pp. 9–10.

[62] See E. G. Wilkins, *The Delphic Maxims in Literature* (Chicago, 1929), P. Courcelle, *Connais-toi toi-même, de Socrate à saint Bernard* (Paris, 1974–75).

[63] Carleton Brown, *Religious Lyrics of the XIVth Century*, rev. G. V. Smithers (Oxford, 1956), p. 141. Cf. Rosemary Woolf, *The English Religious Lyric in the Middle Ages* (Oxford, 1968), pp. 86–7, Wilkins, *Delphic Maxims*, esp. chapter 5.

—a sentiment which underlies several of Henryson's *moralitates*. Another of its implications, the knowledge of the human soul, is widely adapted in more general ways in medieval religious literature. One English devotional work has the significant title 'The Cell of Self-Knowledge'. St. Bernard compares self-knowledge to a ladder by which one advances to the knowledge of all things in the heavens. It becomes a very common theme in devotional literature:

> The highest and most cheaffe learnynge is for a man to know himselffe, for by the knowledge of a mans oune selffe, he shall learne to cum to the knowledge off the bowntie and goodnes of god.[64]

But it is also found, quoted as a maxim, in a variety of non-religious contexts. Chaucer's Monk uses it when he tells the tale of Hercules (the connection with Fortune is significant):

> Lo, who may truste on Fortune any throwe?
> For hym that folweth al this world of prees
> Er he be war, is ofte yleyd ful lowe.
> Ful wys is he that kan hymselven knowe!
> Beth war, for whan that Fortune list to glose,
> Thanne wayteth she her man to overthrowe
> By swich a wey as he wolde leeste suppose.

The proverbial maxim could almost serve as a motto for Henryson's *Fables*. Chantecleir is 'inflate with wind and fals vanegloir' but at the end he speaks with a new wisdom—'I wes unwyse...I wes mair fule'. He has come to a degree of self-knowledge. The idea is implicit in the story of the unwise wether who attempted to transform himself into a dog. He learnt his lesson too late, and the *moralitas* makes it explicit for us:

> Thairfoir I counsell men of everilk stait
> To knaw thame self and quhome thay suld forbeir.
> (2609–10)

It is clearly present by implication in 'The Two Mice'. And indeed the *Fables* as a whole present a mirror for man that he may learn to know himself. As Caxton says in his Aesop: 'For men sayn comynly, who

64 Robert Parkyn, in *Tudor Treatises*, ed. A. G. Dickens, *Yorkshire Archaeological Society Record Series* cxxv (1959), p. 61.

that beholdeth in the glas well he seeth hym self. And who seeth hym self wel he knoweth hym self. And who that knoweth hym self lytel he preyseth hym self. And who that preyseth hym self lytyll he is ful wyse and sage.'[65]

From the *Fables* with all their symbolic images and their complexities, there emerges an attitude which is wise, realistic, tolerant and religious at once. It is an attitude which is perhaps not as unlike that of Chaucer as has been claimed. Henryson's judgement is sometimes severe, and his irony sharp. He has the 'tough reasonableness' of La Fontaine, an awareness of life's cruelty, and a grimmer, and sometimes more macabre imagination than Chaucer. At the same time, his sympathy for his protagonists has more than a touch of Chaucer's *pite*. He achieves almost always a balance of rational detachment and passionate sympathy. As we have seen, there survives into his *Fables* much of the grimness of the Aesopic fable of antiquity. The world of Aesop was forbidding, desolate, and without any hope of change. The human condition was indeed painted in the darkest colours. The world of Henryson's *Fables* is conspicuously one without saints or heroes, and one which has its share of hypocrites and bullies, but it is not quite as hopeless as Aesop's. It is more complex, for he has a broader, more Chaucerian view of man. He has a greater interest in personality as well as in abstract ideas. And beside the scenes of violence and death, there are moments of delight in life—the labourers in the fields, the husbandman driving his oxen, the cadger singing, the two mice celebrating, the poet walking through the wood. Joy coexists with sorrow, and comedy with tragedy. Some of the differences are due to Henryson's Christianity. He no longer sees resignation as a grim necessity, but as the virtue of patience. His Christianity reinforces the sense of the instability and treachery of the world—but although this means that he is keenly aware that joy or prosperity may be short-lived, it also means that he has the hope that wickedness will not last for ever:

> Think that na thing cruell nor violent
> May in this warld perpetuallie indure. (2765–6)

He may not be deeply interested in the possibility of social change, but the vehemence of his satire suggests, despite his Aesop's gloomy words

[65] R. T. Lenaghan, *Caxton's Aesop* (Cambridge, Mass., 1967), pp. 100–1. Cf. p. 193 below.

on the uselessness of preaching, a belief that individual men may be improved. He sees in the hope of salvation a remedy for the ills of the human condition.

His real originality lies in the way in which he has realized the complex possibilities of the traditional form of the fable. In his hands it becomes a subtle and new thing in which, under 'un éclairage oblique d'intensité variable', changing perspectives and ironies, different tones and viewpoints are made to coexist, so that the whole work achieves an imaginative harmony which is surprisingly impressive, and surprisingly reminiscent in miniature of *The Canterbury Tales*.

CHAPTER FIVE

What became of Criseyde

Before going to bed Don Fabrizio paused a moment on the little balcony of his dressing-room. Beneath lay the shadowed garden, sunk in sleep; in the inert air the trees seemed like fused lead; from the overhanging bell-tower came an elfin hoot of owls. The sky was clear of clouds; those which had greeted the dusk had moved away, maybe towards less sinful places, condemned by divine wrath to lesser penalties. The stars looked turbid and their rays scarcely penetrated the pall of sultry air.

The soul of the Prince reached out towards them, towards the intangible, the unattainable, which gives joy without laying claim to anything in return; as on many other occasions he tried to imagine himself in those icy tracts, a pure intellect armed with a note-book for calculations: difficult calculations, but ones which would always work out. 'They're the only truly disinterested, the only really trustworthy creatures,' thought he in his worldly idiom; 'who worries about dowries for the Pleiads, a political career for Sirius, marital joys for Vega?'

Giuseppe di Lampedusa, *The Leopard* (tr. A. Colquhoun)

The Testament of Cresseid is undoubtedly one of the most impressive poems of the end of the Middle Ages, but it is a difficult and tantalizing work, which has provoked an amazing variety of interpretations. Is it a straightforward sequel to Chaucer's *Troilus and Criseyde*, an erotic variation upon it, or a kind of anti-*Troilus*, a 'violent exposure of lust and its bitter consequences'? Is it a solemn tragedy, or 'a little tale of a notorious fallen woman, told with tongue in cheek'? Does its author reveal himself as a humane and sympathetic disciple of Chaucer, or as a grim moralist? Is the moral pattern a Christian one, the story of Cresseid's 'salvation according to the Christian scheme'—or is it non-

Christian, or even anti-Christian? Such contradictory accounts are given of it that we may well begin to wonder if it is not just ambiguous, but incoherent. Indeed, one recent essay on it by Professor J. A. W. Bennett ('Henryson's *Testament*: a flawed masterpiece')[1] criticizes those eulogists of Henryson 'who have obscured his faults by encomiums on "its delicate moral balance", its "reflexion of medieval assurance"', draws attention to vaguenesses, and inconsistencies, and claims that in one place 'he has misread his Chaucer, and misapplied the line in which Chaucer's narrator comments on the same situation'.

The poem's first critic, Kynaston, is clear and tough in his view of what it is about: 'This Mr. Henderson wittily observing, that Chaucer in his 5th booke had related the death of Troilus, but made no mention what became of Creseid, he learnedly takes uppon him in a fine poeticall way to expres the punishment and end due to a false unconstant whore, which commonly terminates in extreme misery'.[2] Similar sentiments about the heroine are voiced by Dryden, speaking (Preface to *Troilus and Cressida*, 1679) of Shakespeare's version: 'The chief persons who give name to the tragedy, are left alive; Cressida is false, and is not punished.' That Cresseid was a false inconstant whore, and that she was deservedly punished, seems to have been the almost universal view throughout the sixteenth and seventeenth centuries. In the popular imagination she had become the 'lazar kite of Cressid's kind', labelled inevitably as 'false'. 'For authors and readers up to 1600,' says Professor Rollins, who has charted her fate in this period, 'Henryson's Cressid was the Cressid; but lacking his sympathy, they regard her as a light-of-love who finally paid for her faithlessness and unchastity by leprosy.'[3] It is likely that the wretched end of Cresseid which so dominated her image in later times was the invention of Henryson, but it is not absolutely certain. There is just the possibility that he found it in some other source. In the Asloan MS. there is a prose

[1] 'Henryson's *Testament*: a flawed masterpiece', *Scottish Literary Journal* i (1974), 5–16. The phrases quoted in the preceding sentence are from Tatyana Moran, '*The Testament of Cresseid* and *The Book of Troylus*', *Litera* vi (1959), 21, Sydney J. Harth, 'Henryson Reinterpreted', *Essays in Criticism* xi (1961), 471, and E. M. W. Tillyard, 'The Testament of Cresseid' in *Five Poems 1470–1870* (London, 1948; repr. as *Poetry and its Background*, London, 1955), p. 17.

[2] Gregory Smith, I, p. ciii.

[3] Hyder E. Rollins, 'The Troilus–Cressida Story from Chaucer to Shakespeare', *PMLA* xxxii (1917), 383–429.

work called *The Spektakle of Luf*, which includes Cresseid in a list of well-known examples (with Eve, Delilah, Helen, Jocasta and others) 'by the quhilk men suld eschew the delectatioun of luf': '...how quyte Cresseid hir trew luffar Troyelus his lang service in luf, quhen scho forsuk him for Dyomeid, and thare efter went common amang the Grekis, and syn deid in great myssere and pane.'[4] The phrase 'went common amang the Grekis' could well be an echo of Henryson's 'scho walkit up and doun, / And sum men sayis, into the court, commoun' and 'go amang the Grekis air and lait'. If it is, it allows us to place the poem before 10 July 1492 (the date given at the end of *The Spektakle*). On the other hand, it could be argued that the phrase is perhaps not so unusual that it must come from Henryson, that if the *Spektakle* is deriving its exemplary figure from the *Testament* it is perhaps surprising that it does not refer to her leprosy, since that particular form of 'great myssere and pane' made such a deep impression later. Moreover, the author claims to be translating his book 'out of latyn'. No trace of such a Latin book has been found, but this does not mean that it never existed. If it did, it must date from before 1492, and this might well suggest that others had thought of making Cresseid end in some kind of misery and pain. Editors and critics are united in preferring the safer solution, that the author of the *Spektakle* had read the *Testament*, but there seems to be still room for doubt.

More important than such speculation is the remark of Professor Rollins that those who were responsible for the wicked Cresseid of later times lacked Henryson's sympathy. Their view comes from a very narrow reading of the *Testament*—and in some cases, one suspects, from no reading at all. However, such an opinion immediately involves us with the knotty problems of the interpretation of the poem. I propose therefore to go through the *Testament*, offering a reading of it, lingering on points of especial interest or difficulty, and attempting to indicate some of the different points of view which have been expressed, but without trying the reader's tolerance by a continual series of skirmishes with other critics.

In the first stanza, the poet introduces his work and himself with a

[4] *The Asloan MS.* ed. W. A. Craigie, STS N.S. xiv, xvi (1923–25), I, p. 279. Cf. B. J. Whiting, 'A Probable Allusion to Henryson's "The Testament of Cresseid"', *MLR* xl (1945), 46–7, J. Kinsley, *TLS* 14 November 1952, 743, J. Gray, *ib.* 13 March 1953, 176, Fox, *Testament*, pp. 17–18.

formal *chronographia*. That it is to be a rather literary poem is suggested by the way the opening *sententia* consciously draws our attention to the appropriateness of the season:

> Ane doolie sessoun to ane cairfull dyte
> Suld correspond and be equivalent:
> Richt sa it wes quhen I began to wryte
> This tragedie—the wedder richt fervent,
> Quhen Aries, in middis of the lent,
> Schouris of haill gart fra the north discend,
> That scantlie fra the cauld I micht defend.[5] (1–7)

This 'doolie sessoun' corresponds profoundly with the 'cairful dyte', for it is not, as we might expect, winter ('a Scottish reversal of the May morning on which so many medieval poems begin'), but something rather more complicated. The season is spring, but it is a spring of a bitter kind, one of those 'winterly springs' which are not unfamiliar in Northern climes.[6] Perhaps in some of its contrasts there are mysterious premonitions of what is to come. The reader may pause later in the poem to reflect that the contrast of temperature presages the heat and cold of love and of lovers, in the persons both of the narrator and of Cresseid. This is a 'perilous' spring, which yokes opposites together. From the beginning, Henryson is carefully selecting and emphasizing images and ideas which are to be developed in the pattern of his story.

It is to be a 'cairful dyte' (we may recall the 'wofull vers that wepen' referred to at the beginning of *Troilus and Criseyde*), for Henryson makes quite clear what its nature is to be: it is a 'tragedie', in its more general medieval sense of a poem with a disastrous conclusion ('tragedie is to seyn a ditee of prosperitee for a tyme, that endeth in wrecchednesse', as Chaucer says in his *Boece*). That it is a poem does not mean that it is undramatic. In its scenic construction, its violent and extreme emotions, the horror of its conclusion, and the urgency of its 'sentence', a medieval tragedy may well remind us of a Senecan play. Professor Norton-Smith has convincingly demonstrated

[5] Quotations from the poem are taken from the edition of Denton Fox (Nelson's Medieval and Renaissance Library, London, 1968). I have modernized i/j, u/v, etc., and have occasionally altered the punctuation.

[6] Fox, *Testament*, pp. 49ff.

this in the case of *Troilus and Criseyde*.[7] Following his lead, I shall argue in this chapter that the *Testament* is in its own rather more pageant-like way, a medieval tragedy in the Senecan mode, and that the tragic pattern which develops in it is of a kind which is not totally unfamiliar to the modern reader. 'Tragedy', says Dante, 'is in its beginning admirable and tranquil, but in its end fetid and horrible' (*in principio est admirabilis et quieta, in fine seu exitu est foetida et horribilis*); it 'begins in joy and ends in tears' (*incipit a gaudio et in lacrimas terminatur*) says John of Garland.[8] It is characteristically an example of the workings of Fortune (cf. *The Monk's Tale*), but individual 'character' and personal choice are by no means excluded. Here it is sufficient to point out that the word 'tragedie' might lead us to expect a 'cairfull' poem, in which lamentation (the 'wailings of tragedies') in the form of rhetorical *planctus* may play a rôle which is as important as realistic or dramatic narrative, a terrible end—'fetid and horrible'—and the combination of extreme emotions and sententious or exemplary matter.[9]

The *chronographia* continues with a further paradox—as the sun sinks

> . . . fair Venus, the bewtie of the nicht,
> Uprais, and set unto the west full richt
> Hir goldin face, in oppositioun
> Of God Phebus, direct discending doun. (11–14)

Henryson seems to mean 'in oppositioun' in its astronomical sense, but, apparently, Venus and the sun are never in opposition. It seems less likely to be 'authoris error' (Kynaston) than a deliberate suggestion of an unnatural cosmological discord.[10] God Phoebus, 'lanterne and lamp

[7] *Geoffrey Chaucer* (London, 1974), chapter 6.

[8] Dante, *Epist*. x, 10 (*Opere* ed. E. Moore and P. Toynbee (4th ed., Oxford, 1924), p. 416); John of Garland, *Parisiana Poetria* ed. T. Lawler (New Haven, London, 1974), p. 136 (cf. pp. 80–2, 102).

[9] I see no hint in Henryson's opening of a 'mock-gloomy setting' for something which is not a tragedy (Harth, *art. cit.*). In answer to one of Dr. Harth's objections—that Cresseid is not of sufficiently high rank to be a fit subject for tragedy, it may be pointed out that Henryson calls her 'lady', and makes her lament her fall from 'hie estait'. One suspects that he thought of her as in Chaucer's poem, where she has a palace, and friends among the most powerful in the city. She would surely have been dignified by her association with Troilus, and had certainly become a famous and exemplary figure.

[10] Cf. Fox, *Testament*, ll. 11–14n.

of licht', and causer of life, as he is described later in the poem, withdraws his beams, but the darkness is illuminated. Venus 'the bewtie of the nicht' is left to dominate the scene—as, in a sense, she does the poem. Her 'golden face' might suggest to us that her aspect is benevolent, that she is one of those 'trustworthy' creatures in whom Don Fabrizio took comfort. Here she seems to be the 'fair planet of love' shining with an extraordinary and perhaps disturbing brightness:[11] 'Throw out the glas hir bemis brast sa fair / That I micht se on everie syde me by...'. Henryson seems to be echoing some lines from the May morning dream in Chaucer's *Book of the Duchess* (ll. 335ff.); the sunlight from a temperate morning, marked by the absence of extremes, has been adapted to an evening scene where one extreme seems to succeed another.

The 'look' of this star does not have to strive to penetrate a pall of sultry air or of Scottish mist and cloud:

> ...The northin wind had purifyit the air
> And sched the mistie cloudis fra the sky;
> The froist freisit, the blastis bitterly
> Fra Pole Artick come quhisling loud and schill...

This, as Professor Fox has shown, is exact in terms of contemporary meteorology—'The Northerne wynde...aryseth under the sterre that hyghte Polus Articus'—and, as he says, the detail emphasizes 'the inhuman and distant origin of the baneful forces'.[12] But the north wind cleanses as well as freezes: 'for the Northe wynde is colde and drye, it pourgyth and clensyth reyne, and dryvyth awaye clowdes and mistes, and bryngeth in clerenes and faire weder'. One suspects that these details have a significance beyond their vividness and realism. It does not seem too fanciful to find in this natural process of 'clarification'—the driving away of the misty clouds, the disappearance of the showers of hail—a suggestion, a kind of symbolic premonition of an inner process, which, cruelly and sorrowfully, will take place in the heart of Cresseid. In a poem in which pollution is to have an important part, the choice of the word 'purifyit' here seems very exact.

[11] Professor Norton-Smith points out to me a remark on the extraordinary brightness of Venus in Douglas, *Eneados* IV Prol. 1–2, for which he has found a source in Martianus Capella, *De Nuptiis Philologiae et Mercurii* VIII, 883 (which in turn derives from Pliny, *Nat. Hist.* II, 6, 37); he compares Musaeus, *Hero and Leander* 111.

[12] Fox, *Testament*, p. 88 (the quotations are from Bartholomew the Englishman).

The narrator considers his own case, in a little scene which was the basis for Gavin Douglas's more extended treatment in the prologue to Book VII of his *Eneados*. From his 'oratur', that place of private meditation and study (it is in just such a place that Cresseid's visionary experience comes to her later), the 'bitter blasts' forced him to 'remufe' against his will, for he 'traistit that Venus luifis quene, / To quhome sum tyme I hecht obedience, / My faidit hart of lufe scho wald mak grene.' He had thought to pray to her 'hie magnificence', but was prevented by the cold: 'Bot for greit cald as than I lattit was / And in my chalmer to the fyre can pas'. It is not only a nice touch of wry self-mocking humour for the poet about to pray to the Queen of Love to have to retreat 'against his will' to a more domestic warmth, but it also shows a tactful, if playful, ambiguity concerning devotion to 'craibit gods'. He achieves a quite Chaucerian balance of tone in this scene; in the following lines in which he reflects on love and age, wit and detachment co-exist with 'faded' sadness and self-pity:

Thocht lufe be hait, yit in ane man of age
It kendillis nocht sa sone as in youtheid
Of quhome the blude is flowing in ane rage;
And in the auld the curage doif and deid
Of quhilk the fyre outward is best remeid;
To help by phisike quhair that nature faillit
I am expert, for baith I have assaillit.

I mend the fyre and beikit me about,
Than tuik ane drink my spreitis to comfort,
And armit me weill fra the cauld thairout...

(29–38)

This fine scene of the 'old poet' trying to come to terms with the fading of love and the coldness of age is a kind of domestic foreshadowing, a serio-comic mirror-image of what is to happen in the poem. That critics differ wildly in their interpretation of the scene—one sees him as 'a kind of medieval Yeats', showing us that 'where an ageing poet can be philosophical, a young girl can only be bitter', whereas another rejects this for a figure 'much more like a medieval Noel Coward... with a drink in his hand', as 'the device of the crusty old man as narrator'[13]—suggests that we are not meant to be forced into an extreme

[13] D. Duncan, 'Henryson's *Testament of Cresseid*', *Essays in Criticism* xi (1961), 132, and Harth, *art. cit.*, 474.

and simple position, but to give full weight both to the underlying seriousness and to the comedy. As we have found in some scenes in the *Fables*, the emotional undertones are varied and complex, and held in tension. There is something almost Shakespearean in the bold way in which the comedy of the scene—stressed by the jokes at his own expense—intensifies, rather than destroys, the tragedy of the story to come, and intensifies the very serious image-clusters and the great oppositions of the poem—cold and hot, 'faded' and 'green' love, age and youth, ugliness and beauty. The narrator's withdrawal to his 'chalmer', says Mr. Spearing, 'is only part of a more general withdrawal from youth into age'.[14] The withdrawal from the more austere setting of the 'oratur', where one might expect him to be visited by a goddess, or by a Lady Philosophy, has also a touch of comic domesticity, but even seated before his fire he is still 'the dreaming man...the man concerned with inner depths'.[15] And his perturbation of spirit, so comically and so seriously expressed, is that which we should expect of a medieval poet about to receive illumination from a vision or a dream.

He certainly has a good deal in common with the narrator of *Troilus and Criseyde*, though perhaps since he admits to having once served Venus, we should not expect quite the 'detached' view which Chaucer sometimes affects. He is no doubt a 'fictive' projection, but it is hard to agree with the view that he is a distinct 'character', an ingenuous narrator who does not fully understand the story he tells, and even harder to see how we are invited to take him as 'a figure illustrating the folly, self-delusion, and sterility of lust...St. Paul's *vetus homo*, the "old man" which represents unredeemed man, corrupt and concupiscent'.[16] His actions in this scene—sitting by a fire and taking a drink—hardly seem to me those of a figure of the sterility of lust or of a *vetus homo*. To make him into an autonomous character quite separate from his creator is as much an exaggeration as the simplest 'biographical' reading. He seems more like the narrator of the *Fables*, sometimes commenting, sometimes dissociating himself from the story, sometimes simply presenting a dramatic scene. As in that work, there is a shifting and complex relationship between 'poet' and

[14] '*The Testament of Cresseid* and the "High Concise Style"', *Speculum* xxxvii (1962), 221.
[15] G. Bachelard, *Psychoanalysis of Fire* (tr. A. C. M. Ross, London, 1964), p. 56.
[16] Fox, *Testament*, p. 55.

'narrator', but the connection seems to be a fundamental one. As Professor Norton-Smith reminds us, we need to consider the presence of the author in the totality of his work, and to be sensitive to the 'tension between an intrusive version of the artistic mind and the total poetic intelligence implied in every word of the poem'.[17] He goes on, in his discussion of the functions of the Chaucerian narrator in *Troilus*, to make some very illuminating connections with Senecan tragedy; he sees the poet now acting as a dramaturge, a presenter of the tragedy (as Lydgate imagined the ancient tragic poet), now participating in a more direct manner, as a kind of chorus, and combining in this aspect the two main rôles of the Senecan chorus—on the one hand morally alert, offering to the audience and the characters advice and philosophical consolation, on the other (a 'Euripidean' rôle), emotionally regressive, fearing all consequences, and wishing to be beyond the reach of reason, anxious to be elsewhere.

The book which the poet takes 'to cut the winter nicht and mak it schort' is *Troilus and Criseyde*, which he describes as 'of fair Cresseid and worthie Troilus'. The opposition of 'the beauty of Cresseid to the moral worth of Troilus'[18] is there, but it is lightly done. What is more important perhaps is that the adjective 'fair' becomes almost the inevitable epithet of Cresseid in the *Testament* (cf. ll. 63, 78, 92, 504, 520, 615). When, within two lines, her beauty is emphasized ('And thair I fand, efter that Diomeid / Ressavit had that lady bricht of hew') the experienced reader of the *Fables* will begin to suspect the beginning of a typical tragic and ironic pattern. The relationship of the *Testament* to *Troilus* is not a straightforward one. It is partly a 'continuation' (the subsequent history of Cresseid), and, since Troilus is not yet dead, partly a companion poem to it (for its time scheme would have to fit into the second half of Chaucer's fifth book).

The poet does not, as we might have expected, fall asleep and dream, but takes 'ane uther quair' which contains 'the fatal destenie' (a reference to the first line of Chaucer's final book) of fair Cresseid 'that endit wretchitlie'—in other words, it too is a 'tragedy'. It is not clear, as we saw, whether this 'other book' actually existed, or whether, as most believe, it is a poetic fiction used by Henryson in the way Malory sometimes uses 'the frensshe book' or Chaucer his 'Lollius' to give authority and an air of objectivity. The famous question that

[17] *Geoffrey Chaucer*, pp. 103–4.
[18] Fox, *Testament*, ll. 41–2n.

Henryson poses, 'quha wait gif all that Chauceir wrait was trew' does not seem meant to question the authority of Chaucer, but to raise once again the question of fiction's 'truth':

> Quha wait gif all that Chauceir wrait was trew?
> Nor I wait nocht gif this narratioun
> Be authoreist, or fenyeit of the new
> Be sum poeit, throw his inventioun....

It is like the witty allusion to the problem of 'feigned' poetry we noticed at the end of 'The Paddock and the Mouse', and combines a self-conscious variation on the affirmation of modesty with a lightly disorienting suggestion of the difficulties of knowing the 'truth' of stories. Its effect, in a curious way, is to enhance the 'authority' of Henryson's narration. Like any medieval poet, of course, he has a great reverence for the material of a story (in Chaucer's *House of Fame* the poets 'bear up' the fame of Thebes or Troy). He may well have remembered too that in the case of the 'fame' of Troy there was notorious dispute about what was 'authorized' and what was 'feigned of the new' ('oon seyde that Omer made lyes, / Feynynge in his poetries...'). Guido delle Colonne, historicizing Benoît's poem, uses cautious formulae like 'some say...', 'according to others'.[19] Perhaps there is also in the background the old notion that 'history' is important in tragedy—'the story is extant', as Hamlet says.[20] Certainly it is to the tragedy that the stanza ends by firmly directing us (and giving us a very accurate indication of what we are to expect—'the lamentatioun / And wofull end' of Cresseid, and 'quhat distres scho thoillit, and quhat deid').

The tragedy of Cresseid begins 'in the fifth act', already *in lacrimis*, and from there, she falls sharply to 'wretchedness'. Her rejection by Diomede is told with brutal abruptness—'Quhen Diomeid had all his appetyte, / And mair, fulfillit of this fair ladie', he banishes her, sending her (the phrase has a cruel legal ring) 'ane lybell of repudie'. Henryson stresses the extreme nature of her plight—she is 'desolait' (a strong word in Middle English), solitary, and an outcast—and of her fall, for she has become promiscuous: '... And sum men sayis into the

[19] Guido delle Colonne, *Historia Destructionis Troiae*, tr. M. E. Meek (Bloomington, London, 1974), p. xvi. The question of truth in relation to the matter of Troy is also raised by Joseph of Exeter at the beginning of his *De Bello Troiano*.
[20] Cf. Helen Gardner, *Religion and Tragedy* (London, 1971), p. 63 and n.

court, commoun.' 'Sum men sayis' is an echo of the technique Chaucer uses in the last book of *Troilus*, where by repeated references to the 'story', the 'book' etc., he contrives to dissociate himself from the terrible story of falsing that he has to tell. He gives no final explicit judgement on Criseyde, except for the words she herself uses in her last speech. In the *Testament*, however, the narrator, leaving his historian's formula, is moved by her evil fortune to utter, in his 'choric' rôle, an eloquent exclamation of two stanzas, which have caused some difficulty:

> O fair Creisseid, the flour and A per se
> Of Troy and Grece, how was thow fortunait!
> To change in filth all thy feminitie,
> And be with fleschelie lust sa maculait,
> And go amang the Greikis air and lait
> Sa giglotlike, takand thy foull plesance!
> I have pietie thow suld fall sic mischance! (78–84)

Two things are immediately obvious. On the one hand, his moral disapprobation is very forcefully and clearly expressed—*fleschlie lust*, *giglotlike*, *foull plesance*—and, significantly, in words implying pollution—*filth*, *maculait*. However, to say as one critic does, that 'in Henryson's view Cresseid was the very embodiment of sensuality, upon which he looked with fierce hatred'[21] is not only a grotesque exaggeration, but totally ignores the other dominant note in the stanza, the expression of earnest regret in the first two lines, and the explicit statement of the last: 'I have pietie thow suld fall sic mischance!' 'Pietie' (as in Chaucer) is an intense, over-flowing emotion, a profound compassion. In the *Testament*, as in other tragedies,[22] it is the great *human* virtue, shown to Cresseid by the narrator, by Calchas, by the leper lady, and by Troilus, but conspicuously not by the gods. Cresseid's plight evokes extreme and conflicting emotions in the poet—a struggle between knowledge and love, between horror and compassion—which he means us to share.

In the following stanza his 'pietie' bursts out:

> Yit neuertheles, quhateuer men deme or say
> In scornefull langage of thy brukkilnes,

[21] Moran, *art. cit.*, 22.

[22] Gardner, p. 79. On Chaucer's 'pite', cf. Gray, 'Chaucer and Pite' in *J. R. R. Tolkien. Scholar and Story-teller*, ed. M. Salu and R. T. Farrell (Ithaca, N.Y., 1979).

I sall excuse, als far furth as I may,
Thy womanheid, thy wisdome and fairnes,
The quhilk Fortoun hes put to sic distres
As hir plesit, and nathing throw the gilt
Of the, throw wickit langage to be spilt. (85–91)

He is echoing Chaucer's words on Criseyde (V, 1093–9). But the way in which the poet is 'impassioned by sympathy for the wronged Cresseid' and blames her troubles 'on a personified Fortune' has disturbed some. 'Nathing throw the gilt / Of the' are words, it has been said, 'which must be forgotten completely if Cresseid's will and death are to have their full tragic force'.[23] An easy solution is to blame an ingenuous narrator, 'a stupid and passionately involved narrator who is able to say, in consecutive lines "...sa giglotlike takand thy foull plesance / I have pietie thow suld fall sic mischance"'.[24] But this narrator, though certainly involved, does not sound 'stupid'—any more than his precursor in *Troilus*. It is surely not more 'stupid' to express compassion than to pass judgement. What of Dante, who after hearing the tragedy of Paolo and Francesca (and the judgement clearly implied), falls down as if dead, because of his *pietade*? It is possible that, as Professor Bennett says, Henryson may have misread Chaucer's 'gilteles', used by Criseyde of Troilus (V, 1084) as denying her own guilt, and that he may have taken 'sely' (V, 1093) to mean 'innocent' rather than 'hapless'. But are the narrator's remarks quite impossible? A number of points deserve consideration. There is, firstly, the possibility that 'nathing throw the gilt / Of the' is not as absolute an excuse as it sounds. 'Gilt' could possibly mean something like 'desert',[25] i.e. that Cresseid, though 'maculait' etc., did not deserve the cruel blows that Fortune gave her. The whole context, and the close link with 'throw wickit langage to be spilt' suggests, also, that the narrator primarily has her reputation (her 'name') in mind. There was certainly a long-standing 'Criseyde question'. She did not fit easily into the rôle either of tragic heroine or of unfaithful mistress. In the tradition, she was a lady of beauty and of eloquence and charm—but of a character which could be variously interpreted ('sober simplicity, courteous

23 'Cresseid in Scotland', *TLS* 9 April 1964, 290.
24 Fox, *Testament*, p. 23 (cf. p. 56).
25 Cf. *OED guilt*, sense 3.

modesty, never-failing compassion' according to Joseph of Exeter;[26] 'pliable because of great compassion' according to Guido, one who 'loved many, although she did not preserve constancy of heart toward her lovers'). Like Chaucer, Henryson is taking care to dissociate himself firmly from the anti-feminist view of her detractors that she is the exemplification of the deceit, fickleness and changeableness of women.

If we take the narrator's rôle as chorus seriously, the difficulties seem much less intractable. It should not surprise us that Cresseid herself, after the emotional crisis which comes to her later in the poem, should express a view of her actions which is not the same as that which is uppermost in the narrator's mind here. I use the word 'uppermost' advisedly. The narrator at this point certainly wants to stress her 'fatal destenye'; he has been careful to show her hitherto as an object moved by external forces (for instance, Diomeid 'ressavit' her, then 'excludit' her) and he continues here with the strong suggestion that his 'desolait' and solitary heroine is the plaything of Fortune. 'Fortunait'... 'Fortoun has put to sic distres' seem unambiguously to suggest an inevitable external force; 'mischance' seems clearly that 'accident which no foresight can prepare against or prudent wisdom evade'.[27] Cresseid thus seems the victim of Fortune, traditionally a blind and fickle *meretrix*, a mistress of arbitrary whims, who 'plays to make her power more known'.[28] And yet, with a change of perspective, it would not be hard to see Cresseid not as the victim, but as the *figura* of such a goddess. Professor Aswell perceptively suggests that in more active verbs like '*go* among the Greikis', '*takand* thy foull plesance' we have just such manifestations of responsible 'choice' rather than an unavoidable 'chance'.[29] The coexistence of these perspectives should not surprise the reader of the *Fables*, and I would indeed suggest that

[26] Book IV (from Dares), tr. Gildas Roberts, *The Iliad of Dares Phrygius* (Cape Town, 1970), p. 43; Guido tr. Meek, pp. 83–4. Lydgate in his defence of her (*Troy Book* III) reproves Guido for speaking 'cursedly' of women, and suggests that her love for Diomede came 'of tendirness and of wommanhede' ('I can noon other excusacioun, / But only kyndes transmutacioun, / That is appropred unto hir nature').

[27] Gardner, p. 50.

[28] Boethius, *Consol. Philos.* II, m. 1, '...sic illa ludit'; cf. H. R. Patch, *The Goddess Fortuna in Mediaeval Literature* (Cambridge, Mass.), especially pp. 56–7.

[29] 'The Role of Fortune in *The Testament of Cresseid*', *PQ* xlvi (1967), 472. Cf. Mr. Dennis Burden's discussion of Milton's treatment of 'hapless Eve' in *Paradise Lost* IX, *The Logical Epic* (London, 1967), especially pp. 94–6.

it is an adumbration of an ancient pattern of tragedy that emerges powerfully later in the poem, a kind of double motivation, in that we believe at the same time that men are helpless before the gods, and yet are moved by emotions and vices within themselves.[30] The narrator here is a true choric figure, morally alert and at the same time full of generous humanity and 'pietie'. Henryson is a good enough poet to let the tensions remain. At the risk of protracting this analysis, I would suggest further that the reader may now have learnt to expect, because of such tensions, to find in places in the tragedy an emotional and agitated style, with violent and intense contrasts, and an exclamatory urgency.[31]

The narrator, again the dramaturge, begins to present his action. He tells us succinctly how 'this fair lady' passed out of the town and went to her father Calchas. The reader of Troy books may be surprised to find that the Greek 'camp' seems to have become rather more permanent, and that Calchas dwells not in a tent but in a house 'far out of the toun'. Diomede too has been elevated (119) to 'Diomeid the king'. In this poem, it seems, Henryson is content to let the background fade into the generalized settings and concepts of popular romance and ballad. Here, as a matter of fact, such phrases suit his purposes quite well: the ballad-like 'Diomeid the king' has a suggestion of mysterious and far-reaching power, and the fact that Calchas lives in 'ane mansioun / Beildit full gay' makes a comforting contrast with the misery which his daughter, who 'desolait...walkit up and doun', has left. Her reception is indeed a kindly one, for Calchas is a much more amiable figure than he is in *Troilus*, and immediately expresses his *pite* with hopeful proverbial optimism: 'peraventure all cummis for the best'. In his usual manner, Henryson sets this in a pattern of dramatic irony, for Cresseid has hardly begun to drink her cup of bitterness. It is perhaps also a further dramatic irony that Calchas is (as he is not in Chaucer) a priest of the temple of Venus and Cupid: 'This auld

30 Cf. H. Lloyd-Jones, *The Justice of Zeus* (Berkeley, Los Angeles, London, 1971), p. 10, and *passim*. On similarities with ancient tragedy, the remarks of A. C. Spearing, *art. cit.*, and I. S. Ross, *SSL* i (1963), 272–3 are suggestive.

31 Cf. Panofsky's remarks (*Albrecht Dürer*, pp. 17ff.) on the dramatic style of Michael Wolgemut and his followers, in which the movements of figures are 'complicated and intensified', draperies are developed 'into tangled masses of angular ridges and hollows contrasting with violent curvilinear contours', and the illusion of depth is 'intensified by bold foreshortenings, strong contrasts in size...'.

Calchas, efter the law was tho, / Wes keiper of the tempill as ane preist...'. 'Efter the law was tho' is a significant phrase, which moves us a little more firmly into the 'antique' world of the Greeks (cf. 'as custome was' (113), 'devoit in thair maneir' (115)). We are being gently reminded that this tragedy is not taking place in contemporary Scotland (although there are plenty of echoes of that: the 'tempill' is almost immediately called 'the kirk', and Calchas has the 'orature' and the medical skill of a Scottish priest), but in the world of 'old stories', that strange world of the *roman d'antiquité* which has in it something of both past and present. Figures from the ancient, pre-Christian world are given contemporary clothes, characteristics, and feelings, and act out their fates in an eternal present. In such a world, remote and yet near, medieval authors like to show ever-recurring patterns of human behaviour, and the ancient figures are readily idealized or made exemplary. Anachronism may sometimes be used to increase the intensity of these stories of passion, so that it becomes 'une manière d'hyperbole plutôt qu'une simple naïveté'.[32]

In this section of the narrative, our attention is concentrated on the intensity of Cresseid's misery. It opens with a pattern of rejection, exclusion and sorrowful departure. She is 'destitute / of all comfort and consolatioun', and alone. She speaks to her father ('siching full soir') with a bitter simplicity:

> 'Fra Diomeid had gottin his desyre
> He wox werie and wald of me no moir.' (101–2)

Under the simple, and often formal surface, Henryson suggests by undertones her emotional turbulence and despair. She comes to Calchas secretly—'richt privelie' and (if this is the correct reading) 'disagysit'. The shame which this implies she feels so strongly makes her shrink from showing herself in public on the feast day: she 'wald not hir self present / For giving of the pepill any deming / Of hir expuls fra Diomeid the king'. It is the dishonour which her ignominious expulsion will bring her in the eyes of others that she feels so keenly here rather than the more profound and more inward shame she comes to

[32] J. Frappier, 'Remarques sur la peinture de la vie et des héros antiques dans la littérature française du xiie et du xiiie siècle' in A. Fournier, *L'humanisme médiéval*, p. 49.

feel later, but her fear of the loss of that 'name' which is an essential part of her being is none the less terrible. Readers of *Troilus* may well recall the insecurity and vulnerability of its heroine, and her terror of 'jangling' tongues. 'Shame' and 'guilt' cannot always be easily differentiated,[33] and though there is as yet not a hint of the latter, one might perhaps wonder if it is not obscurely beginning to play some part in the tautness and extremity of her emotions. She goes into 'ane secreit orature' to 'weip her wofull desteny' alone.

With considerable psychological skill, Henryson has carefully prepared the crucial scene which is to follow. He has not only shown us Cresseid's bitter shame, but has reminded us again and again of the depth of her misery—she is 'destitute of *all* comfort', 'with baill aneuch in breist', 'hevie in hir intent'. A medieval reader might well have begun to suspect such extreme and solitary sorrow, such 'passions and perturbations of the mind' likely to be the cause or the result of melancholy. He would have expected not only tears and sighs to be 'engendrid in the roote of melencolie', but also dreams to proceed from it (as Pandarus says to Troilus). He would not have been surprised to find Saturn playing an important rôle later in the poem, or at the pervasive imagery of blackness. Melancholy was, of course, thought to be the condition of having too much black bile, the effect of an imbalance or excess in humours.[34] One might well associate the disruption of the harmonious mixture of elements in the body with the repeated suggestions of a larger cosmic and spiritual disharmony. There is, however, one quite specific link with the following scene which strongly suggests that we should think of Cresseid as a victim of melancholy. In early use melancholy is always associated with anger (Gower says that it is the daughter of wrath), and in Middle English it can in fact sometimes mean 'ill-temper, anger, sullenness' ('Tundale gruched and wex wrothe...the man speke to hyme curtesly And

[33] Lloyd-Jones, pp. 25ff., E. R. Dodds, *The Greeks and the Irrational* (Berkeley, Los Angeles, 1951), pp. 17, 28ff. Cf. J. K. Campbell, *Honour, Family and Patronage* (*A Study of Institutions and Moral Values in a Greek Mountain Community* (Oxford, 1964), pp. 327–8, J. Peristiany ed., *Honour and Shame: the Values of Mediterranean Society* (London, 1965). Cf. also D. S. Brewer, 'Honour in Chaucer', *Essays and Studies* (1973).

[34] Cf. R. Klibansky, E. Panofsky and F. Saxl, *Saturn and Melancholy* (London, 1964), S. Wenzel, *The Sin of Sloth: Acedia in Medieval Thought and Literature* (Chapel Hill, 1960), esp. pp. 156ff. On disharmony, see L. Spitzer, *Classical and Christian Ideas of World Harmony* (Baltimore, 1963).

brought hym out of his malycoly', 'The kynge beyng in his malencoly, as sone as he sawe hym he sayd in great yre...', etc.).[35]

The scene is introduced with Henrysonian detail—'behind hir bak scho closit fast the dure'—hoping no doubt to achieve complete secrecy and solitude, safe from the eyes of the 'pepill', and (she thinks) of everyone. In this sacred place she falls on her knees, but what comes from her—'angerly'—is not prayer, but a passionate complaint. It is a dramatic moment: from the depths of her melancholy her pent-up emotions burst out:

> Upon Venus and Cupide angerly
> Scho cryit out, and said on this same wyse,
> 'Allace, that euer I maid yow sacrifice!'

Her exclamation is the beginning of a formal *planctus* of two stanzas. It is the first of four which Henryson gives to her at climactic moments, and it is done with typical eloquence. It is no mere decorative set piece, but an integral part of the dramatic action. Professor Norton-Smith has warned us against thinking that Senecan rhetorical decoration is non-dramatic, and reminds us of 'the traditional connection between such ornament and oratory and recitation; such language also has a connection with psychological and emotional revelation, as in Ovid's *Heroides*. These verbally elaborate passages are close to the arias in the older Italian *opera seria*.'[36] This one not only reveals very dramatically the heroine's emotions, but is the vehicle of the 'terrible deed' of the tragedy.

She sees herself as a victim of the gods who gave her 'anis ane devine responsaill / That I suld be the flour of luif in Troy'. Of such a 'responsaill' there is no mention elsewhere in the poem. It may be that this is exaggeration or fantasy on her part. On the other hand, Cupid later (279) says of her 'the quhilk throw me was sum tyme flour of lufe', and in view of the way the 'craibit goddis' behave it would not be impossible to suppose that they may have been up to their old tricks of giving treacherous oracles. It is left ambiguous. It is certainly true, however, that Cresseid does not own any responsibility on her part for having left Troilus (she is, she says, 'clene excludit' from 'Diomeid and nobill Troylus'). There is clearly—and understandably—some self-pity

[35] Gower, *Confessio Amantis* iii, 27ff. The quotations (among those cited in *OED* 'melancholy' (sense 2)) are from the *Vision of Tundale* and Berners's Froissart.
[36] *Geoffrey Chaucer*, p. 184 n. 50.

in her tone, and we recognize her need to have a 'wall of steel' to protect her: 'Quha sall me gyde? Quha sall me now convoy?' Yet there is a genuine sense of betrayal and hopelessness—'now am I maid ane unworthie outwaill', 'excludit, as abject odious'. Her recriminations increase in intensity: 'Ye causit me alwayis understand and trow / The seid of lufe was sawin in my face.' Significantly, Henryson adapts an image used of the well of Narcissus in the *Roman de la Rose*:[37] 'For Venus sone, daun Cupide, / Hath sowen there of love the seed...'. But the seed has ceased to grow green...'but now, allace, that seid with froist is slane'. As she develops the image it inevitably stands in contrast with her implied belief that the flower of love will remain forever the same, and recalls to our mind the 'faidit hart of love' and the frost at the beginning of the poem. Henryson will make us think of this again, when we see the real devastation of her beauty wrought by Saturn's 'frostie wand'. She is vehement in blaming the gods ('is nane to wyte bot thow'), and she calls Cupid 'fals' and his mother 'the blind goddes'. It is possible that this is simply a confusion of Venus with Cupid, often represented as blind. But there seems to be something very deliberate and sinister about the placing of the adjective (we may recall that eyes are of great importance in the literature of love). It causes great offence (cf. l. 283), and the insult is cruelly revenged on Cresseid's own 'cristall ene' (337). Mrs. Twycross suggests that the gods see an offensive implication that Venus is blind like Fortune (with whom the poet later stresses her likeness).[38]

Henryson may have found a hint for this scene in a number of passages in *Troilus*.[39] Indeed Chaucer's Criseyde is—or pretends to be—something of a sceptic—she says at one point that 'goddes speken in amphibologies, / And, for a sooth, they tellen twenty lyes' and quotes the proverb *timor invenit deos* (IV, 1401–8). However, from Cresseid this blasphemy seems at first startling, because unexpected. So far, she seems to have had the passivity and the adaptability of

[37] J. A. W. Bennett, *The Parlement of Foules* (Oxford, 1957), p. 87n.

[38] Margaret Twycross, *The Representation of the Major Classical Divinities in the works of Chaucer, Gower, Lydgate and Henryson*, unpub. B.Litt. thesis, University of Oxford, 1961, p. 407. Cf. Fox, *Testament*, l. 135n. In the *Assembly of Gods* (ed. O. L. Triggs, EETS ES lxix, London, 1896), ll. 374–5, Venus has 'eyen columbyne'. Again, from a different point of view, Cresseid could be seen as the *figura* as much as the victim, sharing in the falseness and the blindness she attributes to the gods.

[39] See Bennett, 'Henryson's *Testament*', p. 11. Cf. III, 1016–22.

Chaucer's heroine and nothing more. Her one active move has been to return to her father. This sudden outburst of anger against the gods is certainly foolhardy, but there is something deliberate about it (emphasized by the details of closing the door, kneeling down) which gives it almost a touch of grandeur. For a fleeting moment this pathetic figure in the 'orature' has something of the great *démesure* of a hero of a *chanson de geste* ('l'ardente révolte d'une âme déchirée').[40] At the same time it seems 'out of character', as if in her extreme misery, this passive figure has been possessed by something like the ancient *ate* (or, as Henryson might more readily have thought of it, has become 'fey', and has proceeded to act in the 'doomed' way one would expect). The pattern of an ancient tragedy does not seem too far away. She has been led to commit the 'terrible deed' through *hubris*. In her arrogance she has forgotten the lot of mortal man, and has presumed to rebel against her gods, and to dishonour them. This will incur swift retribution. Again, Henryson is perhaps suggesting a double motivation. Her action has something of the 'awful necessity' which drives an ancient hero; it is 'determined' by the disorder of humours (caused ultimately by the planets) which produces melancholy, sullenness and anger. At the same time, it is a conscious act of revolt against those whom she sees as the authors of her woeful destiny.

Nemesis comes quickly, and in an eerie way: 'doun in ane extasie, / Ravischit in spreit, intill ane dreame scho fell'. It is important to note that this dream is marked as being of a special kind. 'Ecstasy' can mean 'frenzy' or 'trance'; it is a strong word describing an intense state ('thei weren fulfillid with wondrying and exstasie, that is leesyng of mynde of resoun and lettyng of tunge').[41] Like the equally strong phrase 'ravischit in spreit' it is often used in spiritual and visionary writing. As if in 'incubation' in a sacred place, Cresseid sees in her 'uglye visioun' the judgement of the gods. This episode differs from those dreams of medieval literature which can be classified, analysed, and

[40] J.-C. Payen, *Le motif du Repentir dans la littérature française médiévale* (Genève 1967), p. 160.

[41] *Acts* iii, 10, Wycliffite version, quoted in *OED* s.v. 'ecstasy'. See also *A Dictionary of the Older Scottish Tongue*, ed. W. A. Craigie, s.v. 'extasy'. Cf. *Dictionnaire de Théologie Catholique*, 'exstase', Dom Cuthbert Butler, *Western Mysticism* (London, 1922, 3rd ed. 1967), especially pp. 50ff., 83ff., 115ff. (Augustine describes it as a 'state midway between sleep and death'). For its use in secular contexts of extreme emotion, cf. e.g. *Wallace* ed. McDiarmid, II, 427, IX, 191, Henryson, *Fables*, 490.

interpreted, and failure to realize this has caused difficulty in recent criticism. We are now sometimes told that we should reject an old-fashioned 'objective' reading of it—i.e. taking it 'as a straightforward narrative which gives a definitive account of the causes for Cresseid's sickness' or as prophetic, accounting in causal terms for the sickness—in favour of a more 'subjective' reading—it is 'only a dream', in which Cresseid 'sees mainly what she wants to', or, alternatively, in which 'the gods are projections of her own imagination and fears'. The physical result 'is not due to the fact of the dream itself but due to Cresseid's own actions or choices'.[42] This is not satisfactory; it is too easy, and it implies considerable demythologizing and rewriting. In the flow of Henryson's narrative, the terrible deed—the blasphemy—and the *nemesis* which follows it in this vision are central. It is a kind of dream-epiphany, a symbolic narrative which does not demand that we should choose either a subjective or an objective interpretation. It is a dream, and yet in it something happens. It is a 'self-reflecting' dream,[43] which mirrors Cresseid's cares and her condition—in a precise medical way, moreover, for under the influence of the planets her 'complexion' changes. The planetary gods may well be 'powers of the soul', psychological forces, and at the same time external active and influential powers which sit in judgement on Cresseid.

Henryson's description of the assembly of the gods is perhaps the most splendid of all his set-pieces. He savours each picture for itself, and yet makes it fully a part of the dramatic structure of the poem. His planet-portraits are symbolic images expressing the essence of the power—benevolent or malevolent—embodied in the stars. He has created them by a boldly imaginative development of details and suggestions from traditional astrological and mythographical lore. The ancient gods had gradually come to be astrologized, and the planets had developed personalities (Mars, red and fiery, was thought to be warlike; the distant Saturn, making his slow circuit, to be a slow old man, etc.). They may have been intangible and unattainable, but the influence they had—it was widely believed—on sublunary things meant that they were not entirely disinterested, nor always trustworthy. The new astrology of the twelfth century had blended with an enthusiastic

[42] R. Hanna III, 'Cresseid's Dream and Henryson's *Testament*' in *Chaucer and Middle English Studies in Honour of Rossell Hope Robbins* ed. Beryl Rowland (London, 1974), p. 289.

[43] Bennett, p. 11.

revival of interest in mythological stories about the ancient gods. The ancient gods, endowed with the real power of the planets, could be presented as complex characters; in poetic descriptions in the later Middle Ages they are usually both classical gods and planetary deities (in fact the details of Henryson's 'sevin planetis' owe more to the astrological strand in the tradition than to the mythographical). Gods and planets are described in dozens of books throughout the Middle Ages; they appear in visual form, pictured singly or in groups, now shown surrounded by their 'attributes' from mythology, now by their 'children', those born under their influence and affected by them in appearance, temperament or character (cf. plates 10, 11, 12). My account of Henryson's pictures makes sparing use of this mass of fascinating material, both because of the demands of space, and because it has been discussed fully by Professor Seznec and others (although, unfortunately, a most useful study by Mrs. Twycross, to which I am especially indebted, has not been published in its entirety); I shall concentrate on the imaginative use he made of traditional lore and details.[44]

The assembly is summoned by Cupid, the king 'ringand ane silver bell, / Quhilk men micht heir fra hevin unto hell', and the seven planets descend from their spheres. There is already something strange and unnatural in the setting, suggested by the mysterious and evocative detail, and by the fact that the planets leave their orderly and harmonious course round the heavens. The defendant in this trial does not find herself transported to some hill of justice; her judges descend to her in her secret oratory.

Saturn comes first, as befits the 'supreamest or highest of all the planets', as the seventeenth-century astrologer Lilly calls him,[45] but he is not a noble figure—he is 'ane busteous churle on his manier'. There are reasons to be found in the development of traditional lore which explain how a former god of husbandmen may appear 'rusticus

[44] J. Seznec, *The Survival of the Pagan Gods* (tr. Barbara F. Sessions, New York, 1953), M. Twycross, *op. cit.* (see n. 38). Cf. also the relevant sections in the studies of Stearns and MacQueen, and the notes in the editions of Elliott and Fox. For planet-children in calendar illustrations, see F. Saxl and H. Meier, *Catalogue of Astrological and Mythological Illuminated Manuscripts of the Latin Middle Ages III: Manuscripts in English Libraries* (2), ed. H. Bober (1953), Johannes Graf von Waldburg-Wolfegg, *Das mittelalterliche Hausbuch* (Munich, 1957), S. Samek Ludovici, *Il 'De Sphaera' Estense* (Milan, n.d.).

[45] W. Lilly, *Christian Astrology* (1647), p. 57.

aspectu',[46] but the singling out of this detail, without explanation here, in a god of such power and honourable position cannot but cause unease and trepidation. He comes 'crabitlie', 'with auster luik and cheir', and gives to Cupid 'litill reverence'. We would be right in guessing that he is likely to be hostile to love and to lovers (he is notoriously, as Lilly says, 'a contemner of women'). He is grotesquely, and frighteningly, ugly:

> His face fronsit, his lyre was lyke the leid,
> His teith chatterit and cheverit with the chin,
> His ene drowpit, how sunkin in his heid,
> Out of his nois the meldrop fast can rin,
> With lippis bla and cheikis leine and thin;
> The ice schoklis that fra his hair doun hang
> Was wonder greit, and as ane speir als lang;
>
> Atouir his belt his lyart lokkis lay
> Felterit unfair, ouirfret with froistis hoir... (155–63)

Instead of his traditional sickle, he carries a bow and arrows 'fedderit with ice and heidit with hailstanis'. This makes other fifteenth-century English descriptions of Saturn seem very feeble—in *Reason and Sensuality*, he has a 'frosty beard'; in *The Assembly of Gods* he is clad 'straungely', 'for of frost and snow was all his aray', has 'a bawdryk of isykles about hys nek gay', and wears a crown of lead 'cowchyd with hayle stonys'.[47] Henryson has boldly emphasized two aspects—his age and his coldness. With his sunken eyes, the 'meldrop' running from his nose, and his 'lyart lokkis', he is not only old, but horribly old. He seems almost the embodiment of Winter, with chattering teeth and grotesquely hanging icicles, 'wonder greit, and as ane speir als lang'. Traditionally, he brings intense cold, storms, frost and snow. The reader will recall the images at the beginning of the poem, and Cresseid's more recent lament that the seed of love 'with froist is slane'. He is 'of a pale, wan or leaden, ashy colour', cold and dry and melancholic, and, not surprisingly, is associated with similar maladies: 'my loking', he says in *The Knight's Tale*, 'is the fader of pestilence'. Leprosy is one of the diseases that proceed from his 'cold, dry and

[46] Petrarch, *Africa* III, 146, ed. N. Festa (Florence, 1926), p. 57; cf. Twycross, pp. 126–8, 141. Saturn, once a god of husbandmen, could appear as a peasant, and is sometimes shown as a ragged figure with a crutch; he rules over beggars.

[47] *Reason and Sensuality* ed. E. Sieper, EETS ES lxxxiv, lxxxix (1901–3), l. 1438; *Assembly of Gods* ed. Triggs, ll. 281–7.

melancholly distempers', and, as Professor Fox says, Saturn seems to have the symptoms of leprosy himself: 'a livid and discoloured complexion with a wrinkled face and sunken eyes'.[48] This astrological Saturn is entirely malevolent: 'invidus; longam tenet iram; pauca loquitur; non vult societatem'[49]—Lilly says he 'delights in deserts, woods, obscure vallies, caves, dens, holes, mountains, or where men have been buried, churchyards, etc.' Henryson has totally suppressed his mythographical connections with the Golden Age, civilization, contemplation and poetic inspiration. He has quite ruthlessly pruned traditional 'attributes'—such as Saturn devouring his young, the dragon biting its tail—which are not germane to his purpose, and boldly developed those which are, and so has created a 'speaking picture' of the planetary god's sinister power. What mercy could one 'of quhome the blude is flowing in ane rage' expect from this old 'busteous' churl, with his 'widderit weid' and 'busteous bow'?

In strong contrast comes Jupiter, 'richt fair and amiabill'. Both astrologically and mythologically, he is 'fra his father Saturne far different' ('abhorret Saturnum et eius naturas; prohibet et retrahit eum a suis malis operibus').[50] They are as unlike as Youth and Age, or as Spring and Winter.[51] Where Saturn is cold and dry, Jupiter is hot and moist. Here he wears 'ane garland wonder gay / Of flouris fair, as it had bene in May', and a gay garment of green as if he is a gallant young lord going Maying. He is very powerful—'God of the starnis in the firmament'—but benevolent (his spear is to defend us from the wrath of Saturn). Where Saturn is associated with age, coldness, disease and death, Jupiter is 'nureis to all thing generabill'.

After the serene planet Jupiter comes a frenzied and violent figure, that of the baleful Mars, 'god of ire, / Of strife, debait, and all dissensioun', writhing his face, 'schaikand his sword', foaming at the mouth, blowing a warlike horn. He is dressed, as often in illustrations and descriptions, as a knight, with 'hard harnes' and 'habirgeoun' but Henryson ignores the common depiction of him sitting in his chariot armed with his flail (cf. plate 12) in favour of this turbulent figure, foaming 'lyke to ane bair quhetting his tuskis kene'. It is as if from the

48 Fox, *Testament*, ll. 155–9n.

49 Hali (filius) Abenragel, *De Judiciis Astrorum* (Venice, 1485), f. a iii^{v}.

50 *Ib.*, f. a iv.

51 Twycross, p. 204, compares *Carmina Burana*, 94 (ed. A. Hilka and O. Schumann, Heidelberg, 1930, I, p. 122).

traditional 'attributes' of the violent god ('destructor; iratus...diligit occidere et interfectiones, rixas...stultus, non patiens; cito irascitur ira forti...non ita percipit cum est iratus...prelia facit et destruit populationes')[52] he has distilled a personification of intemperate Ire itself. His eyes—'grislie glowrand ene'—both express his frenzied and choleric nature ('grym as he were wood') and suggest the destruction and strife that come from his 'looking'. That both his falchion and his sword are 'rusty' may suggest that he is a braggart, roaring 'richt tuilyeourlyke', 'as wavering as the wind' as Lilly says.

As befits the central figure of the seven gods, Phoebus arrives with royal dignity in his chariot: 'as king royall he raid upon his chair'. Rather heterogeneous attributes surround him in some mythographical illustrations (cf. plate 12): the serpent Python whom he slew, the Muses because he is the fount of poetic inspiration, his harp, his crow, and—from his renown in divination—the laurel tree and the tripod balanced oddly on his head. Henryson concentrates on the essential features of the planetary god and his power. He is 'lanterne of licht', banisher of night, and the source and renewer of life, 'tender nureis' ('through him is born everything that is born, through him grows everything that grows'). Of all the gods his brightness is overwhelming: 'the brichtnes of his face quhen it was bair / Nane micht behald for peirsing of his sicht'. With a little display of learning, Henryson describes the four horses who draw the chariot of the sun. It seems that he is expanding, very eloquently, two lines from the *Graecismus*, a school-text:

Erubet Eous aurora, pallet Ethous
Fervet Pyrous, se mergit aquis Philogeus.[53]

Time and colour patterns are neatly combined. The sun rises 'into the orient'; Ethios is associated with the morning sun, Peros (= 'fiery') with midday, and Philogye or Philogey with the sun's setting and night. It is more than a learned display, however, for it makes this god's arrival more grand and more spectacular than anyone else's.

Venus[54] is called 'that goddes gay', but it is soon evident that she is not like the 'fair Venus, the bewtie of the nicht' who presided over the

[52] Hali, f. a iv^v.

[53] Ed. J. Wrobel (Bratislava, 1887), IX, 226–7, p. 66. Dorena Allen Wright has shown that Henryson used this in *Orpheus and Eurydice* (see p. 230 below). Cf. also Stearns, pp. 83–9, Twycross, pp. 314ff.

[54] Cf. the discussion of Venus in Twycross, *Representation*, chapter 6, and *The Medieval Anadyomene* (Medium Ævum Monographs, N.S. i, Oxford, 1972).

evening sky at the beginning of the poem. She is not benevolent or 'blisful', but intent on finding redress for her wrongs: 'hir sonnis querrell for to defend, and mak / Hir awin complaint'. Variance is her most obvious characteristic. Her array is 'nyce'—half green and half black—and in her face there is 'quhyles perfyte trouth and quhyles inconstance'. There is treachery and dissimulation as well—under her smiling she is dangerous, 'angrie as ony serpent vennemous', 'richt pungitive with wordis odious'. Her eyes are more grotesque than those of any other of the gods: 'with ane eye lauch, and with the uther weip'. This may be an echo of a detail in the tirade against Fortune in *The Book of the Duchess* (633–4)—'she ys fals; and ever laughynge / With oon eye, and the other wepynge'. It seems quite certain that Henryson (like some other medieval poets)[55] is here deliberately attributing to Venus the fickleness and the scorpion-like qualities of that unstable goddess. In proverbial lore, 'Fortune can both smile and frown', 'Fortune has a double face', 'Fortune is both white and black', 'Fortune is false'. At this point in the poem, it is suggested that the deity who has ruled over Cresseid's destiny is a Venus who has Fortune's most dangerous characteristics. The poet explains the 'taikning' in a way we may feel is a little over-explicit, though not inappropriate in a tragedy with a liking for 'sentence'. 'Fleschelie paramour' ruled by Venus is 'sum tyme sweit, sum tyme bitter and sour'. The description of the goddess embodies the traditional paradox of the duality of love, and expresses her own 'doubilnes', which delights to bring sorrow after joy. The lines are a mirror of the tragic antithesis of prosperity and misery made evident in Cresseid's story:

> Now hait, now cauld, now blyith, now full of wo,
> Now grene as leif, now widderit and ago.

And one cannot but reflect that the affections of this child of Venus who has just turned on her goddess have been similarly 'richt unstabill and full of variance'. When Venus is benevolently disposed, her children are quiet, peaceful, 'loving mirth in...word and actions...oft entangled in love-matters, zealous in their affections', and—as we see in our illustration (Plate 10)—'musicall, delighting in baths, and all honest merry meetings'; but when she is ill placed, these qualities in her child

[55] Cf. Patch, pp. 90–8, Twycross, *Representation*, pp. 404–13. Guido uses the image of the two contrasting eyes when he discusses Briseida as an example of the fickleness of women (xix), Meek tr. p. 157. Cf. Fox, *Testament*, l. 231n.

turn 'sour'—'then is he riotous...wholly given to looseness and lewd companies of women, nothing regarding his reputation, coveting unlawful beds...fantastical, a meer skip-jack, of no faith, no repute...'.[56]

Henryson obviously enjoys himself in the portrait of Mercury, who comes with book in hand, pen and ink, 'setting sangis and singand merilie', in a red hood 'lyke to ane poeit of the auld fassoun'. His attributes quite clearly express his traditional connection with eloquence, the 'polite termis and delicious' of rhetoric (elsewhere he is called 'auctor eloquentiae', has a 'gyldyn tong', etc.) and with music (Lydgate says he 'first in his harpe fond sugred armonyes').[57] He is master of the seven liberal arts, and patron of craftsmen. In our illustration (Plate 11) we can see his children busy at their works; among them may be distinguished one playing an organ (some illustrations have an organ-builder), a painter, a goldsmith, a sculptor, a clockmaker, and a scribe or clerk 'reporting' with his pen. He is also patron of doctors, and comes with boxes of 'fyne electuaris', 'syropis for digestioun', 'spycis belangand to the pothecairis'. In his final lines, where he is thinking of Chaucer's Doctor of Physic, the author of *Sum Practysis of Medecyne* indulges in a little gentle irony:

> Doctour in phisick, cled in ane skarlot goun,
> And furrit weill, as sic ane aucht to be;
> Honest and gude, and not ane word culd lie

—a nice allusion to Mercury's ancient connections with cunning and theft (he is patron of thieves, father of Autolycus, great-grandfather of Ulysses). This god is not entirely trustworthy; his golden tongue makes him into a persuasive and notorious liar, 'the author of subtilty, tricks, devices, perjury' (Lilly). Perhaps we are also meant to recall that even poets of 'the auld fassoun' were sometimes accused of being liars.

The assembly is brought to an end by Lady Cynthia, 'the last of all and swiftest in hir spheir'. Here Henryson gives us a moon-portrait. There is a homely touch in the detail from folk-lore of the churl 'beirand ane bunche of thornis on his bak', but the total effect is eerie and sinister. She is 'of colour blak, buskit with hornis twa', and her appearance gives a very clear premonition of the symptoms of leprosy

[56] Lilly, pp. 73–4.

[57] The phrases (from Servius, *Aeneid* viii, 138, *Assembly of Gods*, l. 367, Lydgate's *Fall of Princes*, II, 2482) are quoted by Twycross, pp. 451, 457, 440.

(with which, like Saturn, she is associated). She has no light of her own, she is 'haw as the leid, of colour nathing cleir' and her cloak is 'gray and full of spottis blak'. Again, there is perhaps a hint of the unstable moon-child in Cresseid, 'a soft, tender creature...unstedfast...easily frighted'.[58]

It seems natural enough that the gods should unanimously choose the swift and eloquent Mercury to be 'foirspeikar' in their parliament. In reply to his question, Cupid makes a cruel and precise speech of accusation, which puts the opposite point of view to that which Cresseid had expressed, placing the blame quite squarely upon her. He begins by arguing that anyone who 'outher in word or deid' blasphemes the name of his god does 'lak and schame' to all gods, and should be punished. In the particular case of 'yone wretchit Cresseid', he and Venus have been blamed 'with sclander and defame' (i.e. blasphemed 'in word'), for her own 'leving unclene and lecherous' (implying perhaps a blasphemy 'in deid'; cf. 'oppin and manifest', l. 305).[59] He puts the case accurately, and without any *pite*. Cresseid, he says, wishes to shift the responsibility for her own unclean living on to the gods. As he goes on to appeal to the interest of all his fellow-gods, his language becomes more exaggerated—'was never to goddes done sic violence'—and his plea for recompense more strident (he repeats the word 'pane'), until in the final line he uses the revealing word 'revenge': 'thairfoir ga help to revenge, I yow pray!' By this point the reader, if he shares any of the narrator's *pite*, may well be recalling the sinister and vindictive nature of some of the gods he has just seen, and wondering if 'yone wretchit Cresseid' may be 'wretchit' in more than one sense. At this dramatic moment, much hangs on the choice Mercury will make. He gives his counsel swiftly and smoothly, and on the face of it the choice of the highest and the lowest of the gods seems as fair a one as any. There is no explicit hint of criticism, but it is hard not to remember the notorious adaptability of Mercury, who takes the quality of the planet with which he is in conjunction ('with the good he is good, with the evill planets ill'),[60] and to feel that he is not entirely disinterested or trustworthy. The choice of those

[58] Lilly, p. 81; the suggestion is made by Twycross, p. 563 (cf. also pp. 528–30).
[59] Cf. 'Cresseid in Scotland', p. 290.
[60] Lilly, p. 77 (cf. the section on the difference of 'manners', pp. 77–8); Hali (f. a v^{v}) says he is 'convertibilis: masculinus cum masculinis: femininus cum femininis: fortuna cum fortuna: infortuna cum infortuna'.

two sinister figures, Saturn and the Moon, neither of them friends of lovers, is, quite literally, disastrous for Cresseid. Astrologically the conjunction is very bad: 'the conjunction, quadrature or opposition of Saturne with the moone causeth an evel unluckye daye for all maters:... nothing shall prosper or come well to passe then attempted.'[61]

The two gods 'proceed', 'quhen thay the mater rypelie had degest' (Henryson is precise in his use of legal language). Cresseid (in a terrible echo of her earlier outcry 'and I fra luifferis left and all forlane') is

> In all hir lyfe with pane to be opprest,
> And torment sair with seiknes incurabill,
> And to all lovers be abhominabill.

In a solemn scene Saturn announces the sentence. He 'passit doun' to where she lay, and, with a gesture which has a terrifying gentleness (quite unlike the frenzied movements of Mars), the slow god 'on hir heid...laid ane frostie wand'. (The 'wand' is probably to suggest both a magic rod, and the white staff of an officer of the court; 'frostie' has by this point in the poem accumulated a series of suggestions, and quite specifically presents a terrible 'confirmation' of Cresseid's own 'that seid with froist is slane'). It is an eerie moment when this silent, cold and profoundly wise god begins to speak. His words have the effect of a commination or a curse, and express a great and sinister power ('Heir I exclude fra the...', 'I change thy mirth...', 'Thow suffer sall'). Her fairness and beauty are to be 'excluded' (an echo of her own word, l. 134) 'for evirmair' (where she had previously said '*now* I am maid an unworthie outwaill'), and her 'mirth' transformed into melancholy 'quhilk is the mother of all pensivenes'. She is being changed, it seems, into a child of Saturn ('thy moisture and thy heit in cald and dry'). Her riches will give way to 'greit penuritie' and she will die like one of his children as a beggar.

At this point the narrator breaks in like a chorus, with an urgent exclamation expressing the audience's horror and *pite*:

> O cruell Saturne, fraward and angrie,
> Hard is thy dome and to malitious!
> On fair Cresseid quhy hes thou na mercie,
> Quhilk was sa sweit, gentill and amorous?

[61] Leonard Digges, *A Prognostication* (London, 1555, repr. Old Ashmolean Reprints, III), p. 36.

Saturn may have spoken 'lawfullie', but he spoke without mercy; he has given a sentence according to law not love. The narrator does not claim that Cresseid is innocent, that it is a case of the righteous suffering unjustly. It is against the excessive cruelty of the retribution—the 'dome' is hard and 'to malitious', the sentence 'wraikful'—that he exclaims. He earnestly pleads with Saturn to withdraw his sentence and 'be gracious', but his plea fades away with the words 'as thow was never', and we are left with the inexorable and malevolent character of the god. From here until the end of the poem the narrator returns to the rôle of dramaturge, presenting the passion of Cresseid. Cynthia descends and reads the 'sentence diffinityve' (the final sentence, which is in a legal 'bill'). The sentence is executed:

> 'Thy cristall ene mingit with blude I mak,
> Thy voice sa cleir unplesand hoir and hace,
> Thy lustie lyre ouirspred with spottis blak,
> And lumpis haw appeirand in thy face...'

Her beauty (the details of which clearly recall the spring-like description of Jupiter) is transformed to a wintry ugliness, to pollution and disharmony. And at last we are told explicitly of her disease:

> This sall thow go begging fra hous to hous
> With cop and clapper lyke ane lazarous.

The 'doolie dreame', the 'uglye vision' comes to an end, and 'all that court and convocatioun / Vanischit away'.

At this point in the poem we should perhaps pause briefly to consider the implications of this scene, for these may have important consequences for the interpretation of the latter half of the poem. This is clear from the wide differences of opinion among critics. We are urged by one, for instance, to see the poem as one which—at least at this point—'questions the divine order quite peremptorily' (the 'bitter core of the *Testament*' is 'a vision of hopelessness, a desolating sense of what a world in which there was no hope of mercy would be like'). To this, another rejoins that the Christian God is not being represented in the poem, and that the planetary deities are not to be confused with Him. Another view is that the planetary gods are the natural forces of growth and decay, operating in a secular universe. Another, that although they may be 'symbols of the inexorable natural order' and exact a mercilessly just retribution, they are in some sense surrogates for

God, and the punishment of leprosy is one sent to Cresseid by God for her blasphemy.[62]

Henryson himself may well have thought that Fortune (whether in the figure of that goddess, or in that of the planetary gods) only seems cruel and arbitrary to mortals in her 'reign' who can see but darkly, and that seen *sub specie aeternitatis* her mutability is a necessary part of an all-embracing Providence. However, if he did, he does not allow a hint of any such view to emerge at this or at any other point in the poem. When the narrator exclaims against Saturn (in words which it is hard to believe represent the views of an uncomprehending unredeemed man attached to sensuality) there is no suggestion that the planetary god is one of our 'hierdes' 'under God' (*Troilus and Criseyde*, III, 619). This is not, however, quite the same as a 'peremptory questioning of the divine order'. Henryson is not writing a theological or a philosophical tract, and there seems no reason for us to expect a coherent and self-consistent *philosophical* system. The question whether the suggestions and attitudes generated form a coherent poetic whole is surely a different one. With this in mind, I suggest that three points need to be remembered. Firstly, it has been already noticed that this is a story of antiquity, one which takes place in pre-Christian times. Any suggestion from the characters in it of a Christian providential scheme would obviously be inappropriate. The deities are not identified with the Christian God, any more than they are demythologized or explained away as demons in a Patristic manner. They act as ancient gods in the strange 'eternal present' of the medieval story. Their actions certainly raise the question of justice. Are we to believe Cupid's version of the 'crime', or Cresseid's? Cupid's accusation, though vengeful, is not irrational nor quite unjust. According to his retributive system of justice, a mortal aggression, a violation of sanctity, a blasphemy needs to be punished in order to preserve the gods' honour and their ordered world. But at the same time we are encouraged to feel a distinct sense of unease about the kind of justice some of these gods are liable to dispense. And we are led to feel a sympathy, which is by no means entirely irrational, for Cresseid's version. The narrator's outcry against the unfairness and the excessive severity of the sentence adds yet another viewpoint. These 'craibit goddis', like those of *The*

[62] Cf. Duncan, pp. 129, 134, Harth, pp. 474–5, Aswell, p. 485, Fox, *Testament*, p. 34, and see Dolores L. Noll, '*The Testament of Cresseid*: Are Christian Interpretations Valid?', *SSL* ix (1971), 16–25.

Knight's Tale, are indeed cruel as well as powerful. That one may sense undertones which are anxious and uneasy is in no way surprising. Doubt was not beyond the imaginative capacity of a good medieval poet. Secondly, it should be remembered that they are planetary gods. Henryson does not commit himself to any abstract statement about the nature and extent of their power, beyond the careful (and quite orthodox) remark that they rule 'all thing generabill' and the weather. No doubt he might have agreed with the common view that they had influence over contingent things; over plants, animals, and perhaps over human bodies, but not over the human will—'astra inclinant, non necessitant'. They may dispose a man to certain actions, but not determine them.[63] His Cresseid brings her punishment upon herself. And yet, without wishing to commit him to a philosophical determinism it must be said that we are also led to feel that in the poem Cresseid is at the mercy of the 'craibit goddis', that they are forces outside her control which govern fate. I would suggest again that Henryson's poetic imagination enjoys using something like the double motivation and double responsibility of ancient tragedy, where the gods are all-powerful, but men are free to decide and are held responsible for their actions. The gods work in and through men. That a human action may be imputed to them does not mean that the human actor is not held responsible. This brings us already to our final point, that we need to remember that this is a tragedy. In the manner of a Senecan tragedy, it generates in the reader an immense sense of unfairness, to which the narrator gives expression in his choric outburst. In the manner of a tragedy it holds contraries in tension. Its pattern of justice will not be a simple one. These gods are disinterested, and yet they are not; 'they care and yet they do not care'.[64]

When her 'uglye visioun' has come to an end, Cresseid 'rises up' and takes a mirror, which immediately reveals a terrible change in her appearance: 'Than rais scho up and taik / Ane poleist glas, and hir schaddow culd luik.' This is a very neat narrative detail, and a significant one. As Professor Bennett says 'an oratory is an unlikely place to find a mirror in'.[65] Perhaps its oddness increases its significance. It

[63] Cf. T. O. Wedel, *The Medieval Attitude toward Astrology* (New Haven, London, 1920), especially pp. 68–9, Chauncey Wood, *Chaucer and the Country of the Stars* (Princeton, 1970).

[64] Cf. Norton-Smith, especially pp. 192ff., Gardner, p. 55.

[65] Bennett, p. 6; on the following remarks, cf. E. Köhler, 'La Fontaine d'Amour

would, of course, be regularly associated with Venus (that 'self-regarding goddess'—cf. our illustration, Plate 10) or with Luxuria. Mirrors may also have magic (cf. the wise and potent mirrors of folk-lore) or prophetic powers—they may open the mysterious world of the future, as in that story of Narcissus already alluded to, which became such a favourite in the Middle Ages (and was sometimes taken as an example against pride or the madness of love). Mirrors, like eyes (the 'mirrors' of the soul), do not just reflect; they can produce an effect. They are, not surprisingly, also associated with self-knowledge, from Socrates to the medieval mystics. Here, it is true, Cresseid sees not much more deeply than the outward self, her 'shadow', but in a poem in which undertones play such an important part, the selection of this detail is suggestive. The mirror recalls the past, the 'seed of love', and the terrible present of fair Cresseid; we may wonder if it is also a hint of the future. A brief *planctus* expresses a recognition of what has befallen her, and (any scepticism and recrimination has gone) some remorse for blasphemy:

> '...Lo, quhat it is...
> With fraward langage for to mufe and steir
> Our craibit goddis; and sa is sene on me!
> My blaspheming now have I bocht full deir...'
>
> (351–4)

The 'common rhythm of life'[66] (which Henryson must have felt in Chaucer's poem) flows back to the solitary Cresseid. A child knocks at the door, and calls out to warn her that supper is ready. Henryson makes the incident marvellously pathetic and ironic. For one who had retreated in shame to the oratory, 'supper' should be a moment of

et Guillaume de Lorris' in Fournier, *L'humanisme médiéval*, pp. 148ff., J. Frappier 'Variations sur le thème du Miroir, de Bernard de Ventadour à Maurice Scève', in *Histoire, Mythes et Symboles* (Geneva, 1976), G. Bachelard, *L'Eau et les rêves* (Paris, 1966), pp. 32–8; W. Deonna, *Le Symbolisme de l'Œil* (Paris, 1965), pp. 290–300, J. von Negelein, 'Bild, Spiegel und Schatten im Volksglaube', *Archiv für Religionswissenschaft* v (1909), 1–37, Bächtold-Stäubli, *Handwörterbuch des Deutschen Aberglaubens* (Berlin, Leipzig, 1927–42), s.v. 'Spiegel', Hastings, *Encyclopaedia of Religion and Ethics*, s.v. 'Mirror' (cf. also vii, 147, a mirror used for self-examination in Shinto shrines); P. Courcelle, *Connais-toi toi-même de Socrate à Saint Bernard* (Paris, 1974), e.g. pp. 22, 49ff., 70–1, E. G. Wilkins, *The Delphic Maxims in Literature* (Chicago, 1929), pp. 68, 77–8, 108ff. See pp. 159–60 above.

66 The phrase is that of Professor J. O. Bayley, *The Characters of Love* (London, 1960), p. 98.

social warmth and domestic security, but the child's call comes at the very moment of the discovery which will lead to her final exclusion from society and family. The irony is bitterly emphasized by the innocent and uncomprehending way the child passes on her father's remarks:

> 'He has merwell sa lang on grouf ye ly,
> And sayis your beedes bene to lang sum deill;
> The goddis wait all your intent full weill.'

The exchange between Cresseid and her father (who is summoned) is wonderfully economical and telling: 'Douchter, quhat cheir?' / 'Allace!' quod scho, 'Father, my mirth is gone!' / 'How sa?' quod he....' As a priest he knows the nature of the disease ('he knew weill that thar was no succour / To hir seiknes'), as a father he expresses grief and love ('wringand his handis, oftymes said allace'). Their last moments together are moments of shared grief—'thus was thair cair aneuch betuix thame twane','...thay togidder murnit had full lang'—before she must leave on yet another solitary journey to 'yone hospitall at the tounis end'. Her parting from her father is more melancholy than her arrival—'all mirth in this eird / Is fra me gane' (that it has turned to 'melancholy' is emphasized by the repetition of the word 'mirth': cf. 316, 368, 384, 409)—and her shame is more profound:

> 'Father, I wald not be kend;
> Thairfoir in secreit wyse ye let me gang...'

Henryson's macabre imagination creates something like the Senecan theatre of the terrible in the sufferings of his leprous Cresseid (and the detail with which he treats the symptoms suggests a good acquaintance with the medical literature of his own time). The horror of the disease hardly needs documentation from social history.[67] Lepers and leper-

[67] Cf. J. D. Comrie, *History of Scottish Medicine* (2nd ed., London, 1932), esp. chapter 9, R. M. Clay, *The Medieval Hospitals of England* (London, 1909), chapters 4, 5, C. Singer, *Journal of the History of Medicine* (1949), 237–9, Saul N. Brody, *The Disease of the Soul. Leprosy in Medieval Literature* (Cornell, 1974), J. Parr, 'Cresseid's Leprosy Again', *MLN* lx (1945), 487–91, P. Richards, *The Medieval Leper and his Northern heirs* (D. S. Brewer, 1977). There is a full discussion, with many further references, in Fox, *Testament*. On Bodel, cf. P. Ruelle, *Les Congés d'Arras* (Brussels, 1965), C. Foulon, *L'œuvre de Jean Bodel* (Paris, 1958), Brody, pp. 87ff., Payen, *Motif du Repentir*, pp. 580ff.

houses would still have been a common sight in late medieval Scotland. There is ample evidence of the revulsion and disgust which the disease provoked. Jean Bodel, a *trouvère*, was smitten by leprosy and in about 1202 wrote a moving poem, the *Congés*, in which he takes leave of his friends in Arras before entering a leperhouse. At the beginning he says that he fears above everything else the shame, and the horror of the people who see him. The same intense emotional revulsion can be found in the various fictional treatments of the disease in medieval literature—*Amis and Amiloun*, *Der Arme Heinrich*, *Sir Aldingar*, etc. Society's fear was not simply of infection from the loathsome, contagious victims. Deep-seated sexual fears were—and still are, apparently—involved as well. That leprosy was thought to be transmitted by sexual intercourse, and was sometimes described as a venereal disease must have intensified the feelings about its corruption and pollution of the flesh.[68] There was 'na succour' for this 'seiknes incurabill'; Bodel says it is the disease 'dont nus hon ne respasse'. Popular medical remedies—adders baked with leeks, etc.—held out little hope; literature offered only miraculous cures, from the blood of children or of virgins.[69] Segregation, of a more or less complete sort, was the usual course of action. Reactions to this 'seiknes incurabill' seem often to have a curious duality. On the one hand it is seen as a blow from heaven; on the other as a disease of peculiar sanctity which sets its victims apart from others in a kind of earthly purgatory. It was often thought to be a punishment for worldliness or for sin, and especially for pride (der arme Heinrich is afflicted with leprosy because of his *hochmuot*). Possibly we are meant to think that in the case of Cresseid's pre-Christian *hubris*, this disease is the punishment which 'most effectively destroys her arrogance'. Bodel can manage to struggle from despair to a Christian resignation. He sees his illness as a

[68] Cf. Brody, *passim*, Fox, *Testament*, especially pp. 26–30. The early history of venereal diseases is obscure, but it seems unlikely that Henryson is describing syphilis (cf. K. Hume, 'Leprosy or Syphilis in Henryson's *Testament of Cresseid*', *ELN* vii (1968–9), 242–5); the quotations in Comrie, pp. 199ff. (e.g. (1497) 'the infirmitey cumin out of Franche and strang partis', (1507) 'the strange seiknes of Nappillis', etc.) suggest that 'grandgore' was much less familiar than leprosy. Cf. F. Saxl, *Lectures* (London, 1957), I, pp. 258–9, for discussion of a broadsheet about the spreading of the new curse. The fear of leprosy and of lepers sometimes produced hysterical panics and terrible crimes (cf. Clay, p. 56, Helen Richardson, 'The Affair of the Lepers', *MÆ* x (1941), 15–25.

[69] Cf. Comrie, pp. 87ff., Clay, p. 65, Brody, pp. 152ff.

punishment and as an example of Fortune's inconstancy, and hopes to find redemption through suffering.[70]

Most importantly, however, as Professor Fox points out, it marks the final stage in Cresseid's isolation and exclusion.[71] The medieval leper was supposed to be completely segregated: 'he must never frequent place of public resort, nor eat and drink with the sound; he must not speak to them unless they are on the windward side, nor may he touch infants or young folk. Henceforth his signal is the clapper, by which he gives warning of his approach and draws attention to his request.' The seclusion of a leper was a kind of 'figure' of death. In the Sarum office, the leper heard mass kneeling under a black cloth set upon two trestles, 'after the manner of a dead man'. The priest is to lead him to the church, from the church to his house 'as a dead man'; before mass he is to make his confession, 'and never again'. He is finally led to the open fields, the prohibitions are read out, and he is left with the words, 'have patience, and the Lord will be with thee'.

Christian patterns of consolation are not available to Cresseid, as she is 'convoyit' by her father (like the passive figure we saw earlier in the poem) through the 'secreit yet', and 'delyverit' in at 'the spittaill hous'. We are reminded again of her altered appearance ('with bylis blak ovirspred in hir visage') at the scene of her reception into her new dwelling place. Her 'hie regrait' and 'still (? quiet) murning' suggest both some dignity in her sorrow, and also perhaps deep emotions barely kept under control. It also suggests to some of the leper folk that she is of noble kin, and, as the poet remarks, 'with better will thairfoir they tuik hir in'. There is a touch of satire here at their snobbishness (even in such ghastly circumstances) but it emphasizes a deeper pathos—neither her noble kin nor their deference to it is of much moment here. Henryson is carefully preparing for another scene. He marks it with a *chronographia*:

> The day passit and Phebus went to rest,
> The cloudis blak overheled all the sky... (400–1)

He reminds us again of her solitariness ('ane sorrowful gest') in that 'uncouth fair and harbery' and of the melancholy and darkness of her spirit ('the bylis blak' on her face suggest the physical effect of her 'humour'). She lies

[70] Cf. Fox, *Testament*, especially pp. 40ff., Brody, pp. 101ff., Clay, pp. 66ff.
[71] Fox, *Testament*, p. 37; for the office of seclusion, see Clay, pp. 273–6.

In ane dark corner of the hous allone,
And on this wyse, weiping, scho maid hir mone.

Her 'mone' is an elaborate *planctus* of seven stanzas in a different metre (and marked as 'The complaint of Cresseid' in the early editions). It is perhaps Henryson's finest piece of rhetorical writing, a great tragic *aria* for his heroine at the lowest ebb of her fortune. Its exclamations are emphasized by heavy alliteration:

O sop of sorrow, sonkin into cair,
O cative Cresseid, now and ever mair
Gane is thy joy and all thy mirth in eird;
Of all blyithness now art thou blaiknit bair...

The antithetical style expresses her conflicting emotions, and the contrasts of her former joys and her present miseries. What has been said of some of the expressions of remorse in the French *romans d'antiquité* seems very true of this lament: 'la douleur poignante de ce remords trop tardif est soulignée par les exclamations et l'invective traditionnelle "Caitive lasse"—malheureuse que je suis—...il s'agit bien d'un *Carpe Diem*, le plus désespéré, celui que l'on prononce alors qu'on est passé à côté du bonheur et que ce bonheur est définitivement aboli.'[72] In the manner of some other medieval laments (cf., for instance, some of the speeches of the victims in the *Dance of Death*) the speaker seems sometimes to step out of a setting in time and place, and to become a universal and exemplary figure. The formality and the 'abstraction' intensify the emotional force. The speech becomes a highly dramatic and self-revelatory set piece.

Cresseid begins by addressing herself, '...O cative Cresseid', as the object of the tragedy, and maintains this for the first four stanzas of the *planctus*, with one exception. At the end of this first stanza, her emotions burst out in a couplet near to despair:

Under the eirth, God gif I gravin wer,
Quhair nane of Grece nor yit of Troy micht heird!

In the second and third stanzas, we have a fine example of the *Ubi Sunt* theme:

[72] Payen, *Motif du Repentir*, p. 304. On the tradition of *planctus* cf. M. Alexiou and P. Dronke, 'The Lament of Jephtha's Daughter: Themes, Traditions, Originality', *Studi Medievali*, 3rd ser., xii (1971), 819–63, M. Alexiou, *The Ritual Lament in Greek Tradition* (Cambridge, 1974).

Quhair is thy chalmer wantounlie besene,
With burely bed and bankouris browderit bene;
Spycis and wyne to thy collatioun,
The cowpis all of gold and silver schene...

and Henryson makes her memory play lovingly over the details of her former life of splendour—the delicate food and the 'gay garments with mony gudely goun'. He is a good enough poet to exploit to the full the possibility of the two 'voices' which this poetic theme offers. That of the wise man, meditating on the presence of death, warns us that all this has passed for ever—but underneath, the voice of memory, clinging to life, recalls the joyous moments of the past, and attempts to save them from devouring time. The final line of the stanza—'all is areir, thy greit royal renoun!'—is a desperate return to the present misery. Henryson's decorum forbids him from suggesting explicitly the Christian and penitential setting in which the poetic theme of *Ubi Sunt* is often (though not always) found. Perhaps in 'wantounlie' (luxuriously) we may hear the moralist's voice warming to the *topos*—or perhaps his heroine's remorse is momentarily tinged with something more like repentance. 'All is areir' is a simple, sorrowful lament for lost happiness. The following stanza is one of pure regret. The voice of memory recreates a wonderful lyrical picture of the past pleasures of courtly life—the gardens (beloved of Venus's children), the Maying, the delights of the singing of the birds, the 'royall rinkis in thair ray'. Only the first interrogative 'Quhair is...' and the context of the lament remind us that spring, love, and delight have passed. The effect is to increase the grief immeasurably. The melancholy person, we may recall, is supposed to remember more clearly and vividly than others, and—proverbially—sorrow is the worse because of the joy that precedes it. The next stanza (425–32) gives us the elegiac answer to the repeated rhetorical questions—'all is decayit' (and 'decayit' is a terribly precise word). We are back in cruel actuality—'darknes dour', the 'lipper ludge' (as against the 'burelie bour', with its suggestions of courtly romance), 'ane bunche of stro' to sleep on, and for food 'mowlit bred, peirrie and ceder sour'. All that remains are the emblems (and the essential equipment) of the leper—'Bot cop and clapper now is all ago'. Now Cresseid's sorrow bursts out in a personal expression ('my' and 'I' are used six times in nine lines)—

My cleir voice and courtlie carrolling,
Quhair I was wont with ladyis for to sing,
Is rawk as ruik, full hiddeous, hoir and hace...

—and she ends with one simple exclamation which, within the formal structure of the *planctus*, expresses the totality of her misery:

Sowpit in syte, I say with sair siching,
Ludgeit amang the lipper leid, 'Allace!'

In the final two stanzas she addresses the 'ladyis fair of Troy and Grece'. She presents herself to them as an exemplary figure, and speaks as one. We are far now from the verisimilitude of the *Fables*; Henryson is concerned with the expressive moment, and makes his heroine address an audience in the manner of Senecan tragedy. It is not, in fact, entirely unmotivated. She is, as it were, now dead, and she speaks as the warning voice from beyond the grave in the medieval religious lyrics (or of Lazarus in the plays)—and even echoes their formula, 'such as I am, such shall ye be':

Be war in tyme, approchis neir the end,
And in your mynd ane mirrour mak of me:
As I am now, peradventure that ye
For all your micht may cum to that same end...

Significantly she offers herself as 'ane mirour'. The final stanza drives home her message: 'nocht is your fairnes bot ane faiding flour...'. Beauty and glory are transient ('exempill mak of me in your memour'). She ends, urgently repeating her appeal for prudence, and a warning of the instability of Fortune:

Be war thairfoir, approchis neir your hour;
Fortoun is fikkill quhen scho beginnis and steiris.

Yet, even though she speaks thus as an exemplary figure, she can hardly accept her destiny:

Thus chydand with hir drerie destenye,
Weiping scho woik the nycht fra end to end....

And it is, as Henryson says bleakly, 'all in vane'. Her grief cannot be assuaged.

Again, there is a little transitional scene in which 'ane lipper lady' attempts to show *pite*, and comfort her—but her proverbial wisdom is cruelly ironic: 'mak vertew of ane neid' (possibly the implication is stronger than simply 'making the best of a bad job', but the Stoic counsel of deriving *virtus* from *necessitas* is hardly more consoling—'thair was no buit'). But we are immediately plunged into another scene (the narrative is now moving swiftly to its close). The Trojan knights, led by worthy Troilus, return victorious to Troy past the leper-house 'with greit tryumphe and laude victorious'—'richt royallie thay raid'—and the lepers ask them for alms. It seems as if once again we are back in the old noble, chivalric life with 'the royall rinkis in thair ray / In garmentis gay...'. It is a fine moment. But the phrase which celebrates their victory—'with greit tryumphe and laude victorious'—cannot but recall Cresseid's phrase in her lament, 'nocht is your famous laud and hie honour / Bot wind inflat in uther mennis eiris'—and we see it all in a new relativity. It is, for the lepers, a splendid reminder of the glory of the life from which they are excluded; at the same time, they remind us of the transience of chivalrous 'tryumphe'.

Recognition scenes are frequent in medieval literature, and often very impressive. Among many, we might recall that in *Sir Orfeo*, where the two lovers meet in the wilderness, and though they recognize each other, do not speak, or the fine scene in Malory, where Isolde sees Tristram 'waxed leane and poore of fleysshe': 'so whan the quene loked uppon Sir Trystramys she was nat remembird of hym, but ever she seyde unto dame Brangwayne, "Mesemys I shulde have sene thys man here before in many placis." But as sone as Sir Trystramys sye her he knew her well inowe, and than he turned away hys vysage and wepte.'[73] But Henryson's stands out among them all. It is a recognition scene in which there is apparently no recognition at all. The lepers cry out for alms, as they might have in contemporary Scotland:[74]

> Than to thair cry nobill Troylus tuik heid,
> Having pietie, neir by the place can pas

[73] *Sir Orfeo* ed. A.J. Bliss (2nd ed., Oxford, 1966), ll. 319–30 (cf. Henryson's handling of this scene, pp. 226 below), Malory, ed. Vinaver (Oxford, 1946), II, p. 501 (quoted by Bennett, p. 13).

[74] Cf. the illustration in MS. Lansdowne 451 (reproduced in Clay and Brody) of a seated leper with a large hat, holding a bell. The *titulus* reads 'sum good my gentyll mayster for god sake'. Clay (p. 69) compares the *Early English Legendary*, where a leper cries to St. Francis, 'sum good for godes love'.

Quhair Cresseid sat, not witting quhat scho was.
Than upon him scho kest up baith hir ene,
And with ane blenk it come into his thocht
That he sumtime hir face befoir had sene,
But scho was in sic plye he knew hir nocht;
Yit than hir luik into his mynd it brocht
The sweit visage and amorous blenking
Of fair Cresseid sumtyme his awin darling. (495–504)

The narrator then gives an explanation in terms of Aristotelian psychology of the way in which Troilus's memory of Cresseid survives.[75] It has a slightly pedantic air—as Professor Bennett remarks, 'it is as if the pedantic and irrepressible Eagle of *The House of Fame* had suddenly intruded as commentator on the last book of Troilus'. It may perhaps be argued in Henryson's favour here that a momentary rest from the high tragedy is effective, especially when it is done in a Chaucerian manner by a pedantic digression on what seems to be a peripheral aspect of the scene. It is rather as if by attempting to explain what is happening in Troilus's mind at this moment, he is drawing our attention to the mysterious undertow in this strange meeting, and preparing us for the working of memory in Cresseid's case. She is 'in sic plye' that he cannot fully recognize her, and she, although she 'kest up baith hir ene' (those eyes which were once 'cristall'), does not even half-recognize Troilus. Henryson's scene, as often, is true if unpalatable—time and long distress have eroded the features and the memory of love. Yet, just as in happier stories of love, love 'comes through the eyes'; this 'luik' produces in Troilus a powerful emotional and physical effect. In place of the dominant imagery of darkness, wintry cold and the 'faded heart of love' we are shown a renewal of the 'fire of love':

Ane spark of lufe than till his hart culd spring
And kendlit all his bodie in ane fyre;
With hait fewir, ane sweit and trimbling
Him tuik, quhill he was reddie to expyre.

It remains mysterious: 'and nevertheless not ane uther knew'. His reaction is immediate and generous. With an impulsive gesture (which

[75] Cf. Stearns, pp. 98–105, Fox, *Testament*, ll. 505–11n. Cf. also M. W. Bundy, *The Theory of Imagination in Classical and Medieval Thought* (University of Illinois Studies in Language and Literature xii, 1927).

seems to form a pattern with Cresseid's action when 'scho kest up baith hir ene') his gifts 'in the skirt of Cresseid doun can swak'. The verb *swak* ('dash, throw') seems to crystallize the tense perplexed emotions of the scene. It seems as contrary to the sinister way Saturn 'laid' his frosty wand on Cresseid, as the 'knichtlie pietie' and 'greit humanitie' of the 'gentill and fre' Troilus is to the gods' cruel verdict: 'and to all lovers be abhominabill'. Troilus rides away to the town, pensive in heart, and with a nice touch the outside world—even if it is merely the constricted one of the group of lepers—is brought in by the slightly 'gossipy' way the other lepers notice the knight's 'affection':

'Yone lord hes mair affectioun,
How ever it be, unto yone lazarous
Than to us all; we knaw be his almous' (530–2)

With considerable skill, Henryson has the little exchange that follows ('Quhat lord is yone, quod scho... 'Yes', quod a lipper man, 'I knaw him weill; / Schir Troylus it is, gentill and fre') trigger a 'delayed recognition' in Cresseid. It comes as a deep emotional shock:

Stiffer than steill thair stert ane bitter stound
Throwout hir hart, and fell doun to the ground.

One can hardly avoid thinking here of her earlier 'ecstasy', and it is perhaps not too fanciful to see other similarities. At a submerged emotional level, what has occurred has also been a vision, potent in significance and in effect, an implied judgement, and perhaps a further 'recognition' of herself as if in a mirror. This emotional scene culminates in her final *planctus* ('ever in her swouning cryit scho thus...'). We are immediately aware of a profound change. She begins with the exclamation 'O fals Cresseid and trew knicht Troylus' and repeats these words twice as a refrain. She speaks forthrightly as 'I':

Thy lufe, thy lawtie, and thy gentilnes
I countit small in my prosperitie,
Sa efflated I was in wantones,
And clam upon the fickill quheill so hie.

For the first two stanzas she maintains this strong opposition of 'I' and 'thou', parallel to 'fals Cresseid and trew knicht Troylus'. The antithetical style we saw in the earlier *planctus* here expresses extreme polarities—'false' and 'true', 'chaste' and 'lecherous'. It is perhaps this passage more than any other which is responsible for fixing the sixteenth-century stereotypes of the two lovers, but it is important to notice that here it is not the poet's judgement, but that of the heroine upon herself. It arises from her psychological and moral state. Although she uses the image of Fortune's 'fickle' wheel, now she blames herself—it was she who 'climbed' upon it. The faith and love she promised to Troilus was a mirror of Fortune: 'in the self fickill and frivolous'.

The effect of these repeated contrasts is to set up an ideal of noble love, embodied in Troilus, which she has totally betrayed:

> For lufe of me thow keip[i]t continence,
> Honest and chaist in conversatioun...

Its qualities are 'lawtie', 'gentilnes', 'trewth'; it is also a knightly love—

> Of all wemen protectour and defence
> Thou was, and helpit thair opinioun...

whereas her love has been ignoble:

> My mynd in fleschlie foull affectioun
> Was inclynit to lustis lecherous.

Her contrast of purity and pollution is powerfully expressed (and arises very naturally from her terrible state and circumstances). It is understandable also that she should exaggerate her depravity. An inclination 'to lustis lecherous', though no doubt real and reprehensible enough, has hardly been a characteristic of her whole life—but in her mood there will be no excusing, no cry like the poet's 'nathing throw the gilt of the'. As in her earlier lament, she speaks out as an exemplary figure, this time to 'lovers':

> Lovers be war and tak gude heid about
> Quhome that ye lufe, for quhome ye suffer paine...

'Richt few' can be trusted to be true—'Tak thame as ye find, / For thay ar sad as widdercok in wind'. She continues in this vein in her final stanza, arguing from her recognition of her own 'greit unstabilnes' ('brukkil as glas' she says, using the word of her detractors, l. 86) to

> Traisting in uther als greit unfaithfulnes,
> Als unconstant, and als untrew of fay.

Pessimistically, she says 'thocht sum be trew, I wait richt few ar thay'. This bleak and bitter view of the *trouthe* of women sounds almost like the misogyny of the old knight in the *Spektakle of Lufe* or of some of the remarks at the end of the *Filostrato*, but there is something sad as well as bitter about the remark 'I wait richt few'. Her pessimism arises directly from her disgust with her own behaviour, which she regards as 'abhominabill' in contrast to the way the noble Troilus upheld the 'opinioun' of women. She ends firmly by assuming responsibility herself: 'nane but my self as now I will accuse'.

Possibly, in the manner of one in the grip of remorse, she has exaggerated her wickedness, and despairingly extended it further than calm reason would allow, but such exaggeration is only too comprehensible psychologically. Her remorse in this last speech is like that of the heroes and heroines of the *roman d'antiquité*: 'le remords, c'est la faute en elle-même, la faute non résolue, ou encore...la faute devenue consciente, et par suite douloureuse' (in contradistinction to repentance, which with its contrition leading to satisfaction, is a 'solution'); '...il y a dans le roman antique un certain désespoir qui est aux antipodes du repentir chrétien.'[76] We might not wish to maintain quite such an absolute distinction, but the tenor of Cresseid's last *planctus* certainly suggests remorse, rather than repentance in a specifically Christian sense. Shame and guilt are intertwined in the speech (as one might expect to find in a work produced by a late medieval Christian culture). Shame, the loss of honour caused by a failure to approach some ideal pattern of conduct, is dominant throughout her opposition of the noble love of Troilus to her own behaviour. It is a public shame—she speaks 'openly' to all lovers—but it is something deeper now than her earlier fear of the jangling tongues of the 'pepill': 'O fals Cresseid'. However, a word like 'fals' in a poem from this period implies guilt as well as shame, guilt in the sense of a *transgression* of interdicted limits, a defiance of the commandments of God (and other words in her speech, like 'wantones', 'fleschlie foull affectioun', would quite clearly suggest this also to Henryson's audience).

Her mind reaches back to the beginning of her calamities, the 'falsing' of Troilus, and conflates it with her later 'fleschlie lust', her

[76] Payen, *Motif du Repentir*, pp. 18 (quoting W. Jankelevitch, *La Mauvaise Conscience* (Paris, 1933)), 19. In the nature of things, Cresseid can hardly make amends (cf. 589–90); the 'royall ring' is to be returned to Troilus 'to mak my cairfull deid unto him kend'.

'leving unclene and lecherous' which Cupid says she throws back on her gods in her blasphemy. What happens, however, does not seem to be 'the resolution of the poem: the true repentance of Cresseid and the salvation of her soul'.[77] Such plainly Christian judgements are kept out of this 'antique' tragedy. The heroine's judgement of herself, 'fals Cresseid', cannot be a fully sufficient description of her as she has been presented to us in the poem, but her remorse clearly marks a change in her attitude. She has come to some kind of self-knowledge ('nane but my self as now I will accuse'). By a pathetic irony she sees more clearly when physically she is almost blind. Perhaps it is as if

> The northin wind had purifyit the air
> And sched the mistie cloudis fra the sky.

If it is not a Christian repentance or conversion, what has happened to her is a spiritual change of some kind. The effects of the delayed moment of recognition, and the marvellous working of memory seem to have brought about a sudden moment of awakening, a moment of self-discovery. Even more than the incidents in the *Fables* discussed in an earlier chapter, this may remind us of a Joycean 'epiphany'. The sudden recalling of the past puts the present in a new perspective.[78]

The ending of the poem has a peculiar nobility and force. Cresseid becomes an active figure again—if only to write her testament and to prepare for death, an important and solemn moment in medieval literature, as in medieval life: 'cet acte essentiel de la vie des gens du moyen âge, accompli non seulement par les riches, par ceux qui possèdent, mais par tous, par ceux qui n'ont que les hardes qu'ils portent sur leur dos...Il est la conclusion de la méditation passionnée de la mort; il exprime le sens du transitoire: constate le terme du pèlerinage accidenté qu'est la vie.'[79] It is as if Cresseid is preparing to embark upon her final journey. Her will is patterned on contemporary wills, but again any explicitly Christian references are suppressed. Now

[77] Tillyard, p. 17.

[78] Cf. M. Beja, *Epiphany in the Modern Novel* (London, 1971), especially p. 15 on the 'retrospective epiphany', 'in which an event arouses no special impression when it occurs, but produces a sudden sensation of new awareness when it is recalled at some future time' (cf. also pp. 40–1).

[79] P. Champion, *Histoire poétique du 15e siècle* (Paris, 1923), I, pp. 245–6. On the popularity of the form, see W. H. Rice, *The European Ancestry of Villon's Satirical Testaments* (Syracuse University Monographs I, New York, 1941). Cf. *Le Testament du gentil Cossois* mentioned above, p. 5.

emptied of 'self', she commits her body to dissolution, 'with wormis and taidis to be rent', her few possessions to the leper folk 'to burie me in grave'. She returns to Troilus the ring he once gave her 'in drowrie', 'to mak my cairfull deid unto him kend'. She 'concludes' shortly, committing her spirit to Diana:

> My spreit I leif to Diane, quhair scho dwellis,
> To walk with hir in waist woddis and wellis.

The implications of these evocative lines are enigmatic. It seems most unlikely that we are to think of Diana as a figure of the Trinity or as some surrogate for God. It seems more plausible to suppose that the spirit of Cresseid, her 'lustis lecherous' now gone, will join the train of that chaste goddess, and return to a purity which lies far beyond the beginnings of Henryson's poem.[80] Her last words are a simple and harrowing exclamation as she is suddenly reminded again of her falsing (and here Diomeid is contrasted with Troilus and his 'trew lufe', not linked with him as he was in her outburst against the gods (l. 122)):

> 'O Diomeid, thou hes baith broche and belt
> Quhilk Troylus gave me in takning
> Of his trew lufe', and with that word scho swelt.

She is buried, and the news of her death brought to Troilus produces in him a kind of 'lesser death': 'he swelt for wo and fell doun in ane swoun.' His remarks are brief and austere—'I can no moir, / Scho was untrew and wo is me thairfoir.' Indeed, nothing can be done; his remarks are just, but merciful (he speaks 'siching full sadlie'). We begin to move away from the 'history' now almost concluded, with the phrase 'sum said'—'sum said he maid ane tomb of merbell gray...', with name and superscription 'in goldin letteris'. Tombs of 'marble grey' with inscriptions in gold are by no means uncommon in

[80] Diana is here probably to be seen primarily as the goddess of maidenhood (cf. *Knight's Tale*, 2300–10); Cresseid wishes for peace, purity and 'fredom'. Henryson does not have her body left unburied among false lovers in a sad valley, as is the fate of Briseida in the fifteenth-century *Hospital d'Amours* (formerly attributed to Chartier; cf. *Les Œuvres de Maistre Alain Chartier*, ed. A. du Chesne Tourangeau (Paris, 1617), pp. 733–4), but he does not give her a heroic apotheosis. Twycross (pp. 543ff.) suggests that her spirit may join the train of the untimely dead and the 'taken', who follow her 'quhilk by the Gentiles was called Diana, and amonst us the Phairie'. It is unlikely that Cresseid would wish for such a fate herself, but Henryson may possibly have had something like this in mind.

medieval literature,[81] but here, as well as removing the story to the generalized and universalized settings of romance, the contrast in colour and especially the 'goldin letteris' of her epitaph are vivid and appropriate. They seem to suggest more than the splendour and happiness of former times. The epitaph is austere, and moving:

'Lo, fair ladyis, Cresseid of Troyis toun,
Sumtyme countit the flour of womanheid,
Under this stane, lait lipper, lyis deid.'

The final stanza, in which the narrator addresses 'worthie wemen', has been criticized as a laboured and unnecessary *moralitas*. Perhaps its wordiness comes as something of an emotional release after the austere ending of the tragedy. The narrator in his choric rôle speaks earnestly and directly to his audience, selecting, as in the *moralitates* of the fables, a single important moral strand from his story for emphasis—'ming not your lufe with fals deceptioun'—and brings it all to an abrupt and enigmatic conclusion—'sen scho is deid I speik of hir no moir'—suggesting perhaps both the proverbial *de mortuis*, 'rayle not upon him that is dead', and the final silence of tragedy—'ther is namore to say'.

If we do not follow Tillyard and others in finding in Cresseid's tragedy 'the story of her salvation according to the Christian scheme' or 'redemption' or 'healing', I would argue that although it contains bitterness and pessimism, and expresses a deep sense of the impermanence of life, it is not totally bleak and hopeless. Cresseid gains some nobility and dignity, and painfully and late achieves some self-knowledge. Though she dies a leper and in misery, the victim both of herself and of the cruel verdict of the powerful gods, we feel that human love and human values are not utterly crushed. *Pite*, that great expression of love, is continually present—in the comments of the narrator, in the kindness shown to her by the human characters in the story. And the spiritual awakening which comes to her at the end seems quite clearly to be caused by a human encounter and by the memory of *trew lufe*, *gentilnes*, and humanity embodied in a person. Noble and 'gentle' love, and the virtues that flow from it, have considerable power. But it would certainly be an exaggeration to

[81] Cf. Lydgate, *Troy Book*, ed. Bergen, EETS ES xcvii, ciii, cvi, cxxvi (1906–20), II, 7520–36 (Teuthras) (cf. also I, 1368, II, 505, 579, III, 2201, Malory ed. Vinaver, I, pp. 72, 91). Heinrich von Veldeke's *Eneide*, 2509–21 has a fine epitaph for Dido, (ed. O. Behagel, Heilbronn, 1882, pp. 102–3).

suggest anything like a 'redemption through love'. The two human lovers remain forever apart—'yone lord' and 'yone lazarous'. Those who would impose neat moral interpretations on this poem would destroy its tragic pattern, which holds its contraries in tension. 'The situation is somewhat Euripidean' says Mr. Spearing, 'gods who are powerful and cruel are set against human beings who are impotent, foolish and wicked, but who yet, in being capable of suffering, demand our emotional involvement, our compassion.'[82] However hopelessly, love and human affection assert themselves, in the worst circumstances and against the curse of the gods. From the contemplation of the suffering comes not only compassion, but understanding: 'the sky was clear of clouds'.

[82] *Art. cit.*, p. 224.

CHAPTER SIX

'New Orpheus'

The usual first reaction of the modern reader of *Orpheus and Eurydice* is one of disappointment, a feeling that this *conte moralisé* does not do justice to the richness of the myth. Gregory Smith says rather glumly that 'while it reproduces the classical story with reasonable accuracy, it superimposes on the plain narrative a philosophical purpose'.[1] Further study shows it to be a rather more interesting work. Our illustration (Plate 13, from a late fifteenth-century copy of Christine de Pisan's *L'Epistre d'Othéa*) is a salutary reminder that the attitudes to the story of Orpheus and Eurydice which were current in Henryson's day differed markedly from our own. The two lovers, in late medieval garb, emerge from the gateway of an underworld which has been transformed into a *città dolente*. Its association with the medieval image of hell-mouth is indicated not only by its demons but by the smoke or flame that pours from the window of the tower behind the drawbridge. Orpheus touches his harp—which had long replaced his lyre—as he casts the fatal backward glance. If we examine briefly the 'mental sets' medieval readers had of the myth, and the versions in which it came to them, we can see that Henryson has contrived to fashion a poem, which, if it is not such an impressive imaginative whole as the *Fables* or the *Testament of Cresseid*, shows some talent and originality, and deserves the title Gavin Douglas gave it—'New Orpheus'.[2]

[1] I, p. lii.

[2] In a note to *Eneados* I, ed. D. F. C. Coldwell, STS 3rd ser. xxv, p. 19 (cf. p. 230 below). On Henryson's poem, see especially K. R. R. Gros Louis, 'Robert Henryson's *Orpheus and Eurydice* and the Orpheus traditions of the Middle Ages', *Speculum* xli (1966), 643–55; cf. also R. J. Manning, 'A Note on Symbolic Identifications in Henryson's "Orpheus and Eurydice"', *SSL* viii (1971), 265–71. On medieval treatments of the legend, see Klaus Heitmann, 'Orpheus im Mittelalter', *Archiv für Kulturgeschichte* xlv (1963), 253–94; also J. B. Friedman, *Orpheus in the Middle Ages* (Cambridge, Mass., 1970).

The immense popularity of the story in the Middle Ages certainly owes something to its mythic potential. It seems to be one of those myths which, as Professor Kirk says, 'palliate a dilemma by revealing its divine and ineluctable origin', demonstrating the impossibility of evading the decree of the gods: 'that mortals cannot as a rule be reprieved from the dead is demonstrated by the tale of how the law was once nearly controverted; yet in the end human frailty means death.'[3] It is also a tragic romance with a chilling element of reality—'the dream of the return of the dead cannot be realized' (Hultkranz). The Greek myth itself is a particularly successful version of a widespread tale. Among the Tungus, legend tells of a woman shaman Nisan who went to the lower world of spirits to bring back the soul of a young man who died while hunting; among the Maori, of Hutu, who went to the underworld to recover the princess Pare who had committed suicide because of him. Many stories of the Orpheus type (with both successful and unsuccessful quests) have been recorded among Indian tribes in North America; here, among the taboos imposed by the lord of the dead, we find a prohibition against looking back, and, although the Indian Orpheus is not usually a musician, he sometimes overcomes the obstacles he meets by means of magic songs.

Around the versions of the classical Orpheus story transmitted to the Middle Ages by the 'authors', Virgil, Ovid and Boethius, there clustered a great mass of commentaries, interpretations, and retellings which are sometimes far from learned.[4] We should even be

[3] G. S. Kirk, *Myth. Its Meaning and Functions in Ancient and Other Cultures* (Cambridge, Berkeley, Los Angeles, 1970), p. 259. On the legend outside Europe, cf. Stith Thompson, *Motif-Index of Folk-Literature* (Bloomington, 1934), F 81.1 (Orpheus), C 331 (taboo against looking back), M. Eliade, *Le Chamanisme at les techniques archaïques de l'extase* (Paris, 1951), esp. pp. 195, 219, 281–2, 331; S. M. Shirokoroff, *Psychomental Complex of the Tungus* (London, 1935), p. 308; J. White, *The Ancient History of the Maori* (Wellington, 1887), II, pp. 163–7. For the North American Indian traditions, see A. H. Gayton, 'The Orpheus Myth in North America', *Journal of American Folklore* xlviii (1935), 263–93, A. Hultkrantz, *The North American Indian Orpheus Tradition* (Stockholm, 1957).

[4] Cf. the fourteenth-century commentary on Boethius by Peter of Paris in which Orpheus's wife Urrices becomes so angry with him that he strikes her and kills her. Unable to rest for sorrow, he goes with his 'vielle' to the entrance of hell. He is given her back on the condition that never again would he see the skies, and that he would be forever blind (A. Thomas, in *Notices et Extraits des MSS. de la Bibliothèque nationale* xli (1923), pp. 69–70, Friedman, pp. 114–16). In another French version, 'Olfeus' visits his wife's tomb and finds there a demon who tells

cautious in using a phrase like 'the classical story', for among the various versions current in antiquity there seems to have been one without the tragic end.[5] Possibly it is this—preserved somehow in popular tradition—which comes to the surface again in the fine English romance *Sir Orfeo*, where the hero regains both his wife, who has been 'taken' by the king of fairyland, and his kingdom.[6] We need not concern ourselves here with trying to isolate the particular combination of the traditions which possibly lie behind this—a recollection of an ancient version of the myth with a happy ending, a contamination with a Celtic story of a recovery from the Otherworld, or the result of an almost universal desire to see Orpheus succeed in his quest. What is important from our point of view is that the myth here appears as a romance—and very easily, for it already has a number of that form's most characteristic elements: a quest with 'adventures' in which the hero is tested, a magic harp, and true love. It appears also as a romance in popular tradition. A ballad recorded in Shetland in the nineteenth century[7] (which would have been accompanied, apparently, by wild

him that he has her 'dedanz mon enfer'. Olfeus goes to the underworld (without music it seems), and as he is on his way out the devils amuse themselves by making a great noise behind him. The fiend makes such a noise that involuntarily Olfeus looks back... (MS. B.N. fr. 7209, f. 41v; cf. L. Moland, *Origines littéraires de la France* (Paris, 1862), pp. 269–77, Friedman, p. 230).

[5] W. K. C. Guthrie, *Orpheus and Greek Religion* (London, 1935), p. 31. See J. Heurgon, *Mélanges d'archéologie et d'histoire* xlix (1932), 6–60, C. M. Bowra, *The Classical Quarterly* N.S. ii (1952), 113–26, P. Dronke, *Classica et Mediaevalia* xxiii (1962), 198–215. Cf. also M. Owen Lee, *Classica et Mediaevalia* xxvi (1965), 402–12.

[6] Ed. A. J. Bliss (2nd ed., Oxford, 1966); see Dorena Allen, 'Orpheus and Orfeo: the Dead and the Taken', *MÆ* xxxiii (1964), 102–11.

[7] F. J. Child, *The English and Scottish Popular Ballads* (2nd ed., Boston, 1882–98), No. 19; cf. Mrs. Saxby, 'Folklore from Unst, Shetland', *The Leisure Hour* (1880), 108–110. On 'King Orphius', see Marion Stewart, *Scottish Studies* xvii (1973), 1–16. J. Frappier, 'Orphée et Proserpine ou la lyre et la harpe', in *Histoire, Mythes et Symboles* (Geneva, 1976), pp. 199–217, draws attention to another curious version which may have popular antecedents in Raoul Lefèvre's *Hystoires troyennes*. In this, Pluto carries off Proserpina, who is the wife of Orpheus, in a ship to 'une cité basse qui estoit appellee enfer' (a euhemeristic explanation is given). Orpheus goes there with his harp, in disguise, and plays before the king. Pluto is moved by Proserpina's sorrow, and promises Orpheus whatever he wishes if he can make her tears cease. Held to his promise, he lets them go, subject to the usual condition. Proserpina is lost, and taken back to Pluto, but she is finally rescued by Hercules and restored to Orpheus. Frappier argues that Lefèvre may have known the lost *Lai d'Orphée* (for references to which, see Bliss, pp. xxxi–xxxii)

music on a violin) has preserved the same, or a very similar, story. The king recovers his queen, 'Lady Isabel', who has been pierced to the heart by 'da king of Ferrie' (no condition is imposed, and there is no backward glance). The hero is, as usual in the West, a musician, although the fact that he 'took out his pipes ta play' suggests that we are a long way from Orpheus and his lyre:[8]

> And first he played da notes o noy,
> And dan he played da notes o joy.
>
> And dan he played da göd gabber reel,
> Dat meicht ha made a sick hert hale...

Two fragments have recently been discovered in a sixteenth-century manuscript of a Scottish romance ('King Orphius'), which, though not identical with the extant ME *Sir Orfeo*, seems very closely related to it. As in the ballad, the queen who is taken by the 'king of pharie' is called 'Issabell'. All this suggests that some such romance or ballad versions of the story may very well have been current in Henryson's Scotland.

Medieval poets were especially fond of Orpheus the lover. They saw him, in courtly garb, as an 'amans fins', as a lover of exemplary faithfulness, a 'loyal amoureux'. Boethius's proverbial lines, 'quis legem det amantibus', which echo through medieval literature, are adapted to courtly elegance:

> Mais la loy d'amour est si fort
> Qu'il ne doubte peine ne mort.
> Dont c'est folie peine et errour
> De bailler loy a fine amour,
> Car Orpheus fu amant fin.[9]

Orpheus and Eurydice had become a legendary pair of lovers. Petrarch in the *Trionfo d'Amore* looks around to see if there are any poets among those who 'were brought to loves daunce'—

which underlies *Sir Orfeo*. On Henryson's poem and romance, see also Carol Mills, 'Romance Convention and Robert Henryson's *Orpheus and Eurydice*', in *Bards and Makars*, ed. Aitken, McDiarmid and Thomson (Glasgow, 1977).

[8] Cf. a similar reference, in jocular vein, in Villon, *Testament*, 633–6, who calls Orpheus 'le doux menestrier, / Jouant des fleustes et musetes' (and gives Cerberus a fourth head). Cf. n. 59 below.

[9] Anonymous French version of Boethius, quoted Heitmann, p. 265 (I give the text of MS. Douce 298).

I saw hym that Erudyce dyd call
Apon Pluto, the great god infernall,
And folowed her (as these hystories tell)
Doune unto the depe dongeon of hell,
And dying dyd his love clepe and call...[10]

Yet this did not prevent them from receiving some very individual treatment. A much earlier Latin lyric poet presents them, as Mr. Dronke says, 'wittily, affectionately, as if they were a pair of lovers in his circle of friends'. Orpheus for him is the philosopher brought down by passion: 'Orpheus, whose habit was to research into the spirits of the sun, the monthly orbit of the moon, the numerically established courses of the stars in heaven, now led to a pursuit of another kind, his studies modified, speaks of kissing, of embracing, and follows his beloved...'.[11]

Orpheus was also known under those two aspects which were to be so important in the Renaissance—as theologian, and as poet-musician.[12] He obviously had a reputation as a cosmologist and astronomer. As the founder of a mystery religion and as the author of sacred and hermetic writings, he was being enthusiastically rediscovered by the Florentine intellectuals of Henryson's time. However, throughout the Middle Ages, his name at least had been remembered as a *priscus theologus* and as a poetic theologian; Dante (*Inferno* iv, 140) places him among the philosophers of antiquity. He was 'the clerke Orpheus'. The Renaissance view, that 'he was a divinely inspired poetic teacher, possessed by Platonic *furor*, who reformed and civilized his barbarous contemporaries, the "stony and beastly people" as Sidney calls them', was also held—though with less stress on the Platonic *furor*—in the Middle Ages: 'homines bestiales et solitarios reduceret ad civilitatem' says Aquinas.[13] Orpheus was the discoverer of music, and the first player of

[10] Tr. Morley, *Tryumphes of Fraunces Petrarcke*, ed. D. D. Carnicelli (Cambridge, Mass., 1971), p. 103.

[11] Peter Dronke, *Medieval Latin and the Rise of European Love-Lyric* (Oxford, 1966), II, pp. 403–6. On misogynistic interpretations, see Heitmann, pp. 266–7.

[12] Cf. D. P. Walker, 'Orpheus the Theologian and Renaissance Platonists', *JWCI* xvi (1953), 100–20. 'The clerke Orpheus' is Fisher's phrase (*English Works* ed. J. E. B. Mayor, EETS ES xxvii (1876), p. 47). On Orpheus and music, cf. Heitmann, pp. 262–3.

[13] Heitmann, pp. 262–3; cf. Trivet, 'homines brutales et silvestres reduxit ad normam rationis'.

the lyre. The etymologies of the names 'Orpheus' and 'Eurydice' as 'optima vox' and 'profunda dijudicatio' offered by Fulgentius[14] allowed an interpretation of the myth in musical terms:

> Si se marient, ce me samble,
> Orpheüs et Erudix ensamble,
> Quand bonne vois en doulce accorde
> Raisons par Jugement accorde
> Dont maries est Orpheus.[15]

One early work of musical theory uses the story of his failure to bring Eurydice back to 'show the fact that men will never be able to penetrate to the intrinsic secrets of music'.[16] He was also the master of poetry and rhetoric, because with Eurydice he combined wisdom and eloquence: 'il fu poetes, ce est sages, e saveit molt bien harper, ce est raisnablement saveit parler. Cil est perfeitement sages qui a sapience e eloquence.'[17] The figure of the wise and eloquent Orpheus could be used in a defence of poetry[18]—Petrarch uses him against the attack of a physician, echoing St. Augustine 'primos nempe theologos apud gentes fuisse poetas.' The fable itself could be used to illustrate the paradox of 'truthful fiction', the 'bella menzogna' of the *Convivio*, the allegory 'that hides itself under the mantle of these tales and is a truth hidden under beauteous fiction'—'as when Ovid says that Orpheus with his lyre made wild beasts tame and made trees and rocks approach him; which would say that the wise man with the instrument of his voice

[14] *Mythologicon* ed. T. Munckerus (Amsterdam, 1681), chapter x, p. 131.

[15] MS. B.N. fr. 576, f. 48, a version of Boethius attributed to the 'anonyme de Meun', quoted by Heitmann, p. 271.

[16] M. Bukofzer, 'Speculative Thinking in Medieval Music', *Speculum* xvii (1942), 173–5; Regino of Prüm (d. 915) ed. M. Gerbert, *Scriptores Ecclesiastici* (1784), I.

[17] A French version of Boethius, quoted Heitmann, p. 273. Cf. Friedman, pp. 101–2.

[18] Petrarch, *Invectiva contra medicum* ed. P. G. Ricci (Rome, 1950), p. 71; Dante, *Convivio* II, i (tr. P. H. Wicksteed, London, 1908), pp. 63–4. The story of Orpheus is cited by others, e.g. Bernard Silvestris, Conrad Celtis, Ronsard. On interpretation of myth in general, see Peter Dronke, *Fabula*, *passim*, W. Wetherbee, *Platonism and Poetry in the Twelfth Century* (Princeton, 1972), esp. pp. 36–66, M. D. Chenu, '*Involucrum*. Le Mythe selon les théologiens médiévaux', *Archives d'histoire doctrinale et littéraire du Moyen Age* xxii (1955), 75–9, E. Jeauneau, 'L'usage de la notion d'*Integumentum* à travers les gloses de Guillaume de Conches', *ib.* xxiv (1957), 35–87, esp. pp. 40–51.

maketh cruel hearts tender and humble; and moveth to his will such as have not the life of science and of art; for they that have not the rational life are as good as stones.'

It is already evident that it is not surprising for a late medieval poet to think that the 'plain narrative' of Orpheus and Eurydice should contain 'a philosophical purpose'. Medieval readers agreed in finding the story deeply significant, and commentators devoted much energy to searching out the mysteries veiled beneath the *integumentum*. The *Ovide moralisé* offers a small anthology of allegorical readings, both ancient—Orpheus as the figure of Christ ('that hevynly Orpheus' as Douglas calls him)—and more recent—Orpheus as ruling reason, Eurydice as the sensuality of the soul.[19] It is, however, the commentaries on Boethius[20] rather than those on Ovid which illuminate Henryson's poem most clearly. He adapts the commentary of Trivet for his *moralitas*, and his view of the story has been profoundly shaped by Boethius. The fine lyric with which Lady Philosophy ('with a soft and sweet voice, observing due dignity and gravity in her countenance and gesture') ends Book III of the *Consolation* begins with a firmly philosophical statement:

Felix qui potuit boni
Fontem visere lucidum,
Felix qui potuit gravis
Terrae solvere vincula

and ends on an equally firm didactic note:

Vos haec fabula respicit
Quicumque in superum diem
Mentem ducere quaeritis.
Nam qui Tartareum in specus
Victus lumina flexerit,
Quidquid praecipuum trahit
Perdit, dum videt inferos.

The opposition of 'boni fontem...lucidum' and 'terrae...vincula' is thoroughly Platonic. In this version of the story great emphasis is

[19] Ed. C. de Boer (Amsterdam, 1936) (the Orpheus stories and interpretations are in Books x and xi). Cf. Friedman, pp. 124ff. Douglas, Prol. *Eneados* I, l. 469.
[20] On the tradition, see P. Courcelle, *La Consolation de Philosophie dans la tradition littéraire* (Paris, 1967), Heitmann, pp. 255ff.

attached to the 'looking back'. The 'quick mind' which, clad with the wings of philosophy, would despise the earth, and find its true home above the starry spheres, allowed itself to be turned aside. But the poem is far from homiletic: 'conceived by Philosophy as an admonitory exemplum' (says Professor Wetherbee),[21] 'it also gives eloquent expression to the very impulse it is intended to curb, the attachment to worldly things which is at the heart of the metaphor of imprisonment'. The force of the tragic paradox that it is love which both inspires Orpheus to his heroic attempt to win back Eurydice from death—so nearly successful ('Vincimur', arbiter / Umbrarum miserans ait)—and causes his failure (Quis legem det amantibus? Maior lex amor est sibi) emerges just as powerfully. The poem is cryptic and allusive, 'plus suggestif qu'explicite', and it invites commentary.

Of the medieval commentators who expounded it, the most distinguished is the twelfth-century Platonist, William of Conches.[22] He is sensitive to the complexities of the lyric, while neatly pointing the Platonic–Christian opposition of the Creator (*fons boni*) and the *delectatio temporalium* (Tartarus), and bringing out those elements in it which make it an interior drama of man's spiritual life—'un drame de la connaissance et de la volonté qui tend invinciblement mais confusément au Bien.' Far from destroying the poetry of the myth, he finds a new poetry in it. Orpheus (*optima vox*) is a wise and eloquent man;[23] his wife Eurydice that natural desire (*naturalis concupiscentia*) which is part of everyone, 'for no one, not even a child one day old, can be without her' (poets, he says, imagine this to be a *genius* which is born with us and dies with us). She is called Eurydice (*boni judicatio*) because everyone desires what he judges to be good. It will be immediately evident that this strikingly non-moralistic and humane interpretation will allow full scope to the emotional tensions of the story. Natural desire

[21] *Platonism and Poetry*, p. 78. Cf. Heitmann, p. 274.

[22] On William, see Dronke, *Fabula*; on this passage, cf. Wetherbee, pp. 96–104, Friedman, pp. 104–9. See also the illuminating remarks of J. Hatinguais (from whom the phrase quoted above comes), 'En marge d'un poème de Boèce: l'interprétation allégorique du mythe d'Orphée par Guillaume de Conches', Association G. Budé, Congrès de Tours et Poitiers, 1953, *Actes* (Paris, 1954), pp. 285–9. Text pr. C. Jourdain, 'Des commentaires inédits de Guillaume de Conches et de Nicolas sur la Consolation de la Philosophie de Boèce', *Notices et Extraits des MSS. de la Bibliothèque impériale* xx (part ii) (Paris, 1862), pp. 40–82.

[23] Friedman's (Orpheus) 'stands for wisdom and eloquence' is not accurate (L. *pro quolibet sapiente et eloquente*).

is pursued by Aristaeus (a figure from the Virgilian version of the story). He is the figure of virtue (*ares enim est virtus*), and follows her because virtue always tries to withdraw natural desire from earthly things. She flees because natural desire gainsays virtue in its wish for its own pleasure, and dies and descends to the lower world, or to earthly delights (*terrenam delectationem*). Orpheus grieves, as a wise man, when he sees his desire and delight fixed in *temporalia*, and although his music overcomes all, it cannot overcome his grief for his lost wife, because however much a wise man overcomes the vices of others by his wisdom and eloquence, he cannot withdraw his desire from earthly things... William is sensitive to the contrast of the ideal wisdom and eloquence of Orpheus and the irresistible earthward tendency of his affections. The story is (Wetherbee)[24] 'at once the embodiment of a subjective view of human experience and an objective exemplum of that experience.' William's allegorical pattern is repeated, with variations, by later commentators who are less enthusiastically Platonist.[25] Nicholas Trivet,[26] for instance, although he is clearly indebted to William in his treatment of the Orpheus lyric, elsewhere takes 'the commentator' to task, and substitutes Aristotelian interpretations for his bold Platonism. Allegorical readings of the story of this and other kinds proliferate throughout the Middle Ages, and beyond.[27] A curious modern reflex has been noticed in the *Orphée-Roi* of Segalen, destined to be set (though it never was) by Debussy, where Orpheus symbolizes the soaring of the soul towards pure sonority, divorced from matter, and Eurydice the soul too closely attached to the reality of the flesh.[28]

Beside the commentaries, there are retellings and expansions of the Orpheus story in French versions of Boethius.[29] It may be that

[24] P. 122. [25] Cf. Courcelle, pp. 306ff.

[26] 'A true polymath' (Smalley, *Friars*, p. 58), the author also of commentaries on Livy and the two Senecas (see A. B. Emden, *A Biographical Register of the University of Oxford to A.D. 1500*). Cf. Courcelle, pp. 318ff., Friedman, pp. 109–14.

[27] Cf. Heitmann, pp. 277–81.

[28] Heitmann, p. 281, E. Kushner, *Le Mythe d'Orphée dans la littérature française contemporaine* (Paris, 1961), pp. 136–76.

[29] See Heitmann, pp. 255ff., Thomas Roques, 'Traductions françaises de la *Consolatio Philosophiae* de Boèce' in *Histoire littéraire de la France* xxxvii (1938), pp. 419ff., L. Delisle, *Inventaire général...des MSS. français de la Bibliothèque Nationale* II (Paris, 1878), pp. 330ff., 334ff. Cf. L. W. Stone, *MÆ* vi (1937), 21–30, R. A. Dwyer, *Boethian Fictions* (Cambridge, Mass., 1976), J. K. Atkinson, *MÆ* xlvii (1978), 22–9. (On other Latin retellings of the story or poems on Orpheus, cf. Heitmann, pp. 260–1, Friedmann, pp. 164–9).

Henryson knew something of this kind. One verse rendering of the lyric (which accompanies the prose attributed to Jean de Meun) follows Boethius directly, telling the story less allusively and with some underlining of emotion:

...Cil s'en va et s'amye apres.
Qui peut donner aux amans loy?
Amour ne veult loy que soy;
Quant ilz aloient leur chemin
Si que pres erent de la fin
Cil se tourne pour veoir s'amye
Et maintenant lui fut ravye.[30]

Another (probably by Friar Renaud de Louhans) is much longer and more leisurely. Orpheus is 'un menestrel de grant maniere' and the musical references are rather more pointed:

Quant il voult en enfer descendre
Ses instruments prist fort a tendre
Si que n'y ot clef ne muance
Qui ne feust selon l'ordonnance...[31]

as are the emotional reactions of Orpheus—

Quant Orpheus vint a la porte
D'enfer adonc se desconforte...

and he 'se porta...Moult tres bien envers Tantalus'. But this is at the cost of a rather heavily explanatory tone: 'a la porte un chien demeure / ...Que l'en appelle Cerberus / ...ce mastin avoit .iii. testes / Ce que n'ont pas les autres bestes.' The mythological references are expanded: the story of Tantalus (some 30 lines) is worked into the text. Even more extensive and longwinded is another verse translation (that of the 'anonyme de Meun') in MS. B.N. fr. 576.[32] It opposes true love to false love, and emphasizes the importance of music by a long disquisition on the art and its power. Music is part of the divine and universal harmony—in the 'doulce consonancie' of the Trinity, the angels, and the harmonies of blessed souls, the music of the spheres,

[30] MS. Douce 352, f. 47ᵛ (also in B.N. fr. 575).
[31] MS. Douce 298, f. 52ᵛ.
[32] Ff. 45–53 (the lines quoted are on f. 49).

Et ossi toutes aultres coses
Sont par musique en vertu closes
Et sont en certain nombre faites.

Again, the mythological references are expanded, here to excessive length, with various legendary stories thrown in for good measure. None of these versions can be claimed as a 'source' for Henryson's poem, but they illustrate the kind of expansive rehandling of the Boethian lyric (sometimes resulting in a rambling and messy whole) which seems to have been the background for it.

In Henryson's own day, the myth was for the first time turned into drama. Poliziano's *Favola d'Orfeo*,[33] composed in June 1480 at the request of Cardinal Francesco Gonzaga, is a pastoral drama, with music and lyrics. It is a thoroughly humanist work. In the earliest editions, just before a shepherd announces the death of Eurydice, Orpheus 'on the mountain' (and presumably dominating the scene) sings some eloquent Latin verses to his lyre in praise of the Cardinal and the beneficence of the house of Gonzaga. It has been suggested that Henryson knew this work, that 'he may have read or even attended Poliziano's piece which was performed as a play before Gonzaga's court in that year' (1480). It would be nice to think that Dunfermline was represented at the court of Mantua, but this claim seems extravagant (it is not even certain that *Orfeo* was performed at the court on that occasion).[34] It is largely based on unproven assumptions about Henryson's humanist training in Italy. Comparison of the two works produces no verbal parallels which are convincing. Any similarities between the two can be explained more easily either as arising from traditional material (it is not notable 'that both heroes must first pass

33 Ed. Ida Maïer, *Opera Omnia* (Turin, 1971), III; tr. L. E. Lord, *A Translation of the Orpheus of Angelo Politian and the Aminta of Torquato Tasso* (Oxford, 1931). Cf. I. Maïer, *Ange Politien. La Formation d'un poète humaniste (1469–1480)* (Geneva, 1966), esp. chapter 3.

34 R. D. S. Jack, *The Italian Influence on Scottish Literature* (Edinburgh, 1972), pp. 8–14. Poliziano left the MS. at Mantua, but (Maïer, p. 390), 'nous ne savons pas si l'*Orfeo* fut alors représenté sur la scène, les cérémonies des fiançailles ayant été annulées'. It was certainly produced later, and was put into tragic form (*Orphei Tragoedia*) probably by Tebaldeo. (In the visual arts, the arrival of the neo-classical Orpheus is especially noticeable; cf. the late fifteenth-century Italian MS. illustration reprod. in Saxl, *Catalogue of Astrological and Mythological MSS.*, III, 2, Abb. 38, or Dürer's 'Death of Orpheus' (1494) (see Panofsky, *Albrecht Dürer*, pp. 22–3).)

the three-headed Cerberus', nor that the power of Orpheus's music is emphasized, nor that Eurydice is called 'mia bella', etc.—she is referred to as his *amie* in medieval versions), or from coincidence. Thus, a shepherd in Poliziano announces Eurydice's death, and a weeping maiden in Henryson brings the news to the king. But, as we shall see, Henryson's episode seems to owe something to popular romance. As in Henryson, Orfeo is given 'a complaint, in which he addresses his harp in strikingly similar language'. But, in fact, it is significant that he does not address his harp, but his lyre (Poliziano's musical symbolism has a humanist's precision),[35] and the language is not really 'strikingly similar'. The complaints develop in quite different ways. Again, it is not surprising that laments should have been given to the sorrowful hero:

O fortuna quantum est mobilis,
Mane leta, vespere flebilis!
Quando magis videbatur stabilis
Tunc est fallax et cito labilis[36]

begins one *planctus* in which Orpheus reviews his story and his final grief. The differences between the two works seem far more striking. Henryson, for instance, has none of the neo-classical machinery—no shepherds called Mopsus and Thyrsis. Poliziano's Orfeo does not go on a heavenly journey, and his story continues until his death at the hands of the Bacchantes. Henryson's poem seems rather to be an individual and original work which is the culmination of medieval traditions.

Orpheus and Eurydice is a tale—'the tale of Orpheus and Erudices his quene', 'Heire begynnis the traitie of Orpheus kyng and how he yeid to hewyn and to hel to sek his quene' are two early headings—and it has something of the narrative art of the *Fables*. When Aristaeus sees Eurydice, a significant detail is picked out:

And quhen he saw this lady solitar,
Bairfut, with schankis quhyter than the snaw,
Preckit with lust, he thocht withoutin mair
Hir till oppress... (99–102)

[35] See E. Winternitz, *Musical Instruments and their Symbolism in Western Art* (London, 1967), p. 175, *Die Musik in Geschichte und Gegenwart* X, 413.
[36] Cf. M. Delbouille, 'Trois Poésies latines inédites', *Mélanges P. Thomas* (Bruges, 1930), p. 179.

In a way which recalls the *Fables*, the formulaic phrase 'quhyter than the snaw' is given a new and mysterious life, and the homely word 'schankis' is pleasingly balanced by the more learned 'oppress'. So, later, 'Watling Street' appears in the learned surroundings of Orpheus's heavenly journey.

Suggestions of popular romances come from more than such stylistic tricks as naming the hero 'Schir Orpheus' or 'Kyng Orpheus', and occasional ballad-like lines—(248) 'far and full ferthere than I can tell' (Asloan), 'fer and full fer, and ferrer than I can tell (Bannatyne). Early in the poem, for instance, Eurydice, 'the michty quene of Trace', hears of the noble fame of Orpheus, and, like the heroine of a fairy-tale or romance, sends a messenger to him, 'requyrand him to wed hir and be king'.[37] There is some nice human detail in the telling—when she saw 'this prince so glorius'

> Hir erand to propone scho thocht no schame—
> With wordis sueit and blenkis amorouss
> Said: 'Welcum, lord and lufe, schir Orpheuss!' (80–2)

Her 'forwardness',[38] of which she is charmingly conscious, also fits neatly (and deliberately) with the allegorical significance given to her in the *moralitas*. As in *Sir Orfeo* it is May when Eurydice is lost:

> I say this be Erudices the quene,
> Quhilk walkit furth into a May mornyng,
> Bot with a madyn, untill a medow grene,
> To tak the air, and se the flouris spring... (92–5)

This little lyrical Maying-scene is in deliberate ironic contrast to the terror of the event which is imminent and the darkness of the world of the dead. It may also be (as is possibly the case in *Sir Orfeo*) that this time is one of those at which the world of 'fairy' is especially active. Henryson certainly follows the classical account of Aristaeus and the serpent, but there are hints of the traditional 'taking' of mortals by fairies (Eurydice is young and fair, and dies an 'untimely death' like

[37] Friedman, p. 197, notes Marie de France's *Milun*, where the baron's daughter hears of Milun, and begins to love him. Cf. also the romantic biography of Jaufré Rudel, who is said to have fallen in love with the countess of Tripoli because of the good report of her from pilgrims. See T. P. Cross, *MP* xii (1915), 612 n. 3, Stith Thompson, *Motif-Index of Folk-Literature*, T. 11.1.

[38] Cf. Rymenhild's love for Horn, *King Horn*, ed. J. Hall (Oxford, 1901), pp. 15ff.

many of the victims of the fairies). His account of the death is not quite as straightforward as it is in the ancient stories. One phrase is very precise—because of the 'crewall venome...so penetrife', 'in peisis small this quenis harte can rife'—but the following is a little more ambiguous: 'and scho annone fell on a deidly swoun'. Proserpina 'calls' her to her court, and she vanishes. The fine dramatic outburst from the maiden which announces the catastrophe to Orpheus gives, however, a significantly different version of the event. She does not say, as Poliziano's shepherd does, 'tua nympha bellissima e defunta'. In contrast to the poet's careful words and terminology (Proserpina for him is 'the goddess infernall'), she gives a 'folk' interpretation:

> Scho said, 'Allace, Euridicess your quene
> Is with the phary tane befoir my ene!'

and goes on to give a more melodramatic version of the 'taking':

> 'Scho strampit on a serpent venemuss;
> And fell on swoun; with that the quene of fary
> Clawcht hir up sone and furth with hir cowth cary.'

At the same time it is evident that *Orpheus and Eurydice* is a learned and rhetorical poem. This is most obvious in the formal *planctus* of Orpheus which is its centre, and is marked off—as was Cresseid's—by a different stanza form. As in the *Testament*, the way is carefully prepared by an emotional scene. After the maiden's first outcry, Orpheus is 'inflamed in ire', and

> ...rampand as a lyoun rewanuss,
> With awfull luke and ene glowand as fyre
> Sperid the maner...

It is a dramatic and extreme human response. His anger may arise partly from the fear of dishonour, partly from the sudden and profound melancholy into which he is plunged.[39] The almost formulaic language in which it is expressed suggests the large emotional gestures of characters in ballads and popular romance. The scene shows Henryson's distinctive sense of narrative rhythm. When the terrible news is

[39] See pp. 177–8 above; cf. the Lefèvre story of Orpheus's loss of Proserpina: 'Orpheus fut si ravy de couroucement qu'il retourna en son palais quant il eut pardu la veue de Proserpine et la se tint dedans sa chambre sans mot dire deux ours entiers' (Frappier, p. 201).

repeated, with its details, the king's grief bursts out—'His hairt neir brist for verry dule and wo'; he is 'half out of mynd'. He takes his harp (although his skill in music has been emphasized, this sorrowful moment is the first time we hear of his instrument) and goes to the wood, that haunt not only of solitary poets, but of those 'half out of mynd' and in despair. He goes

> Wrinkand his handis, walkand to and fro
> Quhill he mycht stand, syne sat doun on a stone

—and the formulaic details catch very elegantly the melancholy, and never-resting anxiety of the king. It is at this point that he makes his 'mone' to his harp:

> 'O dulful herp, with mony dully string,
> Turne all thy mirth and musik in murning,
> And seiss of all thy sutell songis sueit...'

It is a fine melancholy *aria*, with the marvellously evocative line 'Quhair art thow gone, my lufe Euridices?' repeated as a refrain. Dramatically, the great set piece breaks off for a moment at the beginning of the second of the five stanzas, when he tries to comfort himself—'Him to rejoss yit playit he a spring, / Quhill that the fowlis of the wid can sing, / And treis dansit with their levis grene'—but the miraculous power of his music which affects the rest of the creation cannot console him: 'all in vane—that wailyeit [him] no thing'. Like Sir Orfeo, he proposes to give up his kingdom and to live in the wilderness as a solitary:

> 'Fair weill my place, fair weill plesandis and play,
> And wylcum woddis wyld and wilsum way,
> My wicket werd in wildirness to ware;
> My rob ryell, and all my riche array,
> Changit sal be in rude russet [of] gray,
> My dyademe intill a hate of hair;
> My bed sal be with bever, brok and bair...' (154–60)

but unlike him, Henryson's more classically-inspired Orpheus is determined to seek for Eurydice until he finds her.

His 'passing' to the heavens has something of the matter-of-factness of the transitions in the traditional ballad:

He tuk his harp and on his breist can hing,
Syne passit to the hevin, as sayis the fable,
To seik his wife...

The aside may allude once again to the question of 'feigned fables', and may be delivered with some wit, for, as far as we know, no other version of the 'fable' actually has a heavenly journey. The narrator controls this part of the story very carefully, constantly reminding us of Orpheus's failure to find Eurydice—'yit gat he nocht his wyfe', 'bot all in vane' etc. The reactions of the heavenly gods are differentiated—his grandsire Jupiter 'rewit', but the reaction of his father Phoebus is stronger (when he sees his plight, 'it changit all his cheir'). What seems at first to be a digression on celestial music emphasizes yet again that Orpheus's grief is not lessened.

The feeling of the romance 'quest' is even stronger in the journey to hell, which reminds us of the popular medieval stories of voyages to the Otherworld.[40] Orpheus's quest is the more perilous, however, in that unlike most of the heroes in those stories, he goes alone, without a guide:

...I will tell how Orpheus tuk the way
To seik his wyfe attour the gravis gray
Hungry and cauld, [our] mony wilsum wone,
Withouttin gyd, he and his harp allone. (243–6)

He 'passes' for 'twenty days', but as in a ballad, he mysteriously finds the way: 'and ay he fand streitis and reddy wayis'. The boundary of the underworld is a gate guarded by Cerberus, 'a hound of hell, a monstour mervellus'. The landscape of the underworld through which he passes—'our a mure, with thornis thik and scherp', etc.—sometimes has a touch of Scottish scenery; more importantly, however, it is that of the visions of hell and purgatory, with a 'Brig o' Dread' and a 'Whinny-muir'.[41] The furies who guard the bridge are put to sleep by 'a joly spring' (which is a nice contrast to the 'dolereus lay' that

[40] Cf. H. R. Patch, *The Otherworld* (Cambridge, Mass., 1950), D. D. R. Owen, *The Vision of Hell* (Edinburgh, London, 1970), E. J. Becker, *A Contribution to the Comparative Study of the Medieval Visions of Heaven and Hell* (Baltimore, 1899).

[41] MacQueen (*Henryson*, p. 36) makes the apt comparison with 'The Lykewake Dirge'. On the bridges and thorns of the Otherworld, cf. Patch, *passim*, L. C. Wimberly, *Folklore in the English and Scottish Ballads* (Chicago, 1928), pp. 110ff., Becker, pp. 17–18.

Machaut has his Orpheus play).[42] The narrative is lively, and not without a touch of humour. As the furies sleep, Ixion 'stall away', and, later, thanks to Orpheus's harp, 'the watter stude', and Tantalus 'gat a drink'. In the successive scenes of torment, the overtones of Christian descriptions of hell and purgatory, which are always present in this kind of literature, become more and more powerful, until he finally comes to the 'hiddouss hellis houss':

> Beyond this mure he fand a feirfull streit,
> Myrk as the nycht, to pass rycht dengerus—
> For sliddreness skant mycht he hald his feit—
> In quhilk thair wes a stynk rycht odiuss,
> That gydit him to hiddouss hellis houss... (303–7)

The horror of the gruesome place moves the poet to an *exclamatio*—'O dully place, and grundles deip dungeoun...'. It is the pit of despair, from which comes a 'stink intollerable':

> Quhat creature cumis to dwell in the
> Is ay deand and nevirmoir sall de.

Here Orpheus sees, as other voyagers to the medieval underworld had before him, the torments of the wicked—'mony cairfull king and quene, / With croun on heid, [of] brass full [hate] birnand'—the 'maisterfull' and conquerors, other oppressors, and wicked clerics.

In the midst of all these perils and horrors we are never allowed to forget that Orpheus is human. When he first sees Cerberus, he 'began to be agast'; he is still afflicted with his own sorrow, and weeps as he goes; he has the human reaction of *pite* for the suffering inhabitants—he has 'reuth' of Tantalus and Titius whom he sees 'suffir soir'. In the nethermost part where Pluto and Proserpina dwell he at last finds his Eurydice:

> Syne neddirmair he went quhair Pluto was,
> And Proserpyne, and hiddirwart he drew,
> Ay playand on his harp quhair he cowth pass;

[42] *Le Confort d'Ami* (in *Œuvres*, ed. E. Hoepffner, Paris, 1908–21, III), ll. 2313–21:

> Sa harpe acorda sans delay
> Et joua son dolereus lay
> Et chanta de vois douce et seinne...

On 'spring', see *OED sb.* 2, Tobler–Lommatzsch, *Altfranzösisches Wörterbuch*, s.v. 'espringuerie' (associated with tabors, vielles and dancing).

Till at the last Erudices he knew,
Lene and deidlyk, and peteouss paill of hew,
Rycht warsche and wane, and walluid as the weid—
Hir lilly lyre wes lyk unto the leid. (345–51)

His queen has become an inhabitant of the world of the dead; she is 'lyke ane elf'. Once again Henryson handles a recognition scene in a terrible setting with unerring tact. The simple formality of Orpheus's speech to her (his question echoes the *Ubi sunt*) increases the emotional power of the moment:

Quod he: 'My lady leill and my delyt,
Full wo is me to se yow changit thus;
Quhair is [thi] rude as ross with cheikis quhyte,
[Thy] cristell ene with blenkis amorus,
[Thy] lippis reid to kiss delicius?'

Her strange and guarded answer

'As now I der nocht tell, perfay;
Bot ye sall wit the causs ane uthir day'

emphasizes the feeling of peril that surrounds them. The tone of Pluto's words, too, is ambiguous. His humour, which seems kindly and reassuring—suggesting that she is one of the taken, or at least that 'war scho at hame in hir cuntre of Trace' she would soon be restored—may also be ironic and taunting.

The scene which follows is not unlike the romance pattern of *Sir Orfeo*, though without that version's 'rash promise'. Orpheus does not plead or argue (as he does in Poliziano); he simply affects Pluto and Proserpina so much by his music that they 'bad him ass / His waresoun...'. Proserpina imposes her 'conditioun', and sends Orpheus off with his wife. As in *Sir Orfeo*, the reunion of the two mortals is pointed with a touching and evocative detail—'Erudices than be the hand thow tak, / And pass thi way'—but here it is also the beginning of an ironic pattern:

Thocht this was hard, yit Orpheus was fane,
And on thay went, talkand of play and sport,
[Quhill] thay almost come to the outwart port

(Boethius's 'noctis prope terminos' has been transformed, in the manner of our illustration, into the 'outer port' of a medieval walled city.) The poet's exclamation of *pite* at the catastrophe that follows—

> Allace! it wes grit [hart-sair] for to heir
> Of Orpheus the weping and the wo,
> [Quhen that his wyf, quhilk] he had bocht so deir,
> Bot for a luk so sone was [hynt] him fro (394–7)

—emphasizes the contrast of the long toil and suffering 'quhilk he had bocht so deir' and the simplicity of his very human 'fault'—'bot for a luk'. This is the climax of the tale. From the point of view of Proserpina's hard 'law', what has happened is fair; from the point of view of human feelings, it is monstrously unfair. Love has so nearly succeeded in bringing her back from the dead—as the spirits sing in Monteverdi's *Orfeo*:[43]

> Pietade, oggi, e amore
> Trionfan nel'inferno

—and yet has been the reason for her loss. 'Bot for a luk'—the same phrase is used by Orpheus himself, after his anguished exclamation on the contradictions of love:

> 'Now find I weill this proverb trew,' quod he,
> 'Hart on the hurd, and handis on the soir;
> Quhair luve gois, on fors mone turne the e.'
> I am expart, and wo is me thairfoir—
> Bot for a luke my lady is forloir!' (408–12)

The repetition increases the pathos, and emphasizes yet again that the fatal action is the natural reaction of love ('on fors mone turne the e'). It is entirely typical of Henryson to conclude a rhetorical *planctus* with two homely proverbial expressions[44] of the 'law of kind'. The narrative is brought to a simple, sorrowful end:

> Thus chydand on with luve, our burne and bent,
> A wofull wedo hamewart is he went.

Henryson's 'philosophical purpose' in the poem is obvious enough, but it is not quite 'superimposed on a plain narrative'. From the

[43] *L'Orfeo. Favola in Musica* (1607, text by Alessandro Striggio).

[44] Cf. Whiting, H 278 (Heart on the hoard and hands on the sore) (cf. T 386, S 506). The second is probably an echo of L 558 (Where love is there is the eye; cf. variants, E 207, N 39).

beginning the significances of the story are underlined. The opening is serious and sententious:[45] one who wishes to magnify the 'nobilnes and grit magnificens' of a prince should extol his 'ancestre and lineall discens' to inspire him to virtue:

So that his harte he mycht inclyne thairby
The moir to vertew and to worthiness
Herand reherss his elderis gentilness.

The exemplary value of the stories of the deeds of the men of the past is, of course, a commonplace. The *Book of Pluscarden* begins: 'In recalling to mind the praiseworthy deeds of the great men of the past, not only do we profit the men of our day by rehearsing events of interest which have taken place; nay, we also, by the lantern of truth, as it were, show wayfarers the path of virtue through the example of able men of yore; and, while we commemorate their merits, afford the fortunate in time to come a noble opportunity of following in the footsteps of their reverend ancestors.' Henryson, however, is also quite clearly introducing those moral qualities which are directly relevant to his conception of the story of Orpheus—'vertew', 'worthines', 'gentilnes'. When, in the next stanza, he goes on to develop his argument in a particular way (with significant word-play)—

It is contrair the lawis of nature
A gentill man to be degenerat,
Nocht following of his progenitour
The worthe rewll and the lordly estait—

it is hard not to wonder if he may be once again writing for 'ane lord'. It may be for this or some similar reason that he stresses the ideal connection of 'gentilnes' with high birth, rather than that 'nobility of soul' unconnected with rank, of which he would have read in Chaucer. Here it is natural—and in tune with the natural harmony—for nobility of spirit to accompany that of blood. His Orpheus is a king, and from the ancient tradition that Orpheus was a bringer of civilization and 'nurture' it was easy to make him into a model for the ruler. One of the tableaux for the entry of Charles V to Bruges in 1515 represented Orpheus playing to the animals in an enclosed garden, representing the

[45] Cf. Curtius, pp. 156–7; *Ad Herennium* iii. 7. 13 (where descent is linked with education). The lines from the *Book of Pluscarden* are tr. F. J. H. Skene (Edinburgh, 1877).

young prince's kingdom: 'he must tune the instrument of his conduct, that is to say the institution of his reign in perfect consonance and melodious harmony in all excellent virtues'.[46] The harmony of music is frequently a figure of the concord of the well-ruled kingdom. A section in *Les Échecs Amoureux* treats of how 'musique vault et prouffitte a la vie pollitique'.[47] A Scottish poem *De Regimine Principum*[48] opens with the simile

> Richt as all stringis ar cupillit in ane harpe
> In ane accord and tunit with ane uther

—and instructs the king to rule his realm thus, giving 'gud sound and suthfast' to his subjects. It returns to the figure at the end

> Thus sen thow has the harp in generall
> As gud menstrall to rewle it be musik
> Quhilk signifiis thy realme and pepill hale
> With officiaris quhilk governis thy kinrik
> Pull out thy wrast and gar thame sound alyk
> As gud menstrall to play in ane accorde
> All men will say thow art lyk to be ane lord.

Henryson's next lines speak sharply of those rulers who turn from the ideal. They are certainly a statement of a general truth, but it may be that they also have some contemporary reference:

> A ryall rynk for to be rusticat
> Is bot a monsture in comparesoun,
> Had in dispute and [foule] derisioun.

He goes on quickly (whether it is simply his customary briskness of narrative or the delicate leaving of a difficult matter, as we suspected in 'The Lion and the Mouse', is uncertain) to remark 'I say this be the grit lordis of Grew', and if there is any sidelong reference to his own

[46] R. Wangermée, *Flemish Music and Society in the Fifteenth and Sixteenth Centuries* (English version by R. E. Wolf, New York, London, 1968), p. 176, fig. 6, J. Jacquot, *Les Fêtes de la Renaissance* (Paris, 1956), II, pp. 416–17 (on Orpheus as an exemplary figure of the prince, see *ib.* I, chapter 1, *passim*).

[47] H. Abert, 'Die Musikästhetik der Échecs Amoureux', *Romanische Forschungen* xv (1904), 912–14. On music and the concord of kingdoms and men's lives, cf. L. Spitzer, *Classical and Christian Ideas of World Harmony* (Baltimore, 1963).

[48] *Maitland Folio MS.*, ed. W. A. Craigie, STS (1919), I, pp. 115–25, II, pp. 74–91 (the copy in MS. Fairfax 8 has a picture of a harp above the poem).

time it is soon subsumed in his admiration for the wisdom and virtue of antiquity, when

> The anseane and sad wysemen of age
> War tendouris to yung and insolent,
> To mak thame in all vertewis excellent.

The sorrowful kings and queens whose torments Orpheus later sees have forsaken the harmony of 'gentilness', and virtue to become in their different ways 'monstrous' (by 'wrang conqueist', 'foull incest', 'crewaltie', 'grit iniquitie', 'breking of the law', 'oppressioun of Godis folk', 'grit abusion of justice', etc.).

The eloquence and wisdom of this noble Orpheus comes from his exceedingly 'gentill' parentage. From the union of his grandmother Memoria, a goddess 'excellent in bewte, / Gentill of blude', and Jupiter spring 'fair dochteris nyne', the Muses. Their names are given in a learned list, which must have pleased contemporary readers of similar classicizing taste: in a note to his *Aeneid*, Gavin Douglas makes an approving reference, 'Musa in Grew signifeis an inventryce or invention in our langgage, and of the ix Musis sum thing in my Palyce of Honour and be Mastir Robert Hendirson in New Orpheus'. The main source has been shown by Dorena Allen Wright[49] to be the thirteenth-century *Graecismus*, a 'treasury of grammatical, etymological, rhetorical and mythological information and misinformation'. Henryson's lines are not, however, simply a display of knowledge for its own sake. He indicates their significance by expounding the hidden meaning of their names according to traditional etymologies. These emphasize their connection with music—Euterpe 'gud delectatioun' (*Graecismus* bona delectatio), Polimio 'quhilk cowth a thowsand sangis sueitly sing'—with harmony, Melpomyne 'hony sueit in modelatioun' (dulce canens), Urania[50] 'armony celestiall, / Rejosing men with melody and sound', Herato 'quhilk drawis lyk to lyk in every thing' (ex simili simile repperit)—and with wisdom, Thersycore 'gud instructioun / Of every thing' (rerum instructio), Clio 'meditatioun /

[49] 'Henryson's *Orpheus and Eurydice* and the Tradition of the Muses', *MÆ* xl (1971), 41–7. Cf. also Curtius, pp. 228–46, P. Boyancé, 'Les Muses et l'harmonie des sphères', *Mélanges...Félix Grat* (Paris, 1946), pp. 3–16, F. Joukovsky, *Poésie et Mythologie au 16e siècle* (Paris, 1969), pp. 23ff.

[50] *Gr.* caelestis. It seems likely, as Wright suggests, that Henryson is thinking of Macrobius's identification of the Muses and the harmony of the spheres.

of every thing that hes creatioun' (meditatio rerum), Talia 'quhilk can our sawlis bring / In profound wit and grit agilite, / Till understand and haif capacitie' (reddit subtiles animosque...capaces). Caliope (whose name is explained as 'good sound', i.e. eloquence, in Trivet and the *Graecismus*) is supreme, 'of all musik maistress', 'finder of all armony'. From her and Phoebus ('the leader of the Muses' according to Macrobius) Orpheus is born. There is no wonder, says Henryson, that this child of the Muse is 'fair and wyse, / Gentill and gud, full of liberalitie':

> His fader god, and his progenetryse
> A goddess, finder of all armony;
> Quhen he was borne scho set him on hir kne,
> And gart him souk of hir twa paupis quhyte
> The sueit lecour of all musik perfyte. (66–70)

From his divine origin came his 'gentilness', his eloquence and wisdom, and his understanding of music and harmony.

This philosophical matter is continued in the description of Orpheus's journey through the heavens.[51] Medieval readers would expect such a journey to be a source of enlightenment, and, although Orpheus gets no 'knawlege' there of Eurydice, in his descent 'be the way sum melody he lerd'. Like Scipio he hears the music of the spheres, 'passing all instruments musicall':

> 'That', replied my grandfather, 'is a concord of tones separated by unequal but nevertheless carefully proportioned intervals, caused by the rapid motions of the spheres themselves. The high and low tones blended together produce different harmonies. Of course such swift motions could not be accomplished in silence and, as nature requires, the spheres at one extreme produce the low tones and at the other extreme the high tones. Consequently the outermost sphere, the star-bearer, with its swifter motion gives forth a higher-pitched tone, whereas the lunar sphere, the lowest, has the deepest tone...the earth, the ninth and stationary sphere, always

[51] No source for this is known, but suggestions for it could have come from other well-known celestial journeys in the *Somnium Scipionis*, Martianus Capella, etc. (cf. the old notion of Orpheus as a cosmologist, p. 213 above). Is it possible that Henryson found a hint for it in Boethius's phrase, 'inmites superos querens' (taking *querens* for *quaerens*)? Another possible hint may have been found in Trivet's 'ascensus ad caelestia' which he uses of Eurydice in Hades, but which Henryson's *moralitas* seems to link with Orpheus's journey (453–60).

> clings to the same position in the middle of the universe. The other eight spheres. . .produce seven different tones, this number being, one might almost say, the key to the universe. Gifted men, imitating this harmony on stringed instruments and in singing, have gained for themselves a return to this region, as have those who have devoted their exceptional abilities to a search for divine truths. The ears of mortals are filled with this sound, but they are unable to hear it. . . .'[52]

And, like Scipio, he learns something of the *arcana* of the universe, for this melody is the ordered harmony of the cosmos. Macrobius says that the 'soul carries with it a memory of the music which it knew in the sky';[53] perhaps the return of Orpheus to his origins refreshes this memory, though his grief is so great that his music, no matter how closely it echoes this celestial harmony seems unable to assuage it. But he has drunk again of the 'sueit lecour of all musik perfyte'. According to Boethius, whose musical theory is repeated with variations throughout the Middle Ages, we may distinguish three types of music—*musica mundana*, the music of the universe, the harmony which expresses itself in numerical ratios, which regulates the blending of the four elements, the movement of the stars and the seasons; *musica humana*, the harmony of the microcosm of man, the concord of body and soul, the equilibrium of man's 'temperament' (which word itself reflects these ancient theories), the ideal balance of senses and reason; *musica instrumentalis*, the music made by man, which (as Scipio learnt) imitates the harmony of the spheres and follows its laws of proportion. (Henryson, no doubt, thought of harmony in terms of polyphony rather than of ancient monody.) A fine example of this poetic view of the universe is to be found in Fulke Greville's description of Sidney on his death-bed calling for music 'to fashion and enfranchise his heavenly soul into that everlasting harmony of angels, whereof these concords are a kind of terrestrial echo'.[54]

Henryson continues his exposition:

[52] Tr. W. H. Stahl, Macrobius, *Commentary on the Dream of Scipio* (New York, 1952), p. 73. The seven tones are the discrete pitches of a *harmonia* or scale. The following remarks are based on E. de Bruyne, *Études d'Esthétique médiévale* (Bruges, 1946–), I, J. Hollander, *The Untuning of the Sky. Ideas of Music in English Poetry 1500–1700* (Princeton, 1961; refs. from Norton ed., New York, 1970), and Wangermée, *Flemish Music*.

[53] Stahl, p. 195.

[54] *Works*, ed. A. B. Grosart (n.p., 1870), IV, p. 139.

Quhilk armony of all this mappamound
[Quhill] moving seiss, unyt perpetuall,
Quhilk of this world [Plato] the saule can call.

His equation of the celestial harmony with Plato's world soul (if that is what these difficult lines imply) may be an echo of Macrobius: 'the Soul had to be a combination of those numbers that alone possess mutual attraction since the Soul itself was to instil harmonious agreement in the whole world'.[55] From the *Timaeus* the notion of *anima mundi* was eagerly seized on and developed by the twelfth-century Platonists;[56] William of Conches, for instance, identifies cosmic love with it. It is not clear whether Henryson thought this, or whether he imagined it as a generating and ordering force like Nature, or simply, in an Aristotelianized form, as the motive intelligences of the celestial spheres.[57] The following two stanzas expound in detail the mathematical–musical *arcana* of the 'tonis proportionat' which Orpheus has learned. That the digression is shrugged off by the poet with a witty Chaucerian gesture—'Off sic musik to wryt I do bot doit...For in my lyfe I cowth nevir sing a noit'—should not obscure the fact that the information is, it seems, in contemporary terms, accurate, and also strictly relevant to the story. As Professor Hollander says 'it is the perfect Pythagorean revelation in that the "mirry" and "mellefluat" qualities of the music result from the fact that the music is "complet and full of numeris od and even"'.[58] Orpheus has mastered the secrets of the art, and they are to him a source of inspiration and of power. Wisdom has been joined to eloquence.

With his harp (the stringed instrument being the model of harmonious proportion)[59] Orpheus descends to the underworld, and demonstrates his power in a series of encounters with its unharmonious denizens.[60] His performance for Pluto is described more elaborately, in terms which recall his mastery of the 'art':

[55] Stahl, p. 192.

[56] Cf. Wetherbee, *Platonism and Poetry*, esp. pp. 30–6, 26, P. Dronke, 'L'Amor che move il sole e l'altre stelle', *Studi medievali* 3rd ser. vi (1965), 410–12, Tullio Gregory, *Anima Mundi. La filosofia di Guglielmo di Conches e la Scuola di Chartres* (Florence, 1956).

[57] Gregory, pp. 152–4.

[58] Hollander, p. 87.

[59] Hollander, p. 35, mentions the ancient belief in the supremacy of stringed instruments (which have power over the rational part of the soul) as against the wind (associated with passion).

[60] Unlike the fairy inhabitants of the Otherworld in *Sir Orfeo*, they are not said to make music.

Than Orpheus befoir Pluto sat doun,
And in his handis quhit his herp can ta,
And playit mony sueit proportioun,
With baiss tonis in [Ypodorica],
With gemilling in [Ypolerica]...[61]

The echo of celestial harmony which his music brings is powerful enough to affect even the rulers of the underworld:

Quhill at the last for rewth and grit petie
Thay weipit soir that cowth him heir or se.

The unfamiliar emotions evoked are those associated with noble and harmonious love.

We have already seen that Henryson's poem is a story of love, delicately and sympathetically told. From the beginning, however, there is an elegiac note, an awareness of the fragility of human joy:

Off wardly joy, allace, quhat sall I say?
Lyk till a flour that plesandly will spring,
Quhilk fadis sone, and endis with murning, (89–91)

and throughout, strains of melancholy, of irony, and of pathos coexist. Some medieval versions follow Ovid in suggesting that part at least of the motivation for the backward look which loses Eurydice is the fear that she may not be following him. Henryson has none of this. Like Machaut ('Mais amours qui les cuers affole / Et desirs, ou pensee fole / Li fist derrier li resgarder')[62] it is love which causes him to forget the law. The taboo is a condition which is cruelly hard for a lover, for love flows to him from the eyes of his beloved:

Thus Orpheus, with inwart lufe repleit,
So blindit was with grit effectioun,
Pensyfe in hart apone his lady sueit,
Remembrit nocht his hard conditioun. (387–90)

[61] Cf. W. Apel, *Harvard Dictionary of Music*, s.v. 'gymel, gimel, gemell': two part polyphony based on thirds, sixths and tenths. It is described (*c.* 1480) as a style used in England and employing upper as well as lower thirds. May we assume that Orpheus is singing as he plays? (Cf. Boethius: 'illic blanda sonantibus / Chordis carmina temperans', and Machaut (see n. 42).)

[62] *Confort*, 2559–61 (in contrast to *Ovide moralisé* 'douteuz qu'el ne venist mie'). Cf. Gros Louis, 652–3.

There is sadness as well as irony in the Boethian word 'blindit'. The curiously powerful taboo against looking back[63] gives the fateful gesture a great significance in the tale, which is seen as a drama of the spiritual life, and is expounded as such in the *moralitas*. But there is no need to obliterate the scene by an allegory. If we were to *substitute* 'perfect wit' or 'reason' for Orpheus, then there could hardly have been a failure (nor would he have flown into a rage at the loss of his wife). Nor should we make the moral Henryson into a moralistic preacher. That Orpheus's 'backward glance only manifests more plainly the moral backsliding of which, in Henryson's view, he was already guilty'[64] is the view of a critic; Henryson's view, surely, is more complex. It is a human failure, and the hero is left with his sorrow and our 'reuth'. If we were to have a moral at this moment we might wish to set the admiration for human love and for the noble spirit of man of Monteverdi's *Orfeo*—'Nulla impresa per uom si tenta invano...'—against its recognition of its limitations:

> Orfeo vinse l'inferno e vinto poi
> fu dagli affetti suoi;
> Degno d'eterna gloria
> fia sol colui ch'avrà di sè vittoria.

In fact, Henryson leaves us with an open ending, the sorrowful return of the hero. Law not love seems to have triumphed—but love, itself, has a law which is as hard as that of Pluto—quis legem det amantibus? Orpheus in his *planctus* gives full force to its ancient paradoxes and dilemmas:

> 'Quhat art thow, luve, how sall I the defyne?
> Bitter and sueit, crewall and merciable,
> Plesand to sum, till uthir plent and pyne,
> Till sum constant, till uther variable;
> Hard is thi law, thi bandis unbrekable;

[63] Heitmann compares Jung, *Aion* (Zürich, 1951), p. 416. See also W. Deonna, *Symbolisme de l'Œil* (Paris, 1965), pp. 167–8. Hatinguais (p. 287) points out how in William of Conches's interpretation the interdict of the judge of Hades has been allied with the warning in *Luke* ix, 62. Cf. Wetherbee, pp. 116–17. The temptation to look back is used to good effect by confessional manuals on the art of dying (cf. J. McManners, *Reflections at the Death Bed of Voltaire. The Art of Dying in Eighteenth-Century France* (Oxford, 1975), p. 8).

[64] Friedman, p. 208.

> Quha servis the, thocht [he] be nevir so trew,
> Perchance sum tyme [he] sall have causs to rew...'

Human love does not have the serene perfection and harmony of the well-tempered *musica humana*, but it is strangely impressive in its heroic and tragic excess. 'Quhat art thow, luve...?' Henryson, like Chaucer, does not attempt to give a final answer.

Moralitas fabule sequitur. Thus the Chepman and Myllar print marks it off. The metre too is different—stanzas give way to couplets—and the whole *moralitas* is much more elaborate and extended than anything in the *Fables*. As is the case there, it is not a final definition of meaning, but a *queue* which draws attention to some (and to some unexpected) moral aspects of the philosophical tale. Now is the time for the arcane meanings under the *integumentum* to be expounded, for, says Henryson, Boethius wrote this 'feigned fable' for our 'doctrene and gud instructioun', which is 'hid under the cloik of poetre'. He follows the 'noble theologe' Trivet, who 'applied it to good morality'. We shall now see it as a dramatic image of man's nature and destiny. The main characters are given the significances they have in Trivet. Orpheus (son of the god of wisdom and of Calliope, eloquence), is called 'the pairte intelletyfe / Off manis saule' (Trivet has 'pars intellectiva instructa sapiencia et eloquencia', and has a hint for a more particular embodiment: 'eius filius quilibet eloquencia instructus'). Eurydice is 'our affectioun / Be fantesy oft movit up and doun'. Henryson (unlike Trivet) by the word 'our' gently involves us all in the fate of Orpheus (we are reminded of William of Conches's remark that 'no one, not even a child one day old' can be without natural desire). He expands Trivet's more austere 'pars hominis affectiva quam sibi copulare cupit' into a rhetorical and metrical 'imitation' of its instability, its 'moving up and down':

> Quhile to ressone it castis the delyte,
> Quhyle to the flesche it settis the appetyte.

Aristaeus 'is nocht bot gud vertew' (Trivet's 'virtus')—the traditional etymological interpretation. Henryson's

> Bot quhen we fle outthrow the medow grene
> Fra vertew till this warldis vane plesans,
> Myngit with cair and full of variance...

echoes Trivet's 'fugit per prata, id est amena presentis vite' but expands it in a more general devotional fashion (we notice again his use of 'we'). He develops the suggestions of Trivet in his own way: the serpent is 'deidly sin' (= Trivet's sensuality), and our 'effectioun' is 'deid and eik oppressit doun / Till warldly lust' (T. '...ad inferos descendit, id est terrenorum curis se subiciendo'). The account of the various torments mentioned in Boethius's poem follows the same pattern—Henryson selects a suggestion of Trivet's, and then expands it rather in the manner of the French versions discussed earlier. He omits, for instance, the interpretation of Cerberus as 'terra', who is amazed (stupet) 'quod nulla est pars terre in qua non sit admirabilis sapientia et eloquentia' but follows the interpretation (quoted by Trivet from Isidore) of the dog's three heads. Like Trivet he gives the story of Ixion, including, for instance, the birth of the centaurs, but omitting a passage on Juno as 'vita activa', and transforming the rather bald explanation of the stopping of the wheel ('rotacio destitit quando homo sapiencia instructus talia contempnit') into something more poetic:

> Bot quhen ressoun and perfyte sapience
> Playis upone the herp of eloquens.... (507–8)

He expands the stories of Tantalus, the figure of avarice,[65] and of Titius and divination ('Ticius philosophus fuit qui inquisitioni futurorum intentus artem divinandi exercuit',[66] etc.).

Henryson quite clearly told the fable with the *moralitas* in mind—as we have already seen in the description of Eurydice's falling in love. There are also some deliberate echoes (for instance, 'oppress' 102, 443; venom, 105–7, 442, 'wedow', 414, 627). It would be wrong, however, to try to force the allegorical reading offered in the *moralitas* on to every detail of the story. The treatment of Eurydice does not present problems. It is not really 'unusual that Eurydice, the appetite, is described so delicately and tragically...'.[67] Henryson presents 'our effectioun' not as something totally wicked, but as something unstable, wandering, and lost, which when separated from its true

[65] J. Pépin, *Mythe et Allégorie* (Paris, 1958), pp. 173–5, points out that allegorical interpretations of Ixion and Tantalus are ancient (cf. Phaedrus, Perotti's Appendix, ed. Perry, pp. 378–81).
[66] On such strictures against the craft of divination, cf. T. O. Wedel, *The Medieval Attitude towards Astrology* (New Haven, London, 1920), p. 154. Cf. p. 26 above. The French Boethius version in B.N. fr. 576 also has a passage (f. 53) on Ticius and divination.
[67] Gros Louis, p. 654.

consort pulls him away from the 'fons boni lucidus'. The most difficult case is that of Aristaeus. In spite of what some commentators say,[68] it really does seem that in the fable Henryson is insisting on his lustfulness. We can hardly believe that he 'apparently forgot his moral when he was writing the actual poem'.[69] Rather he is deliberately constructing one of those startling 'dark' moralities which we have seen in some of the *Fables*. Whether it is successful from the point of view of literary technique is another matter. The allegorical significances of the other figures in the scene, Orpheus and Eurydice, are also arcane—in the sense that the uninstructed reader might well not see them at this point—but not to the same degree. Aristaeus is an extreme, enigmatic allegory, 'per contrarium', and we are left with the sense of a somewhat awkward mixture of allegorical levels.

The more general themes (and those which are perhaps nearer to the heart of the poem) generate some eloquence:

Than perfyte wisdome weipis wondir soir,
Seand thusgait our appetyte misfair,
And to the hevin he [passis] up belyfe,
Schawand to us the lyfe contemplatyfe,
The perfyte wit, and eik the fervent luve
We suld haif allway to the hevin abuve;
Bot seildin thair our appetyte is fundin—
It is so fast [into] the body bundin;
Thairfoir dounwart we cast our myndis e,
Blindit with lust, and may nocht upwartis fle;
Sould our desyre be socht up in the spheiris,
Quhen it is tedderit in thir warldly breiris,
—Quhyle on the flesch, quhyle on this warldis wrak—
And to the hevin full small intent we tak.
Schir Orpheus, thow seikis all in vane
Thy wyfe so he.... (445–60)

The oppositions of high and low, the freedom of the 'quick mind'

[68] So (following MacQueen, *Robert Henryson*, pp. 34–5), Elliott, p. xviii: 'allegorically beasts are sensual passions, and here such types of carnality are governed...by Aristaeus'.

[69] Gros Louis, p. 654. A more cogent criticism is that suggested to me by Professor Norton-Smith, that the *moralitas* turns into an open excursus on 'this fenyeit fable', i.e. Boethius's 'haec fabula', the original of the 'story', which Henryson's poem has already altered beyond compare.

(implied in 'fle') and the fetters of the earth (in the fine phrase 'tedderit on thir warldly breiris'),[70] light and darkness (cf. the echo of the Boethian 'blindit') are not only those of medieval spiritual instruction, but of the two worlds of Boethius's Platonic vision. The sympathetic, almost consolatory tone of 'Schir Orpheus...cum doun again' reminds us of the eloquent expression Philosophy's poem gives of the impulse it is intended to curb, 'the attachment to worldly things which is at the heart of the metaphor of imprisonment'. The contrast between the tragic division of 'perfect reason' and 'affection' and of an ideal harmony continues throughout the *moralitas*. The torments of Ixion seem to mirror the cares and uncertainties of the world: this 'uglye quheile' becomes that of Fortune. The eloquent power of Orpheus's music ('ressoun and perfyte sapience...upone the herp of eloquens') grants a respite from the 'grit solicitud':

> ...the grit solicitud,
> Quhyle up, quhyle doun, to win this warldis gud,
> Seissis furthwith, and our affectioun
> Waxis quiet in contemplatioun. (515–18)

(Gently and unobtrusively, Henryson is also suggesting a justification for poetry (the 'herp of eloquens', that combination of wisdom and eloquence) as an effective force—it '*makis persuasioun*' to 'draw our will...fra syn' (471–4), it '*persuadis* our fleschly appetyte' (509), '*schawand* to us quhat perrell...' (547); its 'concords are a kind of terrestrial echo' of the divine harmony.) Likewise the avarice of Tantalus for 'vane prosperitie', 'gottin with grit labour, / Keipit with dreid, and tynt with grit dolour' represents the 'solicitud' of temporal things—'ythand thochtis...and besines / To gaddir gold.' The ideal of harmony in *musica humana* is achieved—though briefly—

> ...Orpheus hes wone Euridices
> Quhen our desyre with ressoun makis pess. (616–17)

The two parts together make up the harmony of the soul—as Boethius says (*de Musica*), 'sensus ac ratio quaedam facultatis harmonicae instrumenta sunt'.[71]

[70] Cf. Hugh of St Victor (*PL* clxxvii, 285, quoted by Wetherbee, p. 61): 'Behold the ladder of Jacob. It rested on the earth and the top of it reached the heavens. The earth is the flesh, the heavens God. Our minds ascend in contemplation from the depths to the most high...'. Cf. also Wetherbee, pp. 75ff.

[71] V, chapter 1, quoted by de Bruyne, p. 28.

The 'medievalized' Boethian ideas of the *moralitas* are put into the framework of Christian devotion by a final prayer. The words are carefully chosen. God is asked to allow us to *stand* (with suggestions of Boethian stability and peace) in 'perfyte love',[72] as that which rules the universe ('Terras ac pelagus regens / Et caelo imperitans amor'):

Now pray we God, sen our affectioun
Is allway promp and reddy to fall doun,
That he wald undirput his haly hand
Of mantenans, and gife us [grace] to stand
In perfyte luve....

It makes a fine and eloquent ending, but the reader cannot suppress his doubts about the artistic success of the *moralitas* as a whole. Sadly, it is its ambitious scope and its ingenuity which are the source of its weakness. It is simply too elaborate, and too detailed, so that parts of it begin to resemble the *longueurs* of the *Ovide Moralisé*. The tale, moreover, has been extended too far for the whole to have anything like the emblematic effect of the *Fables*. It is a bold and original work, indeed a 'New Orpheus', but its long *moralitas* does its best to drag it down into the mass of those poems which are simply typical of their age.

[72] See Boethius, II m. 8, III m. 9; cf. Wetherbee, p. 76.

CHAPTER SEVEN

Shorter Poems

The shorter poems attributed to Henryson are not as well known as they deserve to be.[1] They are poems which belong to well-established genres, and they are of uneven quality, but the best show the distinctive and bold handling of traditional form and material that we have come to expect. I begin with a trio of satirical poems, and—with some hesitation—with *The Want of Wyse Men*. It is, in fact, far from certain that this poem properly belongs to the canon. It is not attributed to Henryson in either of the surviving texts, but its association with *Orpheus and Eurydice* in a single Chepman and Myllar tract has convinced most editors of its genuineness.[2] In the attribution of this sort of conventional poetry, internal and stylistic evidence is of little or no value, but one might at least entertain the thought that the poem's learned reference to Saturn and to Octavian could suggest the hand of our poet. *The Want of Wyse Men* belongs to a favourite type of late medieval poetry, the general complaint on 'abuses of the age'.[3] It is not a type of poetry which usually excites the modern reader. He finds its satire too generalized (it is almost impossible not to agree with the poets' denunciations of wickedness or sin), and is quickly bored with catalogues of vices which become steadily less urgent and convincing. Medieval readers, however, seem to have been attracted by the type, and to have used it as a focus for their feelings about particular as well as general injustice. At the beginning of Book xvi of the *Scotichronicon*,[4]

[1] See the full study by I. W. A. Jamieson, 'The Minor Poems of Robert Henryson', *SSL* ix (1971–2).

[2] Cf. Jamieson, 'Minor Poems', p. 126n. The poem will not appear as Henryson's in Professor Fox's forthcoming edition. (Professor Fox also cautions us against accepting the attribution of all the remaining shorter poems as certain.)

[3] Cf., e.g., *Historical Poems of the XIVth and XVth Centuries*, ed. R. H. Robbins (New York, 1959), Nos. 54 *et seq.* (and notes).

[4] Ed. W. Goodall (Edinburgh, 1759), II, p. 474.

Bower pauses to consider the instability of the kingdom, and the need for justice and the enforcement of the law ('Jura enim publica certissime sunt humanae vitae solatia, infirmorum auxilia, tyrannorum frena; unde et securitas venit, et conscientia proficit'). Recalling the remarks of Ovid on the wickedness of the present, he is led to quote a Latin poem on the decline from the Golden Age:

> Aurea tempora primaque robora praeterierunt.
> Aurea gens fuit, et simul haec ruit, illa ruerunt...

and to continue with a personal application: 'propter enim gemitus inopum et miserias pauperum, quos etiam ego, qui haec scribo, praesenti et eodem die vidi et audivi, in proximo et in confinibus meis pauperes denudari vestibus et utensilibus inhumaniter spoliari...'. A quotation from *Ecclesiastes* comes into his mind, and he concludes by moving from prophetic complaint to just such a general poem on the abuses of the time:

> Unde et ego, aeque ut in Trenis Jeremias, idiomate varians, celeumata de cordis penetralibus erumpere cogor, et dicere compellor:
> Lauch liis down our all: fallax fraus regnat ubique.
> Micht gerris richt down fall: regnum quia rexit inique.
> Treuth is made now thrall: spernunt quam dico plerique.
> Bot til Christ we call, periemus nos animique.

The Want of Wyse Men immediately announces the great confusion of a world turned upside down:[5]

> Me ferlyis of this grete confusioun;
> I wald sum clerk of connyng walde declerde,
> Quhat gerris this warld be turnyt up so doun.
> Thare is na faithfull fastnes founde in erde;
> Now ar noucht thre may traistly trow the ferde;
> Welth is away, and wit is worthin wrynkis...

The idea of the decline from that age which 'for gudely governance' was called 'goldin' (Saturn—here in his rôle as the bringer of civilization and plenty—and Octavian are the exemplary rulers who maintain peace and order) is continued in a little scene, faintly reminiscent of

[5] Cf. Curtius, pp. 94–8. In its comic manifestations a favourite subject of the artists (the hunter hunted, etc.); often adapted by satirists (cf., for instance, Skelton's 'The Manner of the World Nowadays').

Piers Plowman, in which the wisdom of the past is slighted by the folly of the present—he who knows 'placebo and noucht half dirige' can come in, while Aristotle, Austin and Ambrose 'stand at the dure'. From time to time, the poem shows signs of losing itself in the disparate manifestations of wickedness, but it is held together by the dominant themes of disorder, of lack of balance—

All ledis lyvis lawles at libertee
Noucht reulit be reson, mare than ox or asse

—and by their contrasting ideals, of 'sad maturitie', 'prudence and policy'. There are moments when the overwhelming threat of the abuses of the age is strongly felt:

Now wrang hes warrane, and law is bot wilfulness;
Quha hes the war is worthin on him all the wyte,
For trewth is tressoun, and faith is fals fekilness;
Gylle is now gyd, and vane lust is also delyte...

As in Bower's poem, the conclusion is a sad 'bot til Christ we call'; a final prayer beseeches the lord of lords to reform 'all thir sayd thingis', 'as thou best thinkis'. Dullness is redeemed by some vigorous homely lines—'into godis neiss it stinkis', or the proverbial refrain 'want of wyse men makis fulis sitt on binkis'.[6]

Another poem against 'fals titlaris'[7] (usually called *Aganis Haisty Credence of Titlaris*) is advice to a lord, the traditional wisdom of the 'mirrors' for princes:

Ane worthy lord sowld wey ane taill wyslie,
The tailltellar, and quhome of it is tald;
Gif it be said for luve, or for invy...

It is a plea for prudence and justice; tale-bearers are motivated by envy, and harm the innocent. It rises to a rhetorical flourish:

O wicket tung, sawand dissentioun,
Of fals taillis to tell that will not tyre,
Moir perrellus than ony fell pusoun,
The pane of hell thow sall haif to thi hyre.

6 Whiting, D 150.

7 Cf. Jamieson, pp. 136–9; Gregory Smith, I, p. lxii, notes similarities with Lydgate's *Fall of Princes*, I, 4243ff. and (possibly) with *The Churl and the Bird*.

More convincing expression of the dangers of tale-tellers and flatterers can be found elsewhere in medieval literature, in set descriptions (as in *The Ancrene Riwle*) or in stories such as *The Manciple's Tale* which demonstrate dramatically that 'a wikked tonge is worse than a feend'. Henryson's poem, however, moves to a strong ending with three vivid images of the backbiter:

> Thre personis severall he slayis with ane wowrd—
> Himself, the heirar, and the man saiklace.
> Within ane hude he hes ane dowbill face,
> Ane bludy tung, undir a fair pretence...

If these two poems are hardly outstanding examples of their kind, the third, *Sum Practysis of Medecyne*,[8] although it presents considerable linguistic difficulty, has a dazzling verve and vigour that is worthy of Dunbar. Some of the 'practices' of medieval medicine were bizarre enough in their own right:[9]

> For eyen that er sore: sethe the rede snayl in water, and geder of the grese and anoynt thin eyen therwith... For the fallyng evel: Tak a yong urchy[n] and roste him to poudre; and of the doust put on thy mete; and drynke the melke of a woman that hath the ferst chyld.

'Urine of a child innocent and mayden' was part of a remedy for 'all evils of eyes'; part of an ointment for gout consisted of 'the grece of a bor and the grece of a ratoun and cattys grece and voxis grece and horsgrece and the grece of a broke', with herbs and 'a litel lynnesed'. Not surprisingly, the idea of a burlesque prescription or 'recipe' had occurred to other writers, as in this 'good medycyn for sor eyen':

> For a man that is almost blynd:
> Lat hym go barhed all day ageyn the wynd
> Tyll the so[n]ne be sette;

[8] Cf. Jamieson, pp. 139–41. Denton Fox, in an important article, 'Henryson's "Sum Practysis of Medecyne"', *SP* lxix (1972), 453–60, draws attention to the French *herberies*, parodies of the selling speeches of quacks (e.g. Rutebeuf's *Dit de l'Herberie*), and suggests that the sixteenth-century parallels to Henryson's poem may well indicate the existence of an earlier 'specifically Scottish tradition of humorous medical poems'.

[9] G. Henslow, *Medical Works of the Fourteenth Century* (London, 1899), pp. 107, 70, 94, 20.

At evyn wrap hym in a cloke,
And put hym in a hows full of smoke,
    And loke that every hol be well shett.

And whan hys eyen begynne to rope,
Fyll hem full of brynston and sope,
    And hyll hym well and warme;
And yf he se not by the next mone
As well at mydnyght as at none
    I schal lese my ryght arme.[10]

Nearer, perhaps, to Henryson's more inventive and fantastic burlesque are some suggestions for 'a good medesyn yff a mayd have lost her madenhed to make her a mayd ayeyn': she should be laid in an 'esy bed' in a 'hot hows', and fed well with chickens and gruel, and other medicinal foods such as the 'neighing of a mare' and 'gnattys smere'—

...She must have allso
The oyll of a mytys too
With the kreke of a henne,
And the lyghte of a glawworme in the derke,
With ix skyppys of a larke,
And the lanche of a wrenne,
She must have of the wyntyrs nyghte
.vii. myle of the mone-lych[t]
Fast knyt in a bladder:
Ye must medyl ther among
vii Wellsshemens song,
And hang yt on a lader;
She must have the left fot of an ele,
Wyth the krekynge of a cart-whele,
Wele hoylyd on a herdyll;
Ye must caste ther upon
The mary of a whetstone,
And the lenthe of Judas gerdylle.[11]

[10] R. H. Robbins, *Secular Lyrics of the XIVth and XVth Centuries* (Oxford, 1952), p. 102.

[11] T. Wright and J. O. Halliwell, *Reliquiae Antiquae* (London, 1841), I, pp. 250–1. Cf. in later mumming plays, the doctor's fantastic speech in R. J. E. Tiddy, *The Mummers' Play* (Oxford, 1923), p. 171. Cf. also A. Brody, *The English Mummers and their Plays* (London, 1971), p. 57.

Such poems, like Henryson's *Practysis*, are of course part of a larger body of satire directed against doctors and apothecaries. The excessive public veneration which the medical profession now enjoys is a relatively recent development. In earlier times, its ways with patients were a favourite target.[12] In one Middle English proverb a painter becomes a physician because where once his errors could be seen by all, now they could be safely hidden beneath the ground. 'On dit un proverbe, d'ordinaire: *Après la mort le médecin*; mais vous verrez que si je m'en mêle, on dira: *Après le médecin*, gare la mort!'—the suspicion that physicians, instead of fighting the good fight against death, were in fact its agents, recurs throughout the centuries from Langland's 'murderers are many leeches', to Heywood's apothecary ('for when ye fele your conscyens redy, / I can sende you to heven quyckly'), to M. Purgon ('M. Purgon est un homme qui a huit mille bonnes livres de rente'. *Toinette*. 'Il faut qu'il ait tué bien des gens pour s'être fait si riche'), and beyond. In the eyes of satirists, their remedies, as well as being often lethal, were sometimes of a drastic simplicity. Poggio has a merry tale of a physician who gave purgative pills to all and sundry, even (quite successfully) to a man who wanted to find his ass; the budding doctor in *Le Malade Imaginaire* gives the correct answer in his 'examination':

...Quas remedia eticis,
Pulmonicis atque asmaticis
Trovas a propas facere?

Bachelierus Clysterium donare,
Postea seignare,
Ensuita purgare.

The impenetrable jargon of doctors and apothecaries constantly provoked satire. Heywood's apothecary offers his wares like an itinerant huckster:

Here be other: as diosfialios
Blanka manna, diospoliticon,
Mercury sublyme, and metridaticon,

[12] The following examples are taken from Molière, *Le Médecin volant*, sc. ii, *Piers Plowman*, ed. Skeat, B vi, 275, Heywood, *The Foure PP*. (J. Q. Adams, *Chief Shakespearean Dramas* (Cambridge, Mass., 1924)), 374–5, Molière, *Le Malade Imaginaire*, I, v, Poggio in Lenaghan, *Caxton's Aesop*, p. 227, *Le Malade Imaginaire*, Intermède at end of Act III.

Pelitory, and arsefetita,
Cassy, and colloquintita.
These be the thynges that breke all stryfe
Betwene mannes sycknes and his lyfe.
From all payne these shall you delever,
And set you even at reste for ever![13]

Incompetent or quack doctors are stock figures of folly. In *The Ship of Fools* Brant ridicules those who test a patient's urine, and take so long in searching through their books for an answer that the unfortunate victim dies.[14] In the 'Cure of Folly', Bosch shows a doctor wearing a fool's cap operating on a foolish patient's head, cutting out the 'stone of folly'.

Medieval medical satire is crude and sharp, and Henryson's *Practysis* is no exception. It is no gentle leg-pulling exercise;[15] rather, its violent and wild language suggests a 'flyting' of the kind we find in Dunbar or Skelton. Its violence and fantasy seem to be the expression of an extraordinary urge to cast off the bonds of normal language and of good sense, but in fact what seems to be a wilful abandonment of the poet's usual delicate rhetorical technique and control of register in favour of a joyously wasteful exuberance turns out to be an artful—if Rabelaisian—choice. Verbal fantasy, parody, and crude invective do more than afford entertainment.[16] The flood of words expresses the anger of the poet, and at the same time creates a mirror of the folly of the victim. Petrarch's *Invectiva contra medicum*[17] defends rhetoric, humanism, and the feigned fables of poets against the real lies of some physicians, but Henryson here ignores such abstract questions, and proceeds directly to a personal attack:

Guk, guk, gud day, ser, gaip quhill ye get it,
Sic greting may gane weill gud laik in your hude
Ye wald deir me, I trow, because I am dottit,
To ruffill me with a ryme...

[13] *The Foure PP.*, ll. 616ff.

[14] Brant, *Narrenschiff*, section 55; for Bosch, cf. M. Whinney, *Early Flemish Painting* (London, 1968), p. 101, pl. 65 (cf. also p. 102).

[15] Jamieson, p. 141.

[16] Cf. R. Garapon, *La Fantaisie verbale dans le Théâtre français du Moyen Âge à la fin du 17e Siècle* (Paris, 1957).

[17] Ed. P. G. Ricci (Rome, 1950).

The tone is not far from Skelton's 'Gup, gorbellyd Godfrey, gup Garnesche gaudy fool!'[18] The railing opening implies a situation, and an opponent to whom Henryson speaks in 'greeting'. The offending 'ryme' is dismissed:

> Your saying I haif sene, and on syd set it,
> As geir of all gadering, glaikit, nocht gude...

and the attack turns to the opponent's incompetence in medicine—'your cunnyng in to cure / Is clowtit and clampit...'. The poetic defence of 'my prettick in pottingary' becomes a kind of vaunt, which rises in crescendo:

> Is nowdir fevir, nor fell, that our the feild fure,
> Seiknes nor sairness, in tyme gif I seid,
> But I can lib thame and leiche thame fra lame and lesure....

He obligingly sends a 'schedule', containing four 'physics', to cure his opponent's malice. The first, for the 'colic', includes such laxatives as laurean (laurel) and culrage (arsesmart); excrement figures prominently, and the tone—as befits a flyting—is deliberately crude and vulgar—'the crud of my culome with your teith crakit'. The poet's fantasy begins to work; in the midst of lists of herbs he recommends

> The hair of the hurcheoun nocht half deill hakkit,
> With snowt of ane selch, ane swelling to swage.

The next 'physic'—'to latt yow to sleip'—becomes even more marvellously fantastic. 'Recipe' (the common opening in such 'recipes')—

> Recipe, thre ruggis of the reid ruke,
> The gant of ane gray meir, the claik of ane guss,
> The dram of ane drekterss, the douk of ane duke,
> The gaw of ane grene dow, the leg of ane lowss,
> Fyve unce of ane fle wing, the fyn of ane fluke,
> With ane sleiffull of slak, that growis in the sluss;
> Myng all thir in ane mass with the mone cruke...

The mad precision of 'fyve unce' is a nice touch. This concoction, steeped with red nettle seed 'in strang wesch' is to be used 'for to bath your ba cod'. By the time we reach the third 'physic', alliterative *impossibilia* are pouring out with surrealist zest:

[18] *Poetical Works*, ed. Dyce (London, 1843), I, p. 119.

...sevin sobbis of ane selche, the quhidder of ane quhaill,
The lug of ane lempet is nocht to forsaik,
The harnis of ane haddok, hakkit or haill,
With ane bustfull of blude of the scho bak...

Prescribed for the cough are (*inter alia*) 'ane grit gowpene of the gowk fart' and 'ane unce of ane oster' 'Annoyntit with nurice doung, for it is rycht nyce / Myngit with mysdirt and with mustart'. At last, the poet takes his leave:

Gud nycht, guk, guk, for sa I began,
I haif no come at this tyme longer to tarry

—and he closes with instructions for the gathering of the herbs ('in ane gude oure', as would have been customary) and for the administering of the medicine:

Ser, minister this medecyne at evin to sum man,
And or pryme be past, my powder I pary,
They sall bliss yow, or ellis bittirly yow ban;
For it sall fle thame, in faith, out of the fary:
Bot luk quhen ye gadder thir gressis and gerss,
Outhir sawrand or sour,
That it be in ane gude oure:
It is ane mirk mirrour,
Ane uthir manis erss.

Where *Sum Practysis* is an extraordinary expression of 'the exuberance, wildness and eccentricity of the Middle Ages', the shorter religious and moral poems exhibit those qualities which Edwin Muir found characteristic of 'the fundamental seriousness, humanity and strength of the Scottish imagination'. Even here, however, there is considerable variety. *The Annunciation*[19] is in its own way as bold an experiment as *Sum Practysis of Medecyne*. The best-known of the English

[19] Cf. S. Rossi, 'L' "Annunciazione" di Robert Henryson', *Aevum* xxix (1955), 70–81, J. Stephens, 'Devotion and Wit in Henryson's "The Annunciation"', *English Studies* li (1970), 323–31, Charles A. Hallett, 'Theme and Structure in Henryson's "The Annunciation"', *SSL* x (1973), 165–74. On the Middle English lyrics, cf. Rosemary Woolf, *The English Religious Lyric in the Middle Ages* (Oxford, 1968), esp. pp. 141–3, Gray, *Themes and Images in the Medieval English Religious Lyric* (London, 1972), chapter 6. On the treatment of the theme in art, cf. the discussion in M. Baxandall, *Painting and Experience in Fifteenth-Century Italy* (Oxford, 1972), pp. 46ff.

medieval lyrics on this favourite topic, 'I sing of a maiden that is makeles', is a masterpiece of simplicity which makes its effects by an unobtrusive precision of detail and by the careful and elegant evocation of emotional undertones. Henryson's poem is totally different; it is dramatic and sometimes flamboyant, and prefers abstraction to detail. It is an elaborate metrical and rhythmical artifact, which has to be read aloud for its effect to be felt. He uses only two rhymes in each stanza, and the *b*-rhyme is carried on throughout the whole poem. As this is on *-is*, it produces an almost breathless series of present tenses, which express very appropriately the surging movement of the poem. Alliteration (sometimes in intricate patterns) gives a meaningful emphasis: Mary 'wox in hir chaumer chaist with child'. There is no sense of strain: the poem is a triumphant metrical performance. Simple conventional epithets ('myld Mary') and formulaic phrases ('barret betis') are in nice contrast to the virtuosity of the form.

Henryson sees the Annunciation as a drama of love. He begins boldly:

Forcy as deith is likand lufe,
Throuch quhome al bittir suet is,
No thing is hard, as writ can pruf,
Till him in lufe that letis,
Luf us fra barret betis.

The proverbial 'love is as strong as death'[20] had been often used in devotional or mystical texts from the time of Rolle; Henryson characteristically extends it by paradox. The *sententia* is exemplified by the narrative which follows—the story of Gabriel's coming, the announcement, Mary's wonder and silence 'as weill afeirit'. Interestingly, Henryson chooses not to give Mary that well-known answer which was the germ of so many Annunciation poems, but allows it to be assumed in the fine and suggestive line 'brichtnes fra bufe aboundis'. His treatment is not visual; he does not encourage us to imagine the scene as the writer of a prose meditation might well have done. Yet his curious blend of abstraction and dynamic narrative is remarkably successful. Gabriel 'glidis' back to heaven, and leaves the Virgin 'blith with barne'. The poet's exclamation:

O worthy wirschip singuler,
To be moder and madyn meir,

[20] Cf. Whiting, L 523.

As cristin faith confidis;
That borne was of hir sidis,
Our maker goddis sone so deir,
Quhilk erd, wattir, and hevinnis cleir
Throw grace and virtu gidis

signals a return to the 'sentence' of the opening lines, and to a meditation on the significance of the great event. The traditional paradoxes—that Mary is both mother and maiden, and that she, a humble creature, bore the creator of all things—are deftly turned. In the following stanza we are reminded of three miracles of love: the bush burning but unconsumed which Moses saw, the dry wand of Aaron which flowered, Gideon's fleece which was moist with dew though the earth around it remained dry. They are, of course, traditional figures of the Virgin Birth, but they are handled with virtuosity. A bold image introduces them:

The miraclis ar mekle and meit,
Fra luffis ryver rynnis[21]

—-and immediately, the burning bush of Moses is identified with the fire of love—

The low of luf haldand the hete,
Unbrynt full blithlie birnis....

Even more boldly, Henryson goes on to remind us explicitly of the omnitemporal present in the eyes of God; for Him these miracles occur at the same moment:

Quhen Gabriell beginnis
With mouth that gudely may to grete
The wand of Aarone, dry but wete,
To burioun nocht blynnis...

'The here and now', says Erich Auerbach, 'is no longer a mere link in an earthly chain of events, it is simultaneously something which has

[21] 'Love's river' (cf. the four rivers which flow from Paradise (*Gen.* ii), and the theme of *Fons Vitae* (*NQ* ccviii (1963), 132)) suggests the idea of an overwhelming excess of love, which in religious and mystical contexts is regarded as most laudable (cf. L. Spitzer, *World Harmony*, pp. 95ff.). Cf. also R. L. Greene, *The Early English Carols* (2nd ed., Oxford, 1977), No. 123, '...Ther sprong a well at Maris fote / That torned all this world to bote...'.

always been, and which will be fulfilled in the future; and strictly, in the eyes of God, it is something eternal, something omnitemporal, something already consummated in the realm of fragmentary earthly event.'[22] When Gabriel speaks, it is the fulfilment of these figures of the event in what mortals regard as earlier history, but the fulfilment coexists with its 'shadows'. We suddenly realize that the insistent present tenses of the poem are more than a simple expression of its own forward movement. The great event, the expression of love, takes place in time, and subsumes its shadows. We have been shown it diachronically in a sequential narrative, and synchronically, as an expression of the 'being' of love. Henryson goes on to tell us that this great expression of love will be perfectly fulfilled in the sacrifice of Christ. Here he lapses into a rather weak rehearsal of the later significant events of Christ's life, but his poem revives with a final prayer to the Virgin—

O lady lele and lusumest,
Thy face moist fair and schene is!—

as the highest human expression of love, and as the eternal queen of heaven:

This prayer fra my splene is,
That all my werkis wikkitest
Thow put away, and mak me chaist
Fra Termigant that teyn is,
And fra his cluke that kene is;
And syne till hevin my saule thou haist,
Quhar thi makar of michtis mast
Is kyng, and thow thair quene is.

Henryson's two poems on old age are not as spectacular as this, but they are none the less interesting. In medieval religious lyrics, old age is usually a topic which is the occasion for a grim *memento mori*. Old men speak with warning voices to the young:

Now age is croppyn on me ful styll,
He makyt me hore, blake and bowe;
I goo all dounward with the hylle...

Now ys this day commyn to the nyght;
I have lost my lewying;

[22] *Mimesis* (tr. W. Trask, Princeton, 1953), p. 74.

A dredfull payne ys for me dyght,
In cold claye therein to clynge...[23]

The Ressoning betuix Aige and Youth begins with a lyrical *chanson d'aventure* opening, and presents a simple contrast between Youth, the 'mirry man', singing sweetly his refrain 'O yowth, be glaid in to thy flowris grene', and Age, 'a cative on ane club', whose appearance is reminiscent of the Saturn of the *Testament*

...a cative on ane club cumand,
With cheikis clene and lyart lokis hoir;
His ene was how, his voce was hess hostand,
Wallowit richt wan, and waik as ony wand.

On his breast he has a 'bill' (perhaps he can no longer sing) with this 'legend': 'O youth, thy flowris fedis fellone sone'. Youth's confidence in his strength and beauty is brash, but endearing; it is sombrely answered by Age:

Thy fleschely lust thow salt also defy,
And pane the sall put fra paramour;
Than will no bird be blyth of the in bouir;
Quhen thy manheid sall mynnis as the mone,
Thow sall assay gif that my song be sour:
O youth, thy flowris fedis fellone sone![24]

Tactfully, Henryson does not award victory to either; they go their different ways, and we are left with their two refrains—'O yowth, be glaid into thy flowris grene!', 'O yowth, thy flowris faidis fellone sone'. In *The Praise of Age*, the old man, though 'decrepit', can sing gaily and clearly 'The more of age the nerar hevynnis blis'. The disorders of the world come from 'covatise', but he is content to be safe from the perils of youth. He represents the other traditional aspect of age—contentment and wisdom—and rejoices in his old age because it brings him closer to

[23] Carleton Brown, *Religious Lyrics of the XVth Century* (Oxford, 1939), No. 147. On old age, cf. G. R. Coffman, 'Old Age from Horace to Chaucer', *Speculum* ix (1934), 249–77, K. McKenzie, 'Antonio Pucci on Old Age', *ib.* xv (1940), 180–5, Gray, *Themes and Images*, pp. 173–5. See Jamieson, pp. 127–31. Cf. the description of Age in *The Parlement of the Thre Ages* ed. M. Y. Offord, EETS ccxlvi (1959), ll. 152–60.

[24] I follow Fox in adopting the Maitland Folio reading *mynnis*.

God. This is a note which is rare—though not unique—in medieval English lyrics.[25]

The Abbay Walk[26] is a simple and eloquent example of that kind of medieval poem in which the poet comes upon an inscription with some startling message. In this case it is written as a *titulus* on the wall of an abbey (there seems to be no need to think of Dunfermline in particular):

On caiss I kest on syd myne e,
And saw this writtin upoun a wall:
'Off quhat estait, man, that thow be,
Obey and thank thy god of all.'

The *titulus* continues for the remaining six stanzas, giving traditional topics of consolation for those in adversity—'blame nocht thy lord', but accept tribulation in humanity, learn patience from Job, and ignore the vanity of the world. The message is driven home by the refrain 'Obey and thank thy god of all'.

The shadows of the great plagues of the Middle Ages may sometimes be seen in the literature and art of the time.[27] The terror of the plague is brilliantly evoked by the description of the stricken city of Florence at the beginning of the *Decameron*, or the drawing by Dürer (who was probably forced to leave Nüremberg in 1505 because of pestilence) of Death as King of the plague, riding a gaunt horse with a cowbell strung around its neck. Humbler memorials are the many prayers (both prose

[25] Cf. Kennedy's 'Honour with Age', *The Maitland Folio MS.* ed. W. A. Craigie, STS N.S. vii (1919), I, pp. 234–5, Gray, *A Selection of Religious Lyrics* (Oxford, 1975), Nos. 91, 92 and notes.

[26] Cf. Jamieson, pp. 132–3. Gregory Smith, I, pp. lxviii–lxix, drew attention to close similarities with a poem in the Vernon MS. ('Bi a wey wandryng', *Minor Poems of the Vernon Manuscript*, ed. F. J. Furnivall, EETS cxvii (1901), II, pp. 688–9).

[27] Cf. Gray, *Themes and Images*, pp. 181–2, 285–6, *Selection*, No. 65 and note. For Dürer's drawing, see E. Panofsky, *The Life and Art of Albrecht Dürer* (Princeton, 1955), p. 106, fig. 147. The plague saints were known in Scotland: St. Roch on an arch at Rosslyn shows the plague spot on his leg; St. Sebastian had a chapel at Easter Portsburgh. Foullis wrote a poem, *Calamitose pestis Elega deploratio*, on an outbreak of plague in Edinburgh at the end of the fifteenth century, sent, he says, by God as a punishment because of a fire in St. Giles (*Humanistica Lovaniensia* xxiv (1975), 108–22). On the plague in Scotland, see J. D. Comrie, *History of Scottish Medicine* (London, 1932), pp. 202–21. There seems to be nothing in Henryson's poem which links it with any one of the several outbreaks in the late fifteenth or early sixteenth centuries. Cf. Jamieson, pp. 141–3.

and verse) against the plague, or the chapels or images of saints whose help was invoked, such as St. Roch, who had a chapel dedicated to him in Edinburgh. Popular images common in German prints (the so-called *Pestblätter*) often show the Virgin Mary protecting suppliants under her mantle from the arrows of a wrathful God. So strong is the faith in the immanent justice of God that the popular devotional attitude is that the plague is allowed to come as a punishment for sin (though possibly one may wonder if the insistence on this suggests the existence of a less pious reaction, and of a need for reassurance). The later chronicler, Pitscottie, describing the 'pestilence without mercy' of 1439, says that it was accompanied by a great dearth sent by 'the verie wraith and yre of god to caus ws knaw our sellfis and throcht that scourge to provock to amendiment of lyffe', but goes on to lament that 'albeit thir thrie plaigues and scwrges [war, famine and pestilence] rang amangis ws yit nevertheless sum men meid thame nevir to amend thair lyffis bot rather became daylie worss, dyveris utheris that pleinyeit upone the enormiteis that thay sustenit gat litill or na redres, quhairfoir the peopill began to warie and curs that evir it chanceit theme to leiwe in sick wicked and dangerous tymes'.[28]

Henryson's *Ane Prayer for the Pest* is a simple prayer addressed to God, 'of power infinyt'. The traditional theological view is put with grave clarity in the first stanza: 'thow dois na wrang to puneiss our offens'. The justice of God, who is all-powerful and all-wise, is not to be questioned; suffering mortals may appeal only to his mercy:

> Bot thow with rewth our hairtis recreat,
> We ar bot deid but only thy clemens.

The petition 'Preserve us fra this perrelus pestilens' is repeated as a refrain in the first five stanzas, and echoed in the following three. We would be glad, says the poet, if God could punish our sins by some other tribulation—by death or sickness, or hunger:

> Wer it thy will, O lord of hevin, allaiss,
> That we sowld thus be haistely put doun,
> And dye as beistis without confessioun....

[28] *The Historie and Cronicles of Scotland*, ed. Æ. J. G. Mackay, STS xlii (1899), p. 30. Cf. Holcot's story of a plague of flies in Norfolk with *ira dei* written on their wings (B. Smalley, *English Friars and Antiquity in the Early Fourteenth Century* (Oxford, 1960), p. 161).

The traditional ideas—the fearful justice of God, the admission of sin, the plea for that mercy given expression by a cruel death on the Cross—are woven together with solemn eloquence:

> Haif mercy, lord, haif mercy, hevynis king!
> Haif mercy of thy pepill penetent;
> Haif mercy of our petouss punissing;
> Retreit the sentence of thy just jugement
> Aganis us synnaris, that servis to be schent:
> Without mercy, we ma mak no defens.
> Thow that, but rewth, upoun the rude was rent,
> Preserve us frome this perrellus pestilens.

As the poem proceeds, the emphasis shifts dramatically from one to the other. Stanza 6, for instance, is a vehement plea to the mercy shown in man's redemption, but ends with a sudden recalling of our 'ingratitude':

> ...Haif rewth, Lord, of thyne awin symilitude;
> Puneiss with pety and nocht with violens.
> We knaw it is for our ingratitude
> That we ar puneist with this pestilence,

which becomes penitential in the following stanzas:

> Thow grant us grace for till amend our miss,
> And till evaid this crewall suddane deid.

The fearsome justice of God is seen as a pattern for justice on earth, in a society which is dangerously inadequate. 'Bot wald the heiddismen that sowld keip the law / Pueneiss the peple for their transgressioun', then there would be no need for such manifestations of divine justice. The last three stanzas have a different refrain—'latt nocht be tynt that thow so deir hes bocht'—, a touch of the aureate diction that Dunbar was to perfect, and a very bold metrical experiment in which each of the first seven lines of the eight-line stanzas generates three internal rhymes. It is as if we are suddenly transported to the 'greater glory and splendour' of Rosslyn Chapel. The effect is that of an exhilaratingly ornamented crescendo, at once an urgent and persuasive plea for mercy, and a paean of praise to the glory and justice of God:

> Superne, lucerne, guberne this pestilens,
> Preserve, and serve that we not sterve thairin.

Declyne that pyne be thy devyne prudens.
O trewth, haif rewth, lat not our slewth us twin.
Our syt full tyt, wer we contryt, wald blin.
Dissiver did never quha evir the besocht.
Send grace with space, and us imbrace fra syn.
Latt nocht be tynt that thow so deir hes bocht...

...Sen for our vyce that justyce mon correct,
O king most hie, now pacifie thy feid:
Our syn is huge; refuge we not suspect;
As thow art juge, deluge us of this dreid.
In tyme assent, or we be schent with deid;
We us repent, and tyme mispent forthocht:
Thairfoir, evirmoir, be gloir to thy godheid;
Lat nocht be tynt that thou sa deir hes bocht.

In Petronius's *Satiricon*, in the description of the lavish feast given by Trimalchio, there is an odd incident:

'...As we drank...a slave brought in a silver skeleton, made so that its limbs and spine could be moved and bent in every direction. He put it down once or twice on the table so that the supple joints showed several attitudes, and Trimalchio said appropriately: 'Alas for us poor mortals, all that poor man is nothing. So we shall all be, after the world below takes us away. Let us live then while it goes well with us."'[29]

Although the *Carpe diem* is usually firmly suppressed, a good deal of this grotesque and sometimes gruesomely playful spirit survives into the later medieval macabre tradition. The sight of skeletons, the warning cry of 'sic erimus cuncti' recur often enough for us to wish to echo Falstaff's 'Peace, good Doll! do not speak like a death's head: do not bid me remember mine end...'. Sometimes the thought of death is intensified by an emphasis on the facts of physical decay or on the grisly end of the body in hell ('...And for thi crisp kell, and fair hair, all bellit sall thou be; / And as for wild and wanton luk, nothing sall thou se...'[30]), sometimes by a dramatic encounter, in which the living

[29] Tr. M. Heseltine (Loeb Classical Library), p. 53. Cf. Herodotus II, 78. On devotional lyrics on death, see Woolf, *English Religious Lyric*, chapters III, IX, and Appendix H, Gray, *Themes and Images*, chapter 10. Cf. Jamieson, pp. 131–2.
[30] *Scotichronicon*, ed. W. Goodall (Edinburgh, 1759), II, pp. 374–5.

person is confronted by a dead man, a skeleton, or a skull, or the figure of Death. The play of *Everyman*, of course, is a well-known example. Skelton's *Upon a Deedman's Heed*, or the legend of the Three Living and the Three Dead, in which three living men are confronted by the horrible spectacle of three dead, are different variations. Henryson's *Thre Deid Pollis* combines both techniques. We have seen enough of the poet's grim imagination to expect something of a *tour de force* in this style, and we are not disappointed. The three skulls deliver their traditional warning ('as ye ar now, into this warld we wair') with macabre detail in stark Scots diction:

Behold oure heidis thre,
Oure holkit ene, oure peilit pollis bair...

They go on to remind us (again in traditional manner) that the time and place of death are ever uncertain. Their warning to 'wantoune yowth' is much more gruesome than that of Age in the poem previously discussed:

...O lusty gallandis gay,
Full laithly thus sall ly thy lusty heid,
Holkit and how, and wallowit as the weid,
Thy crampand hair, and eik thy cristall ene....[31]

And, as is usual in this kind of poetry, the decay of female beauty is not spared. Villon poses the question:

Corps femenin, qui tant es tendre,
Poly, souef, si precieux,
Te fauldra il ces maux attendre?
Oy, ou tout vif aller es cieulx.[32]

Henryson's 'deid pollis' address the ladies in their splendid array:

O ladeis quhyt, in claithis corruscant,
Poleist with perle, and mony pretius stane;
With palpis quhyt, and hals so elegant,
Sirculit with gold, and sapheris mony ane;
Your finyearis small, quhyt as quhailis bane,
Arrayit with ringis, and mony rubeis reid:

[31] With Fox, in l. 20 I prefer MF *laithly*.

[32] *Testament*, 325–8, *Œuvres*, ed. A. Longnon, rev. L. Foulet (Paris, 1932), p. 22.

As we ly thus sall ye ly ilk ane,
With peilit pollis, and holkit thus your heid.

The repetition of words such as 'peilit' and 'holkit' has a peculiarly sinister effect. From the terrible anonymity of death, they put the inescapable 'questioun'—who can now tell 'quha was farest, or fowlest, of us three? / or quhilk of us of kin was gentillar?', that question which so absorbed Villon, the great master of the macabre:

Quant je considere ces testes
Entassees en ces charniers,
Tous furent maistres des requestes,
Au moins de la Chambre aux Deniers,
Ou tous furent portepanniers:
Autant puis l'ung que l'autre dire,
Car d'evesques ou lanterniers
Je n'y congnois riens a redire.[33]

After this reminder of the grimly reductive power of death, the three 'pollis' conclude with a call to repentance and to prayer for their souls.

Even more impressive, and certainly more attractive, is *The Ressoning betuix Deth and Man*. This dramatic encounter is not set in any temporal or spatial background, and, as in some versions of the *Dance of Death*, this absence of particular detail seems to heighten the emotional effect, for the encounter seems to take place in a kind of absolute time and place. The matter is quite traditional—all men must die, death levels all estates, and so on—but the debate is conducted with a genuinely dramatic sense. Death opens with a solemn and forceful speech:

'O mortall man, behold, tak tent to me
Quhilk sowld thy mirror be baith day and nicht....'

His stanza is one long, dignified, and elegant sentence. The sedate lists which are prominent are not simply devices for maintaining this register, but gently, yet inevitably, remind us of his absolute and unlimited power:

'All erdly thing that euir tuik lyfe mon die:
Paip, empriour, king, barroun, and knycht,
Thocht thay be in thair roall stait and hicht,
May not ganestand, quhen I pleiss schute the derte;

33 *Testament*, ll. 1744–51, *ed. cit.*, p. 68.

Waltownis, castellis, and towris nevir so wicht,
May nocht risist quhill it be at his herte!'

Man's first reaction is that of ignorance—'quhat art thow that biddis me thus tak tent...'. He launches into a series of questions (in strong contrast to the flowing dignity of Death's speech) which ends, realistically, with a defiant vaunt:

Is non so wicht, or stark in this cuntre,
Bot I sall gar him bow to me on forss.

The solemn introduction of his interlocutor's name—

My name, forswth, sen that thou speiris,
Thay call me Deid...

—has an immediate and a sobering effect. Man's thoughts begin to turn to penitence (and his phrases become rather more homiletic). When Death calls on Man to repent, we notice that his tone has nothing of the macabre raillery of the *Dance of Death*, and that he does not need to resort to the horrific details of putrefaction. The grim remark

Dispone thy self and cum with me in hy,
Edderis, askis, and wormis meit for to be

is as far as he goes. Nor does he need to offer any physical threat:

Cum quhen I call, thow ma me not denny
Thocht thow war paip, empriour, and king all thre.

Perhaps the nearest visual equivalent to this scene is not to be found in the contortions of Death and his victims in the *Dance of Death*, but in the 'Death and Youth' of the fifteenth-century Hausbuch Master, where a fashionably dressed youth, with an elegant and infinitely sorrowful face, is gently but firmly taken by Death. At Death's feet, we can see a toad and an adder. As Panofsky says '...the theme of Death and Youth was very common in late medieval art, but it is only in this drypoint by the Housebook Master that Death appears as a mystery, awesome yet kindly, threatening yet alluring, merciless yet full of pity'.[34] Henryson's ending, too, is surprisingly gentle and

[34] Panofsky, *Albrecht Dürer*, p. 23, fig. 27 (for a comparable English example, cf. the Cotton Faustina 'Vado Mori' (Gray, *Themes and Images*, pl. 11)).

humane. Confronted by Death confident in his absolute power, Man rejects this 'wretched world', and offers himself humbly to Death's covering cloak:

> 'Sen it is swa fra the I may not chaip,
> This wrechit warld for me heir I defy,
> And to the, Deid, to lurk under thy caip,
> I offer me with hairt richt hum[i]ly;
> Beseiking god, the divill, myne ennemy,
> No power haif my sawill till assay.
> Jesus, on the, with peteous voce, I cry,
> Mercy on me to haif on Domisday.

The shorter poems include two allegorical pieces. That which is now called *The Garmont of Gud Ladeis*[35] is a curious, but rather charming work, with a ballad-like metre setting off its finished and deliberate simplicity. It opens:

> Wald my lady lufe me best,
> And wirk eftir my will,
> I suld ane garmond gudliest
> Gar mak hir body till.
>
> Off he honour suld be hir hud,
> Upoun hir heid to weir,
> Garneist with governance so gud,
> Na demyng suld hir deir

—and goes on to furnish the lady with a complete allegorical outfit. It has been suggested that Henryson took the idea from Olivier de la Marche's *Le Triumphe des Dames*, but this work is longer, more elaborate, and not at all closely similar in detail. The allegorization of clothes would come easily to a medieval writer, not only because of Biblical examples or hints (e.g. *Ephesians* vi, 13–18, *I Timothy* ii, 9–10), but because in life as well as in books, clothes could be signs—for instance the vestments of priests could be given allegorical meanings. Caxton's *Book of the Ordre of Chyvalry* tells us of 'the sygnefyaunce of the armes of a knyght' (his helmet is 'shamefastnes', his habergeon a 'castel and fortresse ayeynst vyces and deffaultes', his gorget obedience,

[35] Cf. Jamieson, pp. 135–6.

and so on).[36] Allegorical significances were attached to the distinctive items of a pilgrim's clothing. *The Pilgrimage of the Life of Man* gives its pilgrim some allegorical armour—his doublet is patience, his habergeon is 'force' ('whiche Jesu Cristes championns wereden in old time'), his helm 'attemperance', his targe prudence, etc. Sartorial imagery is used almost as a matter of course—in Langland, for instance, Haukyn's 'best cote' is soiled with sin. Henryson's poem is rather more than an ingenious list of significances. A dominant idea running through it is that this 'gudliest garment' is one of true and noble love—the lady's kirtle, for instance, is 'of clene constance / Lasit with lesum lufe'. One suspects also that there is perhaps an implied contrast with those fashionable and flashy women's clothes which are the target of moralists and satirists.[37] Moreover, in this case in a very real sense, 'clothes make the woman'. In ordinary life one would expect them to reveal the personality of the wearer rather than her soul. Here, however, quite happily, they are signs both of her outward virtues and of her inner nobility of soul. A single piece of colour symbolism seems to have a special importance:

> Hir sark suld be hir body nixt,
> Of chestitie so quhyt,
> With schame and dreid togidder mixt,
> The same suld be perfyt.

Other items have a protective as well as a symbolic function, for instance,

> Hir mantill of humilitie,
> To tholl bayth wind and weit

or her shoes of 'sickernes', 'in syne that scho nocht slyd'. But although the complete 'garment' is an ideal one, it is not ascetic. Both visually and morally it is attractive; her gown is 'purfillit with plesour. . . / Furrit with fyne fassoun', and she has the elegant 'extras' of the nobility such as the gloves[38] ('of gud govirnance'). It is a 'gay' garment:

36 Caxton, ed. A. T. P. Byles, EETS clxviii (1926), pp. 76–89; *The Pilgrimage of the Lyf of the Manhode*, ed. W. A. Wright (Roxburghe Club, 1869), pp. 58ff. Cf. also P. Meyer, *Romania* xx (1891), 579–615, *The Lantern of Light*, ed. L. M. Swinburn, EETS cli (1917), pp. 65–6.

37 Cf., e.g., Robbins, *Historical Poems*, No. 53 and note, F. W. Fairholt, *Satirical Songs and Poems on Costume from the 13th to the 19th Century* (Percy Soc., xxvii, 1849).

38 Cf. G. F. Jones, 'Sartorial Symbols in Mediaeval Literature', *MÆ* xxv (1956), 69–70.

Wald scho put on this garmond gay
I durst sweir by my seill,
That scho woir nevir grene nor gray
That set hir half so weill.

The *Bludy Serk* is a short *conte moralisé*, an example of that group of stories which tell of Christ the lover-knight who gives his life to rescue a lady, man's soul.[39] It is, as far as we know, Henryson's only excursion into the world of romance, and, interestingly, it is the world of popular romance that he chooses, the world, one imagines, of 'Watschod the tale tellare' and of the 'tua fithelaris that sang Graysteil to the King'. From the beginning the formulaic patterns[40] and the conventional diction are used with relish:

This hindir yeir I hard be tald
Thair was a worthy king;
Dukis, erlis, and barronis bald
He had at his bidding.
The lord was anceane and ald,
And sexty yeiris cowth ring;
He had a douchter fair to fald,
A lusty lady ying...

The tale continues with traditional ingredients: 'adventures', chivalric self-sacrifice, love 'paramour'—and a terrible giant:

He wes the laithliest on to luk
That on the ground mycht gang;
His nailis wes lyk ane hellis cruk,
Thairwith fyve quarteris lang...

At its best the narrative has the pace and the touching simplicity of a good popular romance:

[39] It has some similarities with the version in the *Gesta Romanorum*. Jamieson, pp. 143–5, draws attention to versions in Bozon and a Middle English sermon. On the theme of Christ the Lover-Knight, see Woolf, *English Religious Lyric*, pp. 44–6, and *RES*, N.S. xiii (1962), 1–16. It is a curious fact, probably unconnected with Henryson's poem, that the insurgents of 1489 against James IV adopted as their banner the 'bludy serk' of his dead father (R. Nicholson, *Scotland. The Later Middle Ages* (Edinburgh, 1974), p. 537).
[40] E.g. (l. 6) 'sexty yeiris'; cf. *Sir Orfeo*, l. 90, S. I. Tucker, 'Sixty as an Indefinite Number in Middle English', *RES* xxv (1949), 152–3.

Syne brak the bour, had hame the bricht,
Unto hir fadir deir;
Sa evill wondit was the knycht
That he behuvit to de.
Unlusum was his likame dicht,
His sark was all bludy;
In all the warld was thair a wicht
So peteouss for to sy?

The knight's instructions to his lady to hang his 'bludy sark' before her, and to think of it and of him when she is wooed, and the way this vow is carried out is made into a simple romantic scene, which delicately emphasizes the magic power of the garment and of true love.[41] This is deftly turned to a moral conclusion:

Sa weill the lady luvit the knycht,
That no man wald scho tak.
Sa suld we do our god of micht,
That did all for us mak;
Quhilk fullely to deid wes dicht
For sinfull manis saik...

and a *moralitas* briefly and simply explains the allegorical significance of the story.

It is appropriate to end with a work which not only illustrates Henryson's powers of dramatic narrative at their best, and which is one of those miniature stories which express *multum in parvo*, but which is also—in the best spirit of the 'unbent bow'—a work of delightful and complete gaiety and wit. *Robene and Makene* may perhaps be described as a 'pastoral ballad', but in fact it defies categorization.[42] The names

[41] Cf. the story of how Christ's coat of mercy protects Pilate (Stith Thompson, *Motif-Index of Folk-Literature*, D 1381.4.1, J. Pauli, *Schimpf und Ernst* (1522), ed. J. Bolte, Berlin, 1924, No. 323)—Tiberius wishes to kill Pilate, but when Pilate is in his presence his anger vanishes, because Pilate is wearing Christ's garment.

[42] Cf. Jamieson, pp. 145–6, W. P. Jones, *MLN* xlvi (1931), 457–8, A. K. Moore, 'Robene and Makene', *MLR* xliii (1948), 400–3, and *The Secular Lyric in Middle English* (Lexington, 1951), pp. 188–94. For Baudes de la Kakerie, see K. Bartsch, *Altfranzösische Romanzen und Pastourellen* (Leipzig, 1870), pp. 302–5. On the *pastourelle*, see, e.g., E. Faral, 'La Pastourelle', *Romania* xlix (1923), 204–50, C. Foulon, *L'œuvre de Jehan Bodel* (Paris, 1958), P. Dronke, *The Medieval Lyric* (London, 1968), esp. pp. 200ff. Cf. H. Cooper, *Pastoral* (D. S. Brewer, 1977).

of the characters are those common in the French *pastourelle*, and indeed one *pastourelle* by Baudes de la Kakerie (in Bartsch's collection of *Romanzen und Pastourellen*) has been claimed as its source. The similarities here are not close enough to be convincing, but in a general way *Robene and Makene* does seem to be related to the tradition of the *pastourelle*. There are some obvious differences: the *pastourelle* normally opens as a *chanson d'aventure*. In a common type, the poet-*chevalier* comes upon a shepherdess, pleads with her for love, and is often successful in his pleas. There is nothing of this in *Robene and Makene*; nor does Henryson's poem have anything of the condescension towards rustics which is found in a number of French *pastourelles*. Henryson develops his characters in his own way: Robene is more than a standard comic shepherd, and Makene's reactions are not quite as straightforward as those of the *bergère* (as Faral says 'le trait que les poètes ont accoutumé de mettre en relief chez elles, c'est leur ingénue complaisance, la libre simplicité avec laquelle elles déclarent la satisfaction de leurs sens').[43] However, a *débat*, often an extended argument, plays an important rôle in the *pastourelle*, as it does in *Robene and Makene*, and the central theme is certainly love. In one group, the poet-*chevalier* remains simply an onlooker, who sees Guiot and Robin disputing over the love of Marion, Robin resisting the advances of another girl and remaining faithful to Marion, Marote reproaching Robin for loving other shepherdesses, or similar scenes of rustic love. Henryson completely suppresses any notion of an onlooker, and develops the narrative and dramatic[44] aspects of the story, with the result that his poem comes to sound as much like one of Bartsch's *Romanzen*—brief lyrical narratives of love—as a *pastourelle*. It has been pointed out that the opening (far from the 'riding out' formula of the *pastourelle*) is similar to that of the ballad *Lord Thomas and Fair Annet*:

> Lord Thomas and Fair Annet
> Sate a' day on a hill

—or to that of the narrative carol 'Joly Wat'.[45] *Robene and Makene*,

43 Faral, p. 229.

44 Cf. C. R. Baskervill, 'Early Romantic Plays in England', *MP* xiv, who notes (pp. 238–9) a payment at York in 1447 to 'ii ludentibus Joly Wat and Malkyn' which suggests a 'simple song drama of the pastourelle type'.

45 Moore, *MLR* xliii, p. 402. *Lord Thomas*, F. J. Child, *The English and Scottish Popular Ballads*, No. 73A; 'Joly Wat', R. L. Greene, *The Early English Carols*, No. 78.

however, although it is a narrative poem concerned with love, does not fit quite happily into the category of 'romance' (in Bartsch's sense) or of 'ballad'.[46] Henryson enjoys—as always—his dramatic scenes from rural life, and evokes something like the idyllic background of the peasant feasts mentioned in *The Complaynt of Scotlande*, 'when evyrie ald scheiphyrd led his wyfe be the hand, and evyrie yong scheiphird led hyr quhome he luffit best'.[47] The result of the complete absence of any condescension towards his rustic wooers, and the genuine simplicity of his treatment of the story is to create a true pastoral. As Professor Kermode (quoting Empson) says: 'The pastoral is a leveller—it has to assume that "you can say everything about complex people by a complete consideration of simple people"'.[48]

That the harmony of any rural Arcadia is not proof against the power of love becomes apparent in the first stanza of the poem. The scene is briefly set—not with the traditional meadow, *boschel* or *abespin* of the *pastourelle*:

> Robene sat on gud grene hill,
> Kepand a flok of fe:
> Mirry Makyne said him till...

—and we find ourselves into the action. Henryson has already in these three lines introduced the three main characters. Robene sits keeping his sheep, as medieval shepherds are often depicted. But it is also an appropriate posture for a man who is to prove a slow and recalcitrant lover. 'Mirry' Makene, who characteristically begins the action, is full of life and dynamism, and distinctly flighty as well. We are presented with the first of the many comic oppositions on which the poem is built. The third point of the 'triangle' so often found in a *pastourelle* is here no wandering knight-seducer, but a flock of sheep. The action proceeds—almost entirely in dramatic dialogue. Makene—not a remote and 'daungerous' lady of romance—opens with a direct plea:

[46] Some European ballads (cf. W. J. Entwhistle, *European Balladry* (Oxford, 1939), p. 178) have a gentle lady making overtures to an unresponsive shepherd (cf. e.g. 'Romance de una gentil dama, y un rústico pastor', F. J. Wolf and C. Hofmann, *Primavera y flor de Romances* (Berlin, 1856), II, pp. 64–5). The French 'Occasion Manquée', mentioned by Entwhistle, sounds as if it might be more comparable, but he gives no reference for it.

[47] Ed. J. A. H. Murray, EETS ES xvii (1872), p. 65.

[48] J. F. Kermode, *English Pastoral Poetry* (London, 1952), p. 26; W. Empson, *Some Versions of Pastoral* (London, 1935), p. 137.

'Robene, thow rew one me;
I haif the luvit lowd and still,
Thir yeiris two or thre;
My dule in dern bot gif thow dill,
Dowtles but dreid I de.'

Robene pleads ignorance (an unsatisfactory excuse, as readers versed in the 'law' of love would know):

Robene ansert, 'be the rude,
Nathing of lufe I knaw,
Bot keipis my scheip undir yone wid,
Lo quhair thay raik on raw;
Quhat hes marrit the in thy mude,
Makyne, to me thow schaw;
Or quhat is lufe, or to be lude?
Fane wald I leir that law.'

By the end of this little speech, we can recognize the beginnings of one of those patterns of Henrysonian irony which we saw in the *Fables*. Robene's words, however, also reveal his personality—his innocence, his slowness, his devotion to his sheep (comic in its intensity and pride—'Lo quhair thay raik on raw'), and his totally unconscious cruelty. Makene attempts to give him a lesson in 'lufis lair'. There is a hint of parody of 'fin' amors' when she spells out her 'abc' to one who seems most unlikely ever to become a long-suffering servant in the cause of noble love, but the scene is too delicate and touching to be simply a parody:

Be heynd, courtass, and fair of feir,
Wyse, hardy, and fre
...Preiss the with pane at all poweir,
Be patient and previe.

With nice irony, Robene, in the grip of invincible ignorance, is made to quote a well-known and very appropriate 'sentence':[49]

I wait not quhat is luve;
Bot I haif mervell incertane
Quhat makis the this wanrufe...

[49] Cf. the stanzas in Grimestone's Preaching Book, 'I ne wot quat is love... Owst, *Literature and Pulpit*, p. 21, E. Wilson, *A Descriptive Index of the English Lyrics in John of Grimestone's Preaching Book* (Medium Ævum Monographs, N.S. ii, Oxford, 1973), No. 23.

and he goes on uncomprehendingly—he is not one who readily makes connections—to wonder why she is restless in such idyllic circumstances:

> The weddir is fair, and I am fane,
> My scheip gois haill aboif.

For all his innocence, he seems to know enough of the facts of life to use a phrase like 'play us', but what hinders him is the thought, not of jangling tongues or *losengiers*, but of the disapproval of his sheep:

> And we wald play us in this plane,
> They wald us bayth reproif.

Makene's pleas become urgent and quite open (ll. 33ff.), but once again, Robene's sheep are uppermost in his mind. And in a manner which is quite foreign to the absolute passion of Makene, he thinks of *time*:

> Makyne, to morne this ilk a tyde,
> And ye will meit me heir,
> Peraventure my scheip ma gang besyd,
> Quhill we haif liggit full neir.

He vainly tries to persuade Makene to return to the simple happiness which the mysterious power of love has taken from her, but it comes out as an abrupt and cruel attempt at consolation: 'Makyn, than mak gud cheir.'

The climax of the scene comes in two stanzas of wonderfully dense dialogue, from which the opposing personalities emerge in a way which is at once pathetic and ironic:

> 'Robene, thow reivis me roif and rest;
> I luve bot the allone.'
> 'Makyne, adew, the sone gois west,
> The day is neir hand gone.'
> 'Robene, in dule I am so drest,
> That lufe wilbe my bone.'
> 'Ga lufe, Makyne, quhair euir thow list,
> For lemman I bid none.'

> 'Robene, I stand in sic a styll;
> I sicht, and that full sair.'
> 'Makyne, I haif bene heir this quhyle;
> At hame God gif I wair.'

'My huny Robene, talk ane quhill,
Gif thow will do na mair.'
'Makyne, sum uthir man begyle,
For hamewart I will fair.'

The end of the scene is marked by movement. They separate, and in another contrasting opposition, go their ways. Robene is 'als licht as leif of tre', a simile which not only compares him to a natural object, but to an unfeeling natural object, and which might well suggest to the skilled Henrysonian reader the possibility of change, of an ironic kind. Makene 'murnit in hir intent', and exclaims in her distress:

'Now ma thow sing, for I am schent!
Quhat alis lufe at me?'

In a narrative bridge-passage, we are shown—without a word of analysis—the mysterious ways of love. One might well recall those lines in *Troilus* where Chaucer ponders why this fish and not that comes to the weir. Makene goes home in distress, and Robene, after he has performed his duty and 'assemblit all his scheip', begins to be affected—

Be that sum pairte of Mawkynis aill
Outthrow his hairt cowd creip

—and his reactions are predictable:

He fallowit hir fast thair till assaill,
And till hir tuke gude keip.

The rôles are now comically reversed—one cured, the other fallen ill—and Robene becomes the passionate suppliant:

'Abyd, abyd, thow fair Makyne,
A word for ony thing;
For all my luve it salbe thyne,
Withowttin depairting...

though his passion still acknowledges the temporal limits imposed by his sheep:

My scheip to morne quhill houris nyne
Will neid of no keping.

He deserves the rebuke which is deftly loosed at him, and the proverbial lesson on the nature of opportunity:

Robene, thow hes hard soung and say,
In gestis and storeis auld,
The man that will nocht quhen he may
Sall haif nocht quhen he wald.

'Nosce tempus', as Taverner's version of Erasmus has it, 'know time. Opportunitie is of such force that of honest it maketh unhonest, of dammage avauntage, of pleasure grevaunce, of a good turne a shrewd turne, and contraryewyse of unhonest honest, of avauntage dammage, and brefly to conclude it cleane chaungeth the nature of thynges.'[50] Besides instruction in the mysteries of time, the unfortunate Robene has been taught something of 'love's law'. He continues to plead earnestly—by now he seems to have forgotten the sheep—and eloquently:

'Makyne, the nicht is soft and dry,
The wedder is warme and fair,
And the grene woid rycht neir us by
To walk attour all quhair...'

but his case is doomed—

'Robene, that warld is all away
And quyt brocht till ane end,
And nevir agane thairto perfay
Sall it be as thow wend,
For of my pane thow maid it play...

—and, beneath the 'two smiles' of the moralist, we see him receive the final blow:

'Robene, with the I will nocht deill;
Adew, for thus we mett.'

In the last stanza the reversal is complete, and we take leave of the three protagonists, now placed back in their setting—Robene is no longer 'on gud grene hill' but 'under a huche' 'amangis the holtis hair' (Henryson contrives to make this formula of popular poetry marvellously evocative in the changed circumstances). It is a final 'speaking picture' of the mysterious and unresolved paradoxes of love:

[50] *Proverbes or Adagies* (London, 1545), f. xxiv^{v}. The proverb is common, cf. Whiting, W 275 (and variants), S. B. Meech, *MP* xxxviii (1940–1), 117, W. A. Pantin, *Bulletin of the John Rylands Library* xiv (1930), 108.

Malkyne went hame blyth annewche
Attour the holttis hair;
Robene murnit, and Malkyne lewche;
Scho sang, he sichit sair;
And so left him, bayth wo and wrewche,
In dolour and in cair,
Kepand his hird under a huche,
Amangis the holtis hair.

The shorter poems are a final testimony to the variety of Henryson's achievement, to that 'mark of a generous mind...its power both to rise to great things and to stoop to small ones',[51] to the assurance with which he transforms traditional matter and genre. From the whole of his work, and especially from his major poems, the *Fables* and the *Testament of Cresseid*, there emerges something even more impressive, a poetic personality of considerable complexity and originality. 'Seriousness, humanity and strength' co-exist with irony and wit. Henryson has a profoundly religious vision of man and the world, but it is not one in which a rigid moralist is always in control, rather one which holds—sometimes with difficulty—opposites in tension, and contrives, in an uneasy time, to achieve something like 'completeness and harmony'. As Sir Francis Kynaston says, 'this Mr. Robert Henderson he was questionles a learned and a witty man, and it is pitty we have no more of his works'.

[51] Perrault, *Contes de ma Mère Loye*, tr. G. Brereton (London, 1957), p. 3.

SELECT BIBLIOGRAPHY

1. EDITIONS

B. Dickins, *The Testament of Cresseid* (Edinburgh, 1925).

C. Elliott, *Robert Henryson, Poems* (Clarendon Medieval and Tudor Series, Oxford, 1963, 2nd edition, 1974).

D. Fox, *The Testament of Cresseid* (London, 1968).

D. Laing, *The Poems and Fables of Robert Henryson* (Edinburgh, 1865).

W. M. Metcalfe, *The Poems of Robert Henryson* (Paisley, 1917).

G. Gregory Smith, *The Poems of Robert Henryson*, 3 vols., STS lv, lviii, lxiv (1906–1914).

H. Harvey Wood, *The Poems and Fables of Robert Henryson* (Edinburgh, 1933, revised ed., 1955).

2. SOME CRITICAL STUDIES

Jane Adamson, 'Henryson's *Testament of Cresseid*: "Fyre and Cauld"', *The Critical Review* xviii (1976), 39–60.

A. J. Aitken, M. P. McDiarmid, and D. S. Thomson, *Bards and Makars* (Glasgow, 1977) (contains articles on Henryson by T. W. Craik, M. P. McDiarmid, J. McNamara, C. Mills).

E. Duncan Aswell, 'The Role of Fortune in *The Testament of Cresseid*', *PQ* xlvi (1967), 471–87.

R. Bauman, 'The Folktale and Oral Tradition in the Fables of Robert Henryson', *Fabula* vi (1964), 108–24.

J. A. W. Bennett, 'Henryson's *Testament*: a flawed masterpiece', *Scottish Literary Journal* i (1974), 5–16.

J. A. Burrow, 'Henryson: *The Preaching of the Swallow*', *Essays in Criticism* xxv (1975), 25–37.

Del Chessell, 'In the Dark Time: Henryson's *Testament of Cresseid*', *The Critical Review* xii (1969), 61–72.

G. Clark, 'Henryson and Æesop: the Fable Transformed', *ELH* xliii (1976), 1–18.

'Cresseid in Scotland', *TLS* 9 April 1964, p. 290.

A. R. Diebler, *Henrisones Fabeldichtungen* (Halle, 1885).

D. Duncan, 'Henryson's *Testament of Cresseid*', *Essays in Criticism* xi (1961), 128–35.

D. Fox, 'Henryson's *Fables*', *ELH* xxix (1962), 337–56.

D. Fox, 'The Scottish Chaucerians', in D. S. Brewer, ed., *Chaucer and Chaucerians* (London, 1966), pp. 164–200.

D. Fox, 'Henryson's "Sum Practysis of Medecyne"', *SP* lxix (1972), 453–60.

K. R. R. Gros Louis, 'Robert Henryson's *Orpheus and Eurydice* and the Orpheus traditions of the Middle Ages', *Speculum* xli (1966), 643–55.

C. A. Hallett, 'Theme and Structure in Henryson's "The Annunciation"', *SSL* x (1973), 165–74.

S. J. Harth, 'Henryson Reinterpreted', *Essays in Criticism* xi (1961), 471–80.

R. Hildebrand, *Robert Henryson's "Morall Fabillis" im Rahmen der mittelalterlichen und spämittelalterlichen Tierdichtung* (Hamburg, 1973).

I. W. A. Jamieson, *The Poetry of Robert Henryson: A Study of the Use of Source Material*, unpub. Ph.D. thesis, Edinburgh, 1964.

I. W. A. Jamieson, 'Henryson's "Fabillis": An Essay towards a Revaluation', *Words. Wai-te-ata Studies in English* ii (1966), 20–31.

I. W. A. Jamieson, 'Henryson's *Taill of the Wolf and the Wedder*', *SSL* vi (1969), 248–57.

I. W. A. Jamieson, 'The Minor Poems of Robert Henryson', *SSL* ix (1971–2), 125–47.

I. W. A. Jamieson, 'The Beast Tale in Middle Scots', *Parergon* ii (1972), 26–36.

I. W. A. Jamieson, 'To preue thare preching be a poesye', *Parergon* viii (April 1974), 24–36.

A. M. Kinghorn, 'The Minor Poems of Robert Henryson', *SSL* iii (1965), 30–40.

J. Kinsley, ed., *Scottish Poetry: A Critical Survey* (London, 1955).

C. McDonald, 'Venus and the Goddess Fortune in *The Testament of Cresseid*', *Scottish Literary Journal* iv (1977), 14–24.

D. McDonald, 'Narrative Art in Henryson's *Fables*', *SSL* iii (1965), 101–13.

D. McDonald, 'Henryson and Chaucer: Cock and Fox', *Texas Studies in Literature and Language* viii (1966–7), 451–61.

J. MacQueen, *Robert Henryson: A Study of the Major Narrative Poems* (Oxford, 1967).

J. MacQueen, 'Neoplatonism and Orphism in Fifteenth-Century Scotland', *Scottish Studies* xx (1976), 69–89.

E. Muir, 'Robert Henryson' in *Essays on Literature and Society* (1949, revised ed., London, 1965).

S. Rossi, *Robert Henryson* (Milan, 1955).

S. Rossi, 'L'"Annunciazione" di Robert Henryson", *Ævum* xxix (1955), 70–81.

M. Rowlands, 'The Fables of Robert Henryson', *Dalhousie Review* xxxix (1959–1960), 491–502.

A. C. Spearing, '*The Testament of Cresseid* and the "High Concise Style"', *Speculum* xxxvii (1962), 208–25; also in *Criticism and Medieval Poetry*, 'Conciseness and The Testament of Cresseid' (London, 1964, 2nd ed., 1972).

J. Spiers, 'Robert Henryson' in *The Scots Literary Tradition* (London, 1940, revised ed., 1962).

M. W. Stearns, *Robert Henryson* (New York, 1949).

J. Stephens, 'Devotion and Wit in Henryson's "The Annunciation"', *English Studies* li (1970), 323–31.

Jennifer Strauss, 'To Speak Once More of Cresseid: Henryson's *Testament* Re-considered', *Scottish Literary Journal* iv (1977), 5–13.

E. M. W. Tillyard, 'The Testament of Cresseid' in *Five Poems 1470–1870* (London, 1948; repr. as *Poetry and its Background* (London, 1955)).

H. E. Toliver, 'Robert Henryson: from *Moralitas* to Irony', *English Studies* xlvi (1965), 300–9.

M. Twycross, *The Representation of the Major Classical Divinities in the works of Chaucer, Gower, Lydgate and Henryson*, unpub. B.Litt. thesis, Oxford, 1961.

K. Wittig, *The Scottish Tradition in Literature* (Edinburgh, 1958).

D. A. Wright, 'Henryson's *Orpheus and Eurydice* and the Tradition of the Muses', *MÆ* xl (1971), 41–7.

INDEX

ILLUSTRATIONS

PLATES 1–13

Plate 1. Dunfermline (Slezer's *Theatrum Scotiae* (1693), Bodleian Library).

Che nasce fuori del fior tanto fino
Cogliete il fructo che perfecta chiaue.
Il fior lassate stare al fanciulino
Che legiendo gli tuolle menti praue
¶ Ben che luno con laltro siano boni
¶ Perche la allegoria meglio gli exponi.
¶ De Gallo & Iaspide. Fabula. II.

Vm rigido fodit ore simum dũ qritat escã
Dum stupet inuenta iaspide gallus ait
Res uili pretiosa loco natiq; decoris
Hac in sorde manes nil mihi messis habes.
Si tibi nunc esset qui debuit esse repertor
Quem limus sepelit uiueret arte nitor.
Nec tibi conuenio nec tu mihi nec tibi prosum
Nec mihi tu prodes plus amo chara minus
¶ Tu gallo stolidum tu iaspide pulchra sophie
¶ Dona notes stolido nil sapit ista seges.
¶ Sonetto materiale.
Dice il maestro chel gallo raspando
Dentro al letame per trouar del grano.
Marauegliossi che gli uene amano
Vna pretiosa pietra & el parlando
Disse o preciosa cosa in quanto bando
Sei posta: ascosa in loco si uilano
Sel te hauesse uno artifice soprano
Traria di te sua uita lieta stando
Per me non fai. & io de ti non curo
Amarei piu di te cosa men richa
Che de la fame mi fesse securo
E cosi sempre lo ignorante pica
Contrario di fortuna doue il curo
De laspra pouerta che ognihor limpicha
¶ Si come il gallo sprezza tal semenza
¶ Cossi disprezza il matto la scienza.
¶ Sonetto morale
Mostroui el gallo qui raspar letame.
E questo e lhomo che immortal peccato
Che quando dal bon homo si consigliato
Dice che gli ama piu cercar tal trame
Cioe de peccati il doloroso strame
E cossi contra dio sta sfigurato
Al doloroso tristo e sciagurato
Che non gli ualera poi dir ho fame
Disprezza poi la pietra preciosa
Questa e scientia & ama il tristo pasto.
De la gola crudele e dolorosa.
Cossi lhomo maligno quando al tasto
Si da con mente uile & ociosa
Come la bestia po portar il basto
¶ Ma fa che al gallo tu non assimiglie
¶ Il bon consiglio uo che sempre p'glie.
a iii

Plate 2. The Cock and the Jasp (Zucco's *Esopo Historiado* (Venice, 1497), Bodleian Library, Auct. VI. Q. VI. 74,

¶De Mure & Rana. Fabula. iiii.

M Vris iter rumpēte lacu uenit obuia muri
Rana loquax: & opē pacta. nocere cupit
Omne genus peſtis ſupat mēs diſſona uerbis
Cum ſentes animi florida lingua polit.
Rana ſibi filo murem confederat. audet
Nectere fune pedem: rumpere fraude fidē
Pes coit ergo pedi: ſed mens amente recedit
Ecce natant: trahitur ille: ſed illa trahit
Mergitur: ut ſecum murem demergat amico
Naufragium faciens naufragat ipſa fides.
Rana ſtudet mergi. ſed mus emergit & obſtat
Naufragio uires ſuggerit ipſe timōr
¶Hic iacet ambo iacet uiſcera rupta fluunt
¶Miluus adē: miſerūq; truci rapit unq; duelliū
¶Sic pereant qui ſe prodeſſe fatent & obſunt
¶Diſcat in auctorem pena redire ſuum
¶Sonetto materiale
A L toppo non potendo far ſua uiaˋ
Per lo obſtacol del laco che li giace
Venneli contra la rana loquace
Moſtrando uer di lui la facia pia
E proferiſſe con lingua polia
Di condurlo oltra & a quel molto piace
E quella falſa nel mal far ſagace
Vn filo al pie di quel forte ponia
La rana falſa quando fu nel megio
Ruppe ſua fede per condurlo amorte
Onde conuienne ne ueniſſe a pegio.
Il toppo aitar ſe uol con uolte ſtorte
Ma dal nubio fur preſi dondio creggio
Che ſoſtenero inſieme amara ſorte
¶Coſi periſca chi falſa il ſeruire
¶E poſſa ad inganar pena ſoffrire.
¶Sonetto morale.
C Olui che mai non dorme per far male
E per condurci alo infernal hoſtello.
Fa lhomo deſliale falſo e fello
Per condemnar colui che piu liale
Quando ambi dui nel peccato mortale
Son capulati di ſuo capiſtrello
Lo ingannato ſe chiama meſchinello

Plate 3. The Frog and the Mouse (*ib.*, ff. a iiii^{v}–a v).

Plate 4 (*a*). The Cock and the Jasp (British Library, MS. Add. 33781, f. 7: Walter's Latin with French translation)

Plate 4 (*b*). The Two Mice (*ib.*, f. 19).

Liber

Die ander fabel von dem wolff vnd dem lamp
Esopus seczet von den vnschuldigen
vnd den bößlistigen triegern / ain söl
liche fabel. Ain wolff vnd ain lamp /
baide durstige / kamen an ainen bach
allda ze trinken · der wolff trank oben
an dem bach / vnd das lamp fert vnden · Do der
wolf das lamp ersach sprach er zů im · so ich trinke
so trůbst du mir das wasser · das geduldig lemlin
sprach · wie mag ich dir das wasser trůb machen /
das von dir zů mir flüsset · der wolf errötet nit von
der warhait des lamps vnd sprach · he he du flůch
est mir · antwůrt dz lamp ich flůch dir nit ia sprach
der wolf · vor sechs monet · det mirs dyn vater öch
do sprach das lamp · nun bin ich doch die selben zyt
dannocht nit geboren gewesen. Do sprach d wolf
du hast mir ouch mynen aker gar verwůst mit dy
nem nagen vnd verheret · do sprach das lamp · wie
möcht das gesyn nun hab ich doch der zen nicht /

Plate 5 (*a*). The Wolf and the Lamb (Steinhöwel (Ulm, n.d.), Bodleian Library, Douce 252 f. 62v).

Eproferisse cu lingua polia
De conduzlo oltra et aquel molto piace
Equela falsa dimal far sagace
Vn filo apedi lor forte metta
La zana falsa quando fo nel mezo
Rupe sua fede. p conduzlo amorte
Vnde conuene che uenisse apezo.
Chel tappo aiutandosi cu uolte et storte
Dal nebio foron previ domo crezo
Chen sieme sofrise amare sorte
Cossi perissa chi falsa il seruire
Eper lingano pena soferire.
Comentum.
Olui che mai no dorme p far male.
Eper conduzci alinfernale hostello
Fa luomo desliale falso efello
Per condnar coluy che piu liale.
Quando ambi duy son i pecca mortale
Ecopulati del suo capistrello
Linganato si chiama miserello
Ditar siuuole ma nulla gli uale.
Pero non creder aluomo catiuo
Che facto zana tuopo noti facia
Che lun per laltro male se nutricha
San gieronimo dice chi piu abraza.
Vna cossa gli mancha donde priuo
Chel non cie huomo che uero gli dica :~
De cane et oue.
In causam canis urget ouem sedet arbiter audit
Reddat ouis panem uult canis illa negat
Pro cane stat miluus uultur stat lupus et instant
Panem quem pepigit reddere reddat ut ouis

Plate 5 (*b*). The Frog and the Mouse (British Library, MS. Add. 10389, f. 6; Walter's Latin with Zucco's Italian).

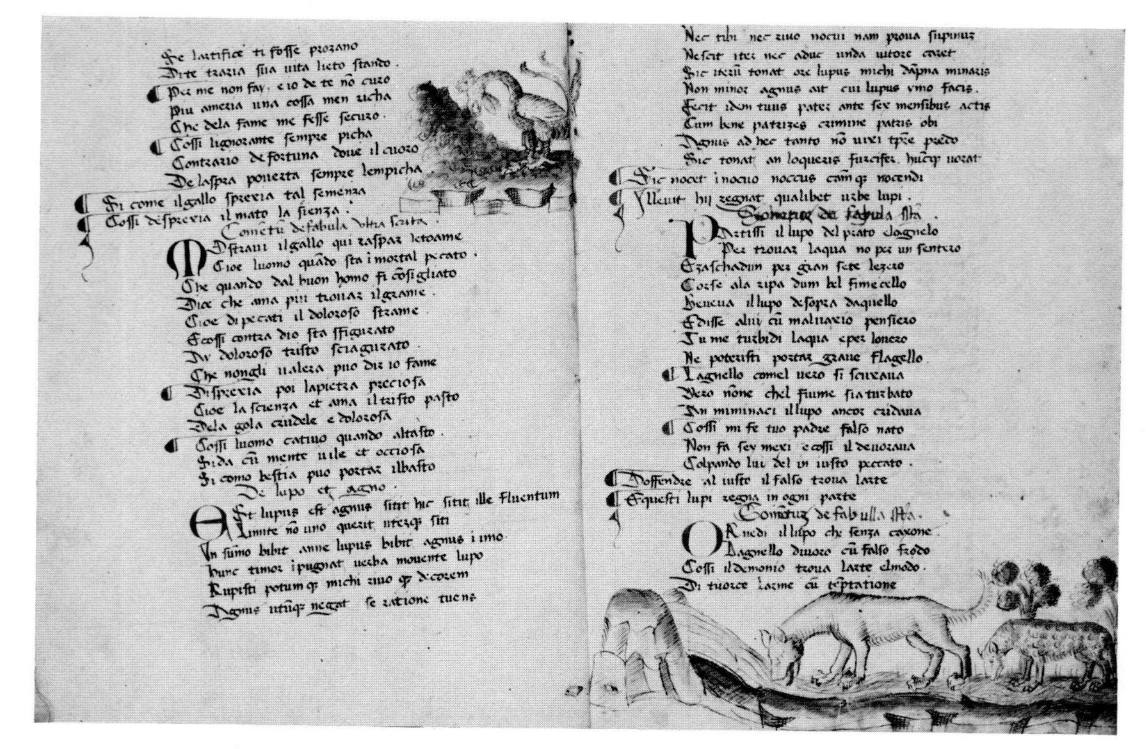

Plate 6. The Cock and the Jasp, and the Wolf and the Lamb (*ib.*, ff. 4ᵛ–5).

42 FABLES CHOISIES.

X I.

La Grenoüille & le Rat.

El, comme dit Merlin, cuide enſeigner autruy,
Qui ſouvent s'enſeigne ſoy-meſme.
J'ay regret que ce mot ſoit trop vieux aujourd'huy,

LIVRE IV. 43

Il m'a toujours ſemblé d'une énergie extrême.
Mais afin d'en venir au deſſein que j'ay pris :
Un Rat plein d'en-bon-point, gras, & des mieux nourris,
Et qui ne connoiſſoit l'Avent ni le Carême,
Sur le bord d'un marais égayoit ſes eſprits.
Une Grenoüille approche, & luy dit en ſa langue :
Venez me voir chez moy, je vous feray feſtin.
Meſſire Rat promit ſoudain :
Il n'eſtoit pas beſoin de plus longue harangue.
Elle allegua pourtant les delices du bain,
La curioſité, le plaiſir du voyage,
Cent raretez à voir le long du marécage :

D ij

Plate 7. The Frog and the Mouse (La Fontaine, *Fables Choisies* (t. ii, Paris, 1678), Bodleian Library, Montagu 159).

Plate 8. Reynard and the fish (Bodleian Library, MS. Douce 360, f. 33; *Roman de Renart*)

Liber Esopi

vide .s.rana ⁊ mus scȝ rana.scȝ murē
Ecce natant.trahitur ille.sed illa trahit
scȝ rana tēdit ad fundū periclitari faciat
Mergitur.vt secum murem demergat in ymo
periculū maris naufragiū patiť .i.fiducia
Naufragium faciens.naufragat ipsa fides
nitiť ad fundū natare .i.eleuat se ↄtrariať
Rana studet mergi.sed mus emergit ⁊ obstat
periculo prāces augmētat .i.pauor
Naufragio vires suggerit ipse timor
talis auis feroci capit .i.bellū
Miluus adest. miserum truci rapit vngue duellum
.s.milu⁹ scȝ rana ⁊ mus intestina fracta narāt
Hic iacet.ambo iacent.viscera rupta fluunt
scȝ oēs illi dicūt impediūt
Sic pereant.qui se fatentur ⁊ obsunt
.i.q̄ intēdit aliū decipe
Discat in autorem pena redire suum

Hic ponit documentū q̄ nemo dȝ alteri aliq̄d pmittere qđ nō intēdit facere.q₂ sepe alios intendētes decipe seipsos decipiūt.qđ innuiť nobis p ranā ⁊ murē.Mure in ostio molendini sup limen residēte. suꝑuenit rana ex campo.⁊ mure salutato cui⁹ illa dom⁹ esset cū interrogauit.quā suam esse rńdit. Rogauit ḡ rana ipm murē vt ipam nocte illa in hospicio susciperet. Qui mus benigne eā intrare ↄcessit.factaqȝ hora cene apposuit ei grossam farinaȝ dicens ei vt lete ↄmederet q₂ bñ sibi faueret.⁊ si meliora haberē etiā apponerē. Et placuit rane locus ⁊ cib⁹.sed cū potus diu expectatus nō venit.rana ḡ potu assueta sitibūda tristis recedit. ⁊ dixit q̄ mallet esse sub molendino absqȝ tali cibo q̄̄ in molēdino sine potu. Cui mus ait molestū sibi eē q̄ oblata sibi nō placerēt.⁊ iurauit se nunq̄ tā bñ pcuratā fuisse.⁊ de illo bñficio recōpensam se velle habere dixit: Illis audit is rana rńdit.q̄ si secū ad sua vellet trāsire sibi reddere vellet cibū cuȝ potu in copia: Cui mus assentiens pariter iuerūt p prata ad fluuiū.erat aūt rana ore plena.⁊ mus incipiebat deficere ex ieiunio.sed ipm rana cōfortauit.et in vicino domū suā esse dixit.tandē itaqȝ prato a mure vix ptransito venerūt ad fluuiū.⁊ ait rana.hanc aquā trāsire debemus q₂ domus mea hic vltra est. Fessus igiť mus ex longa via atrediatus ad ranā sic inq̄t:amiciciā tuā inuite pdo.sed hospiciū tuū adire nequeo.q₂ rore prati grauatus adhuc grauiorib⁹ aq̄s me ↄmittere nō audeo: Ait ḡ rana.turpe est mō desistere ⁊ viā breuē non pficere:si fessus es ⁊ debilis ego iuuabo te ne in aqua deficias.faciamus ergo sic:filo nos alligabim⁹ tu in collo ⁊ ego in pede meo.⁊ sic te adiuuabo. Quius dictis mus acq̄euit. Ipsis itaqȝ in medio fluminis iam positis rana exclamando dixit: ego ↄfisa nimis meis virib⁹ iam deficio ⁊ ad profunduȝ ducor peritura. seqȝ se submergens muri machinata est naufragium.⁊ sic mure ad

Liber Esopi

huc existente ad litus fraudem intellexit. et sic orta est ibi lis magna inť ambas partes:illis in partē trahentib⁹.rana nanqȝ ad fundum traxit ⁊ mus ad litus. Dū eīm sic pariť ↄtenderēt. miluus (qui forte spectatrix erat) miserū dirimit duellum.murem vnguib⁹ arripiens. ⁊ annexā ranā similiter trahens.qui cū se ad mortē trahi videret sic fertur locuta fuisse Qui socio suo parat opprobrium nō immerito cadit in laqueū. Allegorice per ranam pt illigi caro humana.per murē aūt intelligiť anima q̄ aduersus carnē semp militat.caro ↄcupiscit aduersus spūm:⁊ spūs aduersus carnem. Caro eīm nititur trahere animam ad terrena ⁊ carnales delectationes.anima vero resilit ad bona opera.et istis sic litigātib⁹ venit miluus.i.diabolus quasi bolus.i.morsus duoꝝ.scȝ corporis ⁊ anime et rapit ambo. Vel aliter.sicut tangitur in fine littere.per ranā intelligūtur deceptores bonū dicentes sed deceptōem intendentes. ⁊ sepe ↄtingit tales in illam (quam alijs preparauerūt) foueam cadere. Iuxta illud Incidit in foueam quam fecit

corā iudice coberet scȝ ad iudicādū aduertit
In causam canis vrget ouem. ⁊ arbiter audit — De cane et oue
soluat .s.ↄcessum scȝ ouis.s.debere panē
Reddat ouis panem.vult canis.illa negat
in pte canis ↄtra ouē.testať testať testať scȝ isti tres
Pro cane stat miluus stat vultur.stat lupus instant
pmisit restitaere tribuat
Panem (quem pepigit reddere) reddat ouis
soluere scȝ ouis nō teneť scȝ ouis restituere
Reddere non debet.nec habet quod reddere possit
soluat iudex testať agno
Et tamen vt reddat arbiter instat oui
ideo q̄uis adest s^c ouis .i.lanā
Ergo suum licet instat hyems pretendit amictum
.i.frigidū ventū sustinet lana s^c ouis
Et boream patitur.vellere nuda suo
mēdicā acq̄rit pigricia testāte
Sepe fidem falso mendicat inertia teste
innocētia delicti astucia decipi
Sepe solet pietas criminis arte capi

Hic autor ponit aliā fabulā dicēs q̄ quodā tpe canis traxit ouē in cām pro pane quem dixit illi ↄcessisse. sed ouis hoc negauit dicens se nunq̄ panē a cane mutuasse. Iudex ergo canē interrogauit si testes haberet seu fideiussores.qui tres testes noiauit.scȝ lupum miluum ⁊ vulturem.et iudex ab illis veritatē req̄rit.at illi testimonium veritatis cani dederūt.q₂ partē habere sperabant in oue si dānaretť. Iudex ergo precepit quaten⁹ de debito suo cani satisfaceret.exquo idoneis testib⁹ ↄuicta esset. sed illa misera ouis nihil habuit preter lanam quod dare posset. ⁊ hyems erat

A iiij

Plate 9. Aesop with commentary (*Esopus moralisatus cum bono commento* (1492), Bodleian Library, Auct. 5. Q. VI. 80, ff. a iii^v–a iiij).

Plate 10. Venus and her children (Bodleian Library,
MS. Rawl. D. 1220, f. 31v).

Plate 11. Mercury and his children (*ib.*, f. 32).

Plate 12. Mars and Appollo (Bodleian Library, MS. Rawl. B. 214, f. 198).

Plate 13. Orpheus and Eurydice (Bodleian Library, MS. Bodley 421, f. 49^{v}).

While having very charming picture
of Engl life w/out allegory & echoes